THE EBBS

THE EBBS AND FLOWS OF FORTUNE

*The Life of Thomas Howard,
Third Duke of Norfolk*

DAVID M. HEAD

THE UNIVERSITY OF GEORGIA PRESS
Athens & London

Paperback edition, 2009
© 1995 by the University of Georgia Press
Athens, Georgia 30602
www.ugapress.org
All rights reserved
Designed by Walton Harris
Set in 10/13 Janson by Tseng Information Systems, Inc.
Printed digitally in the United States of America

The Library of Congress has cataloged the
hardcover edition of this book as follows:
Library of Congress Cataloging-in-Publication Data
Head, David M.
The ebbs and flows of fortune : the life of Thomas
Howard, third Duke of Norfolk / David M. Head.
xi, 387 p. : ill. ; 24 cm.
ISBN 0-8203-1683-0 (alk. paper)
Includes bibliographical references and index.
1. Norfolk, Thomas Howard, Duke of, 1473–1554. 2. Henry VIII,
King of England, 1491–1547—Relations with nobility.
3. Statesmen—Great Britain—Biography. 4. Soldiers—Great
Britain—Biography. 5. Great Britain—History—Henry VIII,
1509–1547—Biography. I. Title.
DA334.N67 H43   1995
942.05'2'092 B 20   94-28259

Paperback ISBN-13: 978-0-8203-3491-2
ISBN-10: 0-8203-3491-X

British Library Cataloging-in-Publication Data available

For Caroline, Elizabeth, Michael, and Susan

And after him succeeded his sonne Thomas as well in his honors, as in the Office of Lord Treasurer of England, and lived to the time of Queen Mary, tossed to and fro between the reciprocall ebbes and flowes of fortune.

—William Camden, *Britannia* (1637), p. 483

CONTENTS

	Acknowledgments	*xi*
	Introduction	*1*
1	The Howard Family and Early Life to 1509	*12*
2	The Resurgence of the Howards, 1509–1513	*24*
3	The Making of the Duke of Norfolk, 1514–1524	*40*
4	The Peer and the Prelate: Norfolk and Wolsey, 1524–1530	*70*
5	The King's Great Matter and the Rise of Cromwell, 1530–1536	*103*
6	The Pilgrimage of Grace, 1536–1537	*131*
7	Norfolk and Cromwell, 1538–1540	*152*
8	Catherine Howard: From Triumph to Treason, 1540–1542	*179*
9	The Last Years of Henry VIII, 1540–1547	*192*
10	The Final Years, 1547–1554	*229*
11	An English Duke, 1524–1554	*246*
	Conclusion	*287*
	Notes	*293*
	Bibliography	*353*
	Index	*371*

ACKNOWLEDGMENTS

This book has had a long genesis, and there are many people, knowing and unknowing, who have contributed to its writing. My first and greatest debt is to Richard L. Greaves, Lawton Professor of History and Religion at Florida State University in Tallahassee, who first pointed me toward Norfolk as a subject for inquiry and urged me to publish my findings. Without his support and encouragement, this book would not exist at all. I hope that he finds it worthy of his support.

I would also like to thank many others who have read the manuscript in its various stages, some of them known to me by name and some not, but especially including Sir Geoffrey Elton, who read the manuscript when I first thought to seek its publication and made many helpful suggestions on matters of both style and substance. Like all Tudor historians, I have worked in Elton's long shadow, and this book bears many marks of his influence.

My colleagues at Florida State University, Middle Georgia College, South Georgia College, and John Tyler Community College have heard more about Thomas Howard than they ever cared to know, but I have received much encouragement from them, collectively and individually, as well as administrative support for making copies and paying postage as this work went through successive drafts. I have also had assistance from librarians at each of these institutions, especially in getting books on interlibrary loan. I have profited from the suggestions of many people in the writing of this book, but, as is the custom with authors, I accept responsibility for the shortcomings that remain.

Finally, I would like to mention my most constant supporters, my wife, Caroline Smith Head, and my three children, Elizabeth, Michael, and Susan. Although they had very little to do with the research and writing of this work, they have all put up with my preoccupation with "my duke" over the years with a cheerfulness which helped, more than perhaps they know, to make its completion possible. To all of them, my love and heartfelt thanks.

The Mowbray-Howard Connection, with descent of the Dukedom of Norfolk, Earldom of Surrey, and Office of Earl Marshal

```
                                                    (2)
                                    EDWARD I (d. 1307) = Margaret of France
                                                          │
        ┌─────────────────────────────────────────────────┴──────────────────────────┐
various  Thomas of Brotherton,   = Alice Hays         Edmund, earl of   = Blanche d'Artios,
issue    earl of Norfolk (d. 1338)                    Lancaster and Derby  Queen of Navarre
              │                                              │
              │                                         Henry, earl of = Maud
              │                                         Lancaster        Chaworth
    ┌─────────┴──────────────────────────┐                   │
John, 4th baron = Margaret Plantagenet, duchess of      John, 3rd baron Mowbray = Joan Plantagenet
Seagrave          Norfolk for life suo jure (d. 1399)                    │
                           │                                             │
      Elizabeth, baroness Seagrave, eventual sole heiress (d. 1375) = John, 4th baron Mowbray
                                                                         │
                    ┌────────────────────────────────────────────────────┴──────────┐
            John Mowbray, baron Mowbray,              Thomas Mowbray, baron Mowbray and Seagrave. Cr. earl of = Elizabeth Fitzalan, dau. of
            Seagrave, etc. died unmarried 1382        Nottingham, earl marshal for life, 1st duke of Norfolk (1366-99) │ Richard, earl of Arundel
                                                                         │
    ┌────────────────────────────────────────────────────────────────────┼──────────────────────────────────────┬─────────────────────────┐
Constance, dau. and = Thomas Mowbray, earl of      John Mowbray, rest. 2nd = Katherine, dau. of            Isabel = James,     Margaret = Sir Robert
heiress of John Holland, Norfolk and Nottingham,   duke of Norfolk (1425),   Ralph Neville, earl                    lord                   Howard
duke of Exeter           earl marshal (1385-1405)  earl marshal (1392-1432)  of Westmorland                         Berkeley              (1385-1435?)
    │                         │                                   │                                                   │                        │
 no issue                                Eleanor, dau. of = John Mowbray, 3rd duke of Norfolk,                    William,            Sir John Howard, cr. lord Howard
                                         William, lord      etc. Confirmed duke of Norfolk and                    lord                (1470), duke of Norfolk and earl
                                         Bourchier          earl marshal 1445 (1415-61)                           Berkeley            marshal (1483) (1422?-85)
                                                                         │                                                                      │
                                         Elizabeth, dau. and heiress of = John Mowbray, 4th duke of Norfolk, cr. earl              Sir Thomas Howard, cr. earl of Surrey (1483), rest.
                                         John, earl of Shrewsbury         of Surrey and Warenne 1451 (1444-76)                     2nd duke of Norfolk (1514) (1443-1524), earl marshal
                                                                         │                                                                      │
                                         Richard, duke of York, 2nd son = Anne Mowbray, baroness                                   Thomas Howard, cr. earl of
                                         of EDWARD IV; cr. duke of        Seagrave, Mowbray, etc.                                  Surrey (1514), 3rd duke of
                                         Norfolk 1477 (d. 1483?)          (1472-81)                                                Norfolk (1473-1554), earl marshal
                                                                                                                                                │
                                                                                                                                              issue
```

The Howard Genealogy (1)

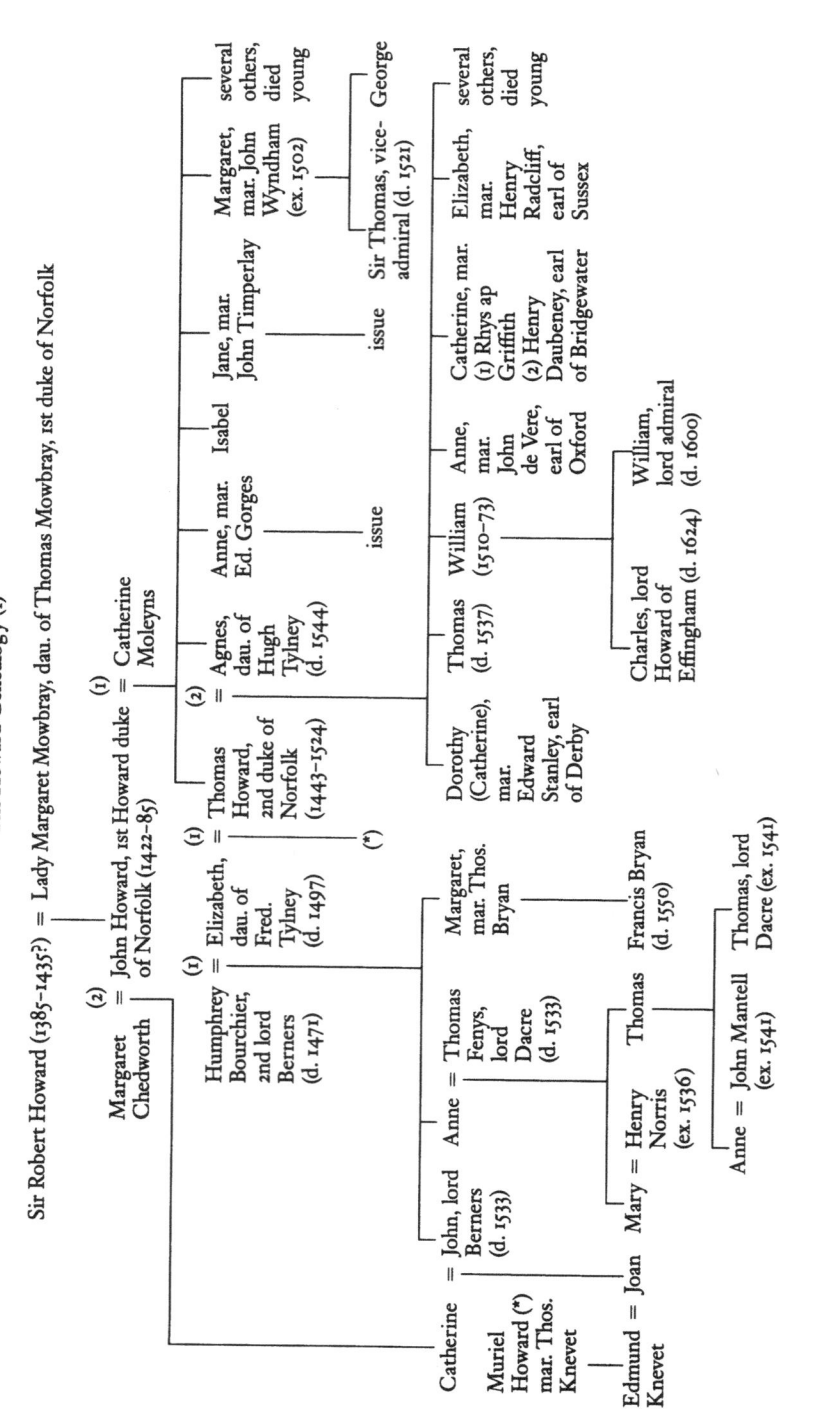

Sir Robert Howard (1385–1435?) = Lady Margaret Mowbray, dau. of Thomas Mowbray, 1st duke of Norfolk

Descendants:

- Margaret = Chedworth (2) / John Howard, 1st Howard duke of Norfolk (1422–85) = (1) Catherine Moleyns

From John Howard & Catherine Moleyns:
- Elizabeth, dau. of Fred. Tylney (d. 1497) = (1) Thomas Howard, 2nd duke of Norfolk (1443–1524) = (2) Agnes, dau. of Hugh Tylney (d. 1544)
- Anne, mar. Ed. Gorges
- Isabel
- Jane, mar. John Timperlay
- Margaret, mar. John Wyndham (ex. 1502)
- several others, died young

Children of Thomas Howard 2nd duke (by 1st wife Elizabeth Tylney):
- Thomas Howard (*) [see following page]
- Dorothy (Catherine), mar. Edward Stanley, earl of Derby
- Thomas (d. 1537)
- William (1510–73)
  - Charles, lord Howard of Effingham (d. 1624)
  - William, lord admiral (d. 1600)
- Anne, mar. John de Vere, earl of Oxford

Issue (Anne, mar. Ed. Gorges): issue
Issue (Jane, mar. John Timperlay): Sir Thomas, vice-admiral (d. 1521) — George

Children of Thomas Howard 2nd duke (by 2nd wife Agnes Tylney):
- Catherine, mar. (1) Rhys ap Griffith (2) Henry Daubeney, earl of Bridgewater
- Elizabeth, mar. Henry Radcliff, earl of Sussex
- several others, died young

From Humphrey Bourchier, 2nd lord Berners (d. 1471) = (first dau. shown above line):
- John, lord Berners (d. 1533)
  - Margaret, mar. Thos. Bryan
    - Francis Bryan (d. 1550)
- Anne = Thomas Fenys, lord Dacre (d. 1533)
  - Thomas
    - Thomas, lord Dacre (ex. 1541)
- Catherine
  - Muriel Howard (*), mar. Thos. Knevet
    - Edmund = Joan Knevet
  - Mary = Henry Norris (ex. 1536)
  - Anne = John Mantell (ex. 1541)

(*) see following page

The Howard Genealogy (2)

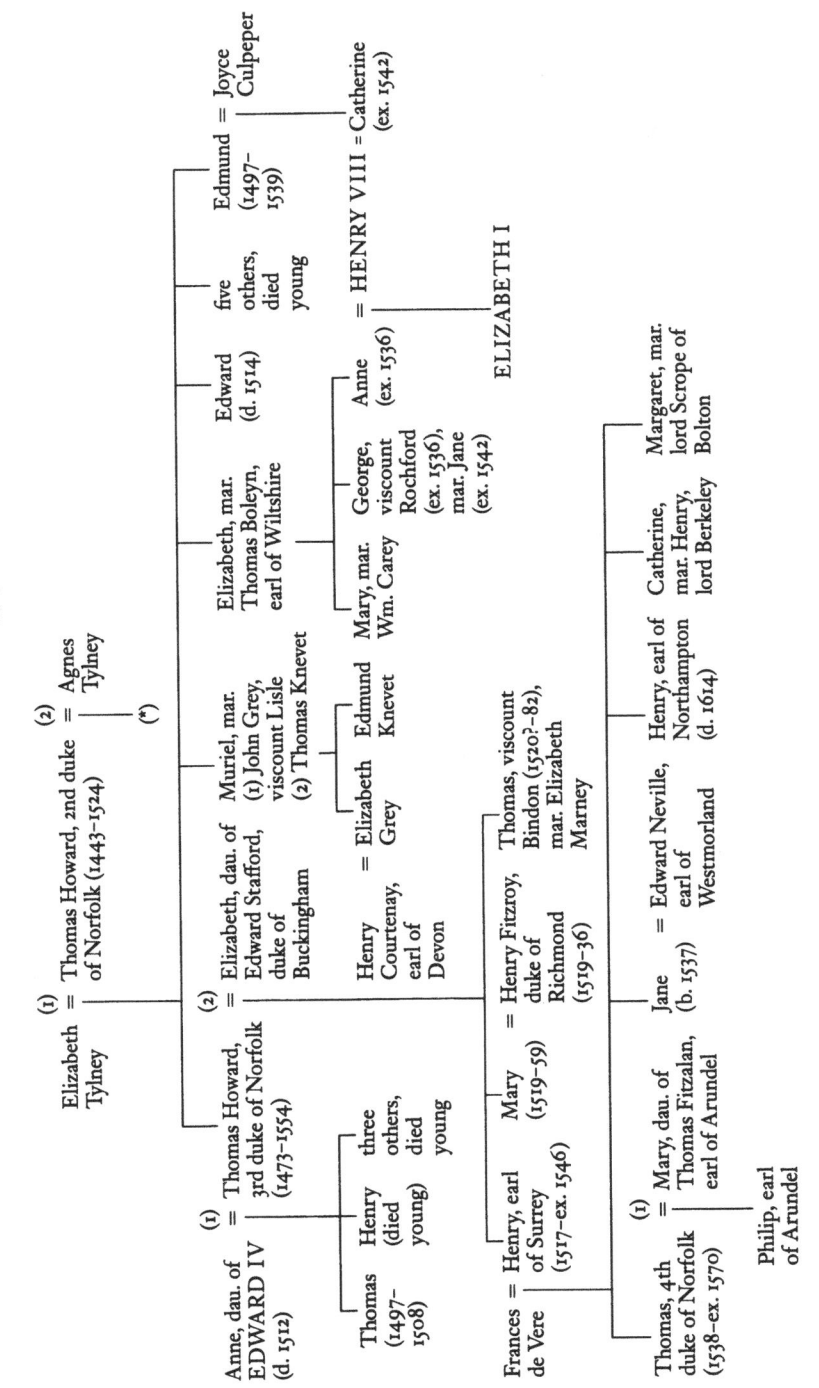

Elizabeth Tylney =(1) Thomas Howard, 2nd duke of Norfolk (1443–1524) (2)= Agnes Tylney (*)

Children of Thomas Howard, 2nd duke, and Elizabeth Tylney:

- Thomas Howard, 3rd duke of Norfolk (1473–1554)
  - (1) = Anne, dau. of EDWARD IV (d. 1512)
    - Thomas (1497–1508)
    - Henry (died young)
    - three others, died young
  - (2) = Elizabeth, dau. of Edward Stafford, duke of Buckingham
    - Henry, earl of Surrey (1517–ex. 1546) = Frances de Vere
      - Thomas, 4th duke of Norfolk (1538–ex. 1570) =(1) Mary, dau. of Thomas Fitzalan, earl of Arundel
        - Philip, earl of Arundel
      - Margaret, mar. lord Scrope of Bolton
      - Henry, earl of Northampton (d. 1614)
      - Catherine, mar. Henry, lord Berkeley
      - Jane (b. 1537) = Edward Neville, earl of Westmorland
    - Mary (1519–59) = Henry Fitzroy, duke of Richmond (1519–36)
- Elizabeth, mar. Thomas Boleyn, earl of Wiltshire
  - Mary, mar. Wm. Carey
  - George, viscount Rochford (ex. 1536), mar. Jane (ex. 1542)
  - Anne (ex. 1536) = HENRY VIII
    - ELIZABETH I
- Edward (d. 1514)
- five others, died young
- Edmund (1497–1539) = Joyce Culpeper
  - Catherine (ex. 1542) = HENRY VIII
- Muriel, mar. (1) John Grey, viscount Lisle (2) Thomas Knevet
  - Henry Courtenay, earl of Devon = Elizabeth Grey
  - Edmund Knevet
  - Thomas, viscount Bindon (1520?–82), mar. Elizabeth Marney

(*) see previous page

THE EBBS AND FLOWS OF FORTUNE

INTRODUCTION

In November 1531, Ludovico Falieri, Venetian ambassador to the court of Henry VIII, sent home a description of the leading figures there after the fall of Cardinal Wolsey. Prominent among them was Thomas Howard, third duke of Norfolk, of whom Falieri wrote: "He is prudent, liberal, affable and astute; associates with everybody, has very great experience in political government, discusses the affairs of the world admirably, aspires to greater elevation, and bears ill-will to foreigners, especially to those of our Venetian nation. He is fifty-eight years old; small and spare in person, and his hair black."[1]

Falieri might have also said that Norfolk was the most accomplished military leader in the realm and perhaps its richest peer, but otherwise it was a very shrewd thumbnail sketch of Howard, capturing both his smooth public persona and his underlying pride and hunger for preferment. At the midpoint of Henry VIII's reign, Norfolk was at the height of his powers and the peak of his ambition, a man who had achieved a great deal but who hungered for even greater prestige and power.

Thomas Howard was born in 1473 and lived until 1554, through the lives of five English monarchs, experiencing the transformations of Renaissance and Reformation alike. His own education and instincts were old-fashioned; in religion and politics, Norfolk was a conservative, unimpressed by the new ideas of the reformers and uncomfortable with the low-born "new men" of the Tudor court. With great pride, the Howards traced their noble lineage back to Edward III, yet their titles and dignities were as much Tudor gifts as was Thomas Cromwell's earldom of Essex. There was a resultant tension in Thomas Howard. He claimed the deference due the leader of the traditional nobility, yet recognized uneasily that loyalty, ability and service counted as much as or more than ancient title to the Tudors. The ambition and self-aggrandizement of the Howards were matched by the grasping aspirations of Wolsey, Cromwell or any other new man, but in one of Norfolk's rank self-service was a dangerous attribute, and one the duke was never able quite to conceal under his cloak of loyal subservience to the royal will.

In many ways, Norfolk was not a very pleasant or attractive man. He was apt to whine and complain in adversity and to resort to fawning flattery when seeking favor. He was capable of considerable charm, as Falieri noted, but he had a violent temper and a savage streak as well. Henry VIII was a notably bloodthirsty king, but Norfolk was willing to match him every step of the way, in his military campaigns in France and Scotland when he burned towns and fields, and as an administrator of justice after the Pilgrimage of Grace, when he hung men by the dozens and lamented his lack of authority to execute more. The Tudor age was no time for the softhearted, but Norfolk seems to have relished even the cruelest work assigned him.

Not surprisingly, Norfolk was equally untender in his personal relations. There is too little evidence to say anything about his first marriage, but it is clear that the second, to Elizabeth Stafford, daughter of the third duke of Buckingham, was a purely political and economic match. Elizabeth bore Thomas three children who survived to maturity, but it was a stormy marriage, with Norfolk eventually taking a mistress, Bess Holland, and sending his duchess off to another house forty miles away. From thence she bombarded Thomas Cromwell with letters complaining of Norfolk's mistreatment, which ranged from miserliness in paying for her household expenses to accusations of physical abuse. Relations with his children and his extended family were not much better; the best that can be said is that it was a harsh age, and being feared and respected might have been all Norfolk expected, for there is little evidence that he was loved by anyone.

Howard's main goal in life was political: to obtain a position of dominance at court and council to match that of Wolsey or Cromwell. In this, his career was ultimately a failure. Perhaps Henry could see that Norfolk's constant professions of loyalty and self-sacrificing obedience were a veil for self-interest; the king may have found it hard fully to trust one whose greed and lust for power were so apparent. Yet desires for honor, wealth and power were hardly uncommon Tudor traits. More likely, Henry found Howard's talents too commonplace for the role which he sought. Norfolk was not unintelligent; certainly he was far brighter than the king's companion Charles Brandon, duke of Suffolk. Nor could anyone doubt his loyalty; as E. W. Ives so aptly put it, "Thomas Howard would have helped his king to hell if Henry had wanted to go there."[2] Yet Norfolk lacked the sharpness and focus of mind that distinguished rare men like Wolsey,

Introduction

More and Cromwell, and the willingness to apply himself to administrative work which made them such valuable servants. Norfolk's lust for power was repeatedly thwarted by his own limitations.

Norfolk was not exceptionally unprincipled for his age; political survival under the Tudors required considerable pliability. Yet Howard lacked the redeeming virtue of believing in something worth suffering, much less dying, for. Certainly his Catholic convictions were nothing like those of John Fisher or Thomas More, who died for their church, or even Stephen Gardiner, whose promising career was derailed by a too-Catholic faith. One wonders if Norfolk would have abandoned the Tudors had he ever thought that rebellion offered greater opportunities. Thomas Howard never took the gamble, for he was also a cautious man, if not always a careful enough one. Family disasters several times brought him under royal suspicion, and he spent the reign of Edward VI in the Tower of London because of the indiscretions of his son Henry, earl of Surrey. Yet he survived to die in his bed, restored to his honors in the reign of Mary.

Norfolk's long life is worthy of study, not only for the stunning successes and equally impressive disasters of his career—the "ebbes and flowes of fortune" of Camden's phrase[3]—but also for the insights it offers into the anatomy of early Tudor politics. Norfolk owed much to his titles and offices of treasurer and earl marshal, all of them inherited from his father. A man of greater talent, industry and daring might have become the dominant figure of the era with these advantages. Thomas Howard, with his ill-concealed pride and his commonplace intelligence, was able to achieve an impressive career, but the preeminence he sought always slipped from his hands as men such as Cromwell and then Edward Seymour overtook Norfolk as Henry's leading ministers.

This study focuses upon Thomas Howard's political career in an essentially biographical framework. Although scholars have given considerable attention to the two Howard women who wed Henry VIII, and the father, son and grandson of the third duke have all been studied,[4] Norfolk, the leader of the Howard clan from 1524 to 1554, has not attracted a biographer. Part of the problem has been the sources; G. R. Elton has insisted, with considerable justification, that the sixteenth century is no age for biography,[5] and it is true that many of the details of the lives and personal affairs of men such as Norfolk are lost. Although the public records provide extensive information on his actions, Norfolk's personality and beliefs can only be assessed at second hand from his and others' letters, most of them "official" papers. The people of the Tudor age were careful about what they committed to writing, and truly revealing observations are few. Worse, almost nothing in the way of "personal" material survives for Thomas Howard; there are no diaries and only a handful of letters not directly concerned with matters of state. Yet a careful reading of his surviving papers reveals much about the man. His often obsequious flattery of the king and his favored ministers did not prevent Norfolk from offering his opinion, even when it was not solicited. He was impatient and had a quick temper, along with confidence and self-importance verging on egotism. He must have thought himself a bit of a scholar and a bit of a wit, for his letters, like Wolsey's, are peppered with Latin and French aphorisms and frequent, even self-conscious, neatly turned phrases. His letters were usually written by secretaries, but those few that are holograph were usually written in great haste under the pressure of the moment and display the atrocious penmanship of one who could not be bothered to master the skills of a mere clerk. Henry VIII, too, wrote a poor hand, even complaining on occasion that it was painful for him to write for himself. The upper class had better things to do than master penmanship, if Norfolk's letters are any indication.

Given all that his letters reveal, both explicitly and between the lines, the historian can deduce a great deal about Thomas Howard. Those who knew him best must have thought him difficult, thin-skinned and a bit thick-headed, but nonetheless dangerous to underestimate. He was charming and vicious by turns, a companion in arms and fellow councilor but seldom a dear friend to his equals, and a demanding and unpredictable master to subordinates.

Considering the limitations of the sources, this study is not a full biography in a modern sense, yet it does, for the most part, focus on a single man and his actions. Insofar as it is a biography, it is a political one, which is fitting, for Norfolk was essentially a political creature, constantly absorbed with the struggle for power and preferment through service to the crown. Despite his long military and diplomatic careers, Norfolk's greatest significance was as a political figure. While it might be anachronistic to call Norfolk a "politician," the modern idea of a person whose career was tied to public service—or in the sixteenth century, royal service—fits Norfolk quite well.

Introduction

Recent works on the mid-Tudor period have greatly expanded our understanding of the nature of politics and the importance of factional competition for influence among Henry's advisors. A "faction" might be defined as a group seeking advantage through gaining influence over policy, from war and peace on the grand scale down to the right to distribute patronage. A faction need not be ideological, although there was an ideological element in later Henrician politics.[6] Elton has argued that factional politics was a major theme of the period: "One thing is clear about the situation between 1509 and 1558; factions at court were trying to get exclusive control but never succeeded in doing so."[7] Ives qualifies this judgment, stating that Henrician factionalism was not yet the dominant force it would become under Elizabeth; long-term parties dominated by great men and clearly oriented toward great issues had not yet arisen. But with the fall of Anne Boleyn and the crisis of 1536, the situation changed, and factional alignments, though often shifting, became the "normal" form of later Tudor politics. To go too far and espouse too unyielding a program was to cross the line from factionalism to opposition, raising suspicions of disloyalty, rebellion, even treason. It was an important but imprecise line, and one that rival politicians constantly tried to convince the king their opponents had crossed—sometimes, as in the fall of Cromwell and Thomas Howard's own arrest, with considerable success.[8]

Other writers have been less supportive of the Elton/Ives model. Retha Warnicke, in her study of Anne Boleyn, disputes Ives's identification of factional membership and motives both in concept and in detail,[9] and Glyn Redworth, in his work on Stephen Gardiner, places considerable emphasis on Henry's decision making and downplays the existence of faction, especially in reviewing the events of Henry's last months and the destruction of the Howards.[10] Likewise, Lacey B. Smith, in his study of Henry VIII, has squarely placed the credit or blame for whatever good or ill came from the reign on the king, and has argued that while Henry could be swayed, he could not be led where he was not already willing to go.[11] In this study I have tried to balance these views; while I believe that factionalism played an important role in mid-Tudor politics, I am persuaded that Henry was more Redworth and Smith's self-aware king and less Ives and Elton's easily swayed figurehead. Thomas Howard seems to have treated Henry as one who could be pushed only so far, and one of his failures was that he sometimes pushed too hard, and was punished with exile from court until he came to his senses. Factionalism as a model can be taken too far, but it cannot be ignored in analyzing Tudor politics.

Tudor factions were not modern political parties with definite platforms, personnel, and organizations in any case. The later Henrician coalition between Norfolk and Stephen Gardiner is a case in point. Eric Ives called the Howard-Gardiner alliance a "permanent conservative front" through the 1540s, while Glyn Redworth doubts that any general cooperative effort between the two existed at all. Although Norfolk and Gardiner shared religious views and a general opposition to progressives such as Edward Seymour and John Dudley, they had significant differences over foreign policy and were as often rivals as allies in the later years of the reign. Nor is there much evidence for an alliance between Howard and Charles Brandon, duke of Suffolk. Despite their cooperation in the fall of Wolsey, the two dukes were never close personal friends, and were also frequent rivals for grants of land and office in the 1530s and 1540s. Suffolk's death in 1545 strengthened Norfolk's position as premier peer without significantly weakening the conservative presence at court.[12] Thus we should be careful about identifying long-term alliances; factions were fluid rather than fixed in personnel and policies; Norfolk, after all, twice attempted to forge a marital alliance with the Seymours, with what potential changes in his personal beliefs or politics we will never know. It is not impossible to imagine Norfolk turning as Protestant as Seymour and the Dudleys had he been convinced it was necessary to his political survival.

Henrician factionalism was limited by several factors. In the first place, political alignments tended to be short-lived and motivated by limited objectives. The important thing was to be on the right side of the political battles when the smoke cleared. Furthermore, loyalty to the crown, or at least the pretence of loyalty, was fundamental to the creed of almost all Tudor politicians; those who forgot this lesson suffered the fate of Thomas More. Ideology was important to conservatives such as Norfolk and Gardiner as well as to progressives such as Cromwell and Cranmer, but when the king had given clear indications of the course of policy, as with the Act of the Six Articles, his councilors almost always fell into line. There must be some doubt about the strength of factional alliances in an environment where the will of the king was the determining factor in politics. Certainly Norfolk had no illusions about the permanency of factions, for he abandoned the Boleyns long before Anne's fall, and made several attempts to ally with the progressive Seymours through the marriage of his daughter Mary and Thomas Seymour. Thomas Howard was a realist. Success, whether measured in wealth, office, or clients at one's beck and call, was what counted. Ideology, though important, was always subject to modification if expediency—or survival—required. Eustace Chapuys, imperial ambassador to England in the 1530s and an important observer of English politics, saw Norfolk's character clearly. At the outbreak of the Pilgrimage of Grace in 1536, Chapuys warned Charles V that, although he hoped that Norfolk's Catholic sympathies would lead him to join the rebellion against Henry VIII, "owing to the said duke's versatile and inconstant humor," no one could rely on him to do so.[13]

Even with the importance of factional battles duly noted, there was much more to Tudor politics than maneuvers in council, for a great deal of wealth and enormous regional and local power were at stake in the contests within the ruling class. Norfolk actively stalked all the available paths to wealth and power. Offices of state and a place on the council were useful sources of patronage, and Norfolk's positions as admiral, treasurer and earl marshal were all vital parts of his political position. As a councilor and a great officer of state, Norfolk collected a wide range of fees and commissions and was able to grant out lower offices and deliver licenses and gifts to his family and supporters. The most tangible and most avidly sought-after source of Tudor wealth was land, and Norfolk used his court connections to build a landed estate spread across the kingdom. When the dissolution of the monasteries was begun, Norfolk immediately sought and won the office of chancellor of the court of augmentations south of Trent, and used his inside position to obtain large grants and gifts; in his home county of Norfolk, Howard obtained three-quarters of the monastic land alienated by the crown, often at bargain prices.[14]

Yet the arena in which Norfolk and his rivals had to operate was not simply one of paper pleadings, writs and letters patent. The court, quite as much as the council, was an important locus of activity, especially when matters less of state than of personal advancement were at stake. Henry was notorious for his love of hunting, games, music, dances, masques and other "pastime with good company." Those who sought the king's favor were wise to join him at his sports, or at least to provide family and friends who could. Norfolk was never a close companion of the king, partly because he was eighteen years older, but he compensated by working to place clients and family members in the royal entourage. His most notable success was with Catherine Howard, an achievement that should not be ignored simply because her career unraveled into one of the duke's most damaging fiascos. Besides Catherine, there were dozens of Howard clients who won preferment because of Norfolk's intervention on their behalf.

Access to the king's household, especially the privy chamber, his most private apartments, was critically important in the battle for influence. Several Howards, including Thomas's brother Edward and his cousins Thomas Knevet and Francis Bryan, were close to the king early in the reign, and others, such as George Boleyn and Charles and William Howard, held places there in the 1530s and early 1540s. After the fall of Catherine Howard, however, Norfolk seems to have had little success in placing his friends and family in the king's innermost circle. The growing interest in the privy chamber in recent scholarship[15] reflects a realization that political power in Tudor England hinged upon personal access to the king. Both Wolsey and Cromwell had known this, and each made concerted efforts to keep rivals such as Norfolk as far from Henry as possible during their periods of power. Those closest to the king stood the best chance of influencing him in matters great and small, for Henry was notoriously disinclined to do business in writing; he generally relied upon those close about him to carry out the work of government. Had Henry been nothing but a pleasure-loving cipher while real power lay in the hands of his great ministers, such personal access would not have mattered. Norfolk's often prolonged absences from court while serving in Ireland and on the borders with Scotland are eloquent testimony to the realities of Tudor politics and to the need Wolsey and Cromwell felt to keep Norfolk away from Henry as much as possible.

The role of the Tudor nobility as a political and social class has also received a good bit of attention lately. Helen Miller and David Loades pay considerable attention to the status of the peerage. One recent writer, G. W. Bernard, has flatly stated that "the nobility was the most important, the most influential and the most powerful segment of society" in Tudor England. Bernard argues that recent scholarship has overstated the modernity of the early Tudor era—a point with which I heartily agree— and that recent writers have made too much of "new monarchy" and "new men."[16] Nor does he think that Henry had any long-term animus against the nobility; those such as Buckingham, Exeter and Norfolk who were ruined during the reign largely owed their fate to Henry's emotional outbursts in response to particular events.[17]

Far from making any concerted effort to cut the nobility down, Henry created numerous titles for his favorites and faithful servants, from Brandon's dukedom of Suffolk in 1513 to William Parr's earldom of Essex at the end of the reign; even the Howards were part of this parade of ennoblements, for they entered the reign holding only the earldom of Surrey, which was certainly a sufficient mark of nobility to serve as royal officers and councilors. The Howards were restored as dukes of Norfolk in 1513 in reward for the victory over the Scots at Flodden, but also in recognition that a dukedom was grander than an earldom; the greater a servant's service to the king, the greater the noble title he should hold in reflection of the honor of that service. Nobility counted for a great deal in Tudor England, as both a source and a mark of status and power.

Since the Tudor ruling class was small, personal contact and family connections were vitally important. The Tudor House of Lords was a gentlemen's club with only forty or fifty members, all of whom had ties of blood and common ambition with the others. Norfolk's own parentage was not terribly exalted; neither his father nor his grandfather had been a duke when he married, and both had found wives among the gentry. Thomas Howard aimed higher and married a princess and the daughter of a duke. By his own and his father's and grandfather's marriages, he was related to many other noble families, including those of the earls of Derby, Oxford, Sussex, Bridgewater, Devon, and Wiltshire and Ormond, as well as baronial clans such as the Lisles and Dacres. If second cousins and in-laws are considered, there was hardly a Tudor peer who was not Thomas Howard's kin. Although Norfolk obviously could not count on all these families to stand beside him in battle, they formed an important web of social, economic and political connections which came into play repeatedly during his career.

Men of inferior rank were equally vital to the prestige and influence of the Howards. The gentry of East Anglia, often Howard cousins in their own right, supplied many of Norfolk's household officials and retainers, and as a class they were counted upon to serve at the duke's side in war and to support his interests in local politics. Attachment to a great lord was one of the main paths of advancement in Tudor England, and one the Howards themselves had followed as clients of the Mowbray earls and dukes of Norfolk. Henry's court and, toward the end of the reign, even the council, included a number of Southwells, Knevets, Gates, Hares, Wingfields, Townshends and others who had passed through Howard service.[18] Not all these ties were permanent, as men such as Sir Richard Southwell and George Blage eventually bit the hand that had fed them. Norfolk's "good lordship" was hardly different from that of a thirteenth-century baron, whether measured in meals provided at the ducal residences, grants to export wine, or places on the county commission of the peace. Lordship provided a vital two-way conduit between the localities and the court.[19]

Tudor politics, from the king down, were not bureaucratic or rigidly institutionalized; the system was based on personal contacts and intimate relationships, a fact that helps to account for the viciousness of the battles which punctuated the reign. Although the period after 1530 has received most of the attention of those studying court politics, there were moments of tension and episodes of brutality earlier. Henry began his reign, after all, by having Richard Empson and Edmund Dudley put to death for their toozealous prosecution of Henry VII's financial policies, and in 1513 Edmund de la Pole was executed for being the closest Lancastrian pretender to the throne that Henry could lay his hands upon.[20] In 1516, Wolsey launched his campaign against abuses of maintenance and livery, hauling the earls of Surrey (as Thomas Howard then was) and Northumberland before the council in Star Chamber, leading to considerable backbiting and fingerpointing among those who feared they might be next. "Her is gret snerling among divers of them," reported Thomas Alen, chaplain to the earl of Shrewsbury.[21] Closeness to the king had both perils and rewards, as the Howards well knew. As Helen Miller noted, "Henry VIII maintained to the end his predilection for men he had known since his youth, in war as at court."[22] Norfolk, sometimes to his benefit and sometimes to his peril, qualified on both counts.

Factional politics involve a necessary element of differences of policy; without that, there would be no factionalism, nor politics as a field of contention at all. Norfolk did, of course, have ideas about how church, state and society ought best to be constituted and have their business conducted. As far as the term applies in the sixteenth century, he was a conservative, a man who saw little benefit in wholesale changes in a system and society in which he and his class were dominant and held wealth and power far out of proportion to their numbers. Norfolk sought power largely for its

Introduction

own sake, and not as part of a program for change. While he had ideas about war and diplomacy which he conveyed to the king when the chance presented itself, Norfolk's main goal seems to have been to preserve and expand his personal wealth, prestige and power. And so we return to the definition of faction offered above. The nature of Tudor politics was such that true ideologues—such as Thomas More, to take the most obvious example—could not long survive. Men such as Norfolk, Thomas Cranmer, and the broad group of Henrician "politiques" who peopled the late privy council, able to bend without breaking, could enjoy relatively long and profitable careers under the Tudors until caught up in a dynastic or religious shift too drastic to avoid. Even so, the highest rungs of the political ladder were slippery indeed, and few of the greatest servants of the early Tudors managed to die in bed; many, like Norfolk, saw the gates of the Tower close behind them.

As a person, Thomas Howard may not have been particularly attractive, but as a figure in Tudor England he was of great importance. He was intimately involved in many of the most controversial episodes of the era, often as a key figure who made decisive contributions to the outcome of events. Thomas Howard lived a long, tumultuous and significant life and, I believe, an interesting one as well. Studying his life and role in Tudor affairs helps to broaden our historical perspective. The age of Henry VIII was not yet modern, while no longer fully medieval. Norfolk serves as something of a symbol for this age of transition: a nobleman, a figure out of the feudal past, adjusting to a changing age that he did not always understand and to which he could never completely accommodate himself.

CHAPTER 1

THE HOWARD FAMILY AND EARLY LIFE TO 1509

THE ACCIDENTS OF BIRTH AND DEATH often play an unforeseen role in history. Before the fifteenth century, the Howards were only one of many gentle families of no great wealth or distinction. Although they had ties to the Mowbray earls and dukes of Norfolk, so did many others. Yet by a combination of luck and determination, through family links and service to the crown, the fifteenth- and sixteenth-century Howards rose to being among the most powerful families in England. The subject of this study, Thomas Howard, third Howard duke of Norfolk, was the beneficiary of his family's earlier luck and labor, and as a result had advantages his father and grandfather lacked. Yet many another nobleman with equal resources ended up having little impact in history. Thomas Howard was different. A man of great pride, enormous ambition and little inhibition, largely by his own efforts he ended up with the most notable career of any Howard. Without the family position his ancestors provided him, Howard might have achieved little. Given the advantages of family connections and opportunities for royal service, Thomas Howard made the most of them.

Like many other English families the Howards claimed descent from a semi-legendary noble ancestor, the Saxon Herwardus, but the historical roots of the family extend no further back than the thirteenth century. The Howards of East Anglia traced their descent from Sir William Howard (d. 1308), chief justice of the Common Pleas, who married well and established a landed estate near King's Lynn.[1] Sir William's descendants continued in royal service for another five generations, but the family's rise from gentry to aristocracy took place only in the lifetime of John Howard (1422–85), lord Howard and first Howard duke of Norfolk. John was the eldest son of Sir Robert Howard, who married Margaret Mowbray, a sister of John Mowbray, earl of Nottingham and Norfolk, in about 1420. In 1425, John Mowbray was restored as second Mowbray duke of Norfolk; as he already had a son, the Howards had dim prospects of succeeding to the dukedom.[2]

In 1442, John Howard married Catherine Moleyns, baroness Moleyns, and they had a flock of children who lived to maturity. As a cousin of the Mowbray dukes of Norfolk, John Howard rose to some stature in East Anglia. He served in Parliament for Norfolk in 1455 and as sheriff of the shire in 1461. Along with the Mowbrays, Howard was a Yorkist. He was knighted for his service at the battle of Towton in 1461, and acted as a gentleman server to Edward IV's queen, Elizabeth Woodville, in 1465. Sir John Howard became a favored, if relatively minor, servant of Edward IV.[3] In return for his military services in France, England and Wales, Sir John was granted land in four counties and in London, was made constable of Norwich castle, and, in 1467, became treasurer of the king's household.[4]

John Howard's eldest son, Thomas, was born about 1443, and entered royal service in 1466 as one of the king's seven henchmen, ceremonial aides of the master of the horse. At some time between 1466 and 1469, Thomas was sent to the court of Charles the Bold, duke of Burgundy, the richest repository of declining chivalry in Europe. Here Thomas continued his education and training as a knight for several years, returning to England shortly before Richard Neville, earl of Warwick, and George, duke of Clarence, forced Edward to flee to the Low Countries while the mentally ill Henry VI was returned to the throne. The Howards remained in England to champion Edward's cause and fought with their king at Tewkesbury and Barnet; Thomas was gravely wounded at Barnet on 14 April 1471 as Edward regained his throne.[5] The king displayed his gratitude to the Howards by appointing Sir John deputy governor of Calais and appointing Thomas one of the four esquires of the king's body.[6]

Thomas Howard's marriage to Elizabeth Tilney the next year was another part of the family's reward. Elizabeth was the widow of Humphrey Bourchier, who had been slain at Barnet. The Pastons, the leading gentry family of Norfolk and frequent rivals of the Howards, had hoped to marry this rich young widow to one of their own clan.[7] By capturing the hand of Elizabeth Bourchier the Howards won the lasting enmity of the Pastons, but also demonstrated their stature in their county. Elizabeth brought her husband the manor of Ashwelthorpe in Norfolk, where they settled. Their first son, Thomas, the future third duke of Norfolk, was born there in 1473, and other children followed: Edward in 1477, Edmund about 1479, and, at some point, two daughters, Muriel and Elizabeth. There were also four or five children who died in infancy. With this growing family, Thomas was granted leave to reside away from court, though he continued to hold the king's favor.[8]

Thomas Howard's stature as a minor but trusted royal servant is demonstrated by a succession of grants and appointments in the 1470s. He was a justice of the peace for Norfolk in 1476, a member of Parliament for the shire in 1477, and sheriff of Norfolk and Suffolk in 1477–78—not an unusual collection of offices for a county gentleman. In 1475, Thomas and his father Sir John accompanied Edward IV to France to meet with Louis XI at Picquigny to discuss Anglo-French peace, and in 1476 and 1477, father and son were commissioned to investigate shipping problems in the east of England. In 1478 Thomas served on the royal commission of inquiry for the lands of George, late duke of Clarence, the king's rebellious brother.[9] For the most part, however, Thomas seems to have concerned himself with family and personal affairs. The survival of portions of Howard household books from this period reveal some details of everyday life and household management. John and Thomas Howard were careful estate managers, patrons of music, literature and the church, and they provided generous if not lavish board to guests and visiting "strangers." Yet even with the household books as sources, the real personal details of biography are largely lacking for the family.[10]

In the last years of Edward's reign, John Howard was somewhat more prominent than his son. Prior to 1467, John was created a baron; all that is certain is that he was summoned to Parliament as lord Howard in that year. John was also appointed admiral of a fleet sent against the Scots in 1479, serving in an office later to be occupied by his grandsons, and was often at court to witness royal acts or to be appointed to royal commissions for sundry purposes. As another mark of favor, Howard was granted reversion of the office of constable of the Tower of London in 1479.[11] Yet none of this was much of a reward, considering the potential honors Edward IV withheld from the family.

On 17 January 1476, John Mowbray, fourth duke of Norfolk, John

Howard's cousin and patron, died suddenly at the ducal castle of Framlingham. At his death, the dukedom of Norfolk and the earldoms of Nottingham and Surrey and Warenne all became extinct, and the hereditary office of earl marshal was vacated, for Mowbray left no direct male heir. His only child and heiress was a three-year-old daughter, Anne. The remaining heirs general were John Howard and William, lord Berkeley, each of whom claimed descent from a sister of the second Mowbray duke. At stake, besides possible revival of the titles extinguished by Norfolk's death, were the vast Mowbray estates in East Anglia, Surrey, Sussex, York, Wales and elsewhere.

Edward IV had no reason to heap rewards and titles on the Howards; they were only a loyal gentry family. Instead, the king took advantage of Norfolk's death to provide for his son Richard, duke of York, at no cost to the crown, while seemingly placing the Mowbray inheritance forever beyond the reach of Howard or Berkeley. Anne was only three, and Richard was hardly older, but nonetheless they were betrothed and, in anticipation of their marriage, Richard was created earl of Nottingham in June 1476 and duke of Norfolk, earl of Warenne, and earl marshal in February 1477. On 15 January 1478 the children were married, and the next day Parliament enacted that Richard, duke of York and Norfolk, was to be granted all lands and rights of the Mowbray inheritance should Anne die without heirs of her body. As what must have seemed a very unsatisfactory sop to family honor, John Howard's son Thomas was knighted at the wedding ceremony. Howard and Berkeley were left with the small consolation of clear titles (guaranteed by the same act of Parliament that had favored Richard) to the manors to which they had right by their Mowbray descent. Neither could have been pleased that the extinguished titles had been granted to the juvenile duke of York rather than revived in their favor—although there is certainly no reason why Edward should have done other than he did as far as Howard and Berkeley were concerned. When Anne died late in 1481 at the age of eight, obviously without heirs of the body, the hopes of the Howards for any share of the Mowbray lands or titles must have seemed faint indeed.[12]

Yet the Howards continued to serve Edward IV faithfully for the remainder of the reign, and after the death of the king on 9 April 1483, John Howard carried the king's banner before the hearse in the funeral procession and was one of the ten knights who kept watch over the corpse the night before the burial.[13] The accession of Edward V, a boy of twelve, did not go smoothly. The events of the next several months, culminating in the seizure of the crown by Richard, duke of Gloucester, brother to the late Edward IV and protector for Edward V, have been rehearsed too often to require further comment except as they relate to the Howards.[14] Were John and his son Thomas disappointed enough by Edward's treatment to plot against his son? Were the Howards more than circumstantial actors in Richard's usurpation? Did they connive at murder, treason and rebellion out of lust for land and title? The murky events of 1483 defy any attempt to answer these questions definitively. Melvin Tucker, biographer of the second duke, makes a circumstantial case for the Howards' close cooperation with Richard, suggesting that John Howard was the murderer of the princes in the Tower, Edward V and Richard of York and Norfolk.[15] Gerald Brenan and E. P. Statham, authors of a not entirely reliable Howard family history, were equally at pains to deny the aid of the Howards in Richard's usurpation.[16]

There is evidence that John and Thomas Howard were intimates of Gloucester between Edward IV's death and his brother's seizure of the crown, but no proof that the Howards helped plot Richard's usurpation or murdered the princes for him. John Howard may have been involved in persuading Elizabeth Woodville to give up her son Richard, duke of York and Norfolk, to Richard's custody;[17] since Richard was the young king's protector, this is not necessarily evidence of sinister intentions. More damning is the allegation of Edward Hall, the Tudor propagandist, that Sir Thomas Howard escorted William, lord Hastings (Edward IV's chamberlain and one of Richard's major rivals for power) to a meeting of the council in the Tower on 13 June 1483 that resulted in Hastings's judicial murder.[18]

In any case, on 25 June Richard assumed the station of king, installing himself in the chair of state at Westminster, with John Howard standing on his right as acting earl marshal. Two days later, the as-yet-uncrowned king created John Howard and the heirs male hereditary earls marshal, with a fee of twenty pounds a year. More important, this was followed immediately by Howard's creation as duke of Norfolk "by girding him with the sword and putting on the cap and golden circlet and delivery of the golden rod," with an annuity of forty pounds. John's son Thomas was then created earl of Surrey, with an annuity of twenty pounds.[19] On 25 July

Richard granted the Howards an array of former Mowbray lands and other East Anglian property seized from John de Vere, earl of Oxford, and the recently executed Earl Rivers.[20]

J. R. Lander has wondered why Richard "was buying Howard support upon a colossally expensive, unprecedented scale. It remains mysterious why they should have obtained so very much more than any other peerage family."[21] Yet Richard's reasons for these creations seem clear enough. Seizing power had entailed the murder of a number of aristocrats—Hastings, Rivers, Sir Richard Grey—and the alienation of others. Richard III and John Howard had been companions in arms at least as early as the battles of Barnet and Tewkesbury, and Richard was keenly aware of his need for the aid of able and loyal soldiers to retain the crown. In fact by October 1483, Norfolk and Surrey provided just such service in quelling the dangerous rebellion of Henry Stafford, duke of Buckingham, an early supporter of Gloucester who became disenchanted and risked everything in favor of Henry Tudor.[22] Without proof that the grants to the Howards were rewards for secret crimes beneficial to Richard, it can only be concluded that the creations were political bribery—a purchase of support that Richard knew he would need, and not payment for services rendered.

During the next year the Howards received additional rewards. On 21 August 1484 Surrey was given an annuity of eleven hundred pounds from the lands of the duchy of Cornwall during the life of his father, and on 7 December the Howards shared the rich wardship of Henry Bourchier, earl of Essex, with custody of his body and right of marriage for this cousin by marriage of Surrey's wife.[23] Surrey was made steward both of Richard's household and of the duchy of Lancaster for all Norfolk lands, and both father and son were appointed to various commissions of the peace, array and jail delivery.[24] The Howards were conspicuous under Richard, frequently employed in royal service, relied upon for loyal support, and well rewarded for their fidelity.

Since they had fared so well under Richard III, it is not surprising that the Howards hastened to the king's support when Henry Tudor, earl of Richmond, landed in Wales. Norfolk began raising troops in Essex, Norfolk and Suffolk, writing even to John Paston, in time of need a "well-beloved friend," to join him with a company of "tall men" dressed in Howard livery and paid at the duke's expense. Paston chose not to comply, and remained in Norfolk while the crown changed hands. He was not, of course, alone, which helps explain Richard's defeat by a pretender with inferior forces and a conspicuously weak claim to the throne.[25] With Norfolk in command of the vanguard and Surrey as his father's lieutenant, Richard met Henry near Market Bosworth on Monday, 22 August 1485. In the ensuing battle, Norfolk was slain and Surrey seriously wounded and taken prisoner. While the body of Richard III was tossed into an unmarked grave at Leicester, Norfolk was granted a respectful burial in the church of the Cluniac priory at Thetford. Surrey found himself in the Tower of London to await the pleasure of the new king.[26]

By early October Lady Surrey was at the priory of St. Catherine's near the Tower seeking word of her husband's fate. On 3 October she wrote to John Paston complaining that the king's servants had disrupted her house at Ashwelthorpe where her children—presumably including the young Thomas, at twelve the eldest child—had remained. Sir John Radcliff, steward of Henry VII's household, had come to Ashwelthorpe to seize the manor, but had to leave it in Elizabeth's hands as it was part of her Tilney inheritance. Even so, most of the servants were dismissed, leaving her, she complained, to keep house with only three or four. Everything that was Surrey's in his own right, or that would have descended to him from his father and the Mowbray inheritance, was forfeited to the crown.[27]

These seizures were legitimized by Henry's first Parliament; in December 1485 an act of attainder was passed against Norfolk, Surrey and twenty-six other supporters of Richard III. By the legal fiction that Henry VII's reign had begun the day before Bosworth, all could be declared traitors, their titles extinguished, and all lands and other possessions seized.[28] The office of earl marshal was granted to John Howard's co-heir and rival, William Berkeley, whom Richard had created earl of Nottingham. Henry also profited from the ruin of the Howards by renting out parcels of Howard lands to loyal peers such as the earl of Oxford and lord de la Warre.[29]

Henry had not decided what to do with the attainted earl of Surrey, but left the door open for rehabilitation by means of a pardon issued on 25 March 1486. Stripped of his dignity as earl and lawfully imprisoned at the king's pleasure, Thomas Howard was nonetheless pardoned of all treasons and felonies.[30] He was kept in the Tower until 1489, but was allowed forty shillings a week for board, as well as three servants at 3s. 6d. a week each. It cost Henry only 6s. 8d. a week for most of his prisoners, who were allowed no servants; the king must have thought Howard a good investment to have allowed eleven pounds a month for his safekeeping.[31]

In the spring of 1489, Henry VII finally gave Howard his liberty. With Surrey in attendance, Parliament reversed the attainders of John and Thomas Howard, but only restored Thomas as earl of Surrey, ignoring the fact that between his father's death in August and his attainder in December, Thomas had by right become duke of Norfolk. Surrey was permitted to enter only the lands from his wife's inheritance and from ancestors other than his father. The main parcels of Howard-Mowbray lands were withheld, perhaps as bond for future good behavior, and the lands rented to Oxford and others were likewise excepted.[32]

With the first session of Parliament ended, Surrey was sent to prove his loyalty by quelling a rising in Yorkshire that had led to the murder of the earl of Northumberland. Surrey dispersed the rebels, driving one leader into exile in Flanders and hanging another before returning to court. In the second session of Parliament Surrey won further rewards, being allowed entry into the rest of the Howard lands still in the king's hands, with rights to negotiate for purchase of the lands granted away.[33]

Only around 1490 do Surrey's children begin to appear as individuals; before then, little can be said about the eldest son, Thomas, and his siblings. We can speculate, based on events of later life, about their education and upbringing. Thomas and his brothers received a medieval education, studying Latin and French—Thomas showed familiarity with the languages throughout his life—and then following the usual course of grammar, rhetoric, logic, some arithmetic and a bit of music. The younger Thomas was old enough before his grandfather's death to have spent time at John Howard's house at Tendring Hall, Suffolk, and he might have read from a library well stocked with works of medieval piety and chivalry. Whether he read these books or not, at his grandfather's house or elsewhere, is not as important as the general intellectual atmosphere in which Thomas was raised and which such books represented.[34] Thomas may have shared the latter stages of his education with his cousin by marriage, John Bourchier, second lord Berners (1467–1533), the translator of the French chronicler Jean Froissart. Bourchier lived with the Howards at Ashwelthorpe during Surrey's imprisonment. If Bourchier's later writings are any indication, the education of the boys in Lady Surrey's household was heavily medieval and chivalric in outlook.[35]

The Howard brothers also trained for war, learning riding, swordsmanship, archery, and the handling of lance, sword, and shield. The Howards were well established as a family of soldiers, and Thomas and his younger brothers followed this tradition. It seems certain that a major aim of their education was to prepare them for knighthood, with training in the militant arts and chivalric conduct alike. Such was the normal regimen for boys of their status.[36]

In 1484, according to Sir George Buck's *History of Richard III*, published in 1619, Thomas Howard was brought to court and betrothed to Anne Plantagenet, Richard III's niece and third daughter of Edward IV.[37] Buck was a partisan of Richard III and had close ties to the later Howards; since Thomas and Anne eventually wed, there is no reason to suspect that this story is a fabrication, although no trace of the betrothal survives in the public records. What is certain is that Surrey's elder sons Thomas and Edward, now styled the lords Howard, were placed in Henry VII's household as pages. There they learned subservience to the new dynasty while being trained as gentlemen and serving as hostages to Surrey's repeatedly tested loyalty. In 1495, Thomas Howard wed Anne Plantagenet. They were married on 4 February at Westminster Abbey, and by 12 February an elaborate settlement had been worked out. Howard would be virtually landless and penniless until the death of the dowager duchess of Norfolk (who survived until 1507), and Anne had nothing but her name, so relatives had to provide for the couple. Surrey gave them the use of a number of manors, and was compensated by the crown with an annuity of £120, probably indicating the value of the lands. Among these manors was Stoke by Nayland in Suffolk which, along with Surrey's house at Lambeth, would be the couple's main residence. Henry's queen, Elizabeth of York, provided her sister Anne with twenty shillings a week for food and drink, and paid for a personal retinue of two women, a young maid, a gentleman, a yeoman, and three grooms, at £51 11s. 8d. a year, as well as an allowance of £16 9s. 4d. for seven horses. Anne's dress would be provided by her sister as the need arose.[38]

In the spring of 1497, Thomas Howard began his military career, joining some fifty gentlemen and knights sent to quell a rising of Cornishmen which culminated at Blackheath on 17 June. Having earned his spurs, Thomas was sent north to join his father, who was serving as lord lieutenant against the Scots. England's northern neighbor had been threatening

The Howard Family and Early Life

invasion for the past year, with James IV offering support to the Yorkist pretender Perkin Warbeck. After a series of skirmishes and raids in the late summer, James and Henry VII made a truce in September 1497 that led to a full-scale peace treaty in January 1502. For their part in the fighting, Thomas and his brother Edward were knighted by their father at Ayton Castle in September.[39]

During the rest of the reign of Henry VII, there are only scattered snatches of information about Sir Thomas Howard. In 1503, when Surrey and his wife escorted Henry's daughter Margaret to Scotland to seal the Anglo-Scots peace by marrying James IV, the earl's entire family went along.[40] Thomas also accompanied his father on an embassy to Flanders in 1507, no doubt a useful addition to his education. Surrey, Fox and several others were given charge of negotiations which led to a treaty in 1508 binding Charles of Burgundy, grandson of the emperor Maximilian, to wed Henry's younger daughter Mary.[41]

For the most part, Sir Thomas and his wife lived quietly at Stoke and Lambeth. Thomas does not seem to have been one of Henry VII's favorite courtiers; he was not present, for example, for the celebrations connected with the creation of the king's second son and namesake Henry as duke of York in 1494, nor was Howard included among the gentlemen and lords who took part in the reception for Catherine of Aragon in 1501, despite his father's part in meeting Catherine at Ambrewsbury. Thomas was involved in a few land deals with his father which have left traces in the public records and in 1506 was pardoned, along with his brother Edward and several other men, for an illegal entry upon a manor belonging to the estate of the late John Grey, lord Lisle.[42] Howard was busy with his wife and family, and does not seem to have been at court often. It is tempting to guess that Henry VII studied Thomas's character and found it wanting. Despite ample contact with the king, Thomas never became a favorite, and was little employed in public business, even as his father's adjunct. There is no way of knowing what kind of man Thomas was at this time, but if his later rough manners and taste for cruelty are any guide, he may already have been a rather unpleasant character.

Nor does much beyond the barest facts survive about Thomas's family. Although Anne and Thomas had a number of children, none lived to maturity. The longest lived, Thomas, was born about 1497, died in August 1508, and was buried in the Howard chapel at Lambeth. What was the boy like? How did Thomas feel about losing his namesake and heir? We have no way of knowing. It is a poignant reminder of how limited the sources of biography really are for the sixteenth century. With the rare exception of collections like the Paston letters, we have very little information on the personal lives of such as Thomas Howard, leaving the biographer to guess at his grief. Anne herself seems to have suffered poor health, leading to her early death from consumption in 1512 at the age of thirty-seven or eight. Thomas was left a childless widower after seventeen years of marriage.[43]

The Howards overcame the disgrace of their support of Richard III largely because Surrey and his sons proved useful to Henry VII. Like Richard before him, Henry needed loyal support to establish and maintain his hold over the kingdom. Surrey proved his worth in the north, and so by 1501 was allowed a larger role in government. On 25 June the earl was confirmed as treasurer and, as one of the great officers of state, became one of the executive triumvirate of Henry's council, along with Richard Fox, lord privy seal, and William Warham, the chancellor. Surrey's post as treasurer, as Tucker has demonstrated, was not necessarily the sinecure Elton regards it. The earl was constantly at court and in council, serving as the only prominent titled noble among Henry VII's heavily ecclesiastical inner circle.[44]

The death of Henry VII in April 1509 was neither a surprise nor cause for a dispute over the succession as had been the death of Edward IV twenty-six years earlier. Henry's failing health had prepared everyone for the end, and the last days were spent in anticipation of the new king rather than in remorse at the passing of the old. Henry VII was a tight-lipped and tight-pursed man, more respected than loved, whose court was frugal and businesslike. In the wings stood young Prince Henry, just less than eighteen, heir apparent since his brother Arthur's sudden death in 1502. Unlike his father, Henry had never known the danger and uncertainty of exile as the pretender to the throne of a troubled realm. Instead, he was brought up in a sheltered royal household, expecting for seven years to be king. Henry VII had kept his son on a tight rein, but with the old king's death, there would be no one to restrain a king who looked to a new dawn of European culture as his inspiration and who was already a patron of art, music and letters—a prince who fully expected to cut a grand figure in the world. Even as Henry VII lay dying the sycophants at court were shifting their allegiance to Prince Henry; the grimmer side of his character had not yet appeared to darken the picture.[45]

The Howard Family and Early Life

Henry VII's last illness was long and painful, and his end almost a relief. Sir Thomas Howard was named one of the lords attendant for the funeral, and with his father was issued black velvet livery of mourning. Sir Edward Howard carried the king's banner in the funeral procession, riding a horse trapped with the royal arms. Surrey was named an executor of the king's will, and at the burial stood by the grave with the other officials of state and household who broke their staves of office and cast them down.[46] For the Howards, the transition from Henry VII to his son was far smoother than that from Richard III to the first Tudor. Nobles only since 1483, the Howards already saw themselves as rightful servants and councilors of the king, and they must have looked to the young Henry Tudor with hope and expectation, perhaps mixed with relief. Surrey and his sons were anxious to prove their loyalty and usefulness. The dukedom of Norfolk still stood as the last great reward to be earned; the Howards were prepared to study the new king, to judge how best to serve him, and to win reward for that service.

CHAPTER 2

THE RESURGENCE OF THE HOWARDS, 1509–1513

THE ACCESSION OF HENRY VIII gave the Howards a great opportunity for improving their position. The new king, born in 1491, knew little about the struggles of the later fifteenth century; the Howard family disaster at Bosworth could be swept under the rug as Surrey and his sons sought to impress the young Henry with their loyalty and usefulness as soldiers and councilors. In the first five years of the new reign, the Howards were spectacularly successful in proving their worth, capped off by their striking defeat of the king of Scots at Flodden.

In the process, Thomas Howard the younger established himself as an important soldier and sailor and, with the prize of the earldom of Surrey won at Flodden, moved out of his father's shadow to became a man of importance in his own right. In the early years of Henry VIII's reign, Thomas Howard's career as courtier and soldier and the outlines of his political personality took shape.

For the first time in as long as many men could remember, a new king came to the throne without battles or bloodshed. Henry VIII succeeded to the crown a few months younger than eighteen. There was no question of imposing a council of regency upon him, but in the early months of the reign, Henry had still to gain the experience of an effective ruler. In this situation, some writers have suggested, Henry VII's veteran councilors took advantage of the young king. The earl of Surrey, as treasurer, has been accused of using his position to encourage the king to lavish expenditure and wasteful pageantry, dissipating the resources of the crown in order to worm the Howard family into Henry's closest circle.[1] Surrey's biographer defends the earl as having merely acted the courtier, studying Henry's character and adapting himself to please the king. Henry VII had been tightfisted, but his son was eager to make his mark, whatever the cost; where the old king had been self-restrained and suspicious, Henry VIII had an easygoing manner with friendship extended, it seemed, to all. Surrey saw the difference between father and son and, with understandable self-interest, sought to advance family interests by playing to the young king's temper. In this, Surrey was not alone, for after the harsh rule of Henry VII, the Tudor nobles were anxious to see that Henry VIII did not emulate his father; instead, his councilors made every effort to encourage him toward pleasure and ease rather than attention to administration. A king occupied with hunting, jousting, feasts and games was much to be preferred to the hardworking, ruthless and suspicious Henry VII.[2]

For Henry VIII was, as all were quick to note, generous and liberal, a magnificent prince who was expected to lead England to martial glory.[3] Lord Mountjoy wrote to his friend and tutor Erasmus of Henry's openhanded patronage and love of learning,[4] and the chronicles agree that Henry's accession was greeted with general relief and expectation.[5] Under the circumstances, Surrey did exactly what any sensible courtier would have done; if as a side effect of his support of Henry's extravagance, Surrey's family grew in royal favor, so much the better.

At the coronation of Henry VIII and Catherine of Aragon, Surrey served as earl marshal.[6] His son Sir Thomas was also involved in the passing of the crown, being paid five hundred marks along with Sir John Carre on 24 May for his services in Henry VII's funeral and Henry VIII's coronation.[7] Thomas Howard also joined in the tournament held to celebrate the coronation. Henry VIII did not attempt feats of arms in his own honor, but there were many knights at court who did. Thomas, Edward and Edmund Howard, as well as Richard Grey (brother of the marquis of Dorset), Charles Brandon and Sir Thomas Knevet (brother-in-law of the Howards) rode as challengers against Henry's answerers, who included Sir John Carre. On the first day, Thomas Howard and Carre won prizes as the most skillful combatants in the tournaments.[8] On the second day, the challenges exchanged indicate that tempers had run high the day before, for there was talk (even if only a chivalric pose) of a fight to the death in the day's swordplay. This was vetoed by Henry and the ladies, but knightly passions did increase to the point that the final event of the tournament, a general battle on horseback, became a near riot. The king's guard was called in, and the contest was stopped only with "grate payn." Even so, it was a splendid spectacle and a fit opening to the reign of a decidedly martial and glory-seeking king.[9]

Most of Henry's closest friends in the early years of his reign, such as Charles Brandon and William Compton, shared his passion for hunting, gambling, dancing and feasting. Fitness as royal advisors had nothing to do with their rise. The king kept court with these men and left government in the hands of carryovers from his father, including the treasurer, Surrey. The earl was too old at sixty-five to keep up with an eighteen-year-old king, but he was well supplied with sons and sons-in-law who could compete for the favor of a vigorous prince. Sir Edward Howard, granted the office of king's bannerer on 16 May 1509 with a fee of forty pounds,[10] became a close royal companion. Sir Thomas Knevet and Sir Thomas Boleyn, wed to Surrey's daughters, were also much at court. The other Howard sons were less favored, although hardly excluded from Henry's circle. Thomas, at thirty-six, may have been too old for Henry. Edmund, not yet thirty, never found the king's fancy for some reason. Even so, they often appeared at court, doing their part to keep the family prominent.

While Sir Edward, Knevet and Boleyn danced and hunted with the king, Thomas Howard was busy reaping family and personal rewards. After being nominated to the Order of the Garter but not elected in 1509, on 27 April 1510 Thomas was added to that select company.[11] Howard was also busy improving his finances through a series of land deals with the crown. Among these were several exchanges that clarified his holdings by virtue of his wife Anne, daughter of Edward IV. In return for scattered lands that had come to Anne through her grandmother, the couple were guaranteed an income of a thousand marks a year, and Howard was granted two East Anglian manors in his own right. Howard also obtained a parcel of lands valued at some seven hundred pounds *per annum* in joint tenancy for life with Anne, in exchange for her rights of inheritance from her father, Edward IV.[12] In another deal in November 1509, Surrey, Thomas and Edmund Howard and Thomas Boleyn obtained the lease of the lands of Elizabeth, daughter and heiress of Sir John Grey, viscount Lisle. Lisle had died in 1504, but had been married to Surrey's daughter Muriel, who later wed Thomas Knevet. Thus the lands of this minor niece were retained in Howard hands pending her marriage.[13]

The younger Thomas Howard was often at court on state occasions to take part in pageants and celebrations. As Sydney Anglo has demonstrated, these displays were an important element in Tudor foreign policy and public relations alike. The prowess at the joust of Henry and his knights lent a martial reputation to a king yet untried in war. Likewise, the processions through London and the tournaments at Westminster were public spectacles, viewed by many of the ruder sort not socially fitted to take part. The steps of the social hierarchy were never more visible than when the king and court appeared in full splendor before the public eye.[14]

On 1 January 1511 the awaited son and Tudor heir was born to the royal couple, prompting the most lavish celebrations of the reign. Prince Henry's birth was commemorated by a spectacular round of banquets, pageants and processions. Thomas and Edward Howard rode in the accompanying jousts, with Thomas honored as bearer of the king's helmet in the closing ceremonies.[15] The celebrations turned to mourning with the death of the newly christened prince on 22 February. Sir Thomas Howard turned with the rest of the court to the sadder observances of a state funeral, riding as one of the six official mourners in the procession to Westminster Abbey.[16]

The court shortly recovered composure enough to go a-Maying. Henry held another tournament early in the month at Greenwich, with Thomas and Edward Howard taking part.[17] Yet the days of martial play-acting were drawing to a close as Henry contemplated more serious matters and the prospect of real war. There was a considerable struggle for influence at court in the resultant effort to mold English policy. Surrey and Richard Fox, bishop of Winchester, had initially been the main contestants for dominance of government. Fox had the support of William Warham, chancellor and archbishop of Canterbury, while Surrey headed a mostly secular party including Sir Henry Marney, chancellor of the duchy of Lancaster; Thomas lord Darcy; George Talbot, earl of Shrewsbury and an associate of Surrey in the exchequer; and Thomas Ruthal, bishop of Durham.[18] The two groups agreed, however, that Henry VII's policy of peace should be continued; Surrey, Fox and Ruthal negotiated a renewed Anglo-French peace in March 1510 even as Henry railed at the French ambassador for daring to speak of friendship.[19]

Thomas Wolsey's rise to prominence changed the balance, supplying Henry with a councilor willing to implement a policy of aggression and war. Wolsey entered royal service as a chaplain to Henry VII in 1507; by November 1510 he was Henry VIII's almoner and a councilor, probably at least at first pushed forward by Fox as an ally against Surrey and the secular party.[20]

Wolsey was soon seeking an independent position on the council and encouraging Henry to seek martial glory in France. Fox reluctantly fell into line, especially after Pope Julius II suggested a Holy League against France and Louis XII responded by calling a schismatic council to meet at Pisa in May 1511. England now had a higher purpose in waging war in France—or at least so the clerical party thought.[21] Surrey still hung back, for continental war seemed an unpromising venture—especially in alliance with the slippery and impecunious Ferdinand of Spain. If there was to be war, the Howards favored action against a nearer and more pressing enemy, the Scots. Yet with Fox and Wolsey allied against him in council, Surrey had to turn to other means to advance his policy with the king.

In the summer of 1511, Surrey's sons took part in a venture that hints at the earl's success in swaying Henry. In August Thomas and Edward Howard were sent out to engage Andrew Barton, a favorite sea captain of James IV. Barton, sailing with letters of marque against Portugal, had taken several English ships on the pretext that they were carrying Portuguese goods. Henry was willing to view Barton as a pirate; without complaining to James, the king turned the Howards loose to capture him. In the ensuing fight, a full-scale sea battle in the Channel, Barton was killed and his two ships, the *Lion* and *Jenny Perwin*, captured.[22]

To Surrey's delight, James was outraged and protested, without effect, that Henry had broken the Anglo-Scots truce solemnized by the marriage of the king of Scots and Margaret Tudor in 1502. James was angry enough to fight had England pursued the matter but, despite Surrey's prodding, Henry still thought it more rewarding to attack France. Wolsey had persuaded the king to risk greater dangers to seek a greater prize. The public acclaim that greeted Barton's death was considerable and the Howard brothers were heroes, but it was not enough. Surrey's opening, so promising in August, was blocked the next month. Surrey may have overplayed his hand in pushing Henry to follow up the defeat of Barton with further action against the Scots, for on 30 September Wolsey wrote to Fox that the earl had been so discountenanced by his latest meeting with Henry that he had retired from court, leaving the field to the anti-French party. Nonetheless, the Howards continued their stirrings against Scotland, for Wolsey complained that Edward Howard used his closeness with Henry to urge the king to war with James.[23]

By November 1511 Surrey returned to court, ready to implement the king's chosen policy. Having lost this round, Surrey made the best of things and tried to reclaim the king's confidence by a show of support for the French war. In October the Holy League was signed at Rome,[24] and Henry and Ferdinand agreed soon after that an English assault on France would commence by 30 April 1512.[25]

With this commitment to war, the Howards found fresh employment. Surrey was sent to watch over the north of the realm, Edward was given a command at sea, and Thomas and Edmund joined the English army supporting Ferdinand's invasion of southern France. Thomas Grey, marquis of Dorset (and a Howard cousin by marriage), was named commander of the army in Spain; Thomas Howard was commissioned as Dorset's second in command and successor should the marquis be killed or incapacitated.[26]

In May 1512 Dorset's company assembled at Southampton. The marquis, as well as Thomas and Edmund Howard and their future brother-in-law Rhys ap Griffith, were among the lords Hall described as "so well-armed and so richly appareled in clothes of gold, and of silver, and Velvettes of sundery coloures, pounsed and enbbroudered." Even the "petie capitaines were in Satin and damaske of white and green [the Tudor colors].... The Baners, Penons, Standerdes and Gittons, fresh and newly painted, with sundry beasts and devises, it was a pleasure to behold."[27] The lords of England went to war dressed as if for a Westminster banquet.

Henry had not yet learned how little he could trust his father-in-law Ferdinand, even though Lord Thomas Darcy's expedition of May 1511 had been a fiasco. Sent with a thousand men to aid Ferdinand in an assault on the Moors in North Africa that was abandoned before it was launched, Darcy had accomplished almost nothing and had let his men run amok in an embarrassing drunken riot in Cadiz. Dorset, with six thousand men, would merely fail on a larger and more expensive scale.[28]

On 1 June, Dorset, the Howards and their army arrived at San Sebastian. Soon after, they marched to Fuentarrabia and then defeated a French force in a skirmish near Bayonne. After that, the English mired down. The allies could not agree on an objective for the English push into Aquitaine, nor did Ferdinand supply the horses and ordinance he had promised. By 8 July, Thomas Howard wrote to Wolsey to outline the English plight but also to assure him that the troops were in good order, not yet troubled by sickness as were the Spanish soldiers. The king's supplies were being preserved carefully in hopes that some action might be taken against the French, but already Howard saw hints of disaster. The Spanish, he wrote, would not extend the English any aid, for they loved money better than their own kin.[29] This letter is the first important surviving document written by Thomas Howard, and it reveals several of his prominent characteristics, both positive and negative: persistence in the face of troubles, studious loyalty to royal policy, and a well-developed ability to shift the blame for problems to any shoulders but his own. Howard was always quick to claim credit for success but equally swift to find scapegoats and blame conditions beyond his control for failure. And so it would be in Spain.

Soaked by relentless rains, with too few tents to cover the men and no carriages to move them elsewhere, short of food and beer and thus forced to local food and wine which made the men sick, and with camp fevers and desertions thinning the ranks, Dorset's army rotted away inactive in northern Spain. Dorset himself fell ill, leaving Thomas Howard nominally in charge. Yet the English lords were loath to accept Howard's command—especially when he urged the army to stay on all winter if necessary to do some notable exploit. The soldiers vented their anger on Wolsey, whom they blamed for their plight, or so reported Wolsey's servant William Knight, who wrote that he feared for his life if it were discovered that he was writing to the king's almoner. By October continued Spanish indifference to the English plight forced Howard to contemplate withdrawing. Ferdinand had long since seized Navarre and, having achieved his own war aims, had no further interest in the English. When word arrived that Henry was planning to send a new commander to replace Dorset, near mutiny ensued. Howard finally hired ships to send the army home, including Dorset, who "was so weake he asked where he was." By December 1512 the tattered remnants of the army were in England. Henry was upset with the performance of his commanders, but even more enraged with Ferdinand, who had so profited by Henry's loss that, according to Hall, "the Englishmen left as muche money there [in Spain] as he [Ferdinand] sent into England" as Catherine's dowry.[30]

The war was in abeyance for the winter. In the spring, Thomas Howard would find new service. In the meantime, he faced another important task. During the winter of 1512–13 his wife Anne died, leaving him a childless widower. This was no fit estate for the son of an earl, and Howard was quick to repair his loss by seeking a match with economic as well as political possibilities—marriage to a daughter of Edward Stafford, duke of Buckingham, the premier peer and richest subject in England.[31]

Buckingham had two eligible daughters, and at Shrovetide 1513 Thomas Howard joined the Staffords at Thronbury to look them over. He settled upon Elizabeth, who was about nineteen to Howard's forty. Elizabeth had been one of Catherine of Aragon's attendants, and perhaps a member of the queen's household, as were several Stafford aunts, Buckingham's sisters. It is possible that Elizabeth and Thomas already knew each other, for both had been at court for Henry VIII's coronation. In any case, the arrangements were made swiftly. Brushing aside the inconvenience of Elizabeth's romance with the young Ralph Neville (later forth earl of Westmorland), Buckingham gave his daughter to Howard, and by Easter they were married. The duke settled an annuity of five hundred marks on Elizabeth and gave Howard a dowry of twenty-five hundred marks.[32]

While this was obviously an attractive financial deal for Howard, the political value of the Stafford match is more difficult to assess. Despite his high status—and royal bloodlines that were at least the equal of the king's—Buckingham was not a courtier except by royal command; his preference was to live in high estate in the west of the realm, exercising his authority as warden of the Welsh Marches. His children's marriages gave Buckingham wide connections within the nobility and made him a potentially powerful force in politics. Yet pride may have stood in the way of Edward Stafford's political influence. As premier peer of the realm, Buckingham was particularly offended by the rise of Thomas Wolsey, the low-born butcher's son, and made little secret of his distaste. By the mid 1510s, Wolsey's political dominance was firmly established, and Buckingham lost, or gave up any effort to hold, significant political power. As a result, the match with Elizabeth Stafford may have been economically attractive to Thomas Howard but in the long run became something of a political liability.

At the time of his second marriage Thomas Howard had little time for family life. On 12 August 1512 his brother-in-law Thomas Knevet was killed in a foolhardy adventure at sea off Brest battling the French. Edward Howard, Henry's lord admiral, vowed to avenge Knevet's death and as a result was himself killed on 25 April 1513 in a daring but ill-advised attack on the French galleys. The English fleet, which had been ravaging the French coast and holding the French navy at bay in Brest, was demoralized by Howard's death and abandoned the blockade, straggling home in shock to Plymouth.[33]

Edward's death deprived the Howards of Henry's favorite of Surrey's sons, but did bring Thomas Howard new duties. On 25 April, he was appointed admiral in succession to his brother, and by 7 May had arrived at Plymouth to view the shambles of the royal fleet. That day he wrote to Wolsey and Henry from the flagship *Mary Rose* to report that the soldiers of the fleet were scattered around the countryside and that morale was at a nadir. The men so feared the French galleys that had taken Knevet's and Howard's lives that "they had as leve go in to Purgatory as to the trade [of battle]." Henry's scathing letters of rebuke to the captains had only made matters worse. Nonetheless, Howard was determined to restore order and discipline; to give the men a sense of purpose, he asked Henry to issue orders for raids into Brittany. Howard also promised to set an example of tough discipline by punishing two men who "did their part veray ill that day my brother was lost."[34]

Henry sent the requested authorization to attack Brittany, providing cover for Charles Brandon (created lord Lisle on 15 May) to invade France with four thousand men while the main body of an army of invasion— to be led by Henry—was prepared.[35] Things did not go smoothly for the admiral. Adverse winds kept the fleet at Plymouth, despite his efforts to move to safer anchorage at Portsmouth. Howard wrote to court constantly, seeking faster delivery of supplies; on 16 May he apologized to Wolsey for all his letters. The king and Wolsey must be "weary of my often writing, but I had rather be judged too quick than too slow."[36]

In his frustration, Howard went to London to seek audience with the king in hopes of speeding the flow of material to the fleet. The king and his war minister were not accessible; even while at Wolsey's own Hampton Court, Howard was forced to communicate with them by letter, for Wolsey was at Bridewell, and Henry and the council had moved to Greenwich. Nevertheless, the mission was a success, and Howard obtained a share of the supplies being collected for the French invasion, although Wolsey instructed Howard to send his own transports to London, as Henry could spare none from his fleet for the admiral.[37] By 8 June, Howard had finished his business in London and rejoined his fleet, which had finally arrived at Portsmouth. With supplies coming in, he wrote the council that he expected to capture Brest while Henry landed in France, since the French were reported to be beaching their ships and sending the men to Calais to repel Henry's landing there. Confident of a successful role in the coming war, Howard declared that he knew of no better service he could do, unless the Scots and Danes invaded.[38]

The last was said in jest, for Howard did not know that his family would have no part in the continental war. The Brittany raid had been intended only to keep the French off balance while the main English invasion was mounted. Bad weather and supply problems delayed action well into June. In the meantime, Henry left London, joining his army in Calais by 30 June. With the king and half the nobility in France, someone had to stay in England to look after Catherine and manage affairs, and Henry chose the Howards. If there were to be any battles on the home front, who better could Henry leave behind than Surrey, veteran of the borders? And who was better qualified to advise Catherine than the experienced councilor and treasurer? So Surrey and his sons found themselves denied a share of the glory of renewal of the Hundred Years' War and relegated to home defense. Surrey doubtless was as enraged and aggrieved as Mattingly portrayed him at Henry's departure for, left behind, the earl was helpless to prevent his rivals, and especially Wolsey, from increasing their influence with Henry at his expense. It was, in reality, both a compliment and an insult to be left to defend the kingdom, but the Howards seem to have been more aware of the insult.[39]

James IV had not forgotten Henry's high-handed treatment of the Andrew Barton affair, and as soon as Henry was in France the rumblings from Scotland increased in volume and tempo. Surrey must have suspected that the Scots would return to their "olde prankes . . . to invade England when the kyng is oute," for Henry had given James ample provocation, even by rough-and-tumble sixteenth century standards. Perhaps Henry refused to believe that James would invade, for the English held the Scots in light regard, seeing them as border brigands and French-paid mercenaries.[40] Even in his later years Henry tended to underestimate the threat of Scotland, but, as he was about to find out, it was a very real peril. At Henry's departure, Anne of Brittany, queen of France, was busy urging James to be her chosen knight against the English—an appeal calculated especially for the chivalric king of Scots.[41] Yet the Scots had reasons for war beyond the obligations of the Auld Alliance. Andrew Barton's death and Henry's refusal to consider Scotland's version of the story, as he was bound to do by treaty, gnawed at James. And this was not the only breach of treaty. James's warden of the East Marches, Sir Robert Kerr, had been murdered by an Englishman, the "Bastard" John Heron of Ford. Heron took shelter in his English castle, and Henry refused to deliver him up as the treaty of 1502 required. Further, Henry had never finished paying Margaret's dowry, a share of which had been due since Henry VII's death. It was an added sore to James that in all his diplomatic wrangles with the English he was forced to deal with Nicholas West, bishop of Ely, whom he personally despised. West shared Henry's contempt for the Scots and made no effort to disguise his feelings. Hardly the least of James's complaints was the continued English claim to the throne of Scotland, publicly rehearsed as recently as in the preamble of the Subsidy Act of 1512.[42]

Given these grievances, the Scots had every reason to invade England in Henry's absence. Why, then, did Henry go to France, leaving Surrey with only a small force to defend the realm? Henry's lust for martial glory in France, which blinded him to the danger from Scotland, must be the main reason. Fox and the other councilors, sounding a loyal chorus, unanimously assured the king that the Scots would not dare attack. Surrey was more cautious. On 22 July the earl left London with his personal retinue of five hundred men, and by 1 August he was at Pontefract Castle in Yorkshire taking musters and surveying defenses. James IV was already gathering his own forces, reported as large as 120,000 men (but certainly far fewer); on 12 August the king of Scots sent his Lyon Herald to France to deliver a formal defiance to Henry VIII. In the meantime, James sent Alexander, lord Hume, to ravage across the borders. When Hume unexpectedly met Sir William Bulmer, English warden of the East Marches, the Scots were routed. In response, James left Edinburgh on 19 August, crossed the Tweed two days later, and laid siege to Norham Castle, which fell by 29 August.[43] The invasion had begun in earnest.

While James moved to assault Ford Castle in revenge for Robert Kerr's murder, Surrey gathered his forces at Newcastle and marched to Alnwick. Provisions were scarce, forcing the English to keep moving to forage for new supplies. Surrey was joined by his son Thomas, the admiral, who brought part of his fleet to Newcastle and by 4 September had marched with about a thousand men to join his father at Alnwick. The opposing armies were now less than twenty miles apart, although separated by rough and hilly terrain cut by several rivers and dozens of streams.[44] James's army, surely never as large as has sometimes been claimed, probably numbered about 30,000. Surrey's force was about 20,000, mostly seasoned militia, veterans of many border campaigns.[45]

With Thomas Howard in camp, assignments for battle formations were made. The vanguard was placed under the admiral, with his brother Edmund and Sir Marmaduke Constable on the wings. Surrey took the rear guard, with Lord Thomas Dacre and Sir Edward Stanley on the wings; from this position, Surrey would be able to view the battlefield and direct troop movements. On the evening of 4 September, Surrey sent his pursuivant to James to offer battle. The earl promised to release the Scottish prisoners in his hands if James would refrain from destroying Ford Castle. The admiral added a personal message that he was ready to answer for Andrew Barton on land since the Scots' navy had gone to hide in France.[46] James answered this challenge by finishing his demolition of Ford Castle, after which the Scots moved across the river Till to a strong position on Flodden Hill overlooking Surrey's line of approach. The king of Scots held Surrey's messenger in his camp to prevent the English from getting details of the new position, but Surrey did not wait for an answer to his challenge. By 6 September the earl had marched to Wooler, some five miles upstream of James's position. From Wooler, Surrey sent another challenge, calling on James to meet with him on Milfield plain or some other "convenient and fayre grounde for twoo hostes to fight on." This James brushed aside with the scornful comment that it was unseemly for an earl to challenge a prince.[47] Surrey was forced to take the fight to James.

The English needed to join battle soon. They had spent a week marching through rain and chill weather, and supplies were nearly exhausted. James meanwhile was encamped, dry, and well supplied. The English could not win a waiting game. Thus Surrey broke camp and moved northeast to Barmer Wood. Here, across the Till from Flodden, the English made camp on 8 September; they could not move from this spot without being seen by James from the high ground of Flodden.[48]

On the evening of 8 September Surrey held a council of war. There are several versions of how a plan of action for the battle was decided. According to Holinshed, the younger Thomas Howard had surveyed the countryside from a nearby hill and had seen that James might be outflanked by a movement across the Till north of Flodden, and thereby "the Scottish king should either be inforced to come downe foorth of his strength and give batell, or else be stopped from receiving vittels or anie other thing out of Scotland." Surrey accepted his son's advice, and thus the English plan of a flanking movement was set.[49] Other authors have disputed Thomas Howard's authorship of this plan, following Hall who, though repeating the story of the admiral viewing the Scottish position from a hill, merely states that "it was concluded betweeene the Erle and hys counsayll" that the Scots' position could be turned.[50]

By five o'clock on the morning of 9 September, the younger Thomas Howard broke camp and marched north along the Till to Twizel Bridge. By noon, he crossed over and moved south toward the Scots' position some three miles distant. Surrey, with the artillery, left camp later and must have traveled more slowly, yet by late afternoon when the battle was joined, had reunited with his sons below Branxton Hill. Surrey may also have crossed Twizel Bridge, following his sons, but probably did not have time enough to do so before reaching the field. Instead, it is most likely that Surrey crossed the Till at Milford, between Twizel Bridge and James's camp. Since Surrey was dividing his forces in the face of a superior force, crossing the Tweed under James's nose was a highly dangerous move, but probably necessary in order to join battle before daylight was lost. There was a degree of confusion among the English when the fighting began at four o'clock—the admiral did not know where his father was and sent a messenger with a token to bring the earl into battle—and it is possible that the separate movements were unplanned and unintended.[51]

During the morning of 9 September, James noted the northward English thrust and broke camp on Flodden Hill, moving several hundred yards north to the high ground of Branxton Hill. Upon leaving Flodden the Scots set fire to their refuse, creating a smoke screen which prevented either side from having a clear view of the other's movements. In moving to Branxton, the Scots deployed in five units. James held the center, with the combined forces of Home and Huntley to his left, and Errol on the left flank. Lennox and Argyll were on James's right, and Bothwell commanded a rear guard. With both armies divided into semi-independent units, the battle became a set of simultaneous but separate encounters.[52]

Thomas Howard advanced almost to the foot of Branxton Hill with his brother Edmund, who had the baggage train, to his right, before the fighting began. At this point, Edmund was sighted by Home, whose troop of borderers swooped down on the outnumbered and overburdened English.

Edmund's forces were routed and the baggage looted;[53] this occupied the Scots long enough for Edmund to retreat under the cover of Dacre's men. Meanwhile, Surrey and James began an artillery duel to the east. The Scots' higher ground now proved a disadvantage. English fire raked the Scottish position, while the Scots gunners could not depress their pieces far enough to hit the English. Disgruntled by this uneven exchange, the Scottish soldiers could not be held; James was forced to abandon the high ground and advance down toward the English. As James engaged Surrey, Thomas Howard found himself facing Errol, supported by a troop of pikemen under Crawford and Montrose.[54] Sir Edward Stanley, finding no enemy in his path, passed around the battlefield to the east, swept around the foot of Branxton Hill, and fell on Lennox and Argyll's rear. Under a hail of English arrows, the Scots broke ranks and fled down the hill in confusion, leaving Lennox and Argyll dead on the hilltop.[55]

The tide of battle turned to the English with Stanley's charge. Lennox and Argyll's men only added to the confusion in the Scottish ranks, while Stanley followed the retreat, placing the main body of James's army under attack from two sides. As in many battles before, English arrows rained down on the massed Scots. On the wet, sloping ground, the Scottish spearmen found the English sword and bill superior in close combat. The spear, or Swiss pike, was five or six yards long, a fine defense employed in formation against cavalry, but unwieldy against foot soldiers. The bill, an oak staff six feet long with a curved blade on the end, was a more versatile weapon, dealing jagged wounds even through body armor.[56]

As night approached, the English ring closed upon the king of Scots. Unlike Surrey, whose gout forced him to direct the battle from a litter, James entered the general melee on foot and fought among his men. Only the poets tell of James's death, for all that is certain is that the dawn found him dead among his slain followers, when he had last been seen alive at dusk, hardly a spear length from Surrey's litter. The field was in English hands. As the admiral's men moved onto the field that morning of 10 September, a last band of eight hundred Scots attempted a counterattack to save their artillery, but Thomas Howard drove them off and seized James's prized brass cannon. The battle of Flodden was over.[57]

The English immediately claimed to have slain ten or twelve thousand Scots, while losing only four or five hundred. The latter figure must be too low, but the former may be realistic. With less than perfect accuracy, Hall listed over forty-five Scottish bishops, abbots, earls, lords, knights and other gentlemen among the dead. Other records confirm that the Scots' casualties were high: of seventy men from the town of Selkirk who left in August, only one man returned in September. A nineteenth-century Scottish genealogist said of Flodden: "The more I look into any Scottish charter-chest, the more I am sensibly struck; almost every distinguished Scottish family having then been prematurely deprived of an ancestor or member."[58] Sir Charles Oman concluded that of twenty-one earls of the Scottish peerage in 1513, eleven died at Flodden; only one who was present survived. Of twenty-nine barons, thirteen fell and only two who fought escaped. The English, on the other hand, lost no peers and only about ten knights, most of whom were with Edmund Howard and died early in the battle.[59] Modern scholars have reached a consensus that something like ten thousand Scots were killed at Flodden. The battle was a disaster of catastrophic magnitude for the Scots.

It remains a matter of conjecture how the Scots, with the advantages of position, superior supplies and probably at least slightly greater numbers could have been so completely routed. Better weapons, more effective use of artillery, superior leadership (especially since James and his commanders joined the fray while Surrey directed his forces from the rear), and superior tactics have all been credited to the English side. As Melvin Tucker, Surrey's biographer, noted, probably not enough credit has been given to the earl's bold generalship—or to the English lack of food and drink which made decisive action necessary.[60] A combination of factors gave Surrey victory, but not least of these was the fierce determination of the Howards not to lose the kingdom left in their care. Sir John McEwen gave a great share of the credit to the ferocious fighting of Surrey's sons; Thomas, the admiral, was in the thick of the fight and lived up to the tenor of his challenge to James to answer for Andrew Barton by giving no quarter and taking no prisoners. Despite the rout he suffered in Home's charge, Edmund fought bravely and was knighted on the field by Surrey, along with forty others, the day after the battle.[61]

While Flodden was fought, Henry VIII pursued the sport of war in France, winning Therouanne and Tournai by siege and, on 16 August, joining a cavalry skirmish which was grandly described as the Battle of the Spurs. Word of Flodden reached Henry on 23 September just as Tournai opened its gates to the Anglo-Imperial besiegers. Catherine's letter, written on 16 September, carefully attributed the victory to God and Henry and not to Surrey, but even as the earl made his way south, public opinion had a strong voice. On 20 September Thomas Ruthal, bishop of Durham, wrote to Wolsey to suggest that Surrey be made duke of Norfolk for his victory and that Henry give special thanks to Admiral Thomas Howard, Lord Dacre, Sir Edward Stanley and the other English leaders at Flodden.[62]

Henry agreed that the Howards had given final, undoubted proof of their loyalty. On the other hand, the king was somewhat irked that the talk of court and country praised Surrey's victory so highly; he did not want his own efforts on the continent ignored. Henry therefore decided to raise Surrey to his father's dukedom and to reward his son with the earldom of Surrey, but at the same time, to honor his commanders in France, Charles Brandon and Charles Somerset, with a dukedom and earldom. Henry's new elevations to the peerage would serve to signal as clearly as possible that England would continue on a warlike course, with these noble warriors sure to take prominent roles.[63]

The victory at Flodden closed a chapter in the Howards' rise into the upper rank of the peerage. During the reign of Henry VII, the Howards had been readmitted to royal trust only slowly and grudgingly. Henry VIII's accession brought greater opportunities to win prestige, and Surrey and his sons were quick to grasp them. The deaths of Edward Howard and his brother-in-law Thomas Knevet were harsh blows to the family fortunes, for Thomas and Edmund Howard would never be as close to the king as their brother had been. For Surrey, the rise of Wolsey as Henry's *alter rex* was all the more bitter in that it was a matter of suitability to do the king's work rather than hunger for influence and power that elevated the priest over the peer. The decision to fight France was probably the turning point in Wolsey's eclipse of Surrey. Yet ironically Surrey and his sons, left behind to guard the rear while Henry sought glory in France, redeemed all by victory over the Scots. Henry brought home battle flags and a few noble prisoners, while the Howards sent him the coat of a king. The end of 1513 and the beginning of 1514 were a time of triumph for the Howards; it remained to be seen how the seventy-year-old duke and his forty-year-old son would capitalize on their newly won prestige and titles.

CHAPTER 3

THE MAKING OF THE DUKE OF NORFOLK, 1514–1524

THE VICTORY AT FLODDEN brought Thomas Howard a peerage in his own right and marked his entry into the upper circles of royal service. Yet several things stood in the way of his further rise. One was his father. Surely no son wishes for the death of a father before his time, but only with the duke of Norfolk's death in 1524 would Howard's path be made clear to the highest rungs of the political ladder. The other barrier was Thomas Wolsey, whose service during the French war cemented his position as Henry's leading minister. Relations between Howard and Wolsey were never good; Wolsey clearly did not trust Howard, and did all he could to keep him away from the king. Yet Howard was too useful to leave unemployed, and during the decade from 1514 to 1524 he had a variety of military and administrative tasks which only added to his prestige. The period from Flodden until his accession to the dukedom served as the final stage of Howard's apprenticeship. By 1524 he would emerge as a seasoned and dangerous rival to Wolsey.

At the beginning of the winter legal term following Flodden and the campaign in France, Henry VIII delivered the rewards he had promised his commanders. Patents of nobility were delivered to the lords on 1 February; the following day, the feast of Candlemas, ceremonies of creation were held at the archbishop of Canterbury's Lambeth palace. The king, the leading nobles, and a crowd of ladies and gentlemen filled the hall as the lords, dressed in velvet and satin, came forward to be girded with swords and created in their new titles. The earl of Surrey was raised to duke of

Norfolk, with an annuity of forty pounds and a grant of forty manors to support his new dignity. Sir Thomas Howard was made earl of Surrey (his father resigning the title) with an annuity of twenty pounds and a life estate in sixteen manors, two castles, and a rent with an annual value of £333 6s. 8d. Further, the senior Howard "and his heirs forever" were granted an augmentation of arms in commemoration of the victory at Flodden and the death of James IV, "viz., on a bend on the shield of Howard a demi-lion gules, pierced in the mouth with an arrow, and colored according to the arms of Scotland, as borne by the said king of Scots." Charles Brandon, viscount Lisle, was made duke of Suffolk, and Henry's lord chamberlain Charles Somerset, lord Herbert, was created earl of Worcester, each with annuities and lands.[1] By rewarding the commanders of the army in France, Henry emphasized that, great as the victory of Flodden may have been, Tournai, Therouanne and the Battle of the Spurs were not to be forgotten.

Nor was Wolsey, the tireless organizer of the French war, left unrewarded. On 6 February he was made bishop of Lincoln, and by the end of the year exchanged Lincoln for the rich archbishopric of York. As further ecclesiastical reward for his service in France, Wolsey obtained the bishopric of Tournai—a see he would visit no more often than York. The new archbishop also moved into prominence on the council, outstripping Henry VIII's early advisors in authority. William Warham, chancellor and archbishop of Canterbury, went into virtual political retirement culminating, in December 1515, in his resignation of the chancellorship to Wolsey. Norfolk asserted himself as much as possible in council and continued to serve as treasurer and earl marshal, but he saw the wisdom of making his peace with Wolsey over the next several years, especially after the duke was seriously ill during the latter half of 1516.[2]

In the months following Flodden, Surrey remained busy with the navy, demobilizing troops for the winter and supervising repairs. Soon after the ceremonies at Lambeth, he was back with the fleet, preparing to raid the coast of France as soon as spring weather permitted.[3] Henry planned a new offensive against France, with Surrey and the navy providing the opening thrust. The admiral had a further motive in resuming the naval war, however, for he still hoped for revenge against the French galleys that had taken his brother Edward's life. While readying the fleet, Surrey quarreled with some of his captains, who feared to face the galleys again, and hinted in disgust that he would be willing to be recalled from his naval duties rather than lead such cowards. If he were to stay at his post, however, Surrey felt that his new dignity required that he be allowed additional personal servants, for he had but eighteen with him at Dover, "which is too few."[4]

Surrey moved back and forth between court and fleet during the spring. On 11 May, his accounts as admiral were examined before the council and found satisfactory. On 21 May, he was again in London for the reception of a papal envoy, and rode in the state procession to St. Paul's as part of the official escort. Although ceremonial and state business alike brought Howard away from his duties at sea, by the end of May he returned to Dover to lead a raid against France. During the spring, the French under Admiral Pregent (the "Prior John" who had slain both Thomas Knevet and Edward Howard) landed in Sussex and burned the coastal town of Brighton before being driven off. Howard was spurred to answer in kind, not only for the sake of his relatives, but to assuage Henry's pride.[5]

On 27 May, Surrey reported a successful foray by ten of his ships along the French coast near Boulogne; a few days later, his full forces assembled, the earl led a major assault on Normandy. Landing near Cherbourg, Surrey's men burned a strip of countryside seven miles long and two miles deep. Another party of seven hundred men sallied far inland, burning villages and fields. The French offered no resistance, but the castle and town of Cherbourg were too strong to attack, so Surrey withdrew, content that the day's work had evened the score with the French.[6]

Surrey's raid was planned as the opening of a new assault on France; while the earl was busy with the navy, musters were being taken and arrangements made to hire mercenaries for the summer.[7] Instead, upon learning that Ferdinand had abandoned his English allies and made a separate peace with France, Henry suddenly shifted sides himself. Plans had long been discussed for Henry's sister Mary to wed Charles of Burgundy, heir to both Ferdinand and Emperor Maximilian, but for months the imperial envoys had dragged their feet on the match. The secret truce of May 1514 between Ferdinand and Louis XII of France led Henry to treat with France himself—not simply to end the war, but to forge a new diplomatic alliance against his father-in-law. An imperial ambassador found Norfolk "much alarmed, and very untrustful" after Ferdinand's about-face, and reported that council and king were determined to have their revenge by turning to France.[8] The key to the new arrangement was the marriage of Mary Tudor to Louis. Because preparations for her marriage to Charles had been well advanced, Mary's wedding with Louis could be prepared with almost indecent haste once she had repudiated her contract with the archduke of Burgundy. Norfolk was one of the English agents who signed the treaty of peace with France on 7 August, and Surrey, as lord admiral, was named one of the English "conservators of the peace."[9]

The treaty was essentially Wolsey's work; having won Henry's confidence by organizing the French campaign of 1513, he was now pushing Henry to seek peace. With Ferdinand's treachery, Wolsey had his way. The treaty with Louis XII was defensive; only if Ferdinand broke the peace would England and France be committed to war. Norfolk seems to have followed Wolsey's lead in turning to the French alliance. Surrey was much less enthusiastic; his attitude toward the French was clear from his raid to avenge his brother, and his prospects for glory and rewards were far greater if war continued. He had little choice, however, but to follow the new policy. The king's honor was at stake, and obedience to the royal will outweighed personal preference. Thus the Howards were among the crowd at Greenwich when Mary and Louis were married by proxy, and when Mary went to France in September, Norfolk was given charge of the escort, with Surrey and Sir Edmund Howard in company.[10]

The ceremonies at Abbeville when Mary was received by Louis were attended by a sparkling array of French and English lords whose rank was indicated by the size of each personal entourage. Norfolk led the English with a party of one hundred horse, followed the marquis of Dorset and the bishop of Durham. Surrey was fourth on the list with fifty-eight attendants.[11] Mary had brought her own court with her, made up mainly of Wolsey's appointees. These servants, Louis complained, insulated Mary from her husband. Norfolk, commissioned to see that all went smoothly, quickly took advantage of the situation by dismissing most of Mary's suite so that Louis could appoint a new court of French ladies. Mary was outraged and wrote to Henry and Wolsey alike to complain, heaping abuse on Norfolk for his presumption. Suffolk, who had gone to France to witness the marriage but also to urge Louis to take arms against Ferdinand, wrote to Wolsey, lamenting that Norfolk had purposely cleared Mary's court of Wolsey's appointees because the Howards had been able to place few of their own clients with the queen. Suffolk went on to say that Norfolk and Surrey hoped to see his negotiations come to ruin, perhaps by having him recalled to London to explain Mary's complaints to Henry. Accordingly,

Suffolk warned Wolsey that Norfolk "be the causer [of the commotions] and loves neither you nor me. . . . Where for, me Lor, I by sche you hold your hand fast that I by not sent for bake; for I am suar that the fader and the son wold not for no good I schold stryke wyet the Frynche kyng; bout [so] I trust to do. And I dowth not bout I knaw hall thyr dreyftes."[12]

The Howards opposed Suffolk's mission to bring France into war with Spain because they feared for the success of any alliance with the decrepit Louis, who was so ravaged by time and disease that few expected him to live long. The Spain of Ferdinand, despite that king's devious policies, seemed a much more likely ally than France, which might soon have a new king of uncertain ambitions and questionable loyalty to an English alliance. A French writer in London had noted in September that there were those in England who opposed the match with Louis because they feared that peace would not last after the king's death.[13] He might well have had the Howards in mind.

Suffolk was not recalled, but neither was Mary's household restored. While the Howards and most of the English visitors returned home after the wedding on 12 October, Suffolk and a few others represented Henry at Mary's coronation at St. Denis on 5 November. Suffolk continued his efforts to lure Louis into war with Spain, dangling the recapture of Navarre before the French.[14] All of this maneuvering came to nothing; on 1 January 1515 Louis XII died, leaving the crown to his twenty-year-old cousin Francis, "a prince who lusted for the heroic and martial as much as did Henry, who was reputed to resemble the devil and would give new and violent impetus to French aggressiveness," as J. J. Scarisbrick noted. Suffolk—who had been in love with Mary even before she wed Louis—promptly allowed her to talk him into matrimony, with Francis's blessings. Mary was thus removed from the international marriage market, which caused not the least part of Henry's outrage with his sister's unauthorized union. The council—including Norfolk and Surrey—urged the king to punish Suffolk, but with Wolsey's aid the duke and his new bride survived the crisis and by the summer of 1515 Suffolk had been restored to favor.[15] The planned Tudor-Valois match ended instead with a Tudor-Brandon marriage and solidification of the alliance between Wolsey and Suffolk.

Perhaps the Howards were pleased by the deterioration of Anglo-French relations during 1515, but the new closeness between Wolsey and Suffolk must have been alarming. Charles Brandon was a careerist of even more naked ambition—if less talent—than Surrey. A man of great physical prowess, with appetites and passions to match, the duke of Suffolk owed his place at court and in council to his friendship with the king, and not to his abilities. Suffolk was basically a courtier and a companion of the king; he was seldom a real political force, nor did he aspire to offices of state for anything beyond their ceremonial and financial value. Suffolk's elevation—with its clear purpose of replacing the recently executed Edmund de la Pole as a magnate in East Anglia—was intended to balance the power of the Howards in those shires. Although Suffolk was not given a large landed estate in his titular home shire, he was granted reversion of all de la Pole lands not in the king's hands, and through the 1510s and 1520s, he made a concerted effort to erect a landed base in Suffolk and to build his power there—both of which threatened Howard interests. Beyond common noble status and military talents, there was little to bind Thomas Howard and Charles Brandon together. For most of the reign, they were rivals or, at best, uneasy allies; a long-term Brandon-Howard alliance never developed.[16]

On 23 November, writs went out for a new Parliament to meet in February 1515.[17] The session was called to raise funds for war, and a subsidy was in fact voted, but most of the legislation was economic reform. By the end of the first session early in April, Henry renewed the peace treaty with France, but the alliance was clearly uncertain, given the ambitions of Francis I. Thus on 5 April Parliament was prorogued to November to await developments in international diplomacy, although as it turned out, the situation was hardly clearer in the autumn than it had been in the spring of 1515.[18]

Suffolk in France and Wolsey in England had charge of English foreign policy, although Norfolk was named a commissioner to treat with the French to renew the peace treaty. Therefore the Howards made sure that they were prominent in the only area of activity open to them, the House of Lords. Of thirty-six sessions for which attendance was recorded in the first session of the Parliament of 1515, Norfolk attended thirty-two times and Surrey thirty-three. Suffolk was in France and Buckingham did not attend; Dorset, the ranking peer after Norfolk and Suffolk, took his seat only seventeen times, and even Wolsey was present only twenty-nine days. William Warham, archbishop of Canterbury, and Wolsey, Norfolk and Surrey headed the committee that explained the reasons for calling

Parliament to the commons on 10 February, and on 14 February, Surrey headed a commission of eight lords to manage conferences between the two houses. These duties were ceremonial; if this was the best the Howards could manage in 1515, Wolsey was clearly in command. Even so, one act of special interest to the Howards was passed in 1515, as the royal grant of land and titles made to Norfolk in 1514 was confirmed by statute. In an interesting and revealing move, Surrey failed in this session to claim precedence among the earls in Lords by virtue of his courtesy rank of marquis (as eldest son of a duke). On 17 February, Chancellor Warham ruled that, while Surrey held precedence outside of parliament, in Lords he would take his seat by virtue of his own station and thus was seated next to last among the earls.[19]

Much of the rest of the year was quiet for Surrey. The earl joined the king's council some time early in 1515, but seems to have had little influence. After Wolsey, the only places of prominence were held by Norfolk, Bishop Richard Fox of Winchester and Bishop Thomas Ruthal of Durham, who succeeded Fox as lord privy seal in 1516. Francis proved a difficult ally. Mary Tudor's dowry could not be recovered despite Suffolk's blandishments, and by September Francis had demonstrated that his real interests lay in Italy and not in helping Henry to beard his father-in-law. While French and English diplomats wrangled, a French army crossed the Alps and seized Milan. In late October, Henry signed a new defensive alliance with Ferdinand. Francis's course of action was so clearly hostile to English and Spanish interests that an Anglo-French alliance was now impossible. Even Scotland was in turmoil by autumn. Henry's sister Margaret fled the country in September after the French-backed duke of Albany arrived to claim his rights as regent for the minor James V. As a result, England's northern neighbor was soon following the Auld Alliance again.[20]

While Wolsey wrestled with these problems, Surrey's activities left few traces. In March, August and November 1515 he was named to commissions of the peace for several shires, but it is unlikely that he attended county court sessions even in Norfolk. Probably Surrey was busy with naval duties, for in a letter of 3 July, the earl complained to Wolsey that payments to a certain William Ellecar, a victualer, were in arrears, which had led to difficulties in supplying the fleet.[21]

Certainly Surrey was at court when Parliament resumed in November, but the international situation was still in flux, and again the subject of war was deferred. Another event of the month was of greater importance; on 15 November the cardinal's hat that Wolsey had sought for several years was bestowed by Rome. Henry required the great nobles to participate in the ceremonies by which Wolsey received his new honor. Norfolk and Suffolk led Wolsey from Westminster Abbey to his palace at Charing Cross, while Surrey walked in the cardinal's train and attended the banquet in his honor.[22]

Norfolk, now over seventy years old, was still willing to harass Wolsey if the chance presented, as in the clearing of Mary's court in France, but otherwise seems to have been content with his family's restored status and his personal influence in the council and as treasurer.[23] Surrey, however, was younger and more ambitious. Surrey was too good a soldier to leave idle altogether, yet Wolsey recognized the earl as a major enemy, and sought after 1514 to give Howard as little as possible to do that would gain him credit in Henry's eyes. Wolsey could not destroy the Howards' social and ceremonial status, but did all he could to prevent the exercise of real power by Surrey. Official relations between Wolsey and Surrey remained outwardly cordial, but there could be little doubt of their basic enmity, as subsequent events were to show.

Great occasions of state required the presence of the Howards, however, and when a daughter was born to Henry and Catherine in February 1516, Norfolk and Surrey held places of honor at the christening of Princess Mary. The duchess of Norfolk and Wolsey were Mary's godparents; at the christening, Mary was carried by Elizabeth, countess of Surrey, assisted by Norfolk and Suffolk, while Surrey carried the ceremonial taper.[24] Only the death of the child's grandfather, Ferdinand of Aragon, word of which reached court just before Mary's birth, prevented another round of tournaments, banquets and celebrations. Henry was glad to have an heir, even if a girl, for, as he told the Venetian ambassador, he and Catherine were still young. "If it was a daughter this time, by the grace of God, the sons will follow."[25] In May, Margaret, queen of Scots, arrived in London for a state visit (since she found it unwise to return to Scotland while Albany held sway) and was lavishly entertained. A tournament was held on 19–20 May, with Surrey riding in the king's band.[26] All seemed well for the earl; then, suddenly, by the end of the month he was plunged into disgrace.

Since becoming chancellor, Wolsey had rigorously enforced the laws against keeping armed retainers and interfering with the courts. On 2 May

1516 the cardinal presided over a special meeting of the council in Star Chamber. With Henry and some thirty lords including Surrey present, Wolsey delivered a harangue on the need for better administration of justice, and the peril of the enormities committed freely in its absence by overmighty subjects. As an example to the gathered lords, Henry Percy, earl of Northumberland, a powerful figure in the lawless north of the realm, was bound over for examination and subsequently sent to the Fleet prison.[27] Nor was Wolsey finished. By 31 May, Thomas Grey, marquis of Dorset, Thomas Howard, earl of Surrey, and George Neville, lord Abergavenney, were put out of the council on Wolsey's orders. Apparently the chancellor had inspected the liveried retinues of the lords attending Margaret's reception and cited offenders to appear in Star Chamber. Caught in flagrant violation of the laws against maintenance, Surrey found himself deprived of even the small voice he had held on the council.[28]

Polydore Vergil recounts a story which, if true, helps explain Wolsey's desire to punish Surrey. According to Vergil, Surrey had drawn a dagger and attempted to stab Wolsey during an argument in the council chamber.[29] Surrey was certainly capable of violent outbursts, but it is strange that such a striking incident would leave no other traces in the records or would have gone without more severe punishment. It is hard to tell whether Vergil, in his own distaste for Wolsey, improved upon a mere threat on Surrey's part, or even made the tale up altogether. Whatever happened between Thomas Howard and Thomas Wolsey, the incident, real or imagined, accurately indicates Surrey's feelings toward Wolsey.

With Surrey's expulsion from the council, Wolsey gained an important victory in finding an offense, or the pretense of one, by which the earl could be held in check. The events of May were symptoms rather than the real cause of Surrey's isolation. His removal from the council was only temporary; by 4 November 1516 Surrey was again in Star Chamber with Wolsey, Norfolk and others to hear complaints concerning the selection of sheriffs.[30] For the most part, however, Surrey was seldom at court during the next several years and was given few formal duties other than his service as admiral. Even that office made few demands; as long as peace continued, he left most of the duties of the office to his deputy, Christopher Middleton.[31] Overall, the paucity of mentions of Surrey in his official capacities during the years from 1516 to 1519 is striking evidence of Wolsey's power and of his success in keeping rivals such as Surrey away from the king and out of the limelight.

Surrey was, nevertheless, useful when emergencies arose. On 1 May 1517, the Howards were called in to quell a riot by the London apprentices on "Evil May Day." Upset by foreign domination of English trade and loss of jobs, with xenophobic hatreds fanned by several indiscreet sermons from the city clergy, the laborers turned to violence. They looted foreigners' shops and threatened bodily harm, not only to foreign ambassadors but (more disturbing in government circles) to Wolsey, the man widely held responsible for the economic malaise. Surrey must have been close at hand, perhaps at Lambeth, for when discontent erupted into violence, he was quickly present. Norfolk and several other lords arrived to secure the city gates and fortify Wolsey's house, while Surrey and his men (perhaps including the retainers for which Wolsey had punished him) moved against the rioters, who fled before a Howard "like sheep at the sight of a wolf."[32] On 4 May, while Norfolk's "xiii C men in harneys" kept order, an oyer and terminer was held at the Guildhall, presided over by the lord mayor of London, Norfolk, Surrey and others. Twenty ringleaders of the riots were turned over to Sir Edmund Howard to be hanged and drawn and quartered, while four hundred others were found guilty of the treason of having broken the peace of Christendom and were bound over to hear the king's pleasure on their fate.[33]

According to Edward Hall, Wolsey thirsted for vengeance against this rabble of ungrateful citizens, but Catherine interceded with Henry to prevent a bloodbath, obtaining pardon for the offenders. On 11 May, while two thousand Howard men kept peace in the streets, the prisoners were brought to the Great Hall of Westminster where, in the presence of the foreign ambassadors and the English court, Wolsey made a long speech condemning the violence of the rioters. Henry listened gravely, then, after the men begged his mercy, granted them all pardon and ordered them released.[34]

Given Wolsey's firm grip on court and council, Thomas Howard's main hope for a return to prominence was a renewal of the continental wars. On 5 July 1517 a new defensive league against France was signed with Emperor Maximilian. The avowed purposes of Wolsey's diplomacy were to preserve the peace by containing France and, not incidentally, to protect the papacy. The accession of Charles Hapsburg, archduke of Burgundy, to the Spanish throne left European affairs in confusion until the end of the summer of 1517; by then it became clear that France and Spain would continue their old rivalry despite the new players, and by early 1518 both

Francis and Charles were seeking English support in the renewal of the Hapsburg-Valois struggle. In the negotiations of 1517 and 1518 Wolsey almost singlehandedly represented England, leaving Surrey to gain what notice he could by taking part in tournaments and diplomatic receptions.[35]

After a fierce summer, the winter of 1517 proved equally extreme, and with it came an outbreak of sweating sickness which scattered the court. Henry fled to the country, and Wolsey himself fell ill, bringing government to a standstill. By early 1518, with the court again gathered for the progress around the royal residences in and near London, Surrey returned to the council, sitting in Star Chamber on 26 January and 11 February.[36] The course of English diplomacy through the thicket of French and Spanish interests was still unclear, but Henry seemed to hope that Wolsey's machinations would lead to renewed war. Thus Surrey was soon busy again with naval duties. In June, Henry visited the fleet at Southampton with Surrey as his host. The king inspected his own ships as well as the galleys of his Venetian allies, and had shipboard cannon fired while he marked their range.[37]

Since early in 1518 Pope Leo X had been pressing for a general European truce and a united crusade against the Turks. Lorenzo Campeggio, absentee bishop of Salisbury and cardinal-protector of England, was commissioned to preach the crusade at Henry's court. Campeggio's entry into England was delayed several months until Leo granted Wolsey a legatine commission as Campeggio's equal, but when Campeggio finally arrived in July, he was treated with all due pomp. Norfolk, Surrey, the bishops of London and Durham and a committee of other lords and clerics met the Italian cardinal at a tent of golden cloth outside London, and then escorted him into the city in a two-mile-long procession of four thousand horses.[38]

Campeggio remained in London until October, but the hoped-for crusade never materialized. Instead, Wolsey seized the moment to organize his own universal peace with London, and not Rome, at its hub. The Treaty of London was sealed by a marital alliance to bind together the recent antagonists, England and France. The infant Princess Mary was betrothed to the equally young Dauphin Francis, eldest surviving son of the French king. On 27 September, Surrey, the English admiral, took a small role in the sealing of the treaty, meeting the French admiral Bonnivet and his suite at Blackheath and escorting them to London. In a splendid ceremony at Greenwich with everyone of note in the realm present, Henry and Catherine gave their consent to the match. Wolsey then placed a ring with a large diamond on Mary's finger, and Bonnivet passed it over the second joint. The blessings given and mass sung, the court retired to the banquet hall, where the two legates sat on Henry's right and Surrey and his French counterpart as admiral on the king's left, with the dukes of Norfolk, Suffolk and Buckingham seated across the table.[39]

Surrey's prominence during the sealing of the Treaty of London was hardly evidence of a new elevation of status. Wolsey was firmly in control of English diplomacy and government in 1518, and thus it was fairly safe for such as Surrey to be allowed ceremonial prominence. In time of peace—such as the Treaty of London presumably assured—warrior families like the Howards could not threaten the cardinal's power. By March 1519, even Spain had joined the peace league; for the moment, there was no war for Surrey fight, no opportunity for martial distinction. For much of the eighteen months following the sealing of the treaty of London, Surrey was of little influence and seldom employed in official business.[40]

With little else to do while Wolsey held sway, Surrey seems to have spent a good bit of time with his family—although from Elizabeth's later account of her marriage, one would hardly describe the earl as uxorious. The couple's first child, Henry, was born in the spring of 1517, and a daughter, Mary, followed in 1519. A last surviving child, Thomas, arrived in 1520. The family spent the summer months from April to October at Tendring Hall, Stoke Neyland, Suffolk, and the winters near London at Norfolk's house at Hunsdon, Hertfordshire; Surrey was never far from court in either case, and probably also spent time at his father's house at Lambeth.[41] Even while in political exile, Surrey had frequent contact with the peers of the realm at his own and his father's houses. The dukes of Norfolk and Suffolk, the marquis of Dorset and the earls of Kent, Essex and Arundel, along with a number of lesser lords and gentlemen, took meals at Surrey's household during these years.[42]

If Surrey needed any further reminder of Wolsey's determination to rule the council and keep the nobility in line, the case of Sir William Bulmer surely provided it. In October 1519, Surrey attended council meetings in Star Chamber dealing with Bulmer, a royal servant who had taken the duke of Buckingham's livery without the king's leave. On 22 October, Bulmer was committed to the Fleet pending further action; four days later, a total of fifty-five councilors (the largest number recorded in the Ellesmere transcripts) heard Wolsey deliver an oration on the establishment of justice—surely a set piece for a captive audience. The next day, 28 October, with forty councilors present, Bulmer appeared to make his submission and beg forgiveness. Wolsey's purpose having been served, Bulmer was pardoned.[43] As Surrey sat through these humiliating sessions, with the painful memory of 1516 in mind, the wisdom of deferring to the cardinal must have been manifest.

In the spring of 1520, after almost four years of inaction, Surrey received a new challenge when he was appointed lord lieutenant of Ireland. With England free of continental war, Henry turned his attention to that troubled land for the first time in the reign. Henry was nominal lord of Ireland, but in fact the island was virtually independent and, worse, a source of almost no revenue despite a number of at least hypothetical payments due the crown. English lordship over Ireland descended from Pope Adrian's doubtful grant of 1154 and Henry II's more compelling campaigns of the 1170s. Through much of the Middle Ages, however, English rule of Ireland existed mainly in theory. Since Henry VII's reign, government there had been in the hands of the Anglo-Irish Fitzgeralds, earls of Kildare. With the small area around Dublin known as the Pale as a base, the Fitzgerald lords deputy had managed to keep Ireland in some sort of order. The English crown was relieved of the expense of trying to subdue the Irish and left free to pursue other matters, but at the price of granting the rule of Ireland to Kildare.[44]

At his accession Henry accepted this state of affairs. In November 1510 Gerald Fitzgerald, eighth earl of Kildare, was confirmed as lord deputy of Ireland with broad powers. Kildare was paid for his services by a grant, in tail male, of all possessions he could recover from any Irish rebel. This method of payment cost Henry nothing, but guaranteed that Ireland would remain in turmoil, as Kildare waged constant private wars of self-enrichment.[45] Fitzgerald died in 1513 and was succeeded by his son Gerald, the ninth earl, who was made deputy under the same terms as his father.[46] This wild young man was even less interested in English control of Ireland than his father had been and embarked on a course of rule marked by increasing violence and disorder. The tension in Ireland was made worse by the death in 1515 of Thomas Butler, seventh earl of Ormond and the leading Anglo-Irish rival to Kildare. Ormond left no direct male heir, but a cousin, Sir Piers Butler, claimed the earldom with the support of most of the Butler clan. Neither Kildare and the Irish council in Dublin nor Henry and Wolsey were inclined to recognize Butler's claim, but he refused in any case to come to Dublin, much less London, to defend it in person. Kildare continued his policy of private war but left Butler alone for fear that he and his allies might be driven into a more effective rebellion than the deputy could contain.[47]

By 1519 enough voices had been raised against Kildare's rule that the earl was summoned to London to explain his actions.[48] Henry took this opportunity to review for the first time the crown's rights over Ireland and the possibility of more effective and profitable rule than that provided by the Fitzgeralds. An optimistic paper, probably first prepared in 1515, was revised in the winter of 1519-20 to show the king how English influence might be increased in Ireland and perhaps even some revenue drawn from the isle. "The State of Ireland and a Plan for its Reformation"[49] detailed a pattern of tribal rule by chieftains constantly at war with each other, with the people reduced to poverty and terror and Henry's authority essentially nonexistent. Yet Ireland could be reduced to obedience and made "a very Paradyce" if the power of the clans could be subdued and English arms and justice placed in the castles and towns. The writer of the plan was vague about the number of troops needed or the cost of the venture, but was certain that reduction by force was possible, practical and necessary: "If the king were as wyse as Solomon the Sage, he shall never subdue the wyld Iryshe to his obeysaunce, without dreadde of the swerde, and of the myght and strengthe of his power. . . . For as long as they [the Irish lords] may resyste and save ther lyffes, they will never obey the king."[50] Henry may have read this paper, but his later Irish policy raises some questions as to whether he took the advice to heart.

Once in London, Kildare quarreled with Wolsey and the two soon developed a mutual dislike; someone else would be needed to restore Tudor rule in Ireland. That the choice fell upon the earl of Surrey has given rise to considerable speculation: why was Thomas Howard, whom Wolsey had kept nearly impotent since 1516, given the lieutenancy of Ireland? Polydore Vergil and Edward Hall, with the modern assent of A. F. Pollard, agreed that Wolsey sent Surrey into exile; Vergil believed that Wolsey was already plotting to destroy Surrey's father-in-law Buckingham and wanted Surrey out of the way.[51] Recent work has cast doubts on this explanation.[52] Wolsey and Surrey were not on good terms in 1520 except in a formal sense, but Surrey was hardly in disgrace. Whatever Wolsey's role in the fall of Buckingham, Henry's wish to subdue Ireland and Kildare's obvious unfitness for the job gave the cardinal a nice opening. Surrey was well qualified for the task; if by being sent to Dublin the earl was banished, so much the better for Wolsey. Moreover, Surrey does not seem to have been reluctant to go; perhaps he was relieved to have something challenging to do. As it turned out, Ireland was not to give Surrey an opportunity for a glowing triumph.[53]

The timing of Buckingham's fall gives further strength to this interpretation. The duke was not arrested until April 1521, when Surrey had been gone for a year and his wife, Buckingham's daughter, had returned to England. In mid-May Buckingham was convicted by a commission of peers of having "imagined and compassed" the king's death and promptly beheaded. This may well have begun Surrey's estrangement from his wife, for Elizabeth never believed that Surrey had done enough to oppose her father's death, a suspicion likely confirmed in July 1522 when Norfolk and Surrey accepted a grant of six manors from the late duke's estate. This act was either a tacit acceptance of Buckingham's judicial murder or, more charitably, mere prudence and greed; there was nothing to gain and much to lose from seeming to sympathize in any way with the fallen duke.[54] In short, there is nothing to prove that Surrey's removal to Ireland had any direct bearing on the fall of Buckingham.

Surrey was appointed lord lieutenant of Ireland in the early months of 1520. The patent itself is lost, but by March arrangements were well under way for the earl's departure after Easter. Surrey, his family, and a hundred men of the royal guard landed at Dublin on 23 May.[55] Money was an immediate and persistent problem; Kildare had already collected the rents due the crown for the year, undermining Henry's plan to finance Surrey's mission out of Irish revenues. Dublin proved expensive for Surrey's troops, and before long the earl was reporting that his men could not live on their wages of four shillings a day.[56] Nonetheless Surrey set to work, and by 23 July wrote to Henry of the success of his early efforts to pacify the island.[57] An emissary was sent to Sir Piers Butler, pretended earl of Ormond, persuading him to remain at peace with his local rival, the earl of Desmond, while Surrey carried out a raid into the country of Connell O'More southwest of Dublin. If the raid was meant to make the new English determination to rule Ireland abundantly clear, it was successful. Butler shortly joined Surrey, bringing with him Mulroney O'Carroll, a troublesome Irish lord who had done "mooche hurt" to the Pale, but who now wished to submit to Surrey. O'Carroll was probably hedging his bets by submitting to the king's deputy, for, as Surrey discovered, the hand of Kildare had been behind O'Carroll's depredations. Kildare had written to the native lords from London urging them to make war on Surrey, apparently in the hope of stirring up so much trouble that Henry would conclude that none but a Kildare could rule the island. Surrey was unable to obtain a copy of Kildare's letter to send to London and, despite his warnings, Henry and Wolsey refused to investigate the matter.[58]

Returning to Dublin, Surrey found Hugh O'Donnell, chief of Tyrconnel, waiting to make a truce. Self-interest was again at work, for O'Donnell wanted Surrey's aid against O'Neill, the strongman of Ulster and O'Donnell's sworn enemy.[59] With one more ally in his camp, by 11 August Surrey felt strong enough to march north against O'Neill's ally McMahon, chief of Oriel. With the aid of Butler, Surrey, doing "such annoysaunce, as I might," drove McMahon back, and O'Neill retreated as well, preventing further battle. Surrey returned to Dublin with much of Ireland in an uncharacteristic state of peace.[60]

The lord lieutenant was still having money problems as the fighting season drew to a close, and so on 25 August he sent Sir John Wallop, the vice-treasurer of Ireland and long a Howard man, back to England to try to hasten payments. Henry had expected Surrey to finance his expedition out of Irish revenues, but the earl had found that nothing could be collected by methods more legal than Kildare's.[61] Late in September Henry sent Wallop back to Surrey with four thousand pounds, but the money was accompanied by warnings that henceforth Surrey would have to raise funds for pay in Ireland. After Christmas, Surrey could begin collecting rents for the new year, and therefore Henry expected "that our chargeis, or the mooste parte of theym, may be bourne upon the same."[62]

Sickness in the Pale meanwhile thinned the ranks of Surrey's troops and undermined morale. As a result, eighteen of the English soldiers plotted to steal a boat, set out to sea, seize a larger ship, and become pirates. Surrey learned of the plan and took the men prisoner, but was disappointed to learn from his Irish lawyers that he did not have the power to hang the mutineers out of hand. Fearful of losing discipline over his men, Surrey requested the power of life and death he held at sea as admiral. Otherwise "if I shall make a proclamasion, upon peyne of deth, as it shalbe nedeful many tymes to doo, I have none auctoritie to put any of them to deth, that shal breke the same."[63]

In September Surrey's cause was aided by a private battle in Munster. Sir Piers Butler's rival Desmond, attempting to ambush an enemy, was himself routed, losing fifteen hundred men and five hundred horses. His power effectively broken, Desmond made submission to Surrey, and other Irish lords of Munster followed suit. Seeking to cement the alliance with the leading Anglo-Irish lords on the heels of this breakthrough with the native chieftains, Surrey wrote to Wolsey seeking recognition of Butler's claim as earl of Ormond and to ask that Butler's son Sir James, then resident at the English court, be sent to Ireland as his father's deputy, since the Irish would only ride under their noble captains and Sir Piers's gout incapacitated him in winter.[64] Butler's claim was not recognized—the earldom of Ormond, along with that of Wiltshire, was granted to Thomas Boleyn, whose claim through his mother was the equal of Butler's—but in intervening for Sir Piers, Surrey did all he could to demonstrate that he made a more useful friend than enemy.

The king, preoccupied with his meeting with Francis at the Field of Cloth of Gold for much of the summer, finally answered Surrey's many dispatches in late September or early October. Henry made it clear that he disapproved of the fire-and-sword policy that had produced what little peace Ireland enjoyed. Henry lacked Surrey's firsthand experience with the independent and unreliable Irish, but it is still hard to believe that the king seriously expected to bring the island under English rule, as he ponderously advised, by "sober waies, politique driftes, and amiable persuasions, founded in law and reason [rather] than by rigorous dealing . . . [and] enforcement by strength or violence."[65] This clearly was the king's plan, however, as he made plain in a letter to an Irish lord who had written to him urging that Surrey be given sufficient forces to conquer the island. Writing at the end of 1520, Henry affirmed that he did not intend to remove Surrey and send Kildare back, but neither would Surrey be sent forces to do more than "hold hymself in termes and lymytes of defence, for the quiet preservacion and tuycion of our Englishchery there." For defenses beyond the Pale, Surrey should look for support from the Irish lord "with such other nobles, your frendes and adherentes, as you have there."[66]

Surrey reacted with caution to this change of course from compulsion to friendly persuasion. In December 1520 he wrote to Wolsey, warning that, whatever Henry's hopes, "this londe will never be broght to dew obeysaunce but only with compulsion and conqwest."[67] Further, Surrey sent Patrick Fynglas, chief baron of the Irish exchequer, to report firsthand on his country's unsettled situation.[68] During the winter of 1520–21 Surrey kept his army at full and expensive strength as rumors filtered into Dublin that the Irish lords who had so recently sworn homage to Henry stood ready to attack as soon as the English let down their guard. Food was in short supply, and desertion and disease continued to thin Surrey's forces, making the task all the more difficult and expensive. By April 1521, Surrey was again writing to Henry to ask for more men and money and warning of treachery from the sworn lords.[69] Henry, Surrey learned, "in no wyse lyketh suche newes, as he hath recevidde" from Ireland,[70] and sent Sir John Pechy to Dublin with word that no more men or money were forthcoming as long as new troubles between Charles V and Francis I threatened the peace of Europe. Pechy was more than a messenger, however; it is clear that Henry wondered where all his money was going and why Surrey seemed unable to subdue Ireland by the "politique waies, driftes and meanes" that the king had advised.[71]

Pechy's report and Surrey's letters must have satisfied Henry, for in June the king sent the earl a thousand marks over and above ordinary wages for his troops, "to be, by your discretion, profitably employed," perhaps to repair some of the damage his Irish service had done to Surrey's private purse. But the king also warned Surrey to "kepe your self in the lymetes of defence, so that We be not put to farther charges, tyll such tyme as it may be perfectly knowen to what issue and end the contraversies and variaunces raysyd betwyxt thEmperour and Frensh kyng schalbe reducyd."[72]

Surrey's answer was to restate his belief that Ireland could be pacified only by military means. Even with an army of six thousand men, Surrey thought the job might take years; Edward I, he noted, had spent ten years subduing Wales, and Ireland was five times as big. Even then, unless Henry colonized the conquered land with Englishmen, Surrey doubted that Ireland could be held under Tudor rule.[73] He was ahead of his time in proposing colonization—a solution tried by both Elizabeth and Cromwell—but this may not have been intended as serious advice. Having laid out his dismal picture of Irish affairs, Surrey came to the real point of his letter. If Henry did not plan a full military conquest, Surrey wished to be relieved of his futile Irish duties.[74] Under the circumstances, Henry might as well have sent Kildare back—an expedient the king would not be ready to consider until another expensive year of Surrey's lieutenancy had passed.

Ireland surely had not lived up to Henry's expectations. The first year of Surrey's tenure had cost at least sixteen thousand pounds, while crown revenues there averaged less than a thousand if they could be collected at all.[75] Worse, by July the sworn lords O'Connor, More and O'Carroll had joined forces to assault the Pale, forgetting their oaths of a year before. Although Surrey was able to seize O'Connor's castle near Edenderry and, aided by Sir Piers Butler, suppress rebellion in the south, new fighting erupted among the chieftains of the north. It was painfully clear to Surrey that he would not be recalled in the midst of this turmoil; instead, he had to begin again in 1521 to pacify the island.[76]

By the autumn of 1521, Ireland was hardly at peace, but the chieftains of the north were so busy fighting each other that, for a change, the Pale seemed reasonably secure.[77] Yet two years in Ireland had accomplished very little for Henry's cause, and now, Surrey wrote to the king, his own purse was bare and his very life in peril: since midsummer the earl had been plagued with dysentery. Thus on 16 September Surrey wrote to Henry begging to be recalled: "I have be, am, and ever shalbe, redy to serve your Grace in what ever place so ever your pleasure shalbe to commande me. Beseeching your most noble Grace so to loke on me, your poore servaunte, that onys, or I dy, I do your Highnes service in such besynes in your owne presence."[78]

Henry consulted with Wolsey, who was in Calais working on what would become an Anglo-Imperial treaty against France. Wolsey agreed that Surrey had done all he could in Ireland and should be recalled because of his illness. If war with France should break out, the expensive adventure in Ireland would have to be ended in any case, and Surrey would be needed in his capacity as admiral.[79] Surrey had long been promising the Irish that Kildare would not return as deputy and so he urged Henry to appoint Kildare's rival Butler. In late October the king sent his lord lieutenant the welcome news: Surrey was to offer Butler the post. If Sir Piers would agree to serve at his own expense, Surrey could appoint him deputy and return to England. Two years of Surrey's expenditures with no end in sight and the promise of war in France were enough to convince Henry of the merits of his father's Irish policy.[80]

By mid-December Butler had agreed to serve on the king's terms, and Surrey left Dublin.[81] Butler was formally appointed lord deputy in March 1522, but the Irish situation was already deteriorating; in February the council in Dublin wrote in reproach to Wolsey of the grave dangers to the land "by reason of this sudden departing of the earl of Surrey and the king's army here," and soon after, the Pale administrators were lobbying Henry's council for the return of Kildare![82] Sir Piers proved a disaster as deputy; his power base in the west was too far from the Pale and Dublin to provide much protection since Butler, incapacitated by gout much of the time, insisted on living on his estates. Thus in 1522 and 1523, constant private wars and rebellions against Butler's authority plunged Ireland into chaos. Kildare meanwhile married an English heiress and gained considerable favor at court. His treasonable actions of 1519-20 forgotten, the earl was restored as deputy in 1524. Kildare resumed his old policy of self-aggrandizement, but at least restored some sort of peace in Ireland. Until Kildare's eventual recall and death in 1534, Ireland remained as Henry VIII had found it, a wild and unruly province hardly more than nominally under Tudor rule.

As lieutenant of Ireland, Surrey performed a difficult task rather well, considering the resources available to him. The Irish lieutenancy gave Henry convincing proof of the earl's abilities and, although the mission did not serve to bring him back to court as a leading councilor, it did lead to further diplomatic service in Scotland and France. Perhaps the Irish service also convinced Henry that Howard's greatest value was as a soldier, for, despite his later political career as treasurer and duke of Norfolk, Howard was most often employed in a military capacity for the rest of the reign.

As Wolsey had suggested, Henry was able to find suitable employment for Surrey away from Ireland, but contrary to the earl's hopes, and probably by the cardinal's design, Surrey was not given service in Henry's "owne presence." Instead he resumed his duties as admiral for a new round of raids in France. Since 1518 and the Treaty of London, neither Francis nor Charles V, who had succeeded Maximilian as emperor in 1519, had kept the peace. Wolsey's Calais conference of 1521, ostensibly held to renew the universal peace, was instead a sham behind which England and the emperor allied against France. Under an agreement ratified in November,

England was to declare war on France in 1522, undertaking at least a small naval campaign that year while preparing for a grand assault in 1523.[83]

Surrey spent much of June getting ready to raid France. He also managed to provoke a nasty diplomatic squabble by trying to force several Venetian galleys at Southampton to join his fleet. By the 1518 Treaty of London, all signatories were obliged to attack any country breaking the peace of Christendom. The designation of France rather than Spain as the guilty party in the latest round of Valois-Hapsburg squabbles was not accepted by all parties, and the Venetians were especially sensitive to the French threat to Italy. Surrey's demand for naval support led to a violent shouting match between the admiral and the Venetians and an appeal to Wolsey by the latter. The galleys finally managed to avoid service with Surrey by stalling tactics. The admiral was ready to sail on 17 June, but the Venetian captains claimed that they would not be prepared for another two weeks. Surrey departed on 21 June in considerable exasperation, convinced of Venetian treachery.[84]

On 1 July Surrey attacked the fortified town of Morlaix in Brittany. By afternoon the English had forced a gate and the defenders and citizens fled, leaving Surrey's men to plunder and burn the rich market town. The next morning, the fifteen or sixteen French vessels in the haven were burned. Surrey then spent several weeks pillaging the coast of Brittany—a violent reminder to Francis that Henry was ready and willing to renew the war.[85]

Surrey was in his element in this kind of campaign. Patience and subtlety were never his long suits; he was at his best in the fire-and-sword tactics of coastal raids and border clashes. Ireland had required more patience and tact than Surrey possessed, but in this kind of war the blunt and brutal Thomas Howard came into his own. Henry heartily approved Surrey's rough tactics, and praised the admiral "for his payne and hardynes." As a reward, Surrey was given command of Calais, where he arrived on 9 August, bringing three thousand new troops and his brother Edmund as his lieutenant.[86] Charles sent several thousand men to join the English in an incursion into northern France, but the allies quarreled, disagreeing on an objective, and finally settled on a policy of small-scale raiding, avoiding laying siege to any major fortress or fortified town. The campaign was costly, and not terribly effective. As Surrey reported it, the emperor's Flemish subjects were only willing to supply their English allies at extortionate prices in cash; worse, before long Charles's German mercenaries were dying of camp fevers at the rate of fifty or sixty a day. The English feared an outbreak of plague in their camp when nine men died in one day, including two of Surrey's own household. They would soon mutiny if the sickness spread, Surrey wrote to Wolsey, for the disease killed with fearful quickness; "he that is whole and merry at noon is dead at midnight, and when they be dead their bodies as black as coal."[87]

As a result of these difficulties, little could be done against the French in the late summer and early autumn of 1522. By 15 October, Surrey had disbanded his army and sent the survivors home; the earl himself was in London by early November. French prisoners and English spies reported that widespread poverty followed the English raids; Surrey bragged that seven years would be needed to recover the losses. For all Henry's costs, however, the results were slim; the campaign had cost Henry at least fifteen thousand pounds, with no gains of territory or fortresses as compensation.[88] Perhaps this helps explain Henry's reluctance to renew the war despite Charles's pleas during the winter and into the spring of 1523.

There was another reason for English caution. Scotland, in the grip of a troubled minority government since the death of James IV at Flodden, was again stirring under the leadership of John Stuart, duke of Albany, the uncle of the young James V. An unstable and passionate man, more French than Scots by upbringing, Albany was nonetheless a magnetic leader who, beside his ties to the Scottish royal house, had considerable French support in the form of money and men—and thus commanded a wide following among the Scots lords. Francis I was hopeful of employing his partner in the Auld Alliance to keep England from bringing her full weight to the Hapsburg-Valois contest; in 1523, as earlier in 1513 and later in 1543, this strategy held considerable promise for France and peril for England. In September 1522, Thomas lord Dacre, warden of the English West Marches, who had fought with the Howards at Flodden and had long held charge of the north, made an unauthorized truce with Albany. This forestalled an immediate Scottish attack, but further conflict was inevitable.[89] Henry recognized the need for a strong presence on the borders to keep the Scots in check, and so he turned again to the Howards, the traditional guardians of the north. On 6 March 1523, Surrey received letters patent as lieutenant general of the English army against the Scots.[90]

Sometime between 16 March, when Surrey signed warrants in London for ships and ordnance to be sent to Newcastle,[91] and 10 April, when he wrote a short note to Wolsey from his new post,[92] the earl arrived on the borders. Almost at once, Surrey succeeded in antagonizing Dacre, who was clearly not happy to be reduced to second in command of a business he had watched over for more than ten years. Dacre had been trying to arrange an extended truce with Henry's sister Margaret, the queen mother, who had returned to Scotland when Albany left for France in late 1522. Surrey, commissioned to fight a war and not to seek a peace, opposed Dacre's negotiations as contrary to his orders. Surrey had, in fact, already begun a correspondence with Margaret before leaving court, undercutting Dacre's influence with the Scots.[93] Further, Surrey and Dacre wrangled over the wardship of Lord Monteagle, a dispute worsened by Surrey's caustic letters to court in which he complained that Monteagle needed to be rescued from greedy hands, and made veiled comments about the erosion of good government in the north—a charge which had to reflect on Dacre, who had served as warden since 1511.[94] With Surrey raising charges of justice for sale and embezzlement from the estates of helpless wards, it is no wonder that Dacre resented Surrey's presence and did everything he could to protect his powerful and profitable situation.

Through April and May, Surrey inspected fortifications, took musters and gathered intelligence for a raid in force into Scotland. On 18 May he led two thousand men across the border north of Flodden and razed several fortresses, including Cesford Castle, seat of the warden of the Scots Middle Marches. By 21 May Surrey was back in Alnwick, a fortified town with a castle that was his major base of northern operations. The lightning raid had greatly heartened the English of the borders, or so Surrey bragged to Wolsey, writing that the king's subjects thought the exploit better than the burning of Edinburgh![95]

Leaving Dacre as his deputy, Surrey returned to London to confer with the king and Wolsey.[96] The earl left Newcastle on 3 June and was at court by 18 June and stayed for ten or twelve days.[97] Although Henry approved the policy of harassing the Scots with small-scale raids, by now it was clear that the Scots would not retaliate until Albany returned from France. When Surrey returned north in July, he carried Henry's plans for a new policy. Surrey was to arrange, with Margaret's aid, an end to James V's minority and thus to Albany's regency. Once declared of age, the eleven-year-old king would become, through Margaret, a pawn of England rather than France, or so Henry hoped. Perhaps Margaret could even be induced to bring her son into England, where he would become a strong lever to control the Scots.[98]

Through August and September, Surrey directed these delicate negotiations, while at the same time preparing for an invasion of Scotland should diplomacy fail. Henry hoped to persuade the Scots to accept England's tutelage, with Surrey's army as added persuasion to the Scots to abandon Albany, whom Henry described as "the most suspect persone of the suretie of the Kings Grace his nephue, of all others."[99] Surrey's spies assured him that the Scots could be won from their allegiance to Albany because he had failed to return to Scotland to oppose the English raiders. Yet it seemed clear to Surrey that Albany would regain his authority immediately if he did return, the optimistic reports of Scottish traitors notwithstanding. Margaret held power only in Albany's absence and only because no one else was available as a counterweight. Margaret herself recognized the weakness of her position, and anxiously sought Surrey's aid in escaping Scotland if Albany could not be kept away or crushed militarily upon his return.[100]

Henry remained hopeful of erecting an English party among the Scots even as events of late August and early September demonstrated the vanity of this design. To show the costs of resisting his advances, Henry ordered Surrey to attack Jedburgh, a strategic fortified town ten miles into the Middle Marches. Surrey warned Margaret of the coming blow, but she reported that the lords believed that Surrey did not dare to march on Edinburgh, and, worse, "the Lordes set not by the hurt of the pore foulkes, but lawhis at the same." Surrey suspected that Margaret was urging him to attack Edinburgh so that she could escape with him. The earl wrote to Wolsey on 21 September, "I am advertised by dyvers wayes, that the Quene hath no credight now amonges the Lordes, considering that they looke every houre to here of the Dukes arryval."[101] While Margaret continued to claim a following among the Scottish nobility, her letters revealed the growing weakness of her position. Surrey's spies reported Margaret's waning power and Albany's growing strength; even while the queen negotiated with Surrey, the Scots lords were mustering forces to support Albany. With nothing to lose in launching the raid, Surrey wrote to Wolsey at 3:00 A.M. on 22 September that "at the ceasyng here off I woll go to horsbak and do the most hurt I can."[102]

Surrey and Dacre led more than six thousand men into the Middle

Marches. Burning the corn in the fields and throwing down houses and towers, the English marched westward to Jedburgh. The defending garrison put up a stiff fight, and both sides suffered heavy losses before the Scots were overwhelmed. The city was burned, and even the abbey church was ransacked and set afire. With insufficient food and drink to sustain a longer raid, the English withdrew as quickly as they had entered, and by 27 September Surrey was in Berwick writing an account of the raid to Wolsey.[103] Already he knew that the attack had been a strategic failure, for word had reached him that Albany had landed at Kirkcudbright on 21 September, sailing south of England and through the Irish Sea to avoid the patrols watching for his return. Albany brought French soldiers, guns, supplies and money with him; Surrey's spies said that there were 8,000 Frenchmen, while Margaret reported 6,000 foot, 100 men-at-arms and 200 light horse. Even if, as Surrey thought, these estimates were too high, the message was clear. Albany had returned in strength to follow the example of 1513, forcing England to open a second front to the north in the face of war with France. Worse, it was widely rumored that Richard de la Pole, the surviving Lancastrian claimant to the English throne, would either join Albany in Scotland, or lead an invasion of his own from the continent in concert with Albany's attack. Surrey was not sure how seriously to treat these reports, but even in passing them on to Henry he gave them added weight.[104]

Henry had initially been reluctant to renew the invasion of France on a large scale in 1523, but events of the summer proved too promising to pass up. After ten years of relative peace, the king was ready to throw himself into continental war again with all his old enthusiasm. In the early summer, a potential English ally appeared in France in the person of Charles, duke of Bourbon and constable of France. Bourbon was driven to rebellion when Francis seized the lands the duke held by right of his deceased wife. It took months of negotiations, but by June Bourbon had turned traitor and agreed to aid Henry and Charles V against his king. Thus encouraged, Henry sent Suffolk to the continent in August with ten thousand men. Even as Surrey finished the destruction of Jedburgh and Albany marched toward Edinburgh with his French forces, Suffolk began a drive toward Paris that showed initial promise before bogging down in late October. With England heavily committed to the continent, Albany found the time more than ripe for a renewal of the Auld Alliance.[105]

Once Albany reached Edinburgh, control of the government and of the young king fell out of Margaret's hands with startling swiftness. More than ever, the queen was anxious to get out of Scotland with her son, but Wolsey agreed with Surrey that it would serve no useful purpose to aid her escape without her son. The earl noted that it would cost one or two thousand marks a year to support Margaret in England, where she would be of no use, while only three or four hundred pounds would keep her content in Scotland.[106] Margaret has been unable to prevent Albany from invading, but she remained useful as a source of information, even if of questionable reliability.

Surrey and Dacre spent the first weeks of October studying reports from their spies, but could not be sure where Albany would strike. Therefore they spread their forces, Surrey remaining at Newcastle but in communication with lieutenants at Berwick and Norham, while Dacre moved to Carlisle. Each had four to six thousand men under him, but across the eighty miles from Berwick to Carlisle every able-bodied man stood ready to join battle on a day's notice. Although rumors placed Albany's host at up to thirty thousand men, no one believed that such a large army of Scots could be held together long enough to invade. Wolsey, almost prophetically, added his doubts. The ill weather and lack of food along the borders would be troublesome enough, but the cardinal also expected the memory of Flodden to hold the Scots back, and predicted that no serious invasion would occur.[107] Surrey, less confident of the outcome, wrote to Wolsey asking for more money, troops and "some noble men and gentlemen of the South partes to helpe to ordre the batayles"; the northern lords, and especially the Percy earl of Northumberland, "will not come onles your Grace Doth wright streitly to hym by post."[108]

When first sent north in early 1523, Surrey had been promised that he would be recalled by the feast of All Hallows (1 November), before the fierce northern winter set in. Now, in October, he reminded Henry and Wolsey of this promise. The king responded by appointing Thomas Grey, marquis of Dorset, warden of all the Marches, but while Dorset came north with a band of lords to help provide leadership for the defense of the Borders, Surrey was not recalled. Although (as he claimed) worn out in body and purse by his service to the crown, Surrey would remain in the north until Albany had done whatever hurt he could.[109]

Albany was meanwhile finding out that, true to Wolsey's prediction, many of the Scottish lords were opposed to an invasion; men willing to defend their own soil against Surrey were much less enthusiastic about marching into England in support of France. Perhaps fearing that his attack, already postponed, would be impossible in the face of such reluctance, Albany tried in mid-October to arrange a truce to comprehend England, Scotland and France. Surrey answered with Henry's stiff terms; only if Albany were expelled and his French troops sent home could he treat with Scotland for peace. As Surrey warned the lords of the Scottish council, war was inevitable unless the Scots would "open their ien and be no longer blinded with the feigned frauds and abusions of the said Duke and Frenchmen."[110]

For Albany, no truce was possible on such terms. Nor could he afford to keep his French troops in Scotland indefinitely; if they were to be used, it had to be soon. Therefore, on 23 October, having sent his artillery train ahead, Albany marched south toward Berwick.[111] Surrey, receiving news of Albany's actions, wrote to Dacre from Newcastle on 25 October, ordering him to move east. By 28 October Surrey had himself moved to Alnwick, still thirty miles from Berwick, but well placed to move quickly to any point in the East and Middle Marches that Albany might strike. Surrey still doubted that Albany would actually invade England in force; Wolsey must have agreed, for he wrote in the margin of Surrey's letter "this was alwais the kinges opinion and myne bothe."[112]

Albany sent a few men across the Tweed west of Berwick to burn the countryside, but it was a futile gesture; the Scottish army, supplied off of the land, had already done more damage to their own country than would be done to England. By 30 October Albany reached Coldstream, where his worst fears were realized; although there was no sizeable English force nearby to oppose a crossing of the Tweed, most of the Scots refused to invade. Desperately, Albany sent a challenge to Surrey, hoping to tempt the earl onto Scottish soil. Albany even promised to put Surrey to "curteous raunsome" if captured in battle. Surrey declined, citing his orders which, he said, prohibited entering Scotland, but promised Albany that "yf the sayd duke were taken prisoner by hym or his menne he would strike of his head and send it to the kyng of England his Master."[113] So much for chivalric courtesy.

Thwarted in his effort to force a battle, Albany determined to achieve something notable for his pains. On the night of 30 October the duke sent several thousand Frenchmen and what Scots would join them across the Tweed to besiege Wark Castle. After two days of bombardment, the invaders stormed the keep on 2 November. Sir William Lisle's force of one hundred men held off the attackers for most of the day; then, in the afternoon, word reached Albany that Surrey was advancing to the relief of Wark with twenty thousand men. In fact, Howard had only a quarter of that number, but before the English were in sight Albany's courage broke. He called his men back from Wark, where they had gained the outer yard, and suddenly every Scot knew that the invasion was over. As Albany and his Frenchmen pulled back to Edinburgh, the Scots melted away. Although Albany protested loudly that his countrymen had deserted him, and refused all blame for his "onhonest jowrnay," the duke's credit with the Scots was shattered. Albany had himself done what Surrey and Margaret had been unable to do, as the events of the next several months were to prove. Surrey wrote to Henry and Wolsey alike, bragging of Albany's shame, "how cowardly he fled this daye, when I came to presente hym batayle." The Scots, he claimed with ironic understatement, had not done twenty shillings' damage to the realm.[114]

Nonetheless, Surrey was relieved to see Albany withdraw, for winter was upon the north, and he knew he could not have kept his army together for long without food, clothing and shelter, all of them in short supply. Surrey had moreover fallen sick, and said he could not keep down food or sleep more than an hour at a time. Fearing that a winter in the north would cost him his life, the earl renewed his pleas to be recalled. Surrey distrusted Dacre, but was willing to see him appointed deputy if it would get the earl away from the borders. Surrey was sure that the Scots would cause little trouble during the winter, and in his anxiety to escape the north he was not interested in reminding Wolsey of Dacre's vices.[115]

On 12 November, Henry authorized Surrey to appoint Dacre as deputy and come south. Wolsey wrote on 26 November with orders for setting defenses and providing for pay and provisions for the border garrisons. These things done, Wolsey wrote, "ye, aswel for recoverye of your helthe, as of your good counsail and avice to be geven unto the Kinges causes and affaires here, wol retourne at your pleasure."[116] This message reached Surrey at Newcastle by 29 November, and three days later Howard wrote that he would depart for London the next day. By 5 December, Surrey was already at Tuxford, Nottinghamshire, fifty miles south of York, when another letter reached him. Henry, worried about events in Scotland, wanted Surrey to return to Newcastle. Although a council of regency had been appointed for James V, Albany had not yet, as hoped, returned to France. Margaret and her pro-English party remained powerless. In early November, Albany had presided over a Parliament at Edinburgh, and there was talk of a French marriage for James. Margaret's letters to Henry—not necessarily the best evidence of the truth of Scottish affairs, as Surrey had learned—indicated that Albany's power was growing again. In the face of this uncertainty, Henry wanted continued negotiations with the Scots in Surrey's experienced hands.[117]

Surrey demurred, arguing that Albany's authority was ruined beyond repair and that the duke would slink away to France as soon as he could make a graceful escape from the morass of Scottish politics. More to the point, Surrey was reluctant to return to Alnwick on a temporary assignment that might keep him in the north all winter. Although he sent his baggage back to Newcastle, Surrey insisted that, having headed south, he would lose all credit with the Scots if he did not speak to Henry in person before his return to the borders. Therefore, he wrote, he would continue toward Windsor. Surrey arrived at his house at Hunsdon, Hertfordshire, on 7 December, and was at court two days later. He must have pled his case successfully before king and cardinal, for he shortly wrote to Dacre to ask that his servants and goods be sent south again. Dacre sent several letters to Surrey with details of repairs to fortifications and musters of men, but on 21 January the earl told Dacre to send such news to Wolsey. Surrey expected that someone else would be lieutenant the following spring and was therefore anxious to leave details of Scottish affairs in Wolsey's hands.[118] At court, Surrey took his place on the council, tended to his duties as treasurer, and attempted to recover his health and set his personal affairs in order.[119]

Since being sent to Ireland in 1520, the winter of 1524 was Surrey's first extended stay at court. The earl found much to occupy him: family, friends, personal affairs, and reacquaintance with the state of the many alliances the Howards held at court. Norfolk had been in poor health for two years, and made his last appearance at court in April 1523.[120] It was clear that there would soon be a new duke, and many old ties needed to be reaffirmed. Thus Surrey's stay in and around London was valuable for more than rest. From 22 December to 8 January, Surrey and his countess were at court for Christmas and New Year festivities, no doubt renewing old friendships in the process. Even in his few days at Hunsdon, as the Howard household books make clear, Surrey received visits from a stream of family and political connections, including Sir Henry Grey; Lord Fitzwater (Robert Radcliff, later earl of Sussex); Thomas Grey, marquis of Dorset; and a servant of the earl of Kent.[121]

Surrey was still lieutenant of the north as winter turned to spring in 1524. Henry VIII was bound by his treaty with Charles V to invade France in May, and doubtless Surrey hoped for a leading place in that war. But Henry demurred and delayed and finally left the fighting to Bourbon; Surrey was left in charge of the north.[122] Although the evidence is confusing, it seems clear that Thomas Howard did not return to the borders until July 1524[123] for, after years of failing health and a final lingering illness, the second duke of Norfolk died at Framlingham on 21 May. Surrey spent the next month preparing his father's funeral and obtaining entry to his new lands and titles. By Henry VIII's patents of 1514, Thomas Howard succeeded his father in titles and lands as heir male; no new creation or legal act was required. But the will had to be proved and the inquisition *post mortem* prepared before the new duke could enter his inheritance, and all of this took time. The second duke was buried on 22 June at the Cluniac priory church at Thetford, an institution long patronized by the dukes of Norfolk. On 16 July, the new duke was granted livery of lands. The Norfolk lands, worth £4,500 a year in 1519 and yielding £2,241 net in 1524, now passed to the third duke, minus the portion retained by Agnes, the dowager duchess. As earl of Surrey Thomas Howard held lands worth over £1,000 a year. With fees from offices, the third duke became one of the wealthiest men in England, with an income over £4,000 *per annum*.[124]

In 1524, at the age of fifty-one, Thomas Howard had finished his apprenticeship. The new Duke Thomas stood at the pinnacle of the English peerage, no man but the king by ancient right his better. It had been a long, slow, and hardly steady rise to this station, but Norfolk arrived as a seasoned soldier and an experienced diplomat and councilor, a man who had proved his worth on many occasions. From 1509 to 1524, Thomas Howard had served Henry VIII loyally, at great professed cost to his own health and private wealth; there could be no doubt that the family's sin of Bosworth Field had been expiated. The question remained whether this duke of Norfolk would succeed where his father had failed in gaining political primacy to match his titular and ceremonial status. One man stood in Thomas Howard's way—his old nemesis Thomas Wolsey.

CHAPTER 4

THE PEER AND THE PRELATE: NORFOLK AND WOLSEY, 1524–1530

BECOMING DUKE OF NORFOLK changed matters little for Thomas Howard in his struggle for political power. Wolsey reached the apogee of his political power in the 1520s, and Norfolk quickly learned that his ducal status did not guarantee primacy in court and council. Yet the period from 1524 to 1530 gave Norfolk his first opportunity to take a leading role in Henry VIII's government. During these years, his career took on the form it would have for most of the later reign of Henry VIII—wide-ranging service to the crown, offered with a great show of loyalty, but often with an underlying churlish air of one who felt he deserved greater honor and rewards than Henry saw fit to give him.

For the moment, Norfolk was distracted from court affairs by diplomatic concerns. Henry did not renew the war against France in 1524; after Suffolk returned from his unsuccessful invasion, the fighting was left to Bourbon. The Hapsburg-Valois struggle continued as the main focus of English policy, but Scotland was also worrisome.[1] As Norfolk had predicted, Albany was unable to recover his authority after the fiasco of 1523, and England's always tenuous influence in Scotland was in danger of disappearing altogether until a new tool fell into Henry's hands in the person of Archibald Douglas, earl of Angus and Margaret's estranged husband. At Henry's urging, Angus and his brother George slipped across from France to England in the summer of 1524, and by 6 July Wolsey was plotting to use Angus in some fashion to turn Scottish affairs to English advantage. With this tantalizing prospect at hand, Norfolk was ordered north.[2]

By late July Norfolk reached Newcastle and took up the thread of diplomacy. The main problem with Angus was that both Margaret and her main ally, James Hamilton, earl of Arran, had personal grudges against him. In her husband's absence Margaret had occupied herself with a series of lovers; the queen, Norfolk noted, "was not gretely joyffull off the commyng of the Erle of Angushe." Arran had his own reasons for opposing Angus. Angus had killed Arran's brother Patrick and had threatened more than once to kill Arran as well if he could lay hands on him.[3] Neither Margaret nor Arran wanted to see their own power reduced, and both knew that Henry did not need several pensioners contesting for control of Scotland. Arran was James's cousin, and the nearest native-born Scot to the throne (Albany having been born in France); he did not intend to yield without a struggle, even if he had to abandon England and turn to France for support. On 1 August Wolsey sent Norfolk detailed instructions on feeling out the Scots' reactions to Angus's proposed entry. If the earl could counteract Albany's influence and assure a pro-English presence in Edinburgh, Norfolk was to send Angus into Scotland; the price of destroying the inconstant Margaret as an ally would be worth paying.[4]

The quest to neutralize Albany proved needless; early in August James was taken to Edinburgh and declared of age, formally assuming government in his own right. By this fiction, Albany's regency was ended, leaving Margaret and Arran in control of the twelve-year-old king. It was now clear that Albany was no longer a factor in Scottish politics. But could Margaret and Arran be counted upon to follow Henry's lead? If they could not, would the Douglas brothers be any more likely to dance to England's tune? Henry, Wolsey and Norfolk had to weigh the costs of supporting Angus against the potential gains. In mid-August, Margaret announced that David Beaton, chancellor, archbishop of St. Andrews and a notable friend of France, had been imprisoned as proof of the loyalty that she and Arran owed to Henry.[5] By early September a truce was signed to pacify the borders, and James promised to send ambassadors to Henry to treat for a permanent peace.[6]

Despite the promise of these events, Margaret had learned of Henry's dealings with Angus, and she wrote several letters to Norfolk in September and October 1524, protesting that the duke should not believe what anyone else in Scotland told him. The country would turn to France if Angus returned, she warned, and further, James's own authority and reputation would be damaged. "Preyeng you hartly, my Lord," she wrote, "as een of my specyal fryndyz, that ze vyl labor at the kyngs Grace my brotharz hand, that the said elr of Angus com not in Scotland."[7] Arran, too, wrote to Norfolk on 3 October, proclaiming his loyalty to Henry VIII but urging the duke to hold Angus back. Arran's letter was more revealing than he intended, for there was an undercurrent of desperation to his words. Arran understood that his personal position was at stake and was willing to do almost anything to retain his grasp on power—perhaps a fatal hint that he was not to be trusted and had to be destroyed if England was to gain ascendancy over Scotland.[8]

Wolsey had hoped that Arran and Margaret could be reconciled with Angus, but tortuous negotiations during October proved this wishful thinking. Arran was ready to turn to France rather than share his rule with Angus. The young King James was reported to favor Angus, leading Arran to fear the Douglas faction all the more.[9] Norfolk warned of the dangers of employing Angus, but Angus was able to convince Wolsey that he and his brother could command the loyalty of a pro-English party of lords around James, protecting the king from the baleful influence of the pro-French Beaton and his party.[10] On 4 October Wolsey and Angus agreed to a set of articles whereby Douglas promised, once in Scotland, to support James and not to oppose Margaret and Arran unless they threatened James's authority or turned to France. Angus also swore to serve Henry VIII against any prince but his own, and to follow the advice of Henry, Wolsey, Norfolk and Dacre in all things. This pact sealed, Wolsey sent Angus north into Norfolk's care, giving the duke the task of monitoring Scottish reactions to Angus's proposed entry. If, in his judgment, it would aid England's cause, Norfolk was to set the earl free to return to his homeland.[11]

Norfolk was well aware that Margaret, infatuated with a new lover, was unlikely to be reconciled to Angus, nor would Arran accept such a dangerous political and personal rival. The question became one of measuring risks. Would Arran and Margaret remain useful to English interests if Angus was held back? Wolsey pressed Norfolk for his opinion, but the duke protested that "this matier is of so great emportance, and the persones of so unstable demeanor that be the chief parties, that I dare not gif myne advyse to thone or thoder."[12] Norfolk wanted to avoid the blame if the Angus affair proved a disaster. Yet he knew that Margaret's party was in danger of losing power in any event; the very threat of Angus's return was enough to undermine their position. On 10 October, Norfolk made a final attempt to reconcile Margaret to Angus. In a long letter, pleading, cajoling and threatening by turns, Norfolk concluded by urging Margaret to "shewe yorself now to be contented to folowe the kingis highnes pleasure." Henry and Wolsey had decided to send Angus home; it was now up to Margaret and Arran. If they would not cooperate, the English leaders would throw their support to the presumably more tractable Angus.[13]

As late as 24 October, Norfolk wavered. He was sure that Angus could command a pro-English party in Scotland and prevent the return of Albany, but at the cost of permanently turning Margaret and Arran to France.[14] Perhaps Norfolk hesitated to release Angus because of his long correspondence with Margaret and a sense of loyalty to the erratic queen. But on 24 October news reached Norfolk that changed his view of the situation. Sir George Douglas reported from Berwick that Margaret had freed the francophile chancellor, Beaton.[15] This seemed proof that the queen preferred a pro-French policy to the ruin of her rule; unless Norfolk acted quickly Scotland would again fall under French sway. By 30 October, the Douglases, with Norfolk's blessings, entered Scotland. Wolsey wrote that he and the king wished to "moche commende and allowe" Norfolk's decision, and well they might. Wolsey had effectively destroyed Margaret and Arran by playing with Angus. The threat of a turn to France was a self-fulfilling prophecy, for Margaret's only other choice was to be an English puppet, which the Scots lords would not have tolerated. Yet even after all this Norfolk was instructed to make one more effort to reconcile Margaret to her husband. Meanwhile, the final insult, no pensions were to be paid the queen or Arran.[16]

In reviewing the Scottish correspondence of 1524 the reader is left with the impression that Wolsey was not very pleased with Norfolk's work, not so much because of the outcome—for Angus proved a useful ally—but because Norfolk lacked the finesse that Wolsey's schemes required. Wolsey wanted to use Angus not to drive Margaret and Arran into the arms of France or undermine their support among the Scots lords, but as a means of gentle persuasion that English friendship was the best guarantee of their continued rule in Scotland. Norfolk felt that he did the best he could with an all but impossible situation; Wolsey, however, believed that Norfolk did less than full justice to the delicate work that the cardinal tried, in some frustration, to conduct by remote control. Perhaps Wolsey was attempting the impossible—not for the only time in his career—but it may be that Norfolk's pedestrian intelligence was not up to the task that Wolsey set him. Norfolk was more a soldier and man of action than a diplomat; burning towns and throwing down castles were more his line. Dealing with twisted and uncertain affairs such as the Scottish situation of 1524 required delicacy he lacked, a shortcoming which may help to explain his failure ever to hold on to political primacy for very long.[17]

At the end of October Thomas Magnus and Roger Ratcliff arrived as English residents at James's court.[18] Their reports to Norfolk revealed that Arran was, as expected, intransigent. Not only would he not make peace with Angus, but Arran was gathering his forces to fight if necessary and daily wearing his French Order of St. Michael as a badge of his allegiance. "Whosoever have hym best," Norfolk wrote of Arran, "is no more sure of hym, than he that hath an ele by the tayle." Margaret, too, was obstinately having nothing to do with her husband, the very mention of whom drove her to frenzied outbursts against Henry and Norfolk for having betrayed her. Fearing Angus would gain control of the government when the Scots Parliament met in November, Margaret tried without success to persuade Norfolk to invite the earl to Berwick and detain him while Parliament sat. As Magnus and Ratcliff wrote Wolsey, any move to patch things up with Angus would ruin Margaret and Arran's credit with most of their supporters, for Hamiltons could have no peaceable dealings with Douglases.[19]

Angus made the first hostile move. Late in November the earl entered Edinburgh with a band of four hundred men headed by Matthew Stewart, fourth earl of Lennox. Publishing a proclamation "shewing that they were commen as the Kingges faithfull subjectes to serve His Grace," Angus summoned the council and declared that James "required the said Lordes of the Counsaill that they [i.e., Arran and allies] wolde take the rule and guyding of the said King thayr Maister." Any royal officer who disobeyed Angus would face punishment for treason. Margaret took refuge in an abbey until the earls, at James's request, withdrew from the town. The queen took her son to Edinburgh Castle that evening, only to find no lords willing to join her against Angus. The rule of Scotland had fallen to Archibald Douglas and, after Beaton switched his allegiance to Angus, Margaret was finished as an independent force in Scottish politics.[20]

Angus and his followers were supreme for the next several years until James began his personal rule in 1528 and Angus fled to France. A council of regency, with Angus, Lennox, Arran, Margaret and Beaton uncomfortably yoked together, was erected in the spring of 1525 and, although no formal peace was signed with England during Angus's rule, neither was the war resumed. Henry did not gain direct control of Scotland or of James through Angus; on the other hand, it is doubtful that Margaret and Arran would have been able to resist the anti-English and pro-French sentiments of many of the lords as Angus did. Under Archibald Douglas's rule, Scotland at least ceased actively to threaten England's northern border while continental war beckoned. This was all that Henry VIII ever really sought in his Scottish diplomacy; Angus proved wholly satisfactory as regent.[21]

Norfolk returned south at the end of 1524. On 19 September he had asked to be spared another winter in the north or, if he were to stay, permission to send for his wife and goods to set up household at Sheriff Hutton. As late as 24 October Wolsey, expecting Scotland to remain in turmoil, relayed Henry's command for Norfolk "to make your abode ther for a season." Following Angus's entry, however, Norfolk renewed his pleas; on 16 November he wrote from Newcastle "mooste humble beseching your Grace [Wolsey] tadvertise me how I shalbe ordred conservnyng my departure hence."[22] Angus's seizure of power and the Scots' decision to send ambassadors to London to treat for peace finally brought Norfolk release from his duties. On 29 November Norfolk and Dacre signed a truce with the Scots for two months, and as the Scottish ambassadors headed for London, Norfolk seems to have followed without awaiting final permission, as he had asked, to "comme forwardes towardes the Kinges Highnes."[23]

Norfolk was in London in mid-January, taking charge of the talks with the Scots. The truce was renewed for another two months in late January with Norfolk and Dacre signing the articles for the English.[24] The duke also took his place in council where he was in frequent attendance early in 1525.[25] Perhaps more important, Norfolk joined the court circle that hunted and feasted with the king. Several of this group had Howard connections, such as Norfolk's brother-in-law Thomas Boleyn and cousin Francis Bryan, but Henry's closest companion was Charles Brandon, duke of Suffolk. In 1515, Suffolk had gratefully accepted Wolsey's aid in overcoming Henry's ire at his unauthorized marriage to the king's sister. By

1520 Suffolk had learned that Wolsey's friendship was unnecessary as long as he had the king's friendship. It was, after all, the king and not the cardinal who raised Brandon to a dukedom. Suffolk was slow to become Wolsey's open enemy but, like Norfolk, he had chafed under Wolsey's close supervision and parsimonious control of funds while waging Henry's wars. While Wolsey sought to insure peace and win England advantage by diplomacy, Suffolk shared Norfolk's preference for a policy of war; how else could such as Brandon and Howard win honor and rewards? Norfolk and Suffolk were not close friends, but they often served together during the 1520s, and by inclination and attitude had a good deal in common.[26] By 1527 at the latest Norfolk and Suffolk were allied in support of Henry's divorce project and in opposition to Wolsey. It was during this period at court in 1525 that the Norfolk-Suffolk alliance must first have taken shape.

With Scotland and England at peace and Charles V and Francis I at odds, the prospects for renewed English entry into the continental wars still were dim in early 1525. Then, on 14 February, a French army was crushed by imperial forces outside Pavia, and Francis was taken prisoner. Word of this disaster reached London by 9 March, inspiring a round of celebrations and reviving plans for military action. There seemed no question that Henry would now fulfill his treaty obligations to Charles and invade France. Even before an English embassy left for Madrid, the foreign ambassadors were reporting plans for Norfolk to go to Normandy at the end of May with 10,000 men if Charles would but provide 3,000 horse and 1,000 foot in support. The old Angevin empire, perhaps the crown of France, lay before Henry. Charles, of course, could take Languedoc, Burgundy and Provence, linking his dominions, and Bourbon could recover his patrimony. The prospect of carving up a defenseless France was heady wine even for Henry, a man who had never lacked for extravagant vision.[27]

Yet with a full fighting season open and France lying helpless before her enemies, there was no English invasion of the continent in 1525. Charles was out of money and had already won a considerable victory by taking Francis hostage; he had no interest in redrawing the map of Europe, much less in placing Henry on the throne of France. Despite the enthusiasm by Henry, Norfolk and Suffolk, Wolsey saw Pavia as an opportunity to seek peace rather than war; the cardinal quickly opened unofficial negotiations with the queen mother of France and treated Charles's ambassadors with hostile suspicion. But most decisively, England proved unable to afford

The Peer and the Prelate

war. The Amicable Grant, an extra-Parliamentary tax in the form of a forced loan, not only failed to raise sufficient funds, but nearly caused a full-scale rebellion in East Anglia, in the process derailing any possibility of England going to war in 1525.[28]

Henry's council was enthusiastic for war; knowledge of Wolsey's pacific desires only inspired greater clamor for an invasion of France. With time too short to obtain a subsidy from Parliament, the council drew up plans for the more expeditious collection of funds by means of a benevolence or forced loan at the rate of one-sixth of the income and moveable goods of the laity, and one-third for the clergy—the latter an extraordinarily high and ruinous rate. By the end of March commissioners were off to the shires to begin collections while Wolsey took charge of administration of the scheme. Norfolk and Suffolk went into their counties, and William Warham, archbishop of Canterbury, began work in Kent. This step, according to Edward Hall, was Wolsey's doing. Normal practice would have been, as with the subsidy commission of 1523, to appoint local gentlemen to make collections. Instead, Wolsey saw to it that the great men of the counties—many of them his opponents in and out of council—would actually "practice" the Grant. This had the effect of leaving Wolsey alone with the king while placing the ill-will sure to be engendered by the Grant on the authors of the war policy.[29]

By the end of March Norfolk was in his home county organizing collection of the loan. On 1 April he wrote Wolsey from Kenninghall to report early progress. Having met with the merchants of Norwich on 29 March, Norfolk had found then willing enough to support the French war but unable to make full payments in cash due to coin shortages. Norfolk urged Wolsey to take payments in plate instead, accepting what the gentlemen offered. Perhaps, Norfolk suggested hopefully, Henry could coin dandiprats for the army in France from the plate. Already, however, Norfolk could see trouble looming. If the rich were short of coin, how could the commons be expected to subscribe their full rates?[30]

Norfolk planned that, once the leading men of the shire agreed to the loan, he would send them out as agents to collect from the commons, following the normal practice of subsidy collections by gentry commissioners. Wolsey's instructions authorized no such action, and Norfolk's requests to have the men added to his commission were refused; the duke was to rely on his own authority to collect the Grant.[31] Yet by taxing the wealthy first, Norfolk caused a host of problems. The clothiers and merchants paid what they could, but then were forced to dismiss their laborers. The Grant was but the last straw, for low woolen prices and trade disruptions because of continental war had already drained much of the coin from East Anglia. With no jobs, no pay, and faced with demands for a forced loan to the crown, the commons were swiftly pushed to desperation.

By 4 April Norfolk was aware that the full rates from his county were unlikely to be collected, but he put the best face on things he could, suggesting that he and Suffolk would be able to collect most of their levies within another week. The common people were unhappy that the church was not being taxed as well (the clerical loan apparently had not yet been collected in Norfolk—more of Wolsey's doing?), but the duke thought that he had mollified his people sufficiently and expected no more than grumbling. Aware as well that absence from court while plans for war should have been going forward left the king too much to Wolsey's influence, Norfolk and Suffolk sought permission to return by St. George's Day, 23 April, for the meeting of the Order of the Garter. Norfolk had already been nominated to lead the vanguard into France, and he wished to begin preparations for that "great voyage." Wolsey initially agreed that the dukes could return, and on 14 April Norfolk wrote that he would be at court within a week. In the meantime, however, resistance to the Grant had begun in other areas of the realm, and problems arose in East Anglia that made it clear that the duke's presence would be needed there to prevent trouble. As rumblings of discontent with the Grant began to be heard, the dukes were told to remain at work, "wherin the kinges grace trustith undoubtidly . . . that no difficultie shalbe made."[32]

By 10 April collections had slowed to a trickle. The commons were reluctant or unable to pay, and threats were heard against those who did; Norfolk was forced to use personal persuasion on a group of two hundred men who only agreed to pay their shares after the "sheding of many salt teares." Still, most of the wealthier had made their benevolent grants; Norfolk reported that less than twenty of the men in the shire with over twenty pounds had not. Since the commons had little funds, collections were going about as well as could be expected. Again, Norfolk asked if he was to be at court by 23 April, only to be ordered by Wolsey to stay in Norfolk and redouble his efforts.[33] Despite the difficulties with the Grant, on 11 April Norfolk was commissioned to command the army of invasion, leading him to write three days later thanking Wolsey for his aid and promising continued friendship.³⁴ Norfolk did not yet expect anything to stand in the way of war. Nonetheless, he realized that his own political position, as well as the success of the French invasion, were tied to the Amicable Grant. No letters from Norfolk survive from 14 April to the end of the month, while Norfolk made a furious effort to finish "practicing" the Grant, all with the aim of assuring war with France, his own command, and a favorable reception at court.

While Norfolk had difficulty obtaining the full rates in his county, the loan ran into trouble elsewhere as well. Hall noted problems in Berkshire and Huntingdonshire, and reported the grudge of people "through England" against the Grant.³⁵ By mid-May there was resistance in the Isle of Ely, Essex and Cambridgeshire, while in Lincoln there seemed no point in asking those with less than twenty pounds for anything. The duke of Suffolk had troubles in his shire, especially because of a corn shortage which had drained coin from the county, and Warham faced resistance in Kent.³⁶ Wolsey himself took charge of London, tried very hard to wring money from the capital—perhaps too hard?—and ran into problems of his own. The Londoners flatly refused to pay the sums demanded, and a city councilor quoted a statute of Richard III against benevolences to the cardinal's face, even after Henry apparently relented on 26 April and decided to accept whatever the city freely offered.³⁷

Things had already gone too far in Suffolk. Norfolk had worried about commotions in his shire, but by the first week in May Suffolk's rough handling of his county led to open resistance. When Suffolk, expecting trouble from unemployed wool workers in the south of the county, ordered the constables to disarm the commons, an outburst ensued in which four thousand men of the Stour valley marched to Lavenham, just west of Wolsey's home town of Ipswich, threatening Suffolk and his lieutenant Sir Robert Drury with physical violence. The local constabulary would not face the rioters but only broke down the bridges to prevent a wider disturbance.³⁸ By 8 May Norfolk arrived with a force of his own men and retainers, but the two dukes wisely chose negotiation over battle. Norfolk sent John Spring, a Lavenham clothier, and Sir Thomas Jermyn, Spring's brother-in-law and a Howard man, to ask the rioters their intent. Assured that they "would live and die in the kynges causes, and to the kyng be obedient,"

Norfolk asked to speak to their captain. John Green came forward to state the commons' position:

> My lorde . . . you aske who is our captain, for soth hys name is Povertie; for he and his cosyn Necessitie, have brought us to this doyng. . . . I speke this my lorde, the cloth makers have put all these people, and a farre greater nomber from work[. T]he husbande men have put away their servauntes, and geven up household, they saye, the kyng asketh so much, that thei be not able to do as thei have done before this tyme, and then for necessitie, must we dye wretchedly; Wherfore my lorde, now according to your wisedom, consider our necessitie.[39]

On 8 May Henry wrote the commissioners to proceed "douceley rather than by violence"; thus the dukes sought the rioters' submission, offering to "send to the kyng, and make humble intercession for your pardon." The dukes were painfully aware that the rising had taken place in the counties under their care, and so while writing to Henry "mooste humbly beseching your highnes to contynewe good and gracious Lord unto us," they blamed their troubles on Wolsey, who had, after all, written the commissions and directed collection of the Grant. Further, they warned Henry that the rising in Suffolk might inspire rebellion elsewhere. For prudence's sake, and especially considering the violent comments against Henry that Warham had reported from Kent, the dukes suggested that Henry Stafford (son of the attainted duke of Buckingham) and Edward Neville, two scions of houses with disloyal histories, be given a "gode regard" lest the disorders be seized upon as a pretext for rebellion.[40]

During the next several days Norfolk and Suffolk, armed with a commission of oyer and terminer, were busy accepting the rioters' submissions. Four men of Lavenham were held as principal offenders, but the rest were charged to warn the men of other towns to come before the dukes to seek pardon and allowed to depart. Norfolk and Suffolk bitterly noted that the men of East Anglia had some right to be aggrieved, as their reward for goodwill in submitting to the Grant had been to see the rest of the realm, less hasty to pay, freed of the obligation.[41] Having done his job better than any other commissioner in collecting the Grant, Norfolk gained only blame for a rebellion and the ill will of the citizens of his shire. On 12 May he and Suffolk reported to Wolsey that talk of resistance continued in Essex, Cambridgeshire and at Cambridge University, keeping the situation tense. The dukes remained ready to resist any trouble, but thought it imperative that the king's council should meet to decide what should be done. Clearly, they were anxious to return to court to tell their side of the story; they knew Wolsey was doing them no good by his monopoly of the king. Still, Norfolk and Suffolk wrote, they would stay in their shires until hearing from the king whether the Grant would be rescinded.[42]

On 14 May, Henry relented and sent out letters revoking the commissions for the loan and extending free pardon to all who had resisted, openly or secretly; with this announcement the uproar against the Amicable Grant quickly subsided. By 17 May Norfolk and Suffolk were reading the king's letter in their counties, and within a few days the dukes had returned to court, bringing along their token prisoners to face royal justice. On 19 and 20 May, Norfolk sat with Wolsey in Star Chamber as the men of Lavenham and other rebels were treated to Wolsey's chastisement and then granted Henry's promised pardon; Norfolk and Wolsey pledged themselves as sureties for their fellow East Anglians.[43] The risings against the Amicable Grant thus ended without bloodshed, but the limits of his power were demonstrated to an angry Henry VIII. Tudor rule was essentially cooperative; taxation was more voluntary than coercive. With the economic slump of the 1520s, the forced loan of 1522, and the subsidy of 1523, the Grant proved too heavy a burden, and the king's subjects, "lambs already close-shorn," made it clear that they would not, could not, pay more. When the Grant was finally withdrawn, Henry disingenuously claimed that "he never knew of that demand," and Wolsey was allowed to take the public blame. As the king knew, ministers and not monarchs had to bear the odium for unpopular policies.[44]

Wolsey suffered little loss of prestige from the fiasco of the Amicable Grant. Despite Charles V's rebuff of Henry's offer to partition France, Wolsey's diplomatic skills were still of paramount value. Charles, although content with his victory at Pavia, was unhappy with one of the basic terms of his English alliance—his betrothal to a child princess, Henry's nine-year-old daughter Mary. The emperor was ready to marry, and had cast his eye upon Isabella of Portugal, a richly dowered woman of twenty-two years. To force Henry's hand, Charles demanded that Mary, with her full dowry, be sent to Spain at once. When this was refused, Charles insisted that he be released from his obligation to wed Mary; the Anglo-Imperial alliance abruptly collapsed by the summer of 1525.[45]

Wolsey may already have planned for this, although the breakup of the alliance was Charles's work and not the cardinal's. Secret negotiations with the French were under way by 22 June; this resulted in the initialing of an Anglo-French treaty on 18 August. Norfolk and Suffolk joined Wolsey in signing the still-secret Treaty of the More and, on 29 August, Norfolk took a prominent place in the public unveiling of the pact which bound England to aid in freeing Francis from captivity.[46] This was a complete reversal of English policy, although not the first of Henry's reign. As in 1514, the king turned to France when Spain insulted and disappointed him. For Henry, dynastic pride was more important than diplomatic consistency; in pursuing what certainly was to him the chivalric sport of war, he always seems to have been looking for the next fight rather than cleaning up the consequences of the last one.

Wolsey worked furiously to gain Francis's release, as did the French. In January 1526 Francis signed a punitive treaty with Charles and was escorted out of Spain after delivering his sons as hostages in his place. Francis assured the English that the treaty would be disavowed as having been made under compulsion, and, once safe in France, he did exactly that. The culmination of Wolsey's new diplomatic offensive was the League of Cognac signed in May 1526 which bound England, France, Milan, Venice, Florence and the pope against the emperor. Through the year from the failure of the Amicable Grant to the League of Cognac, Wolsey proved his worth to Henry beyond all doubt. No one else could have orchestrated this grand about-face and realignment, and the king knew it. By mid-1526, Wolsey stood supreme, ruling court and council and so firmly holding the king's confidence that none dared oppose him.[47]

From the autumn of 1525 until the middle of 1527 Norfolk was pushed into near-retirement by Wolsey. Even so, in this period the seeds of Wolsey's fall were sown. The jilting of Mary by the emperor and the breakup of the Anglo-Imperial alliance was a great if initially unappreciated turning point in Henry's reign. What was at first merely an annoyance, a diplomatic insult, would soon become the central crisis of the reign. Catherine was almost forty; the chances for further children from the royal marriage were slim. Henry had hoped that the marriage between

Charles and Mary would provide an heir to knot forever the bonds that Henry VII had initiated by the Treaty of Medina del Campo in 1489; England and Spain would have been joined to the perpetual ruin of France. With Charles now married elsewhere, and with no faith in queens regnant, Henry adopted other expedients. His first effort to ensure the succession was to recognize an illegitimate son, but later the king would turn to the more enticing prospect of divorcing Catherine to wed a younger woman capable of bearing an heir. Having presided over England's diplomatic reversal, Wolsey would find himself obliged to aid these other designs as well. In pursuit of Henry's dynastic schemes, Wolsey would stick at expedients easily accepted by Norfolk and his fellows, and the aristocratic party would enjoy a resurgence.

Henry Fitzroy was the beneficiary of Henry's first effort to preserve the succession. Fitzroy was born in 1519 to Elizabeth Blount, a lady in waiting to Catherine and a cousin of Lord Mountjoy. Until 1525 Fitzroy lived in obscurity, but on 16 June Henry brought forth his bastard son for all to see when Fitzroy was created earl of Nottingham and duke of Richmond and Somerset in ceremonies at Bridewell Palace. The dynastic overtones of the titles were unmistakable, harkening back to Tudor earls of Richmond and Beaufort dukes and earls of Somerset. Norfolk attended the ceremonies, but not as earl marshal. Wolsey had seen to it that reversion of that office had been granted to Suffolk before the second duke's death. A further insult to Howard's pride followed on 16 July when Richmond was made admiral of England. Norfolk took until 16 August to surrender his patent, but Wolsey could afford to wait. Finally, Richmond was sent north as warden general of the marches and later made lord lieutenant; although a council did the actual work, this appointment relieved Norfolk of his last official position within Wolsey's reach.[48] The loss of these family dignities was a sore blow to Norfolk which was hardly lessened by his token appearances to sign the new treaties with France. Norfolk and Suffolk ratified the Treaty of the More for the sake of ceremony; everyone knew who was the real architect of the arrangement.

Following these humiliations, Norfolk was not prominent at court again for two years until fresh diplomatic events and Henry's growing interest in a Howard niece, Anne Boleyn, brought him into renewed favor. Norfolk was occasionally at court and in council during the interim,[49] but for the most part he was away from London. With time on his hands, between

1526 and 1528 Norfolk busied himself with erecting a new mansion on the site of the old Mowbray hunting lodge at Kenninghall. Built in the new, unfortified, style, Kenninghall was in the form of an "H" with two wings joined by a central hall. This lavish palace, faced with ornamental brickwork and adorned with Turkish carpets and rich tapestries, was intended to rival Wolsey's Hampton Court and York Place. The construction of Kenninghall, Norfolk's main residence in the 1530s and 1540s, occupied a considerable portion of Norfolk's time and money during his exile.[50] Even if shunted into country seclusion, the duke was determined to reside in a fashion befitting his station, and make as strong a statement about his prestige and wealth as his situation permitted.

Norfolk was not without honors and grants of favor during these years, but they hardly made up for the loss of the earl marshalship or admiralty. He continued to be named on commissions of the peace—for twenty-four counties at once in February 1526[51]—and in July 1525, he was confirmed in ownership of the estates granted him at his creation as earl of Surrey. Although the service due was increased from one red rose to two knights' fees, the grant was improved from life tenure to tail male.[52]

Norfolk was also busy advancing family interests through a variety of wardships, guardianships and marriages. In July 1525, he was the leading member of a group licensed to supervise the estates of Richard Southwell inherited from the dowager countess of Oxford. When Oxford himself died on 14 July 1526, the estates of this Howard brother-in-law were taken over by Norfolk. Oxford had been under the care of the Howards since 1514 because he had proved incompetent to manage his own affairs. Oxford had been married to Anne, half-sister of the third duke, and Norfolk saw that the young dowager countess entered the de Vere estates. Norfolk's ties to the family did not end there, for in 1532 his eldest son Henry was wed to Frances de Vere, daughter of the new earl, a de Vere cousin.[53]

Norfolk also pursued the wardship and marriage of Elizabeth, daughter and co-heir of John, lord Marney, although he found it necessary to write to Wolsey asking aid in gaining the favor from Henry. This letter (like a similar one concerning the earl of Oxford) was written while Marney was on his deathbed—hardly in good taste, but haste and determination were essential in obtaining choice wardships to exploit. Norfolk was able to marry Elizabeth Marney to his younger son Thomas; a settlement was worked out in 1530, and the couple was wed in 1533, when Lord Thomas was no older than thirteen—young enough to underscore the financial and dynastic aspects of the match.[54] Norfolk also attempted to arrange at least one other marriage in 1526, between his half-sister Catherine and a son of Thomas, lord Berkeley, a descendant of the Berkeley co-heirs to the Mowbray estates. Although this match fell through, whether because the couple were distant cousins or for other reasons, another Berkeley married a Howard granddaughter in 1554.[55]

There are traces of some of Norfolk's other activities during the period that reveal something about the lifestyle and pursuits of an English duke. Norfolk fancied falcons, for in June 1526 the chancellor of Poland mentioned in a letter to Henry VIII that Norfolk's falconer had visited there after finding no suitable birds in Denmark.[56] There is evidence, too, of the duke's business enterprises. From January 1525, Norfolk was involved in a dispute with Charles V's sister Margaret, regent of the Netherlands, over a ship that had been captured and sold "some time ago" (perhaps during the Anglo-French war of 1523?) as a prize of war, mistakenly so in Norfolk's view, as Henry and Charles had been allies. After an exchange of letters in 1525–26, the matter was settled to no one's satisfaction. Margaret lost the sureties she had paid on the duke's behalf, and Norfolk recovered his cargo only after making restitution for other goods that had allegedly been lost through his actions as admiral.[57]

By the spring of 1527, English policy had developed new complexities that provided an opening for Norfolk's talents, and the duke began to appear at court more frequently. Despite England's obligations under the League of Cognac, Henry had provided neither troops nor funds to aid Francis in his Italian war with Charles. In the spring of 1527, in hopes of reviving the flagging Anglo-French alliance, a team of French ambassadors came to England, offering to match their king with the spurned Princess Mary. From the end of February to late April, Wolsey was almost constantly engaged in the talks, which led to a new treaty signed on 30 April at Greenwich. The pressure of diplomatic events brought Norfolk to court, but while Wolsey was closeted with the French, the king kept council with Norfolk, Suffolk, Thomas More, Rochford and others. While Wolsey labored to bind England closer to France, there were loud voices in council against the new alliance and repudiation of the traditional ties to Spain. Norfolk seems to have been a leader of this noisy opposition. Sometime before 16 April, the duke had high words with Wolsey on the subject in

Henry's presence; the cardinal's rage helped to send him to bed with a fever, delaying completion of the treaties.[58]

More than foreign policy was involved in Norfolk's resurgence. Henry had known for several years that Catherine would bear him no sons; the elevation of Richmond was an admission of that. Now, in the spring of 1527, the king's conscience settled into a certainty that his marriage to his brother's widow was invalid before God, papal dispensation notwithstanding. Surely this explained the succession of miscarriages and infant deaths that had been the fruits of Catherine's pregnancies; could this be other than evidence of divine punishment for the king's great sin? In April, Henry queried his council on the possibility that the marriage was illegal, and then, in May, had Wolsey convene a secret legatine court to consider the question before asking Rome for a binding judgment. Before the arguments could be heard, however, word reached England that the unpaid imperial troops of the duke of Bourbon had mutinied, sacked Rome, and driven Clement VII into the Castel Sant-Angelo, where he became a virtual prisoner of the emperor.[59]

Wolsey's secret court was adjourned; it appeared foolhardy to press the pope for a judgment against his jail-keeper's aunt. Yet Henry's determination to be free of Catherine quickened nonetheless, for by now he had set his heart on a replacement, Norfolk's niece Anne, daughter of Thomas Boleyn, viscount Rochford. By May 1527, Henry's infatuation with a girl who might have been but another casual mistress became something more serious, and Anne's uncle became a much more frequent resident at court as her position with Henry took shape. After a largely French upbringing, Anne had come to court, probably in March 1522. Her father, Thomas, treasurer of the household, and her sister Mary, formerly a mistress of the king but now wed to William Cary of the privy chamber, provided Anne an entry to the inner circle which lived in close contact with Henry. Probably Norfolk had little to do with Anne's first coming to court, and little intention of using her as a political pawn. When Henry first began to take an interest in Anne in 1525, Norfolk was in exile at Kenninghall. Whether by the design of the family or her own initiative, Anne refused to do as her older sister Mary had done and become Henry's concubine. She held out for the prize of being queen, and this perhaps was part of Henry's fascination with her. By the spring of 1527, in addition to his scruples that Leviticus declared his marriage to his brother's widow sinful, Henry had a tempting alternative. As the king's "great matter" became a major theme of English policy, Norfolk profited from his blood ties to Anne and returned to favor as a close and trusted councilor and royal companion.[60]

At the end of 1526, Charles V sent a new ambassador to England. Iñigo de Mendoza, bishop of Burgos, arrived only after being detained in France, and his instructions did not reach him until negotiations between Wolsey and the French were well under way. Even considering Mendoza's obvious bias against Wolsey and his friendship with the anti-French Norfolk, his reports are valuable accounts of Norfolk's resurgence and of the events leading to Wolsey's fall. On 18 May Mendoza reported that Wolsey and the French alliance were both widely unpopular and that Henry might relieve the cardinal of part of his duties. Mendoza was overly optimistic, but he shrewdly identified the two major groups in opposition to the cardinal. Norfolk led the aristocrats who chafed at Wolsey's control of government—a service more properly dominated by the king's rightful advisors, the ancient nobility—and who resented the low-born cardinal's social pretensions. Cuthbert Tunstall, bishop of London, and many other clerics resented Wolsey's domination of the English church as papal legate and archbishop of York. Norfolk and Tunstall made no secret of their distaste for Wolsey; Mendoza thought it worthwhile to offer pensions to the pair because they favored Charles and opposed Wolsey and France.[61]

Wolsey certainly knew of the opposition of Henry's councilors, but he only became aware of the threat posed by Anne Boleyn in the summer of 1527. In July, Wolsey was confident enough of his power to go to France to work on the details of the alliance with Francis and to seek an end to the crisis in church government caused by the sack of Rome. Charles V would be neutralized and the pope made useless as a pawn by the simple expedient of Wolsey taking church government into his own hands. It was a grand scheme, and, as a minor point, Wolsey believed he could arrange Henry's divorce; the cardinal was already planning a new marriage to a French princess.[62] Wolsey was, in fact, overplaying his hand; he soon learned that Norfolk, Suffolk, Rochford and Tunstall were holding close counsel with and being entertained merrily by Henry in his absence. On 19 August William Knight, one of Henry's secretaries (and long a Wolsey man), wrote to the cardinal reporting that the dukes, Rochford, and Anne's cousin William Fitzwilliam were all privy, with the king's knowledge, to Wolsey's personal correspondence with Henry.[63]

Worse was to come. Even as Wolsey sought papal approval of a bull declaring the royal marriage void, Henry sent Knight to Rome to propose that the king be licensed to enter a bigamous marriage. Knight also carried the draft of a bull permitting Henry to marry within prohibited degrees of consanguinity. None of this was told to Wolsey, but when he discovered the details of Knight's mission the import became distressingly clear. Anne's sister Mary had been Henry's mistress, and under canon law the liaison was sufficient to place Anne within the first degree of collateral affinity with the king. No such relationship existed with any French bride Wolsey had considered. Thus, when the cardinal returned to England in late September—having failed to seal the isolation of Charles by a firm agreement with Francis, to take control of church government, or to obtain Henry's divorce—he faced a new crisis. Wolsey arrived to find Norfolk and his friends in high favor and Anne closeted with Henry. At Anne's demand, Wolsey conducted his first interview with the king in her presence.[64] The struggle between Wolsey and a loose coalition of enemies was joined in earnest, with the focal point, Norfolk's niece, now alarmingly evident.

Yet Wolsey survived this scare with relative ease. Henry, determined that Clement would dissolve the royal marriage, knew that Wolsey was indispensable for that purpose. Anne, too, had learned the lesson that Wolsey had long known, that Henry's favor was everything; as long as she stood in the king's good graces, Wolsey could not harm her—and probably only help her. Although there was no great love between Anne and Wolsey, they were forced by circumstances into an outward show of amity. Anne wanted Henry free to marry her, and needed Wolsey. The cardinal, on the other hand, dared not oppose one whom the king loved and wanted for a wife. As a result, the hostile coalition was forced into retreat; in the autumn of 1527, Wolsey weathered the first storm.[65]

The result for Norfolk was renewed exile. Wolsey kept the duke away from court with a succession of tasks that both knew better suited the gentlemen of East Anglia. In December Norfolk surveyed grain production and the state of the eastern export economy which was threatened by the prospect of war with Charles V, since his territories in the Netherlands were East Anglia's major trading partner. After a brief sojourn at court around Christmas, Norfolk returned to East Anglia to put down a small-scale revolt against controls on the sale of corn. As a result of this rising, on 4 March 1528 Norfolk wrote to Wolsey asking the king's pleasure on hanging several men for unlawful assembly at Bury (ten miles from Lavenham, center of the troubles in 1525). The duke asked leave to come to court when he was done, but on 10 April was told by Rochford that Henry wished him to remain in his shire for the Easter legal term.[66]

Exiled from court for the moment, Norfolk probably attended the court sessions, and busied himself with work at Kenninghall. In mid-April, he put down yet another series of disturbances brought on by economic problems. When informed on 23 April that he was to stay in Norfolk through May to prevent further trouble, the duke rather petulantly demanded that the earls of Essex and Oxford and Lord Fitzwater be commanded to go to their houses as well, in case any "business should chance."[67] Norfolk recognized the government's concern with the continuing disturbances in East Anglia, but felt that others should join him in the country as proof that necessity, and not court politics, justified his banishment from court.[68]

In May Norfolk was still busy hearing complaints against the ruin of trade when he fell ill. Henry was sufficiently concerned to send his personal physician William Butts to treat the duke, who nonetheless complained that he would have recovered more quickly had he been allowed to consult "cunning men" in London. Again on 2 June he requested leave to come to court for the next legal term, but the petition was denied, perhaps on the pretext that his recent illness might be contagious.[69] Thereafter Norfolk took up a new theme in his requests to see the king. Ireland, where he had served as lieutenant in 1520–22, was suffering a near civil war among the Anglo-Irish nobility, leading Norfolk to emphasize his expertise in Irish matters and seek permission to advise Henry on problems there. The duke could even display a letter from the Irish council begging him to intercede with the king to prevent chaos, ending with the plea, "our especial esperance is in you."[70]

This tactic availed nothing, and Norfolk was not able to return to court until late 1528. It was not Henry's need for advice on Ireland but Wolsey's failure to wrest a divorce out of Clement VII that made Norfolk useful to the king again. Wolsey was in a quandary. His only claim to power was the service he could give the king, yet to support policies leading to a marriage between Henry and Anne would surely strengthen domestic enemies such as Norfolk and Rochford. On 18 September Mendoza told Charles V that Wolsey was dragging his feet on the divorce. Henry suspected the same, for in August he had openly sworn at his minister because the case had not gone forward more quickly.[71] Several English envoys at Rome including

Stephen Gardiner were attempting to prod Clement into action, but Henry was not satisfied, even after Lorenzo Campeggio, absentee bishop of Salisbury, cardinal-protector of England and papal legate, arrived in London in October with a decretal commission to hear Henry's case. Clement had secretly ordered Campeggio to delay, seeking a settlement without a trial, and, if all else failed, to recall the case to Rome rather than allow a verdict to be reached in England. Henry had looked to Campeggio's arrival as the last step before his wish would be granted, but instead only more delay and irritation would result.[72]

Norfolk was in London by mid-November, perhaps bolstering Henry's spirits with his hearty support of the king's cause.[73] Norfolk's return was linked to a short-lived project to prod Campeggio into action by preparing a document signed by the great of the realm, attesting that "the abrogation of this marriage is much desired by the people of England." Only Norfolk, Rochford and Anne's brother George signed the paper before the scheme was dropped; the whole heavy-handed project may have been Norfolk's idea.[74] Henry was casting about for a solution to his problem, and neither Wolsey nor Norfolk seemed able to provide it. The duke was at Kenninghall for Christmas, but back at court by 2 January for the reception of new Venetian envoys; Norfolk was seemingly in high esteem at the dinner that followed.[75] After spending much of the spring in his county, by mid-1529 Norfolk began to appear at court more often than at any time in the previous several years. The reason seemed clear to the foreign ambassadors who, reporting Wolsey's growing peril, saw Norfolk as his main critic and enemy. The effort for papal approval of the divorce had gone so far that, if it failed, Henry would surely lay the blame on Wolsey. Yet the cardinal still had considerable resources. The French envoy, Jean du Bellay, bishop of Bayonne, wrote that "the duke of Norfolk and his party already begin to talk big, but certainly they have to do with one more subtle than themselves."[76] Mendoza, despite his optimism a year before that Wolsey was in great danger, had a similar impression. On 4 February he noted the importance of Henry's favor as the key to power, and indicated that Wolsey, though in danger, was hardly yet ruined:

> This lady [Anne], who is the cause of all the disorder, finding her marriage delayed, that she thought herself so sure of, entertains great suspicion that the Cardinal of England puts impediments in her way, in a belief that if she were Queen his power would decline. In this

suspicion she is joined by her father, and the two dukes of Norfolk and Suffolk, who have combined to overthrow the Cardinal; but as yet they have made no impression in the King, except that he shows him in court not quite so good countenances as he did, and that he said some disagreeable words to him.[77]

Henry's show of disfavor to Wolsey while the outcome of Campeggio's commission hung in the balance must have encouraged Norfolk to bring his opposition into the open. In March Wolsey learned how audacious Norfolk had become when Brian Tuke reported that, in a council meeting with the king, Norfolk, Suffolk and Rochford showed open contempt when the cardinal's letter was read.[78] The aristocratic faction clearly was determined to trap Wolsey on the divorce and destroy him.[79]

By 22 May, du Bellay was certain that Wolsey's downfall was imminent unless the divorce was granted soon. "I assure you," he wrote to a French correspondent, "Wolsey is in the greatest pain he ever was." The dukes, among others, were busy daily reminding Henry that Wolsey had not done all he might to promote the divorce.[80] In June, Suffolk let the mask slip further, writing Henry a letter full of veiled castigation of Wolsey and reminders that one whom the king trusted had deceived him.[81]

The last chance for Wolsey to make a complete recovery was the legatine court. Henry had hoped to avoid a trial of his case, and had long sought direct papal action to dissolve the marriage. By the spring of 1529 the king despaired of any such easy solution from Clement VII, and on 29 May the cardinals were given permission to open court. On 18 June proceedings began at Blackfriars. Catherine refused to recognize the jurisdiction of the legates and appealed to Rome for justice, even kneeling before her husband, begging him not to divorce her. After weeks of pointless arguments, on 23 July Campeggio announced that the court would be adjourned for the traditional Vatican summer recess until October! Henry sent Norfolk and Suffolk to demand that the sessions continue until sentence was given, but to no avail. On 31 July the court adjourned. Long before October Clement's letters revoking the case to Rome would arrive to insure that the recess was permanent.[82] What Henry had long sought to avoid, and what Wolsey had seemed indispensable in blocking, had come to pass. Henry's suit would be heard in Rome under the very nose of the emperor; the king's case was ruined before it was heard.

On the heels of this failure, Wolsey narrowly averted a disaster in foreign affairs. French and Imperial diplomats had been meeting at Cambrai for some time with no apparent prospects of agreement, but suddenly in July the talks turned productive. Wolsey had all but ignored this potentially dangerous meeting; an English delegation arrived in time to preserve appearances, but More and Tunstall had no influence over the terms of the "Ladies' Peace" signed on 5 August. Wolsey had been taken in by Francis's promises of love for Henry, and the miscalculation was obvious to everyone, including the king.[83] Wolsey's League of Cognac had failed to keep Charles and Francis at odds, and now Wolsey barely missed being left out of the new treaty. It was a far cry from his grand design for a universal peace with England and himself at the hub.

Wolsey was in peril, for he had failed in the two areas of his greatest value. Norfolk, Suffolk, the Boleyns, Tunstall, and the rest of Wolsey's domestic rivals now had an opening, and began pressing Henry to ruin Wolsey. Wolsey's servant and biographer George Cavendish believed that Anne was especially effective in swaying Henry against Wolsey, but there is evidence that others were at work as well. On 29 August Wolsey sent his servant Brian Tuke to speak with the king, but Tuke was unable to see Henry because he had gone hunting with Norfolk, Suffolk and du Bellay. On 1 September, Wolsey was still not at court and not expected to come soon. A French envoy was already writing that the good offices of Norfolk, Suffolk and Rochford were essential for success at court. Nor did Wolsey appear when a new imperial ambassador arrived later in the month to present his credentials. Eustace Chapuys echoed the French impression that the dukes and Rochford had become Henry's leading advisors, transacting all state business and monopolizing Henry's attention.[84]

Henry went on progress at the end of July while Wolsey remained in London. Norfolk joined Henry at Woodstock on 28 August and followed the court to Grafton the next month. It was here that Henry and Wolsey had their last meeting. Wolsey arrived with Campeggio on 19 September. Campeggio was given rooms at Grafton—a manor house too small to accommodate the whole court—while Wolsey was assigned lodgings nearby. That day, Henry and Wolsey had a long conversation, sometimes jovial, sometimes angry; at one point Henry produced a packet of letters, demanding to know if they were in the cardinal's hand. Perhaps the king had uncovered or been shown evidence of some of Wolsey's more devious twists in diplomacy and the conduct of the divorce; had Henry not been warned that Wolsey placed his own desires over those of the king? At dinner that day, Norfolk sat with Wolsey. When the cardinal suggested that arrangements for the coming Parliament might be enhanced if the bishops were sent to their sees, Norfolk urged Wolsey to go himself, not to Winchester, but to York, "where consisteth your greatest honor and charge." Wolsey warily answered, "Even as it shall please the king."[85]

Anne also pressed the attack against Wolsey at her private dinner with Henry. Reminding the king of the "great slander and dishonor" Wolsey had done him, Anne protested that the cardinal could not be allowed to go unpunished: "There is never a nobleman within this realm that if he had done but half so much as he hath done but that he were well worthy to lose his head." Perhaps all this took effect. The next day, when Wolsey returned to resume his talk with Henry, he found the king ready to go out riding with Anne. Henry terminated their discussion "hastily but kindly," sending Wolsey home to ponder his fate.[86]

On 9 August, Henry had ordered Wolsey to send out writs for Parliament to meet on 3 November. By October, the king decided to strip Wolsey of the writs he normally controlled—perhaps a hint of plans to use the session for an attack in the cardinal. Stephen Gardiner, who had entered royal service through Wolsey's household, had by now joined the camp of his former master's enemies.[87] On 6 October Gardiner wrote to Wolsey asking him to send writs for elections in five shires. Those in Nottingham and Derby were to be executed by Norfolk, while the others would be employed as the king wished.[88] It was no secret now that Wolsey was to be prevented from having a party in the Commons; du Bellay wrote on 4 October, "I see clearly Wolsey is to lose his influence entirely in this parliament. I see no chance for the contrary." Du Bellay was sure that Wolsey's former proteges had deserted him, contributing to this turn; he referred certainly to Gardiner and probably to Brian Tuke and Thomas More.[89]

Wolsey made his last appearance in council on 6 October. Three days later, even before Parliament met, the first legal blow was struck. On the opening day of the Michaelmas term, Henry's attorneys entered an indictment for the offenses of provisions and *praemunire* against Wolsey— charges that he had unlawfully interfered in appointments to ecclesiastical benefices and, as papal legate, had violated the fourteenth-century statute against exercising a foreign authority in the realm.[90] Even before the case was heard, Henry took a further decisive step, certainly at the urging of Norfolk and Suffolk, both of whom had been with the king at Windsor before returning to meet with the council in London. On 17 October the dukes appeared at York Place to demand the great seal from the chancellor. Wolsey refused to comply without written authority from the king, forcing Norfolk and Suffolk to return the next day with Henry's letters ordering the surrender and demanding that the deprivation be made public. By 20 October Henry used the seal at Windsor on several documents before delivering it to Gardiner for safekeeping.[91]

Although Wolsey's fall from power had not been Norfolk's work alone by any means, the duke was quick to assert himself. On 18 October, he appeared at court in a gleeful mood. Chapuys noted that Norfolk cheerfully asked how Charles V would take the news of Wolsey's troubles, and the ambassador answered carefully that the emperor would be glad to see affairs fall to those qualified by birth and nobility to conduct them.[92] With Wolsey stripped of office, Norfolk and his allies were seemingly in firm control. Yet du Bellay noted their insecurity. To make sure that Wolsey or another like him could never rise again to such eminence, "these lords intend, after he is dead and ruined, to impeach the state of the church, and take all their [i.e., the ecclesiastics'] goods. . . . They proclaim it openly." To cement their position, du Bellay noted, the dukes had put Wolsey out of York Place, forcing him to take up more humble lodgings, and Norfolk had been named president of the council and Suffolk vice-president. Du Bellay did not know yet who would be chancellor, but predicted that it would not be a priest.[93]

Even while a struggle to decide that issue went on in council, Chapuys attested to Norfolk's new power, reporting on 25 October that administration had fallen largely to the duke, who told Chapuys that mismanagement of the council by former advisors was at an end. Wolsey, Norfolk said, had been replaced because of his falsehoods and lies and because he followed his own rather than the king's will. In a lengthy report to Charles V on his meeting with the duke at Lambeth House, Chapuys ridiculed Norfolk's claim of love for the house of Burgundy, noting that all those in power were saturated with French money.[94] Nevertheless, Chapuys urged Charles to write personal letters to Norfolk and Suffolk, as they stood highest in Henry's favor. Norfolk showed the loyalty to the king's causes that made him such a valued royal agent at this troubled time by protesting at length to Chapuys that only scruples of a tender conscience compelled Henry to set Catherine aside. He would rather lose a hand, the duke swore, than have anyone believe that he wished Catherine removed for the sake of putting another in her place. Only Charles's failure to remain neutral had caused the affair to drag on so long![95] One wonders if even Norfolk believed this.

The day after this letter was written, a new chancellor was finally chosen. Warham, archbishop of Canterbury, was too old, and a cleric besides; Suffolk's nomination seems to have been blocked by Norfolk, who did not wish another noble to hold the seal; Anne's candidate, Gardiner, declined, preferring the bishopric of Winchester which Wolsey shortly was forced to resign. Even Anne's father, Rochford, was passed over, although he was made keeper of the privy seal; Thomas Boleyn, like Charles Brandon, was too great an incompetent to trust with the chancery even as a sinecure. Instead, the choice fell upon Thomas More, a lawyer, scholar, and experienced diplomat and administrator. A veteran of a dozen years of royal service, More had been Speaker of the House and chancellor of the Duchy of Lancaster, as well as one of the envoys to Cambrai earlier in the year. More had risen to prominence in Wolsey's service, but had ties to the Howards as well. Most important, his recent service had been to Henry rather than to Wolsey, and he seems to have taken at least a passive role in the opposition to the cardinal. However, More was not a member of Anne's circle (and viewed the whole divorce project with some dismay) and, despite his friendship with the king, was not part of the rather dissolute court circle that hunted and feasted with Henry. He was certainly fit for the post, yet obscure enough that it was thought necessary for Norfolk to make a public declaration of More's qualities—an unheard-of step in appointing a new chancellor.[96] More was to serve two and one-half years, never comfortable with Henry's policies toward Rome and Catherine, but never a serious threat to the dominance of Norfolk and his cronies. The real replacement for Wolsey would rise from another quarter and never hold the post of chancellor.

Wolsey meanwhile submitted to the provisions and *praemunire* charges in the court of king's bench, was convicted, judged forfeit of his goods and lands—and then pardoned by Henry, allowed to keep his house at Esher, and restored to the archbishopric of York! If this ambivalence was not enough to worry Norfolk, Henry also sent Wolsey several rings as tokens of affection even as the cardinal rode from London into exile.[97] With

Henry wavering dangerously toward the fallen minister, Wolsey's enemies turned to Parliament for what they hoped would be a final blow. More opened the session in November with a lengthy and vehement attack on Wolsey, urging the assembly to go beyond the "gentle correction" thus far administered to the cardinal. Hardly needing such encouragement, the lords set to work on what looks like a draft act of attainder; by 1 December Norfolk, Suffolk, Rochford and the nonpeers More, Fitzwilliam and Sir Henry Guildford presented forty-four articles, which the House of Lords ratified. The indictment was not cast as a formal bill of attainder, however, and Henry let it go no further. The Commons never considered the bill, and no legislative charges with any legal force were to be made against Wolsey.[98]

At the same time, the council encouraged the king to torment Wolsey further by carrying off a new gallery recently built at Esher to the royal palace at Westminster. Henry was not sated, however, and he followed this up with the remarkable announcement that the crown would have York Place, which belonged, not to Wolsey himself, but to the archbishopric of York. Despite Wolsey's angry reminder to Henry that "there is both a heaven and a hell," the transfer took place and, by the end of November, York Place was a royal residence.[99] According to Cavendish, Norfolk was at dinner with Wolsey when Sir William Shelly arrived with Henry's demand for York Place. By this account, Norfolk met Wolsey's courtesy and deference with courtesy of his own, offering to find places for Wolsey's servants. Wolsey conceded his defeat with a verse:

> Parcere prostratis, scit nobilis ira leonis;
> Tuquoque fac simile, quisquis regnabis in orbem

—gracious words, meaning, "The wrathful noble lion knows how to spare those who are prostrate before him; go and do likewise, you who will reign over the earth."[100]

Despite the seeming cordiality of this meeting, Norfolk was still determined to destroy Wolsey. A bill was entered in the Lords early in the session, probably with Norfolk behind it, to cancel royal obligations to repay money lent on privy seals and letters missive, a sum of thirty-five thousand pounds or more. The purpose was to ruin Wolsey's financial supporters who had made loans to the crown at his request, backed by little more than his standing with the king.[101]

Henry's maddening refusal to prosecute Wolsey to the extremes of the law kept Norfolk in constant apprehension lest the cardinal somehow return to favor. Chapuys's reports at the end of 1529 and early in 1530 show the uncertain cast of events. He wrote that Henry now bore Wolsey no personal grudge and that only pressure from Anne and her party had pushed the king so far. At the same time, Chapuys's letters show Norfolk as Henry's new diplomatic spokesman. In October Norfolk had conducted talks with the imperial envoy on settling debts between the shaky allies of Cambrai, and in November the duke delivered Henry's congratulations to Charles on the Turkish retreat from Vienna. Chapuys noted sourly that the English refused to offer any real aid to the emperor, but only lit bonfires of celebration. "I wonder," Chapuys wrote, "whether the king and he [Norfolk] intend to pay us out in smoke!"[102] While he referred to Norfolk as "the most powerful man in the kingdom" on 12 January, by 6 February Chapuys was beginning to see that Henry intended that no new all-powerful minister would take Wolsey's place. Henry named Suffolk president of the council, replacing Norfolk, and appointed several new councilors to balance the influence of the Howard-Boleyn faction.[103] Wolsey learned of this uncertainty at court, for in early 1530 he set to work to build a new party of supporters and friends, writing soothing letters and offering bribes and favors in return for news from court and council. Perhaps as part of this effort, John Russell approached Norfolk early in February to feel out the duke's attitude toward the fallen cardinal. Norfolk, offended, countered Russell's inquiry by asking if Wolsey cherished hopes of regaining power. Russell replied that Wolsey was a man of courage who would never reject a chance to serve the king. Norfolk flew into a rage, swearing that he would eat Wolsey alive before permitting him to return to power.[104]

The danger of that resurgence seemed imminent. On 11 February, More, Norfolk and several others acknowledged before the king receipt of a deed for the recovery of Wolsey's possessions to royal use by terms of his *praemunire* conviction. Yet the next day Henry granted Wolsey a general pardon. The fallen chancellor wrote to Gardiner on 17 February after he received word of Henry's action: "My owne goode Mastyr Secretary. I cannot express how muche I am bowndyn to my Lord of Norfolkes grace and yow to whom with my dayly servys and prayer I beseche yow to geve my mooste humble and effectuall thanckes, lyke as I do the semblabyl to yow."[105] What had happened? Surely Norfolk's animosity had not abated. On 22 February Norfolk smoothly insisted to Chapuys that he had obtained the pardon to placate Henry's lingering affection for the cardinal. In fact, Norfolk probably had opposed the pardon as firmly as possible but, seeing Henry's determination, gave in to the inevitable and even tried to claim credit for it afterward. Chapuys doubted Norfolk would be able to keep Wolsey from court, for the cardinal had avoided Henry's real wrath. Still, for the moment Norfolk's position seemed strong for, as Chapuys noted, nothing was done at court without Thomas Howard.[106] Indeed, Norfolk's sway was amply demonstrated when he committed the normally serious offense of abducting the underage Edward Stanley, earl of Derby, to marry him to a Howard half-sister. Norfolk and Derby were pardoned for the offense, and excused the heavy fine that might have been imposed.[107]

Much to Norfolk's distress, Wolsey lingered up the Thames at Esher, and at Lent Henry allowed the cardinal to move even closer to London at Richmond. The threat of Wolsey's easy return to court gnawed at his enemies, and in the spring of 1530 they finally were able to do something about it. Behind Cavendish's bald statement that Henry was "lightly persuaded" to order Wolsey to his benefice at York, there must have been considerable maneuvering. It is hard to believe that Henry thought that York, a province Wolsey had never entered, needed his personal attention. It seems more likely that Henry was made aware of Wolsey's continued communication with the court and foreign ambassadors behind his back. In March Norfolk sent Wolsey's secretary Thomas Cromwell to order his master to "go to his benefice, where lieth his cure." Wolsey responded by agreeing to retire to Winchester. Upon hearing this from Cromwell, "Norfolk answered and said, 'What will he do there? Nay,' quod he, 'let him go to his province of York, whereof he hath received his honor, and there lieth the spiritual burden and charge of his conscience, and so show him.' "[108] On 28 March, Henry sent Lord Dacre to assist Wolsey in his move in accordance with a cardinal's dignity. Wolsey was slow to set out, awaiting a thousand pounds in moving expenses which did not arrive until 5 April. Meanwhile Norfolk fumed impatiently, sending Cromwell with another message: "Show him that if he go not away shortly, I will, rather he should tarry still, tear him with my teeth." Only on 28 April, after a journey of slow stages, did Wolsey reach Southwell and enter his province for the first time. Here, barely past Nottingham, still fifty miles from York, Wolsey halted. He would remain as close to court as the king would allow.[109]

If Norfolk wished to retain his grip on power, he needed to do more than push Wolsey north; it fell to the duke to do something about the king's divorce. Between April and October 1530 Norfolk busied himself with the case, overseeing collection of English and European university opinions on the legality of the marriage, as well as continuing to manage Henry's somewhat forlorn diplomatic effort to pressure Clement.[110] In March, Clement issued a bull revoking Henry's case to Rome and prohibiting his remarriage. Henry and his ministers had been working furiously to prevent just such an action. When word reached England, Norfolk apparently suggested simply ignoring the bull, but when he rehearsed this notion with Chapuys, the imperial envoy had a chilling response. Charles V would not need, as Norfolk feared, to declare war on England, Chapuys was sure, for Henry's own subjects would rise in rebellion against their heretical king should he thus defy the pope.[111]

Still, something had to be done to persuade Rome to grant Henry's wishes. Perhaps to counteract Chapuys's reports of widespread English opposition to Henry's divorce, on 13 July a majority of the English temporal lords and a number of spiritual lords signed a petition to the pope, praying him to consent to the king's desires. Norfolk, Suffolk and Rochford were prominent among the signers; even Wolsey signed the petition (although More did not).[112] Yet the petition broke no new ground. The best that Norfolk could suggest was a policy of delay, trying to stall an adverse decision in Rome while searching for some way to gain papal approval of the divorce.

In September Norfolk informed a papal nuncio that, although he was as devoted to Rome as any man in England, he was obliged to stand by Henry in insisting that the case could not be taken out of the realm.[113] This was hardly a new or useful idea. In fact, Norfolk was proving with each day that he did not have the original ideas and subtle insights necessary to solve Henry's problem. For two years after Wolsey's fall, England was not so much without a policy to gain the divorce as overwhelmed with useless ones. It awaited the arrival of Thomas Cromwell in Henry's confidence to bring new life to the campaign and carry much of what Henry and Norfolk had only threatened to a logical, if revolutionary, conclusion.[114]

Even while occupied with Henry's business during 1530, Norfolk had not forgotten Wolsey, nor Wolsey Norfolk. The cardinal launched a major effort to appease the duke during that year. In May, Cromwell reported a disappointing interview with Norfolk, undertaken at Wolsey's behest: "The D. of Norfolk," Cromwell wrote, "promiseth you his best ayd but he willeth you for the present to be content and not to much molest the king (concerning payment of your Debts, etc.) for, as he supposeth, the time is not meet for it."[115] In August the cardinal directed a placating letter of his own to the duke, but to no avail. In October, Thomas Arundel approached Norfolk, seeking some abatement of his hostility toward Wolsey, assuring him that the cardinal had no aspiration to greater authority. Norfolk retorted that no man could convince him of that. Wolsey, he said, "desired as much authority as ever [he] did." Arundel, reporting the conversation to Wolsey, tried to reassure the cardinal that at least no one—including Henry—intended to lower his estate further.[116]

Meanwhile Norfolk struck another blow in October, taking personal charge of the dismantling of Wolsey's pet project, his college at Oxford. Cardinal College was eventually refounded by Henry, but Norfolk reclaimed Felixstowe priory and several manors he had reluctantly contributed to the foundation.[117] Yet despite the pillaging of Wolsey's college and his other possessions, it is clear that Norfolk and his party had pushed Henry as far as they could. Had Wolsey not drawn suspicion upon himself by his own actions, it is doubtful that any more harm would have befallen him, and Henry would have left him as archbishop of York to live out his days.

Since his fall from grace Wolsey had been playing a dangerous game of private diplomacy, writing to Francis and Charles and their ambassadors as well as friends in Rome, seeking assurances of goodwill and news of international affairs. None of these communications was, in itself, treasonous, but in combination with other actions on Wolsey's part they could be used to construct a case against him.[118] In October 1530 Wolsey made his final mistake. Despite the prorogation and pending dissolution of Parliament, he called a convocation of the northern clergy to meet at York on 7 November. Tunstall, bishop of Durham and president of the council in the north, reminded Wolsey of the precedent of awaiting the meeting of the Canterbury convocation before summoning the northern clergy. But Wolsey persisted in his plans, summoning "all the lords, abbots, priors, knights, esquires, and gentlemen of his diocese" to be present for his enthronement as archbishop sixteen years late; no one knew what might be done by or with such an assembly.[119] Several other pieces began to be fitted into a case against Wolsey. On 23 October word reached England of a new papal brief forbidding Henry to remarry and threatening excommunication. Wolsey's chaplain had recently been arrested leaving the country with letters for Rome. These were innocuous enough in themselves, but the communication was unauthorized; who knew what might have been passed out in earlier letters? Possibly Wolsey had encouraged the unfavorable brief; Norfolk must have reminded Henry of that chance. In fact the duke denounced the brief to the papal nuncio, calling the threatened sentence of excommunication outrageous, and insisting that Henry was a loyal son of the church who had never offended the pope.[120]

Norfolk's hand in incriminating Wolsey is revealed most clearly in his dealings with the cardinal's physician Antonio de Augustini, who was detained while trying to leave the realm with Wolsey's letters. These were even more incriminating than those found with the cardinal's chaplain, for they contained a few lines in cipher. After his arrest, Augustini was taken to Norfolk's house where, according to Chapuys, he was examined without violence and sang the tune the duke wished to hear. The Venetian envoy also reported that Augustini had found great favor with the duke. Facing who knew what punishment for his service to Wolsey, Augustini wisely came to terms with Norfolk. The arrangements are obscure, but on 12 December (after Wolsey's death) the doctor entered into a bond to pay one hundred pounds to the crown if he ever revealed the contents of a "secret book" he had given to Norfolk.[121]

During the last days of October, while Norfolk prepared his case against Wolsey, London was aflame with rumors that the cardinal was raising forces in the north to seize power; the Milanese and Venetian ambassadors alike reported such stories.[122] The combination of Wolsey's clandestine communication abroad, the brief against Henry, and the foreboding assembly at York finally convinced the king to act. On 1 November Walter Walsh, a groom of the king's chamber, set out for York with a warrant for Wolsey's arrest. Norfolk and Suffolk assured Chapuys vaguely that they had "many important causes" against the cardinal and that a room in the Tower awaited him. Lady Anne especially, Chapuys said, had urged

Henry to act against Wolsey, weeping and wailing, insisting on the cardinal's treachery, and warning Henry that they would never be wed until Wolsey was gone.[123]

Walsh arrived at York on 4 November, and two days later Wolsey began his trip south, moving as slowly as he had gone north the spring before. Wolsey never faced trial, for he fell ill along the way and died on 29 November at Leicester Abbey. By his death, Wolsey "passed out of Henry's jurisdiction" and finally ended the long months of tense pursuit by Norfolk and his faction.[124]

When word of Wolsey's death reached court, Norfolk made no effort to conceal his jubilation and relief. The Howards and Boleyns celebrated their fortuitous triumph with savage crudity. In December, Rochford gave an entertainment at court featuring a masque in which the spirit of Wolsey was carried off to hell by a band of demons; Norfolk was so pleased that he had the masque printed. At court, Wolsey was spoken of with such violent disrespect that the foreign ambassadors were shocked.[125]

Wolsey's fall reveals the essentially negative character of Norfolk's political career; he was always more successful in bringing others down than in making constructive contributions to royal policy. Despite the opposition of such as Norfolk, had Wolsey been able to accomplish Henry's divorce, he would likely never have fallen from power, or at least would not have lost out to Norfolk and his faction. Norfolk was a man of action and not a deep thinker, a soldier and not an administrator. This more than anything else explains his short tenure as leading minister after Wolsey's fall, for others proved more inclined to shoulder the burden of administration and better able to find new directions for royal policy.

Yet at the end of 1530 Norfolk momentarily stood supreme. His long fight to obtain his rightful place was, to all appearances, successful. Even with Anne not yet crowned queen, the prospects for continued Howard dominance seemed extremely promising. The triumph would prove a chimera.

CHAPTER 5

THE KING'S GREAT MATTER AND THE RISE OF CROMWELL, 1530–1536

WITH THE DEATH OF WOLSEY, Norfolk's triumph seemed complete. Chapuys, the imperial ambassador, treated the duke as the cardinal's successor, and in November the Venetian envoy said of Norfolk, "His Majesty uses him in all negotiations more than any other person. Since the death of Cardinal Wolsey, his authority and supremacy have increased, and every employment devolves to him."[1] For the next several years, Norfolk remained constantly at court and in council, preoccupied with the king's "great matter" of the divorce from Catherine of Aragon and marriage to Anne Boleyn. Yet Norfolk proved unable to offer any significant new ideas; his policy was essentially a continuation of Wolsey's on a cruder level. There seemed no alternative to a Roman settlement of the case, and so Norfolk labored vainly to bully Clement VII and to entreat Charles V to abandon his aunt as a sacrifice on the altar of diplomatic necessity. None of this proved effective. Instead, while Norfolk held shaky supremacy, the king turned increasingly to others who, like Wolsey, would prove that talent and industry were as welcome in Henry VIII's service as noble lineage, as long as the king's work was satisfactorily done.

While the career of Anne Boleyn may seem the most prominent element of the years from 1530 to 1536, from Norfolk's viewpoint the rise of Thomas Cromwell from insignificant clerk to dominant minister was of far greater ultimate importance. Born around 1485, the son of a prosperous blacksmith and innkeeper of Putney, Cromwell pursued a merchant career in Flanders and France before entering Wolsey's service in 1514 as a

The Ebbs and Flows of Fortune

collector of revenues. Cromwell served in the Parliament of 1523 and went to the Inns of Court in 1524. By the time of Wolsey's fall, he was the cardinal's personal secretary and a minor but well-known court figure.[2] The Parliament of November 1529 gave Cromwell his chance to begin building an independent political position. He sent his servant Ralph Sadler to Norfolk to ask if he might have a seat. Norfolk, through his servant John Gage, replied that Cromwell was welcome to find a seat, "so ye wolde order yourselfe in the saide rowme accordynge to the instruccyons as the said duke shal give you from the kinge." Norfolk offered the king's favor, but no seat. Therefore Sadler contacted Thomas Rush, who controlled the writs for Wolsey's town of Orford, and William Paulet, who had the cardinal's pocket borough of Taunton, to see if a seat might be purchased.[3]

Perhaps Rush was unable to deliver; in any case, the day before Parliament opened Cromwell was elected for Taunton.[4] Cromwell won his seat with Norfolk's approval, but hardly entered his service; during the first session of Parliament Cromwell tried, with little success, to prevent any further attacks on Wolsey. The proposed bill of attainder was withdrawn, but this was certainly done at Henry's insistence, despite the legend that Cromwell gave an impassioned speech which swayed the Commons.[5]

Henry was nonetheless quick to notice Cromwell's abilities. By early 1530 Cromwell was sworn of the king's service and by year's end was admitted to the council. After Wolsey's death Cromwell was given charge of the division of spoils from his estate, with the result that all who wished a share had to deal with him. As each grant required royal approval, Cromwell had constant access to the king. While others appeared supreme to the eyes of the outside world, Cromwell rapidly gained the confidence of the king through sheer ability. Until 1534, when he was named the king's secretary, Cromwell was employed mainly in domestic affairs, which tended to obscure his importance in comparison with Norfolk, Gardiner and others who had charge of foreign policy.[6] By the spring of 1533, when Norfolk went on a diplomatic mission to France, Cromwell had become the leading royal minister and advisor. This was possible because he succeeded where Wolsey and Norfolk alike had failed in attaining Henry's divorce.

By early 1531, the political line-up at court had become quite complicated; at least three loose factions can be identified. Norfolk's group was momentarily supreme, but hardly unchallenged, and in fact the "aristocratic" faction that had worked to topple Wolsey was beginning to unravel. With the exception of Anne's father Thomas (made earl of Wiltshire and Ormond in December 1529), Norfolk's partners in power were less than enthusiastic about Anne's continued rise. Suffolk was not happy as titular head of the council, and Anne and her grasping family irritated him personally. Other members of the aristocracy had, like Suffolk, gotten what they really wanted with the fall of Wolsey and had no interest in the further rise of the Boleyns. William, lord Sandes (the lord chamberlain), the earls of Sussex and Exeter, Thomas lord Darcy, John lord Hussey and Sir William Fitzwilliam—the inner circle of the council that, with Norfolk, profited most from Wolsey's fall—must be counted among this group.[7]

The "conservative" faction at court was likewise shaky, as many loyal Catholics had doubts about the divorce project or opposed it altogether. While many clerics had opposed Wolsey, his fall left them without a rallying point. Gardiner, Henry's secretary, was a conservative Catholic whose support of the divorce was always personally painful; Gardiner's main aim was to extort action from Clement VII. His support for Anne seems to have declined after September 1531, when he was made bishop of Winchester and achieved an independent political position. Gardiner was uneasy about the Protestant connections of Anne's chaplains; he was also consistently pro-Imperial in his politics, and never liked the pro-French tone of the circle around Anne.[8] Many conservatives like Thomas More, John Fisher, Cuthbert Tunstall, the earl of Shrewsbury, and others, were opposed to the entire divorce project; their loyalty to Catherine of Aragon has led to their identification by recent historians as an "Aragonese" party.[9]

The "progressives," led by Thomas Cranmer and Edward Fox among the ecclesiastics, were joined by Thomas Audley and Sir George Boleyn. It appears that they presented Henry with a comprehensive program for action, part of which survives in the form of a document known as the *Collectanea satis copiosa*. The *Collectanea* supported the contention that England was an independent empire, autonomous and therefore immune against the claims of outside—that is, papal—authority. Other canonical and theological materials which no longer survive *in extenso* were also prepared by Cranmer's group to support the argument that Henry's marriage was invalid by God's law and that, more important, there might be a purely English solution to the king's case. Within the program of the progressives lay the seeds of Henry's claims as Supreme Head of the English church and much that would be done by the Reformation Parliament. But in 1530–32, Henry was not yet prepared to follow this course. The role of Cromwell became the decisive element. Cromwell initially floated between the camps of Norfolk and the progressives, retaining Norfolk and Henry's political support while awaiting the chance to push forward the progressive plan. Cromwell's personal views in 1530–32 are open to debate; not until the parliamentary session of 1532 does Cromwell emerge as an independent figure. But from mid-1531, Cromwell courted Anne's favor as a means of maintaining Henry's; he was in fact one of the few at court willing so to do.[10]

In the midst of this political turmoil, Norfolk pursued the royal divorce determinedly. Early in January 1531 he treated Chapuys to a harangue on Henry's imperial powers. Since England was a self-sufficient empire, the king could prohibit the publication or execution of papal bulls and decretals in his realm. Norfolk, somewhat inconsistently, nevertheless warned the imperial envoy not to publish the rumored papal pronouncements in favor of Catherine that Henry so feared. Chapuys countered by insisting that the pope had the right to punish disobedience and that it would be better for the English to remove the cause of papal displeasure than to offer defiance to the Holy See. Norfolk ignored this argument and went on to show Chapuys a scroll, supposedly copied from the tomb of King Arthur, referring to him as "emperor." This was the first public rehearsal of English imperial rights, and Norfolk's use of the argument shows that he was aware of the *Collectanea* and the line of reasoning later to be exploited so effectively by Cromwell. Chapuys was evidently puzzled by the episode, missing Norfolk's real point, and he reported it to Charles with the sarcastic comment that he wondered that Henry did not also claim to be "Emperor of Asia."[11]

Norfolk and Chapuys had another tense meeting on 22 March. The duke asked if the Turks had renewed their attacks on Charles's eastern dominions. Chapuys, knowing of Henry's hope that the emperor would become too busy with the defense of his lands to interfere in Henry's Roman case, answered that he thought the infidel would attack for no other reason than to please those who seemed so to desire it. This barb, Chapuys noted, stung Norfolk. In the same letter, Chapuys reported that Henry, when told by the papal nuncio Borgho of renewed Turkish invasion, was quite pleased with the news that the emperor would again be expensively occupied.[12]

A few days after this meeting, the second session of Parliament drew to a close. All was obviously not well with public support of the divorce, for More was compelled to make a speech to the Lords attacking those who accused the king of seeking to wed Anne out of mere lust. Further, when the collected European university decrees on the validity of the king's marriage were read to the upper house, an unexpected debate began. Bishops Stokesley and Longland were allowed to speak in support of Henry, but when Standish and Clerk tried to defend Catherine, Norfolk interrupted to say that the decrees had been presented for information only, and not for debate, and discussion was abruptly ended. In the Commons, the reading of the decrees was met only with sullen silence.[13]

Perhaps as a result of this unenthusiastic reception, on 6 June 1531 Henry tried to cow Catherine into submission. An imposing delegation made up of Norfolk, Suffolk, Dorset, the earls of Shrewsbury and Wiltshire, the bishops Stokesley, Longland and Gardiner, as well as Rowland Lee, later bishop of Coventry and Lichfield, was sent to confront the queen. Accused of bringing the kingdom to ruin by her reliance on Rome and defiance of Henry, Catherine refused to yield. Instead, she declared that her visitors were neither her counsel nor her judges, and therefore not fit to discuss the case with her. They were, she charged with considerable justification, more devoted to Henry than to the truth. Catherine could not be bullied. According to Chapuys, Norfolk reported to the king that the queen would not yield, for she owed obedience to two others before the king. Henry, Chapuys wrote, expected Norfolk to name the pope and the emperor, but instead the duke said they were God and her conscience. Nothing in this world would make Catherine forsake them.[14]

Norfolk's obsession with the king's case was made clear in another conversation with Chapuys during the summer of 1531, when the duke recited such a list of councils, chapters and laws on Henry's side that the ambassador asked the duke if he had suddenly become a great doctor of the laws. Yet Chapuys thought that Norfolk was motivated largely by self-interest because Charles V had failed to renew the duke's pension.[15] Chapuys missed the point; it was not Charles's pension, but Henry's will, that motivated Norfolk. If Thomas Howard could succeed where Wolsey had failed in solving the king's dilemma, he would be assured of the lasting gratitude of a king who could offer him far greater gifts than the emperor.

Despite the slow progress of Henry's case, the end of the year found Norfolk in continued favor. He weathered smoothly the arrest of his brother-in-law, the Welshman Rhys ap Griffith, who went to the Tower in September for allegedly plotting a Scottish-aided Welsh revolt.[16] Norfolk demonstrated his untarnished authority by dominating a council meeting on 18 November when a new imperial ambassador arrived to present his credentials, addressed to the king, Chancellor More, and Norfolk, perhaps included as treasurer and therefore deserving of ceremonial precedence, but certainly in recognition of where power then lay. This new ambassador thought that Wiltshire, Gardiner, More and Fitzwilliam were the most important of the other councilors, but Norfolk was clearly supreme. The duke demonstrated his sway by suspending the meeting several times for private consultations with the king, leaving the others to wait before business was concluded.[17]

Despite his role in other state business, Norfolk remained preoccupied with the divorce case. He met with Henry and Gardiner to draft William Benet's instructions for a new mission to Rome at the end of 1531, for example.[18] Henry was starting to consider a non-Roman resolution of his case, and Norfolk was in the middle of an abortive scheme to gain support for an English settlement. According to Chapuys, in February 1532 the king sent Norfolk to meet with an unnamed group of "influential persons" in hopes, apparently, of winning a general consensus that the divorce case belonged to the temporal rather than the spiritual jurisdiction and could thus be settled by Henry as emperor of his realm. Lord Darcy (who would later be executed for complicity in the Pilgrimage of Grace) led the opposition to Norfolk's reasoning, and the matter was, for the moment, dropped. This failure may have marked the beginning of the breakup of the "aristocratic" party, although not the end of Norfolk's influence; shortly after this meeting, Chapuys reported that Norfolk and Wiltshire had visited Archbishop Warham to pressure him to grant the king a divorce on his own authority. Forewarned, Warham refused. Cromwell would be the architect of a parliamentary Reformation, but Norfolk was obviously aware of the theoretical justification for unilateral action to end the king's marriage. Where Norfolk and Cromwell would part company was over the extension of Henry's divorce case into a general assault on the practices and beliefs of the English church.[19]

English diplomacy was also affected by Henry's divorce case. The University of Padua had been slow to produce a decree favoring Henry. The Venetian ambassador, Carlo Capella, learned the consequences when Norfolk told him bluntly that Henry's favor would be withheld until the Signory sent a positive verdict. In the meantime, Venetian merchants were told that there was no wool available for sale, and their galleys were not allowed to leave English ports.[20] On 25 February 1532, after a month of these delays, Norfolk informed Henry that Capella wished to see him; the Venetians were now ready to support Henry's case.[21]

The end of February also found Norfolk penning new instructions to Benet in Rome to use the "infenyte clamor of the temporalyte here in Parlement agaynst the mysusyng of the sprytuell jurysdiccion" as a threat against the pope. The English people, Norfolk wrote, were ready to forsake Rome if anything was done to proceed wrongfully against Henry. More specifically, Benet was instructed to prevent Catherine's case from coming before the Rota by raising before the cardinals these threats of an England about to be driven from the arms of Rome. Whatever eventually happened, Norfolk said, he had done his duty by these warnings: "At the lest I have lyke a trew catholyke man discharged my consience, wher best remedy may be provyded."[22]

Norfolk's interest in Henry's case naturally extended to concern with the affairs of Charles V, England's greatest potential enemy. In January 1532 Norfolk responded to Chapuys's news of troubles in southern Italy with a sigh, saying, "Things look bad indeed!"[23] The next month the duke and the ambassador discussed Flemish affairs, and in March Norfolk received a detailed report from an English agent on Charles's troubles in Germany. Several days later, Norfolk again spoke to Chapuys and offered insincere condolences for the pains being suffered by the emperor and the pope.[24] The difficulties of Henry's opponents seem always to have been a welcome subject for Norfolk's conversation.

Norfolk's motives in supporting Henry's projects were always suspect to Chapuys, but events in the spring of 1532 demonstrated that even Norfolk supported the divorce because it was the royal will, and not out of blind devotion to Anne Boleyn and his family. There had been rumors as early as June 1531 that all was not well between Norfolk and his niece; Anne rightfully suspected that Norfolk was more interested in his own power and prestige than in her welfare. In April 1532 further rumors circulated that Norfolk was seeking to wed his son Henry to Princess Mary, guaranteeing Howard ascendancy as long as the Tudors reigned—as well as making Anne superfluous to the family. Norfolk finally broke the suspense by marrying his son to Frances de Vere, daughter of the earl of Oxford. Chapuys believed that Anne had all but compelled the match out of fear that, should Henry Howard wed Mary, Norfolk would be willing to dispose of his niece.[25]

Nor was all well in the camp of the king's supporters. Not all of Wolsey's enemies had become champions of Anne; Suffolk in particular resented the Boleyn ascendancy. Norfolk and Suffolk had long contended for influence in East Anglia, and bad blood had developed between their followers—men whose standards of discretion were somewhat lower than their masters'. The rivalry turned violent in April 1532 when Richard Southwell, a Howard client, led twenty men on a foray into the sanctuary of Westminster to murder Sir William Pennington, a gentleman follower of Suffolk.[26] The whole court was in an uproar, and Suffolk set out to dislodge the murderers by force, threatening revenge on Southwell "although it were in the kinges chamber or at the high aulter." Henry sent Cromwell to calm the duke, and things were settled peacefully only after Southwell paid a fine of a thousand pounds. The Venetian ambassador reported that the real cause of the quarrel was that Suffolk's wife Mary had slandered Anne Boleyn; the result seems to have been a settling of old East Anglian grudges in the guise of defending family honor. Henry was reported very displeased by the whole affair.[27]

In the first sessions of the Reformation Parliament, Henry tried to prod the papacy into action by attacking the abuses of the medieval church—popular legislation which hinted that English anticlericalism might be directed more effectively toward Rome if need be. At the same time, Henry continued the tactic of mobilizing European intellectual opinion on his side by means of the university decrees in support of his case. Neither effort had produced the desired result of a papal declaration that the royal marriage had been void *ab initio*, thereby freeing Henry to marry Anne.[28] In early 1532 the third session of the Reformation Parliament began. Parliament was for the first time under Cromwell's management, and although the divorce was not achieved in 1532, there was a developing militancy in the acts passed against Rome in the session, with many hints that the king and Parliament would resort to more extreme measures if the divorce were delayed longer. Cromwell was working toward the same goals as Norfolk at this point, and the duke apparently still saw Cromwell was a useful tool rather than a potential rival for power. Only when the radical implications of Cromwell's work and his connection to the backers of the *Collectanea satis copiosa* became clear—not before the summer of 1532—did Norfolk begin to have doubts about Cromwell's role.

The other major figure who would play a role in the opposition to Cromwell was Stephen Gardiner, bishop of Winchester. Gardiner and Norfolk shared only a distrust of Cromwell at this point, for their motives were very different. Gardiner opposed the arguments of the *Collectanea* and those who put them forward, but had little of Norfolk's disdain for low-born new men, being one himself. While both men were Catholic in their faith, Norfolk had no qualms about dismantling the church to enrich the nobility, while Gardiner shared Wolsey's desire to preserve the independence of the clergy. A proud and difficult man, Gardiner was never happy with the Protestant tendencies of the growing English Reformation but, like Norfolk, placed loyalty to the king above personal beliefs.[29]

Norfolk was concerned with the mounting pace of events, and avoided conversation with Chapuys on the excuse that he was too busy with his managerial duties in the House of Lords.[30] Much was done by this spring session, including the act in conditional restraint of annates, empowering Henry to halt by letters patent the payment of fees for entry into benefices usually sent to Rome. Despite the radical implications of this act, Norfolk saw it simply as another means of pressuring the pope; as he wrote to Benet in Rome, he believed that "nothing hurtful shalbe done, unless the fault be in Him [Clement] in proceeding wrongfully and ungrately against the King."[31] In explaining the act to Borgho, Norfolk claimed that the measure was not Henry's work, but was only proof of the feelings of loyal English subjects who believed Henry, and not the pope, to be the sole arbiter between God and subject.[32]

Yet by now it should have been clear that the pope could not be bullied. Henry was unwilling to make the act in conditional restraint of annates effective; instead the king shifted his aim by applying coercion against the English church. *Praemunire* charges lodged against fifteen English clergy in 1530 had been little more than a means of raising money; radical plans for a full-scale assault on the church had no support from Henry, much less Norfolk and his circle.[33] Now in 1532, a new weapon was unveiled to force the English clergy into obedience, in the form of the "Supplication Against the Ordinaries," a list of complaints against clerical abuses, especially in the ecclesiastical courts. The Commons had considered the

Supplication in 1531 and 1532 but no legislation resulted. In April 1532, the Supplication was laid before the Convocation of the Clergy at Canterbury. Convocation, under Warham, did not submit to the charges, instead drafting an unyielding reply which king and Commons alike found unsatisfactory; Henry told the Speaker, Audley, "we think their answer will smally please you, for it seemeth to us very slender." On 10 May Henry ordered Convocation to submit to three articles which had the effect of reducing that body to a rubber stamp for royal demands.[34] Warham tried at first to resist, but the king replied by threatening to push a bill through Parliament to reduce the status of the clergy "below that of shoemakers," as Chapuys expressed it.[35] Instead of taking such a radical course, however, Henry sent a delegation of notables led by Norfolk and Wiltshire (and including Sandes and Exeter from the rapidly shrinking aristocratic party) to confront Convocation with a slightly different version of the articles. Warham backed down before this show of royal determination, and, with several of the king's staunchest opponents prudently absenting themselves, Convocation voted a nearly unanimous approval of Henry's articles. Only John Clerk, bishop of Bath and Wells, dissented. On 16 May, the day after Norfolk's visit, the king was presented the enacted articles of submission.[36]

In the meantime, Clement VII initiated a new offensive. On 21 May, the nuncio Borgho arrived at court to present a new papal brief. By this time, Henry lived in constant dread of excommunication, and therefore Borgho was refused access to the king until he had revealed his business to Norfolk. When at last Borgho's message had been passed in to Henry, the nuncio was admitted to the king's presence to present a brief which, to Henry's great relief, merely ordered him to return to Catherine and live with her as husband and wife. Henry and Catherine had not seen each other since July 1531, and the king had installed Anne Boleyn in the royal household in a state nearly that of a queen. Not even the most obtuse observer could have failed to see the import of this. Therefore, the brief ordered Henry to set Anne aside and return to his duty. Henry listened patiently, but insisted on his right to discipline his own wife and refused to yield, rejecting the nuncio's argument that Clement was acting only in the name of simple justice.[37]

Norfolk was well chosen as the king's watchdog; in the midst of uncertain support at court, in Parliament and Convocation, there was no one more loyal to Henry's schemes than the self-interested duke. This was clear to foreign observers as well as to the king. At the end of May, an imperial report characterized Norfolk as man who would work willingly to destroy Catherine if that was the king's will and would suffer anything for the sake of power.[38] Despite his social and theological conservatism, Norfolk had no love for the papacy, sharing Henry's suspicion that allegiance to any power outside the realm smacked of disloyalty to the crown. Where the royal will was stated clearly, Norfolk would obey, even if some rationalization of his principles was involved. As long as the Henrician Reformation attacked the authority of Rome without destroying the beliefs and practices of medieval Catholicism, Norfolk could remain comfortable with change.

Wolsey's enemies had not uniformly become supporters of Anne Boleyn, in large part because Henry's intentions toward Anne and Catherine were clear if he could have his own way about it. Thomas More perceived this state of affairs as distinctly as any. For More, the submission of the clergy was the step that made Henry's course both clear and repugnant. Seeing Henry determined to wed Anne, More saw that events would lead to a point where he could no longer subordinate conscience to his duties as chancellor. Therefore, on 16 May 1532 More asked Norfolk to convey to Henry his wish to resign the office.[39] Norfolk carried the request to the king, and as a result on 5 June, in the presence of Henry, Norfolk, Cromwell, and others, More resigned as chancellor. Henry delivered the Great Seal to Thomas Audley, knighting him and appointing him keeper.[40] More's resignation was evidence that the secularly oriented councilors, with Cromwell as leader, were taking precedence over the clerics and their allies who had been reluctant to support Henry's policy in seeking the divorce. It only slowly became clear, to Norfolk's discomfiture, that this new secular party would be a religiously progressive one as well.[41] More's resignation signaled the beginning of the end of Norfolk's preeminence; one wonders if Norfolk was aware of his shaky position at the point of More's resignation.

With the session of Parliament over, Norfolk spent much of the rest of the year preoccupied with foreign affairs. He spoke repeatedly with Chapuys on subjects ranging from the progress of the Imperial Diet at Nuremburg and the war with the Turks to Scottish affairs. Norfolk also led talks with the Venetians, seeking support for the divorce in exchange for trade concessions.[42] More important, Norfolk was involved with plans for a meeting between Henry and Francis at Calais. News that the Diet had worked out a peaceful settlement in Germany, leaving Charles with one less distraction, spurred Henry's resolve to win French support for his case. Henry had been unable to have any of his own bishops made cardinals in succession to Wolsey, but France had two new princes of the church who might lead a pro-English party in the Rota. By the spring of 1532, Francis seemed amenable to a meeting to work out a joint program to isolate Charles and win Henry's divorce. After a summer of rumors and half-secret planning, Norfolk arrived at Calais in early autumn as Henry's advance agent, meeting with Francis on 14 October to finalize details for a meeting of the kings a week later.[43] As long as Henry looked to Rome and to France, Norfolk retained considerable influence. Despite the progress made by the progressive party, any significant papal concessions would have undermined the progressive position and might have resulted in Norfolk's continued preeminence.

The French were pleased to find Norfolk acting as Henry's envoy. He was, as Chapuys had often and anxiously noted, a French pensioner and, to all appearances, still Henry's leading minister. Thus the French were as eager to maintain his friendship as they were to reach an understanding with his master. During the festivities after Henry arrived at Calais, Norfolk and Suffolk were made knights of the French Order of St. Michael, while Montmorency, the constable of France, and Charles, duc de Bourbon, were elected to the English Order of the Garter. As an additional mark of goodwill (and a thinly veiled bribe to obtain his future friendship), Norfolk's pension was raised to three thousand crowns (around six hundred pounds) a year.[44] When the real business of the meeting was conducted, Henry and Francis agreed that the two French cardinals would champion Henry's cause in Rome, and plans were laid to have Francis and Clement meet somewhere in France with an English representative— perhaps Norfolk, perhaps Henry himself—in attendance.[45]

All of this proved to be a sidetrack, never to be followed, for events forced the king to other expedients. Prior to the meeting at Calais, on 1 September 1532, Anne had been created marchioness of Pembroke in her own right in ceremonies at Windsor.[46] Henry took Anne with him to France, displaying her as queen in all but name. Whether this peerage was the final bribe that won over Anne's earlier resistance, or whether the success at Calais made marriage seem near at hand, Anne gave in to Henry some time in the autumn of 1532. By December she was pregnant. The opportunity for a legitimate son—the object of the exercise, after all—was too great to be squandered. On 25 January Henry and Anne were secretly married. A point of no return had been reached. Henry could no longer wait for Rome, but had to take matters into his own hands if the child were to be legitimate.[47] In the process, Thomas Howard would find himself outflanked by the progressive party. The king's success in marrying Anne would be a disaster and not a triumph for Norfolk.

Thus, while the business of state went on seemingly as usual, with Norfolk continuing his rambling talks with foreign ambassadors on all manner of subjects,[48] there was intense activity behind the scenes. Although Henry and Francis had agreed that a special envoy should be sent to France to join in the French king's meeting with the pope, and the names of Norfolk and Wiltshire were even advanced as nominees,[49] the king and Cromwell were busy rendering the whole project meaningless by lining up support in Convocation for an English dissolution of the royal marriage. Clement VII still had an ironic role to play in Cromwell's plans. William Warham, archbishop of Canterbury, had died in August. On 21 February, Henry's nominee, Thomas Cranmer—a religious progressive, a former Boleyn chaplain and a married man to boot—was approved by the Roman consistory, and his bulls of appointment and pallium were shortly sent to England. In the next few weeks, Henry's case was presented to Convocation, and, by the end of March, Cranmer was granted permission to judge Henry's marriage—though the king pointedly reminded his new archbishop that clerical authority over the case was only possible by royal sufferance.[50]

Henry pressed Convocation for a decision so relentlessly that, according to Chapuys, the members hardly had time to eat. No one watched the events of the spring of 1533 with more anxiety than the imperial ambassador, who sadly told his master that there would be a quick judgment in the king's favor; only John Fisher was expected to stand in open opposition.[51] Chapuys was correct. On 5 April the kind of marriage that existed between Henry and Catherine—that of a man and his brother's widow—was declared contrary to divine law and not subject to papal dispensation; this was a position Cranmer had first mooted in 1529. In the meantime, Parliament produced an act in restraint of appeals to Rome to prevent papal review of English decision.[52] While Cranmer prepared to open a court at Dunstable to try Henry's case, Norfolk was sent to Catherine to ask her, for the last time, to renounce her titles and claims concerning her marriages to Arthur and Henry. The queen refused, and also ignored Cranmer's summons to Dunstable. As far as Catherine was concerned, her case had already been recalled to Rome and was out of Henry's hands. She therefore refused to add the color of legality to what she considered but a flimsy charade.[53] On 23 May, the particular marriage of Henry and Catherine was declared void by Cranmer's court, and on 31 May, Anne was crowned queen in lavish ceremonies at Westminster.[54] Henry's divorce and remarriage had been carried out with unseemly haste; it now remained to be seen if the child Anne carried would be the boy required to make it all worthwhile.

Perhaps to his relief, Norfolk had already left for France and missed Anne's coronation. By now, Thomas Howard knew how little he had gained from his niece's rise, and he rather bitterly told Chapuys that he had been neither the originator nor the promoter of Anne's elevation, "but on the contrary had been always opposed to it and had tried to dissuade the king therefrom." Chapuys—hardly the most disinterested commentator—assured Charles that the English people were indignant with Henry for putting aside Catherine in favor of Anne; the coronation, he wrote, was more like a funeral than a celebration.[55]

Norfolk's mission to France may have been his last chance to retain power against the rising influence of Cromwell. Henry intended to go through with the marriage to Anne regardless of papal opinion, but still hoped that Clement could be weaned from Charles V by the proper French and English blandishments. Clement was clearly hesitant to accept a unilateral English judgment on the king's marriage, and needed the gentle prodding that Francis and Norfolk were expected to provide.[56] Gregory Casale wrote to Norfolk from Rome with assurances that the imperialist pressure on Clement was negated by the cardinals, who wished only peace and would therefore prevent any action against England for the moment.[57] In fact Norfolk's mission and Casale's reports were based on grave misconceptions. The English rightly perceived that Charles could not afford war, but they had not counted on any open act against Henry from Clement. The pope was normally hesitant, but events in England pushed him into action. Henry had often been driven to distraction by the endless delays from Rome; now, in mid-1533, when he counted on such hesitation, it was not forthcoming.

Nor was Henry's cause aided by Francis, who was beginning to doubt the merits of having his policy shaped by the whims of a none-too-stable Henry VIII. Although Norfolk had intended to meet Francis at Lyons by 23 May, the duke was still in London on the 26th awaiting word from France on a new meeting date. On 30 May, having missed a message that requested him to await further notice before leaving for France, Norfolk was in Calais. There he paused for instructions from Henry and news of Francis's location. Henry wrote on 6 June and again a week later, urging Norfolk to prevent a Franco-papal meeting unless a favorable decision could be assured; otherwise Norfolk was to accompany Francis to the meeting with Clement, reminding the French king at every step of his obligations to Henry.[58] These instructions seemed difficult enough to fulfil, but at the same time Henry was preparing a secret appeal to the next general council of the church against Clement's authority! Word of this leaked out to Chapuys and thus to Rome, effectively sabotaging any meeting between Norfolk and the pope before it could occur.[59]

Norfolk finally met with Francis at Riom, in the Auvergne, and the two began a procession through a series of French towns. Francis insisted upon meeting Clement and suggested that Norfolk proceed to Marseille by way of Lyons while the French court continued its progress. Accordingly, Norfolk left Francis and reached Lyons by 21 July. It was here that a messenger brought Norfolk the news that Clement, outraged with English presumption, had declared peremptorily on 11 July that Henry's divorce was invalid and his marriage to Anne Boleyn void. Effective the end of September, Henry was excommunicate. Norfolk was said nearly to have fainted at the news.[60]

Henry reacted to Clement's sentence with surprising calm and pondered his next move for several weeks before sending new instructions to Norfolk. Even these were unusually mild; Norfolk should dissuade Francis from meeting with Clement on grounds that the new marriage and the decisions of the English clergy could not be appealed or touched by any other authority. Should Francis insist on the meeting, Norfolk was "sadly" to take his leave.[61] Not surprisingly, Norfolk was unable to keep Francis from his audience with the pope. Therefore Norfolk left for Calais and by 30 August had returned to London. François de Tournon, one of the two French cardinals whom Francis had pledged to plead Henry's case, believed that Norfolk would still have been useful at a meeting with Clement, for the differences between Henry and the pope were not yet beyond resolution. Norfolk had to obey his orders, but nevertheless carried home assurances of Francis's love for Henry and a written pledge that the French king would treat Henry's matter as his own.[62]

Perhaps Henry was too stunned by the news of his excommunication to appreciate the loopholes the sentence offered him. Norfolk could have been sent to soothe the pope with all manner of promises, assurances and lies; the delay in the sentence made it clear that Clement was willing to be lenient, even to compromise. Instead, Henry chose to make his position irreversible and to wreck relations with the papacy by retaliation. On his return Norfolk was set to work collecting all available writings in support of Henry's position in order to arm Gardiner, who was chosen at the last moment to rush to Marseille as Henry's representative. Gardiner harmed Henry's case considerably by losing his temper and lecturing Francis on the canon law of Henry's case. Francis responded by demanding Gardiner's recall. The meetings between Francis and Clement began on 13 October, but by 7 November the English fiasco was complete when Edmund Bonner, on Henry's orders, harangued Clement with threats of an appeal to a general council. Henry blamed the ensuing ill will of the pope on Francis, saying that he had not done all he might to advance his brother's cause. In fact, as the French retorted, Francis had done much and Henry had ruined things, quite unnecessarily, himself.[63]

In the interim, the event for which so much had been risked took place when Anne was delivered of her child. To Henry's bitter disappointment and the chagrin of the astrologers who had confidently predicted a son, a daughter was born. Elizabeth was christened on 10 September 1533, with Norfolk serving as earl marshal for the first time since recovering the office from Suffolk in April. Norfolk's daughter Mary bore the basin, while his half-brothers William and Thomas helped carry the canopy. The dowager duchess of Norfolk carried the infant Elizabeth and served as godmother. Even if Norfolk and Anne were not on the best of terms, the value of Elizabeth as a Howard and the ceremonial precedence of the family could not be forgotten.[64]

With the birth of this daughter, Henry had forsaken one princess for another. Still, Anne was young; who knew but that she might soon bear a healthy son. Certainly it was too early to abandon hope. By November it was also too late to turn back, although Chapuys was busy urging Crom-

The King's Great Matter and Cromwell

well to accept the friendship of the emperor and abandon France and Anne alike. Henry was so enraged by Francis's failure to save the English cause that relations between the two princes worsened perceptibly. Norfolk was warned by the French ambassador that Francis could not be expected to declare himself against the pope, for it would only drive Clement into the arms of Charles again. Norfolk agreed that such a course would not serve, but hesitated so to advise Henry, who, the duke said, was loathe at the moment to trust anyone. Norfolk circumspectly held his peace.[65]

By the end of 1533, Cromwell held a near monopoly on Henry's attention. Norfolk found himself pushed aside and, worse, suffering at the hands of his haughty niece. In September, Chapuys reported that Anne had accused Norfolk of being too familiar with the imperial ambassador, leading the duke nervously to refrain from his usual talks with Chapuys for fear of further outbursts from the queen. Chapuys also noted in December that Norfolk, who had been one of the few courtiers to show respect for the pope to this point, had begun to bow to the will of the king and to speak blasphemously about Clement. Chapuys reported that Norfolk acted as he did because he feared to lose the influence left to him, which hardly exceeded what Cromwell wished it to be, so great was the latter's sway with Henry.[66]

With the divorce from Catherine accomplished and the breach with Rome worsening, and with Cromwell assuming administrative control, Norfolk had become expendable at court, and found himself given few official tasks. Those that fell to him were as unpleasant as the realization that Wolsey's former servant had become the new master of court. On 15 December Norfolk was sent to the former princess Mary to order her into the service of Anne's daughter, now to be known as the Princess of Wales. Mary angrily insisted that the title was hers and could not be given to another. Nonetheless, she was forced to do as Norfolk commanded.[67] The duke retained only a small role in foreign affairs, limited mainly to writing occasional letters to Montmorency urging that Francis continue to press Clement for Henry's divorce. This was a rather futile duty, considering the shoddy treatment Henry had accorded Francis and Clement alike.[68] Despite his eclipse, Norfolk's influence at court was not entirely ruined, for Lord Lisle sought the duke's help when he found his efforts to enter the lands left him by his late wife blocked by legal tangles. Further, Gregory Casale, charged with misconduct as Henry's Roman ambassador, thought it expedient to write a separate letter to Norfolk along with one to the whole council seeking exoneration.[69]

Yet for the most part, Norfolk was shoved aside while Cromwell dominated the government. Cromwell deserved his newfound power, of course, for he had done that which Wolsey and Norfolk alike had failed to do: Rome was distressed, and neither Francis nor Charles pleased, but Henry's marriage had been unmade and no foreign hosts had yet descended on English shores. In early 1534 Norfolk was absent from court on his own and not the king's business for the first time in several years. Chapuys explained Norfolk's disinclination to be at court by pointing out that many of Anne's former supporters had opposed Henry's renunciation of Rome. Norfolk was rumored to have told the French ambassador that neither he nor his friends would consent to a final breach. Henry had heard these rumors, much to his displeasure, had made inquiries, and Norfolk had retreated to his shire.[70] Howard returned to London in early 1534, and attended the House of Lords on thirty-eight days between 15 January and 30 March,[71] being present for most of the deliberations on the important acts of the fifth session of the Reformation Parliament: a statutory enactment of the submission of the clergy; absolute restraint of annates; prohibition of Peter's Pence and other payments to Rome; the succession act in favor of the children of Anne Boleyn; and a companion act reasserting the nullity of Henry's marriage to Catherine and thus Mary's bastardy.[72] Norfolk did not take a prominent place in the passage of this barrage of legislation. Chapuys spoke to the duke on 24 February, seeking permission to address Parliament in favor of Catherine and Mary, but was denied access by order of the king. When Parliament was adjourned on 30 March in royal session, Norfolk was commissioned along with Audley, Cranmer and Suffolk to take the oath to support the act of succession on behalf of the Lords.[73]

The implications of all this require some sorting out. Much of what we know of the opinions of men at court in the period comes from Chapuys, whose reports became increasingly unreliable as Henry's assault on Rome went on. The imperial ambassador was inclined to believe that a conspiracy in favor of the princess dowager, as Catherine was now known, was forming after 1533. Most recent writers have been skeptical of this interpretation, but G. R. Elton has turned back to Chapuys and the idea of an "Aragonese" group whose influence can be seen through the rise and fall of Anne Boleyn to the Pilgrimage of Grace and the Exeter Conspiracy.[74] The main support for this party came from conservative clerics, northern aristocrats and old gentry families. There is no real evidence, Chapuys's wishful thinking notwithstanding, that Norfolk had any part in these seditious activities. Norfolk was bitter over the rise of Cromwell, and increasingly uneasy with Henry's venom toward Rome and the old faith. But Norfolk was also a realist, and Chapuys's report of 7 March that Norfolk's show of opposition had landed him in trouble seems evidence of a last outburst before he regained his self-control. Whatever his personal sympathies, the duke could not afford to be anything other than the king's man. Unquestioned loyalty was the greatest service he could offer Henry. Thus from the middle of 1534, although Norfolk continued political efforts, increasingly in concert with Gardiner, to steer Henry toward a more conservative religious settlement, he kept well short of the line between political maneuvering and the treason that real opposition was deemed to be. If the 1534 session of Parliament was a turning point for England and the Henrician Reformation, it was a turning point for Norfolk as well. The duke's period of rule after the fall of Wolsey was over. Cromwell had assumed command and Rome was to be forsaken. Norfolk, however reluctantly, accepted this state of affairs and turned his full energies to winning back his influence with the king.

Norfolk was able to subordinate his pride and conscience, and bend to the king's will. There were others who could not. The foremost among these were Thomas More, who had resigned as chancellor two years earlier because of his qualms of conscience, and John Fisher, bishop of Rochester and since 1527 an outspoken defender of Catherine and opponent of the campaign against the church. Both More and Fisher were implicated in the affair of Elizabeth Barton, the "Maid of Kent" who had prophesied disaster should Henry wed Anne. Barton and several others were condemned by attainder and ended up on the scaffold at Tyburn in April 1534 for their treasons and heresies. More was examined by a commission which included Norfolk, Audley, Cranmer and Cromwell in March 1534 and escaped for the moment by disavowing Barton and any sympathy for her defense of the old faith. Gardiner, who might have sympathized with More, took no part in his examination, having been sent to his diocese after the prorogation of Parliament on 30 March with orders not to return to court until summoned. Cromwell replaced Gardiner as principal secretary in the spring of 1534 as further evidence of the bishop's fall from grace.

Yet Gardiner was no More; while Sir Thomas remained defiant and ended on the executioner's block, Gardiner used his time in exile to write his *De vera obedientia* in defense of the royal supremacy, and eventually returned to Henry's good graces.[75]

By April 1534, More was again in trouble for his refusal to take the oath to the act of succession. Confined to the Tower (in blithe disregard of Henry's promises not to force his conscience), More was examined again by Norfolk's commission. Now the former chancellor stood firm. "By the mass, Master More," Norfolk is said to have urged him, "it is perilous striving with princes. And therefore I would wish you somewhat to incline to the king's pleasure. For, by God's body, Master More, *Indignatio principis mors est*." Norfolk had lived by this servile creed, but More could not, as his answer indicated. "Is that all, my lord? Then in good faith is there no difference between your Grace and me, but that I shall die today and you tomorrow." In July 1535, Norfolk sat on the commission that convicted More of treason for denying the royal supremacy and sent him to his death.[76] Perhaps Norfolk's religious convictions were so shallow that he could not imagine taking the stand that More felt compelled to take. More likely the possibility of dying in futile defiance of the king never crossed Thomas Howard's mind. If the judicial murder of one of England's greatest men was demanded by the king, Norfolk was willing to play his part; loyalty far outweighed conscience.

More's death was overshadowed at the time by the destruction of Fisher, who followed More to the block after Rome had assured his martyrdom by making him a cardinal priest.[77] Henry's willingness to destroy two of the foremost men of his kingdom was a clear indication of the loyalty he required. One was either wholly on the king's side or an enemy to be destroyed. Clearly the lesson was not lost on Thomas Howard.

While this drama was played out in 1534–35, Cromwell took firm hold of politics, and Norfolk was relegated to subsidiary service. In July 1534 he served as lord high steward for the trial of William, lord Dacre, son of the Thomas Dacre who had served with Norfolk in the north, a man whose honesty Norfolk had questioned in the 1520s. Dacre was charged with treason on the basis of vague but probably essentially true charges of disloyalty to Henry, opposition to the divorce, and plans to lead a rebellion in favor of Princess Mary. At the least, Dacre had used his position as warden of the West Marches for private profit, making him vulnerable to attack. To the astonishment of everyone and the deep chagrin of Norfolk, the hand-picked jury of peers acquitted Dacre. In general tenor the charges against Dacre were probably true, but they were brought forward by the countess of Northumberland, an old family enemy, at the urging of Queen Anne, and the peers were unwilling to pursue a personal vendetta.[78] Dacre's acquittal is also evidence for the strength of the Aragonese party at court, although hardly proof that Norfolk was a sympathizer. The duke was left with no excuses to offer Henry for his failure to deliver the expected verdict; the fiasco only confirmed the king's suspicions about Howard's dispensability.

Still, Norfolk was not entirely excluded from court. At then end of July 1534, he served with Audley, Cranmer and others on a commission to hear a dispute between the town and University of Cambridge.[79] In August, he witnessed the ratification of a new Anglo-Scots peace treaty; the duke's lowered status was indicated by his absence from the commission that negotiated the pact with a state that had long been the special concern of the Howards.[80] In September Chapuys reported that Norfolk had retired to his country house because the council, discussing Irish affairs, had rejected his expert advice. Perhaps Norfolk was also aware that, should he press his services upon the king or stress his experience with Ireland, Cromwell might do as Wolsey had done and send him off to Dublin. According to Chapuys, Norfolk had sworn not to go unless Henry would "first construct a bridge over the sea for me to return freely whenever I like."[81]

Norfolk remained in a precarious position as long as he gave Henry reason to doubt his loyalty. When word arrived that Clement VII was near death, Chapuys reported that Norfolk and Dorset urged Henry to seize the opportunity to return to loyalty to Rome once a new pope was selected. Henry angrily insisted that no man could make him go back; it was an unmistakable rebuke to Norfolk and his fellow conservatives. Yet Norfolk remained in sufficiently good grace to be sent, along with Cromwell, private reports of the election of Alexander Farnese, who took the name Paul III.[82]

Norfolk's ceremonial position as earl marshal made him an essential figure on state occasions such as the reception of Phillipe de Chabot, admiral of France, in November 1534. The admiral was escorted from France by George Boleyn, lord Rochford, brother of the queen, and Norfolk met them at Blackheath to escort the ambassadorial party into London.[83] Chabot came to England for a new round of negotiations aimed at patching up Anglo-French relations. He was dispatched in expectation that the change at Rome would permit England to take a less radical course and seek reconciliation, but at his arrival the conservative party was in eclipse and Parliament, called into session on 3 November, had just passed the act of supremacy declaring Henry head of the church in England. Chabot's mission was thereby doomed to failure. The issue of a new marital alliance was raised, but the French insisted on considering Mary legitimate and bargaining for her hand. This Henry could not countenance, and the talks collapsed.[84]

In the meantime, a final break between Norfolk and his niece seems to have taken place. Bad relations between them had been smoldering for some time, but by the end of 1534 it became evident that all ties of affection and family interest had been severed. Chapuys sent Charles V a thirdhand story (told Chapuys by the earl of Northumberland) that, at court, Anne had heaped more abuse on Norfolk than a dog deserved, so much so that the duke left the queen's chamber in a rage. Once in the hall, he vented his spite by muttering that Anne was nothing but a "great whore."[85] The duke remained at court for the next six weeks, but by about 10 February, he departed for Kenninghall, complaining to Chapuys before leaving that he was no longer held in any esteem at court.[86]

The Anglo-French negotiations meanwhile continued; in March Henry decided to send an new embassy to France. Henry nominated Norfolk, Cromwell and Sir William Fitzwilliam for the task. Cromwell, leery of involving himself in unsuccessful diplomacy, protested his ill health, and Rochford was named in his place.[87] Before leaving for France, Norfolk took part in an investigation of several monks accused of denying the royal supremacy, presiding over their trial on 3 May. The next day Norfolk, Richmond, Wiltshire, Rochford and others were seemingly enthusiastic spectators at the public execution of the unfortunate monks. Clearly, Norfolk was doing all he could to assure Henry of his support of royal policy. The duke also attempted to patch things up with Cromwell; on 6 May he wrote a restrained but friendly letter to the new leading minister, full of reassurances that he would always be a faithful friend, "grudge who will."[88]

By the middle of May a sheaf of detailed instructions had been drawn up for the French embassy, and on 20 May Norfolk and his fellows arrived in Calais. Initial discussions proved that the French expected Henry to make concessions to prevent a Franco-Imperial alliance, while Henry still believed himself the injured party after the failure of Francis to shield England from papal condemnation. As a result, Rochford was sent back to London to report and seek new instructions.[89] Henry responded on 6 June, sending a letter to Norfolk denying him authority to relent on any point, giving the duke the thankless task of convincing Francis that Henry's desires were completely fair, honest and in France's best interests! Henry also insisted that, should the French agree to wed Francis's youngest son, the duc d'Angoulême, to Elizabeth rather than to Mary (an unlikely concession in any case), the prince would have to be brought to England for his upbringing.[90]

In fairness to Henry, it should be said that Angoulême stood a good chance of eventually becoming king of England should he wed Elizabeth and should Henry have no male heir. Under the circumstances, Henry was seeking to guarantee that Angoulême would be Anglicized before he could become king, but not surprisingly the French considered the entire idea absurd. Norfolk's instructions allowed no flexibility to offer other terms, and, as a result, the talks quickly collapsed. To the delight of Chapuys, Norfolk and the French representatives parted on 14 June amidst mutual recriminations.[91]

Following this fiasco, which Cromwell had foreseen, perhaps even planned, and certainly welcomed, Norfolk found himself again disgraced at court. According to Chapuys, Anne and Cromwell had allied to arrange the duke's ruin, Anne out of spite because her uncle made no secret of his distaste for her, and Cromwell out of a desire to solidify his own position by humbling the great men of the realm, starting with Norfolk.[92] As a result, Norfolk spent the summer after his French mission and the executions of More and Fisher at Kenninghall. On 9 September he wrote a letter to Cromwell seeking news of the state of the French negotiations, a clear demonstration that he had lost any share of that business. Hoping to curry favor, Norfolk also mentioned that he had heard that commissioners collecting the parliamentary subsidy in Norwich had found no one who admitted to an assessment over a hundred pounds, which he knew to be untrue. Norfolk offered to pressure the leading men of the city for a more honest evaluation.[93] The strategy of deference to Cromwell seems to have worked; the duke was called to court in mid-September and must have traveled in his usual estate, for he wrote Cromwell on the 24th asking that places be found at court for the twenty-four horsemen in his train.[94]

Norfolk's return to court was probably connected with the opening of Parliament scheduled for 3 November. The session was postponed until February 1536 because of plague in London; probably Norfolk returned to his county through the year's end.[95] He was back at court early in January when Catherine of Aragon died, prompting Henry, in a display of incredibly bad taste, to dress in yellow and order a round of celebrations. Norfolk was also present on 21 January when the king fell from his horse after a run in the lists and was unconscious for two hours, for the duke carried the news to the queen. Anne was several months pregnant at the time with what Henry hoped would be his long-sought son. Considerably shaken by the news of Henry's fall, Anne miscarried a week later on 27 January, the day of Catherine's funeral. Anne tried to blame Norfolk, the bearer of the frightening tidings, for the consequences of her scare, but rumors were already flying that Anne, incapable of bearing a male child, was herself to blame.[96] Having conspicuously failed in the duty for which Henry had married her, Anne found herself in serious danger.

In the late winter and early spring of 1536 Norfolk was busy with Parliament and with diplomacy. The rivalry between Charles and Francis was again escalating toward open war, and both sides were bidding for England's support. Chapuys told his master that Norfolk and other pro-French councilors could be won over since they had been in political decline, and Charles responded with instructions for his envoy cautiously to offer the duke the emperor's friendship.[97] Francis meanwhile was ready to offer Henry a bribe of fifty thousand crowns as an inducement to enter the war on his side. Norfolk assured a French ambassador that Henry could never love Charles, but ten days later he indicated to Chapuys that a renewed French alliance was out of the question.[98] The duke obviously enjoyed being courted by both sides—and must have relished this diplomatic double-dealing as much as did Henry.

Beyond all this, however, more serious events were slowly taking shape, events in which Norfolk would be little more than a spectator. The coup that brought about the fall of Anne Boleyn is perhaps the classic case of Henrician factionalism. Norfolk, who had distanced himself from Anne, and who, despite the fond hopes of Chapuys, had never supported the Aragonese faction, played a curiously passive part; except for presiding over the trials of his niece and nephew, he seems to have had little or nothing to do with the grim events of April–May 1536.

Anne's failure to produce a son upset Henry greatly, but, worse for the queen, the king had grown tired of her jealousy and her noisy complaints against enemies at court. Early in 1536, Henry's flirtation with Jane Seymour—the latest in a series of casual liaisons—became something more serious. Anne now found herself alone at Greenwich while the court went elsewhere. By April, the king had decided to rid himself of Anne and to ask his subjects to accept a dissolution of the marriage that had been made at such great cost.[99] Cromwell, who may have put the idea into Henry's head in the first place, was ordered to investigate the possibility of a divorce on grounds of Anne's precontract to Henry Percy, who had since succeeded as earl of Northumberland. Unfortunately, Percy had denied an engagement to Anne under oath before the king in 1532. This tactic showing little promise, Henry appointed Norfolk and Cromwell to head a commission to investigate Anne's conduct since her marriage. If the marriage itself was valid, perhaps there was something wrong with Anne's living of it.[100]

Certainly Henry was persuaded there was, although not by Norfolk and Cromwell but probably by members of his court hostile to the Boleyns. The party that pushed forward Jane Seymour remains rather obscure, in part because the main beneficiary of Jane's rise was her brother Edward, a man of too little influence in 1536 to have engineered Anne's destruction alone. It seems probable that the real leaders of the faction seeking to topple the Boleyns were second-rank political figures at court. The leading figure in terms of status was Henry Courtenay, marquis of Exeter, a man of high rank and noble blood but rather slim power at court. Exeter's main goal in replacing Anne with Jane Seymour seems to have been to restore Mary to the succession and to halt the religious progressivism which the "Lutheran" Boleyns represented. A less prestigious but actually more powerful member of the group was Nicholas Carew, master of the horse, a household official and royal companion. Carew was particularly angry with the Boleyns because Anne had persuaded Henry to select her brother George for a recent vacancy in the Order of the Garter which Carew had coveted. He was supported by Anthony Browne, Thomas Cheney and John Russell, all gentlemen of the privy chamber.[101] The importance of the locus of the conspiracy is shown by the status of the men destroyed with

Anne, all of them (save her brother and the hapless Mark Smeaton) members of Henry's household. The fall of Anne Boleyn was the occasion of a factional struggle at court, but Norfolk was not personally a party to it; his own clients were neither victors nor victims as far as can be determined.

Jane Seymour was pushed forward as an object for Henry's infatuation in much the way that Norfolk had employed Anne against Catherine. The object of the ploy was precisely the same, to obtain political preferment through alliance with the new queen. Like Anne, Jane appears to have been coached by her backers and instructed not to give in to the king's amorous advances.[102] Between 25 April, when Cromwell and Norfolk began gathering evidence against Anne, and 1 May, when the first arrests were made, Carew and his fellows were already certain that the queen was ruined, or so they assured Chapuys.[103] The first to be arrested was Mark Smeaton, an organist in Anne's service who was detained secretly by Cromwell. On 1 May Henry Norris, a gentleman of the privy chamber, was sent to the Tower only hours after he had been celebrating May Day with the king; legend has it that Norris was undone when Anne dropped a handkerchief to him as a love token. The next day Anne's brother George, viscount Rochford, was taken into custody, and in short order Anne herself, conducted in near hysteria by Norfolk and a body of men at arms, joined the men in the Tower. By 4 May William Brereton and Sir Francis Weston were also in custody, and by 10 May all were charged with adultery and conspiracy to murder the king.[104] Anne had certainly been at the center of a cult of courtly manners and love-posing that could be twisted for the benefit of a suspicious mind such as Henry's into charges that she had presided over a treasonous orgy. Yet the idea that Anne had actually had carnal relations with her brother and the other men, or had plotted the death of the king, must have seemed far-fetched even to Cromwell and his agents as they gathered the evidence. As a result E. W. Ives has concluded, with Elton's concurrence, that the real purpose of the arrests of Norris, Weston and Brereton was to effect a purge of Henry's household to the benefit of the Aragonese Exeter-Carew group.[105]

Perhaps even the investigators were nervous about the charges; with the memory of Dacre's acquittal still fresh, there may have been doubts about the certainty of a trial. Norfolk and several other councilors visited Anne in the Tower to try to extort a confession from her. She was told that Norris and Smeaton had admitted their crimes (which they had not), and Norfolk accused Anne of plotting Henry's death in order to marry one of her lovers. Anne refused to crack, and the delegation left without satisfaction.[106] Nonetheless, the grim charade continued. Since Smeaton, Norris, Weston and Brereton were all commoners, they were tried apart from Anne and Rochford and were the first to meet their fate. On 12 May they appeared before a commission headed by Norfolk, Suffolk, Audley, Wiltshire, Cromwell and Fitzwilliam. The judgment, based largely on Smeaton's confession obtained through torture, was swift and merciless. The four were found guilty of treason and ordered executed.[107]

Anne and Rochford did not have to wait long; on Monday, 15 May 1536, Norfolk presided as lord high steward over their trial. Anne staunchly denied all of the charges, and Rochford's impassioned defense led some to expect his acquittal. But certainly the judgment that both were guilty was a foregone conclusion. Henry had decided that Anne had to go, and Rochford could not have been released without casting serious doubts on already dubious proceedings. On 17 May Rochford was beheaded with the other men at Tyburn; two days later Anne followed at the hands of a French swordsman brought over from Calais for the occasion.[108]

Not content with the execution of his wife for her adultery, Henry also procured Cranmer's judgment that the union had been void *ab initio* due to his previous relations with Mary Boleyn. To his credit, Cranmer tried to intervene in Anne's favor and had to be summoned before the council and ordered to cease. Yet the archbishop's pliability was soon evident. On the day of Anne's execution Cranmer issued a dispensation allowing Henry to marry a second cousin, Lady Jane Seymour.[109]

The fall of Anne Boleyn was a blow to the fortunes of the Howards, even considering the queen's hostility to Norfolk the previous two years. Norfolk gained nothing from his show of loyalty at Anne's trial. Worse, the field was opened to a rival clan, the Seymours, who swiftly began reaping the rewards of their ties to the new queen after Henry and Jane were wed at York Place on 30 May. By 5 June the queen's brother Edward was created viscount Beauchamp in a first step toward the earldom of Hertford and, in Edward's reign, the dukedom of Somerset.[110] The rise of the Seymours, coupled with continued ascendancy of Cromwell, would serve to keep Norfolk in relative eclipse for much of the next four years until the fall of Cromwell and the rise of Catherine Howard.

Norfolk's position was actually little changed by Anne's fall. He remained subordinate to Cromwell, but not without some influence. A new Parliament was elected to meet in June 1536 for the express purpose of dealing with the muddled succession question, and Norfolk had considerable influence in the elections. He controlled ten seats in Sussex alone and seems to have managed other elections, for he reported to Cromwell that in all the other shires in his commission, such persons would be returned as "I doubt not shall serve his highness according to his pleasure."[111] The foreign ambassadors continued to treat Norfolk as an important councilor, indicating that he still held a place at court.[112] Norfolk gained very little in the long term from the career of Anne Boleyn. The rise of Thomas Cromwell was a bitter blow for Thomas Howard, all the more so since Cromwell proved to have both ability and a taste for power rivaling those of Wolsey. Yet Norfolk's pride was undiminished, his hunger for position and power unsatisfied. The duke had no choice but to bide his time, awaiting the opportunity to reassert himself against Cromwell and the newly arisen Seymours. In this respect, nothing had changed. Norfolk was not a creative or innovative politician; Cromwell, like Wolsey, was more than his match. But Thomas Howard remained a dangerous political figure. Should the opportunity present itself, he would seek to do to Cromwell what had been done to Wolsey.

CHAPTER 6

THE PILGRIMAGE OF GRACE, 1536–1537

THE FALL OF ANNE BOLEYN confirmed Thomas Cromwell's dominance. By 8 July he had been raised to the peerage as Lord Cromwell of Wimbledon and replaced Wiltshire as keeper of the privy seal. Norfolk, though often at court and in council and active in Parliament, was clearly no longer the leading figure in government.[1] If he had expected rewards for his role in the trial of Anne, Norfolk was sorely disappointed. Anne's destruction, if anything, had proved the value of Cromwell and shown that Norfolk had little to offer beyond his servile obedience. Cromwell had managed Parliament ably for Henry, and was proving as resourceful and crafty an administrator as Wolsey had been—reducing Thomas Howard again to the roles of soldier, diplomat and councilor, a royal servant of considerable value, but no longer the leading minister.

Norfolk's few official duties in mid-1536 were as often onerous as honorable. In May, Henry sent Norfolk to rebuke Princess Mary for her refusal to accept the succession act and her own bastardy. Mary eventually gave in, but even so Henry saw that his daughter, as a living symbol of Catholic and Imperial sympathies, was too dangerous to legitimize, and the new act of succession left Mary a bastard while casting aside Elizabeth, thus placing the hopes of the kingdom on the fruits of the Seymour marriage. Failing male heirs there, the king reserved the right to name a successor by letters patent.[2]

Although the Seymours profited greatly from the fall of the Boleyns, Cromwell was the real beneficiary of Anne's disaster as he proved able to

131

block the ambitions of the Darcy-Carew-Exeter faction. Edward Seymour, viscount Beauchamp, quickly accepted a role as Cromwell's ally. Beauchamp was every bit as ambitious as Norfolk, but as the king's brother-in-law he would gain enormous leverage as soon as Jane provided an heir. Cromwell handled the Seymours carefully, treating them as allies rather than rivals for the time being. Accepting these social upstarts was galling enough to Norfolk, but to make it worse the Seymours were religious progressives as well. The rise of Edward Seymour coincided with the emergence of a progressive party at court, led by Cromwell and Cranmer, while Norfolk and Gardiner increasingly assumed leadership of the conservatives. By 1539 a clear polarity would appear in court and council.[3]

Norfolk's diminished status was attested to in July 1536 when his half-brother Thomas, lord Howard, was sent to the Tower for the offense of having contracted to marry the king's niece, Lady Margaret Douglas (daughter of the Queen Mother of Scotland, Margaret), without royal consent. Several years before, Norfolk had been pardoned for an illegal marriage between his half-sister and the earl of Derby, but this was a more serious offense and, given his reduced status, Norfolk was unable to do anything for Lord Howard. In July an act of attainder passed the House of Lords, with Norfolk in attendance, and received royal assent. The unfortunate Lord Howard remained imprisoned until his death in November 1537.[4]

Family troubles continued to plague Norfolk in the summer of 1536. On 22 July Henry Fitzroy, duke of Richmond, the king's illegitimate son and the duke's son-in-law, died at St. James. Henry had once thought to name Fitzroy as his heir, but Richmond had become more of an embarrassment than an asset to the king. The task of giving Fitzroy a quiet burial fell to Norfolk. Richmond's coffin was carried to the Howard chapel at Thetford under a load of hay and laid to rest without fanfare under Norfolk's direction.[5]

Once away from court to carry out this task, Norfolk discovered to his dismay that Cromwell blocked his return. Chapuys had earlier reported that Norfolk alone had opposed the Imperial alliance in council; Cromwell was irritated enough with Norfolk's recalcitrance to complain to Chapuys that the duke was a fickle man, and rather too ambitious. Having gotten Norfolk away from court, Cromwell was anxious to keep him away as long as possible. On 4 August a French observer reported that Cromwell had taken advantage of the duke's absence to poison Henry's mind against Norfolk.[6] The duke soon received word of the king's anger that Richmond had not received a more honorable burial. Although the quiet manner of the funeral was Henry's idea in the first place, on second thoughts— or at Cromwell's suggestion—Henry had decided that Richmond's burial had dishonored the Tudor dynasty, and Norfolk even heard rumors that a room in the Tower awaited his return to London. Howard wrote several soothing letters to Cromwell, protesting that "Totenham would turn French" before he deserved such a fate. Instead, Cromwell ordered him to collect the subsidy voted by Parliament in 1534 in Norfolk and Norwich. As late as 10 September Norfolk was occupied with this task and isolated in the country while Cromwell monopolized Henry's attention.[7]

The outbreak of disturbances in the north in the autumn of 1536 was Norfolk's salvation from the isolation into which his enemies at court had thrust him. The dissolution of the lesser monastic houses, begun in April 1536 under the direction of Cromwell as Henry's vicar general in matters spiritual, was an important step in Cromwell's drive to consolidate the reformation of the English church. By dissolving the monasteries the crown stood to gain forty thousand pounds a year in rents and other revenues. Henry could enjoy the income himself, but was also able through grants and sales to tie the ruling classes to the Henrician church.[8] The willingness of the nobility to accept church lands was remarkable, and even the conservative dukes of Norfolk and Suffolk were quick to petition for their shares.[9]

Yet in the north, this policy sparked tremendous upheavals. Monastic houses served many purposes besides religious ones, providing schools, almshouses, hospitals and orphanages and offering employment on their estates to landless freemen. The loss of much of this was viewed with deep suspicion and foreboding. In addition, the monasteries were major landlords, renting to farmers across the northern shires. Transfer of these estates to new owners suggested a round of rack-renting, enclosures and, at the least, collection of stiff entry fines, all at the expense of renters faced already with poor harvests and a steady population rise that exacerbated unemployment.[10] Northern society was not uniquely conservative in the 1530s; most of provincial England was far more medieval than modern. But the basic economic and religious conservatism of the north, coupled with the relatively large number of northern religious houses involved in the first wave of dissolutions, does much to explain why the north revolted in 1536, while the equally conservative west waited until 1549, and the south, though restive in areas, never came to open rebellion over these issues.[11]

The situation in the north was complicated by the position of the aristocracy. Government of the north, as in all of England, was possible only through the local notables and the justices of the peace, generally gentlemen of the shires. A number of noble families had long held sway in the north, ruling almost as princes in their distant realms far from the notice of London. The deaths of Thomas Stanley, second earl of Derby, in 1521, and of Lord Monteagle in 1523, each leaving a minor heir, left a power vacuum in Lancashire. Edward, third earl of Derby, reached his majority in 1531, but he was considered "half a fool" at best. As Christopher Haigh observed, "In the mid 1530's, when the Cromwellian religious changes had to be enforced, the county [of Lancashire] was ruled by a vacillating young man who could not preserve good order."[12] There were similar problems in Yorkshire. Thomas, lord Darcy, warden of Pontefract Castle, was staunchly opposed to the progressive influence at court, and may have been plotting with Chapuys to use Catherine of Aragon as a focus of rebellion before her death in January 1536. After the demise of the princess dowager the plotting turned to the aim of establishing a semi-autonomous Catholic state in the north. And Darcy was not alone. The Percy earl of Northumberland and his son Sir Thomas were widely suspected of disloyalty.[13] Lincoln, too, was unsettled in 1536, in part because of the efforts of Charles Brandon, duke of Suffolk, to build a landed power base there through the connections of his third wife, Catherine Willoughby. In the face of the decline of the old baronial families, and in the midst of unrest caused by the religious innovations of the previous years, the Tudor north was ripe for trouble.[14]

Much of the discontent of the northern aristocracy focused on Cromwell and his progressive allies such as Cranmer and Audley. Cromwell had pushed forward the reform of the church, but also had insisted on royal and not baronial administration of justice in the north—this was at least in part the import of the abortive trial of William, lord Dacre—and had blocked Sir Thomas Percy from entering any part of the lands his predecessor had willed to the crown. Thus while the commons had economic and religious grievances, their betters were unhappy with political affairs.

The result was that the northern lords, and especially Darcy and Percy, abdicated responsibility to keep order in their shires once an outbreak began, and may have incited rebellion.[15]

The thesis that the Pilgrimage of Grace was not a spontaneous uprising but rather the work of disaffected conservative aristocrats such as Darcy is not new, nor is the idea that the leaders of the rebellion of 1536 were connected with the Exeter conspiracy of 1538. This interpretation was put forth by M. H. and Ruth Dodds in 1915.[16] More recently, Elton has expanded on this theme, tracing an "Aragonese" faction at court from the early 1530s through the fall of Anne Boleyn and, after failure to gain control of government through her destruction, on to the Pilgrimage of Grace. According to this view, Darcy, John, Lord Hussey and Robert Constable were the real leaders of the Pilgrimage of Grace, and their aim was to force the restoration of Mary and a return to a conservative religious policy. The importance of this thesis is that it ties together a number of actions during the 1530s that hint of opposition politics, underlining Elton's theme of the progress of Cromwell's Commonwealth programs.[17] The Pilgrimage of Grace may or may not have been orchestrated by a few disgruntled barons, but certainly the people of the north were upset enough with economic, social and religious grievances to resort to rebellion in 1536 and 1537 once the spark was struck, and the northern aristocracy did much less than it could have to contain the troubles. The Pilgrimage of Grace did not come close to overturning Tudor rule, but the northern risings gave Henry a very serious scare.[18]

From Norfolk's viewpoint, most of this causal background was unimportant. What mattered was that, with several northern shires in rebellion, an angry and worried Henry VIII needed his experienced hand. After months of sporadic rioting and unlawful assemblies, the first concerted northern rising of Henry's reign took place in Lincolnshire in October. There was some bloodshed, including murder of the bishop of Lincoln's chancellor, but the main product of the affair was a series of petitions to the crown for redress of grievances, with the restoration of the church and the removal of low-born councilors such as Cromwell leading the demands. Lancashire was also restive in early October, and by the middle of the month a band of over a thousand rebels had gathered in the west of that shire.[19]

As the gravity of the troubles became evident, orders went out across the realm for gentlemen and nobles to raise forces to subdue the northern rising. Henry initially appointed Suffolk commander, but planned to lead the royal army north in person. Norfolk fully expected a major role in the business, and, after a brief visit to court around 7 October, returned to his shire to raise his troops.[20]

According to Chapuys, Norfolk was in high spirits, bragging that he would crush the rebellion easily. Better still, the duke hoped that the affair would work the ruin of Cromwell, since his policies had been the greatest cause of the troubles. Chapuys also reported that Norfolk secretly believed that the tumult would put an end to dissolution of the religious houses. That innovation, Chapuys wrote, had cut across Norfolk's Catholic grain; it was owing in part to his earlier expressions on religious matters that he had lost favor at court. Norfolk did, in fact, share the rebels' opposition to such religious progressives as Cranmer; however, he chose to fight them not by supporting rebellion, but by continued political intrigue.[21] Norfolk may have hoped that a grateful king would reward success in the north by a return to favor and influence, and perhaps by establishing the Howards as the leading magnate family of the region. Had Norfolk been of a less calculating nature, his convictions might have led him to support the rebels. As it stood, loyalty to Henry seemed a more promising course than civil war. This was clear even to Chapuys, who, while hopeful that the risings would restore the old faith and return Mary to the succession, warned Charles that, "owing to the said duke's versatile and inconstant humor," no one could "rely on him" to support the rebellion.[22]

Henry or Cromwell must have shared Chapuys's doubts about Norfolk. On 8 October, Howard received orders to remain in East Anglia to prevent trouble there while Henry led his army north. The duke reacted with anger and shock. "Alas, sir," he wrote the king, "shal every noble man save I only eyther come to your parson or els go towardes your enemys? Shall I now sit still lyk a man of law? Alas, sir, my hert is nere ded as wold to God it wer." Unless Henry sent him confirmation of the order to remain in his shire, Norfolk vowed to march north with his retinue rather than "to remayne at home with so moche shame as I shall do." Several other letters to Henry, Cromwell and the council followed, leading to a change of heart at court, and Norfolk received new orders authorizing him to march to Ampthill to join the assembling army. On 11 October Norfolk left Kenninghall with his son Henry, earl of Surrey, in his train; the duke's second son Thomas was left at home with several hundred men to preserve order in the shire. When word of this arrangement reached the king, Henry immediately ordered Norfolk to send Surrey home.[23] Norfolk's sons would remain under Henry's watch as pledges for his loyalty—a safeguard which only underlines Henry's doubts about Norfolk's religious sympathies.

Even while Suffolk and Shrewsbury suppressed the Lincolnshire rising, the northern rebellion of 1536 received its lasting name when Robert Aske raised the banner of the five wounds of Christ in Yorkshire at the head of the self-proclaimed Pilgrims of Grace who had gathered under his direction. The ranks of the Pilgrimage were swelled in the following weeks by men from Lincolnshire, with the result that Aske's forces grew into the tens of thousands before Norfolk could march north to face them.[24] By 18 October Norfolk, with the marquis of Exeter as his second in command, reached Ampthill, Bedfordshire, with about four thousand men—a force that would have seemed more than sufficient to face any Tudor rebellion, but one that would shortly prove inadequate before the ranks of the Pilgrimage.[25] As Norfolk moved toward York, dispatches flew back and forth between the duke and court. Henry had decided not to come north until he was sure of the situation, leaving Norfolk to face the rebels with the forces at hand. Aske and his followers were remarkably peaceful, but, following the violence in Lincolnshire, Henry was determined not to negotiate. Lancaster Herald was sent to Aske with a demand that the Pilgrims recall their duty to God and king and return to their obedience; in return, the king offered pardon to all who submitted to Norfolk, but no promise of redress of grievances. On 21 October Henry ordered Norfolk and Exeter to join with Shrewsbury at York and disperse the rebels by force if politics failed. As yet, the king had no idea of the magnitude of the rising.[26] Neither, apparently, did Norfolk, for on 23 October he wrote to the king hoping that Shrewsbury would not give battle to the rebels before his arrival, for there were many knights in his train who would be disappointed not to have a part in the expected rout.[27]

Two days later Norfolk was at Welbeck. Fourteen miles away at Doncaster, the Pilgrims had occupied a strong natural defensive position on the northern banks of the river Don. Now Norfolk first learned of the size of the host facing him. Aske had gathered about forty thousand well-fed and well-armed men, and most of the leading men of the north had either fled or joined the rebels. Darcy surrendered Pontefract Castle to the

Pilgrims, while Edward Lee, archbishop of York, and most of the king's council in the north entered Aske's camp; even the city of York was in rebel hands. Norfolk, having gathered loyal northern levies along the way, had about eight thousand cold and hungry men at his disposal; no wonder he approached the encounter with Aske with increasing apprehension. Besides learning of the rebels' strength, Norfolk also discovered, probably to his intense relief, that Aske was willing to discuss grievances before resorting to arms. Norfolk thus wrote Henry a cautious letter reporting that he would meet with the rebels to hear their terms. The duke hoped the king would "take it in good part" if he negotiated with Aske, for he assured Henry that he would not abide by any promises made to the rebels that were contrary to the king's policy, and swore that he would "rather be torne in a myllion of peces than to shew one poynt of cowardise or untrouth to your maiestie." Yet the outcome of the encounter was far from certain, for Norfolk closed by asking the king to look after his children if his plans should "myscary."[28]

While Henry dictated a new set of instructions for Norfolk on 27 October, the duke came face to face with Aske and his followers. Still unaware of the situation at Doncaster, or, if aware, unable to bring himself to treat with rebels, Henry ordered Norfolk not to fight unless he could be assured of success, advising instead that the duke withdraw to Nottingham or Newark "tyl, with our Army Royal, which we doo put in aredynes, We shall be hable to bere down the traitours befor us." Henry made no mention of negotiations, nor did he offer a pardon in order to persuade the rebels to disperse; he still expected to crush the Pilgrims by force.[29]

Norfolk meanwhile found himself outnumbered and unable to advance or retreat without risking suicidal battle—or worse, the defection of his army to the ranks of the Pilgrims. Therefore he did the only sensible thing and entered into talks with Aske. Norfolk had detected a rift within the rebel ranks, for Aske, although acknowledged as leader of the Pilgrimage, was able only with some difficulty to persuade his followers not to resort to immediate violence against Norfolk's army. Therefore Norfolk, Exeter and Shrewsbury issued an open letter to the rebels which boldly reminded them of the loyalty they owed the king and threatened their utter ruin at the hands of a vast royal army under Henry's command should they not disperse. Under the circumstances, this was a rather audacious document, and it bears quoting in full:

The Pilgrimage of Grace

Alas, ye unhappy men! What francy, what folye, hath ledde and seduced you to make this most shameful rebellion against our moost noble and rightouse King and Soveraigne; who is more worthye, for his innumerable graces, and noble vertues, and gentle conditions, to be King, maistre and governor, or all Christendom, than of so small a realme as Englonde? And if ye fynd fawte, that he hath had moche good of youe, then ye owght to considre and thinke the same to be well imployed; for he hath not only spent the same, but also an infinite som of his owen treasure, to maynteign and kepe youe in peax, against all enemyes. Fye for shame! How can ye, of all those parties, fynde in your hartes to rebell against His Highnes, who hath soo often, in our cumpany, obteigned great victories against the enemyes of the realm? Fye for shame! How can ye thus doo, and over and besides for offences to your naturall Soveraigne Lorde, yeve us too, that have loved you better than any parte of the realm, occasion to fight with youe, that we have taken for our best frendes? We can say no more; but trust ye, surelye, that unles ye doo, incontinent, draw home, every man to his house, we woll yeve youe bataill; and though we shalbe sory soo to doo, yet we shall shewe youe the most hard curtesye, that ever was shewed to men, that have loved youe soo well as we have don. Alas! that ever it shold be sayde that ye Northern men, that have so well served their Prince, in our cumpanies, and in many other quarrell, against them! Finallie, it is nowe at your choyse, whether ye woll abide the dawnger of bataill against us, or els go home to your houses, submitting youe to the Kinges mercy. If ye goo home, ye may be assured to have us most humble sewters to His Highnes for youe; and if ye doo not, then doo your worst to us, for soo we woll doo to youe. And yet ye have occasion to say, that we deale like honest charitable men with youe, to yeve youe this warynyng, more gentle than your desertes doth require.[30]

On 27 October Norfolk and Aske met at Doncaster Bridge. Aske, to his credit, had no desire for battle but hoped through a show of force to persuade Henry to accept the seriousness of the rebel grievances.[31] Norfolk's offer of a pardon and promise to relay the rebels' complaints to the king was enough for Aske, who agreed to order his men to disperse peacefully. Aske knew he could not force the king's hand by marching south, for many of his followers were farmers who would not leave their lands at harvest time; the season was too late to begin an extended military campaign. Aske thus was forced to rely on the king's mercy, and to hope that his complaints would receive a fair hearing. This was not all naïvete; Aske and the Pilgrims did not see themselves as rebels at all, but as loving subjects attempting to free the king of his evil councilors. Once rescued from Cromwell's influence, Henry would restore the true church and the monasteries—and thank his pious and loyal subjects for their service in bringing him to his senses. Alas that it was not so simple.

Aske agreed that Norfolk and two representatives of the Pilgrims would carry their petitions to Henry; until their return, a truce would be observed. On 28 October Norfolk reported to Henry that "uppon the declaration there of your most gratious free pardon, [I] have dispeached home, to their howses, all the said commons." In a letter to the council the next day Norfolk candidly admitted his relief that the Pilgrims had dispersed peacefully, for he knew now how precarious his position had been at Doncaster.[32] The duke then headed south; by 6 November he was at Windsor to discuss the rebellion with king and council.[33]

Although he had shown not the least sign of going over to the rebels, Norfolk feared with considerable justification that the king would not approve of his handling of the affair, and he wrote to Darcy on 6 November and again two days later, urging him to write to the king to disprove the suspicions voiced at court that Norfolk had abetted the rebellion by his lax handling of Aske and the Pilgrims. Norfolk, not entirely sure of Darcy's loyalty, asked him to prove his devotion to the king by arresting Aske and meeting the duke at Doncaster at the end of December to begin the task of restoring the north to obedience.[34] If indeed Darcy was behind the rebellion, it was no wonder that he demurred. In a long rambling letter to Norfolk, Darcy protested his loyalty, but refused to move against Aske, leaving his options open if continued support of the rebellion should prove a more promising course.[35]

By mid-November, Henry drew up new instructions for Norfolk and Sir William Fitzwilliam's negotiations with Aske. Norfolk, Henry noted, was sent as a man "with greate wisedom and pollicye," one "thought a personage whiche is right acceptable, before many others, to the people of those parts." Norfolk and Fitzwilliam were to remind the rebels of their duty to God and king and demand a full submission to royal mercy. Those

Pilgrims who submitted and swore loyalty were to be pressed into service in rounding up all who refused to yield; those who remained contumacious would be excluded from the king's pardon. Norfolk and Fitzwilliam were given leave to deal with anything not covered in the instructions by their own circumspection, with "full power and auctoritie in all things to devise, set forth, procede, determyn and conclude, as they shall thinke most expedient for His Graces honor, and the good conducing of this affayr to his desired purpose." Henry's attitude toward any obstinate Pilgrims was clear, for at the close of his letter he promised "the utter extinguishment of those traitours, their wyves and children, with fire and sworde accordingly."[36]

Yet Henry's instructions hardly gave his commissioners a free hand to deal with Aske. The two main demands of the Pilgrims were the removal of "symple and evyll dysposed persons" from the council, and "the perservacyon of Chrystes Churce," that is, the Catholic faith.[37] In an article appended to his instructions, Henry offered his answer. His council, the king insisted, was well stocked with men of noble birth, and he lightly ran over a list of dukes, lords and bishops. No mention was made of Cromwell, the real target of Aske's complaints, or of the "heretical" bishops Cranmer, Longland and Latimer. As for as the state of the church, Henry coolly insisted that he was a true Christian man, "mynded to dye and lyve in the puryte" of the "Faith of Christe."[38] These bland answers would give no satisfaction to the discontented northerners, nor be any help to Norfolk in bringing them to terms. Aske himself recognized the danger of allowing Henry to stall, for with winter coming it would be impossible to keep a rebel army in the field. Thus on 19 November, Aske told a supporter that he would meet with Norfolk at Doncaster either to agree on a set of articles or to resort to battle; there could be no further delays or negotiations.[39]

Norfolk and Fitzwilliam set out for Doncaster on 21 November, already worried that the rebels had been given too long to organize defenses. Suffolk, who remained in Lincoln, warned that Aske and Constable were too strong to be taken except by surprise. By now it was clear that Darcy had thrown his lot in with the rebels. Norfolk was fearful that Darcy, Aske and Constable would "essay some new business" and wreck his peace mission before a meeting could take place.[40] The duke wrote several apprehensive letters to Henry warning that the rebellion could not be suppressed by sheer force. Therefore, Norfolk planned to agree to Aske's demands for a full pardon and the calling of an extraordinary Parliament to meet at York to discuss the grievances of the north. On 2 December Henry responded, sending new instructions for the talks with Aske. Henry, as usual, brushed aside the doubts of his servants, serene in his expectation that all would work out according to the royal will, regardless of the obstacles. "We mervayl moche," the king wrote, "that you doo all write unto Us in such extreame and desperate sorte, as thoughe the world shold be, in manner, turned uppe so downe, onles We wolde, in certain pointes, condescende to the petitions of the rebels." Norfolk and Shrewsbury could treat with the rebels, but were warned that under no circumstances were they to issue the full pardon they carried or to agree, in Henry's name, that a northern Parliament would be held. If the rebels demanded a Parliament, Norfolk was to ask for twenty days in which Henry might consult with his council; the duke would use this period to gather forces "in the closest and secretest maner you canne" to fortify and defend the River Don against a rebel advance.[41] In his dealings with the Pilgrims, Henry showed himself not as a loving king who had the best interests of his subjects at heart, but as a harsh and demanding master who expected loyal obedience to the royal will. Perhaps the ensuing bloody suppression of the Pilgrimage of Grace could have been avoided; that it was not is largely owing to the king's thirst for vengeance against his disloyal subjects. One of Henry's greatest strengths as king was his unshakable belief in his God-given sovereignty and righteousness, but the cost paid by his subjects for this self-assurance was a high one indeed.

Not realizing that Henry never intended to give an inch to his rebellious subjects, Aske and Constable had taken Norfolk's promises to present their grievances seriously, and had presided over a series of meetings at York and Pontefract to draw up demands. These reiterated the already expressed aims of the uprising: the dismissal of Cromwell, restoration of the Catholic Church, and calling of a northern Parliament to express the true sentiments of the region. The meetings were well attended, orderly and well organized, all of which bespoke Aske and Constable's impressive organizational and political skills. Yet the delay Henry had won, stretching the negotiations into December, proved decisive in the suppression of the rising. The momentum of the Pilgrimage of Grace had been lost. When Aske and Norfolk had met on 27 October, nearly forty thousand men had stood in the rebel ranks. Now when they met again on 6 December, Aske was supported by only thirty of his followers. Norfolk listened gravely to the Pilgrims' articles, promised that the king would grant a pardon and call a Parliament (but himself did neither in the king's name), and ended with vague promises that all complaints would be given a hearing. Within two days, Aske had announced the king's promise of pardon and, laying down his own badge of the five wounds of Christ, exhorted his followers to return home. The Pilgrimage of Grace was over.[42]

Henry's Lancaster Herald was soon reading a promise of pardon throughout the north, and Norfolk returned to court, arriving at York Place by 15 December. Henry was disappointed that none of the rebel leaders had been executed, but he must have been satisfied with Norfolk's conduct, for by the end of the year, plans were being drawn up for the duke to go north in the spring as the king's lieutenant, heading a reestablished Council of the North.[43]

Norfolk was at Kenninghall looking after local affairs, his instructions not yet drafted, when new troubles in the north began. Aske had accepted Henry's invitation and come to court in December, but when he returned to York on 8 January, he could offer his worried followers nothing more than the king's vague assurances that Norfolk would soon return to hold a northern Parliament at York, and that Henry might bring Jane Seymour there for her coronation as well. There was no pledge to dismiss Cromwell, nor to slow the assault on the church. It was all too clear to many, if not yet to Aske, that Henry was stalling and had no intention of keeping his promises. In January, Sir Francis Bigod and several others renewed the rebellion and led unsuccessful attacks against Hull, Scarborough and Beverly.[44] When word of these troubles reached the king, it gave him the excuse he had certainly wanted to revoke Norfolk's promises of pardon and to take revenge against his ungrateful subjects.

On 16 January Norfolk received instructions to return north. Howard wrote a series of letters to Darcy, Constable and others to meet him at Doncaster or Pomfret to hear the king's new orders for the rule of the north.[45] Norfolk headed north late in January, reaching Lincoln by the end of the month. At Doncaster on 2 February Norfolk displayed his banner and proclaimed his commission as king's lieutenant north of Trent. All unauthorized assemblies were prohibited, and Bigod was declared a traitor with a reward of forty pounds offered for his capture. Perhaps to Norfolk's relief, these new risings were much smaller and less well organized than the original Pilgrimage of Grace. Most of the trouble was from small groups of landholders and laborers who feared that Aske had betrayed them and believed that the king's pardon would not save them from prosecution. As Norfolk noted, the gentlemen of the shire were no longer in rebellion, but instead had taken the lead in putting down the disturbances.[46] The artificial social unity of the Pilgrimage of Grace was no more; those gentlemen who might have sympathized with Darcy now made haste to flock to Norfolk's banner and dispel any hint of treason by aiding the suppression of the rebellion.

By 11 February Norfolk reported that Bigod had been captured and that executions of the rebels would begin the next day. The disturbances were not yet over, however, for on 14 February the village of Kirk-by-Stephen rose against one of Norfolk's men when he tried to arrest a suspected rebel and, more seriously, the same day a mob of nearly six thousand rose in Cumberland and marched on Carlisle. This last arose out of the general mood of despair over the failure of the northern risings of 1536–37, but may have been directly sparked by the earl of Cumberland's eviction of tenants and enclosure of arable land. The city resisted the ill-armed mob, and by the time Norfolk arrived at Barnard Castle with four thousand men on 17 February there was little to do but accept the submission of the rebels and round up the leaders for punishment. Norfolk reported that seventy-four men would be hanged as an example, a dozen at Carlisle and the rest at their home villages. To obtain even this many convictions, Norfolk had been forced to proceed under martial law. Local juries, he said, would not have convicted one in five of the rebels.[47]

More executions followed as Norfolk moved through the north. The duke was aware, nonetheless, that too severe a retribution would not chasten, but would cause bitter resentment and, perhaps, new troubles. Therefore, he suggested to Cromwell on 8 March that about twenty men each should suffer in Durham and York; of twenty-four under arrest in Newcastle, the duke would hang as many as "good evidence" would allow, and then he would move on to seek convictions in the smaller towns. Sixteen were eventually condemned in Durham and another thirteen hanged at Lancaster.[48]

While most of Norfolk's victims died quickly under martial law, the leaders of the risings were brought to justice more slowly. Darcy and Sir Robert Constable went to London to face Henry of their own will, perhaps hoping to brazen their way out of the treason charges they faced. Robert Aske traveled south under a safe-conduct issued by Norfolk. The duke, however, had no doubt about what should be done with all of these men. He advised Cromwell to examine Aske in order to obtain evidence against Darcy and Constable—all of whom Norfolk thought deserving of punishment for their offenses. "Hemlock," he noted, "is no worse in a good salad than the remaining of any of them in these parts should be to the commonwealth." Bigod alone went to London as a prisoner, sent in chains in March along with a dozen other ringleaders of the 1537 risings. To insure that none of these men would escape punishment, Norfolk convened two grand juries, one of friends and relatives of the accused and the other of men Norfolk could expect to do as he wished. By this means, the kinsmen of the rebels could prove their loyalty by indicting the chosen victims—or paint themselves with the same color of treason if they refused. With this threat hanging over their heads, the men of the first jury returned indictments against all of the accused.[49]

By 7 April Aske, Darcy and Constable joined Bigod in the Tower. None of them confessed to treason, but the outcome was beyond doubt and all were convicted. Aske and Constable were sent north in late June and, under Norfolk's supervision, hung in chains at York and Hull. Bigod was hanged at Tyburn as a lesson to Londoners on 2 June, while Darcy was accorded a peer's beheading on Tower Hill on 30 June.[50] In all, around two hundred died for their parts in the northern rebellions—over a third of them at Carlisle for a rising that had little to do with the Pilgrimage of Grace or Bigod's revolt.[51] Norfolk supervised most of the executions and, in the process, was reminded again of the cost of disloyalty to Henry VIII. The vigor with which Howard carried out the king's revenge was the most decisive statement he could make about his own loyalty, but Norfolk showed a taste for blood in his own right that was just as grim as his king's.

During the turmoil of the Pilgrimage of Grace and its aftermath, several dissolved religious houses had been reoccupied, and others, scheduled for destruction, had gained respite. While Robert Radcliff, earl of Sussex, set to work dissolving several Lancashire houses, Norfolk took charge of the dissolution of Sawley Abbey, Newminster Abbey and St. Agatha's Priory, all in Yorkshire, and Lanercost Priory in Cumberland. Henry was in no mood for opposition, and he ordered Norfolk to "cause all the monkes and chanons that be in any wise faultie, to be tyed upp, without further delaye or ceremony, to the terrible example of others."[52] The fate of the residents of these houses is not clear, although the abbot of Sawley was executed for treason along with at least one of his monks. Norfolk also personally directed the dissolution of the monastery at Hexham, apparently peacefully, as well as the seizure and dismantling of Bridlington Priory. Most of the monks executed in 1537 suffered for treasons committed during the rebellions. The most striking deaths for religious reasons involved two monks from Hull, John Rochester and man named Walworth, who attempted to persuade Norfolk of the error of the royal supremacy. This affront touched the duke deeply—or so he told Cromwell in reporting the incident. "I believe he [Rochester] is one of the most arrant traytours of all the others I have heard of," the duke wrote. "Two more wilful religious men, in manner unlearned, I think, never suffered."[53]

By the end of March Norfolk had begun to chafe under his enforced absence from court. On 31 March and again on 2 April, he wrote to Cromwell complaining that his own affairs were going to ruin while he labored in the north. In the meantime, the cold damp climate was damaging his health. If he remained longer, he wrote, those who wished his life shortened would have their desire.[54] Norfolk felt that his work in subduing and pacifying the north had not been properly rewarded. Instead of being allowed to return to court in renewed authority, he found himself isolated in Yorkshire carrying out tasks better suited for the local justices of the peace. Henry tended to forget those not in daily attendance at court, granting favors to men about him at the moment. Norfolk had learned this lesson in his own battles against Wolsey, and now, as the forgotten servant, he was impatient to return to London. Norfolk's pleas were answered by assurances that he was not kept away from court through lack of favor, but because his presence was essential for the good ordering of the north. On 8 April Henry sent Norfolk a personal letter assuring him that he cherished the duke's good health as much as his own, but ordering him to remain where he was until further notice.[55]

There was, in fact, another reason for Norfolk's continued residence beyond Trent. The Henrician Reformation had created new tensions with a still-Catholic Scotland and especially with James V, who had reached manhood in the years since Flodden and had deep resentments against Henry VIII and England. In January 1537 James sailed to France to marry a daughter of Francis I, thereby reaffirming the Auld Alliance.

Further, James took as his leading councilor David Beaton, archbishop of St. Andrews in succession to his uncle James; Scottish policy was now dominated by a staunchly pro-French Catholic party. For the moment, Francis was immersed in an Italian war with Charles V, ignoring the pleas of Paul III to turn against England instead. Should France give the signal, however, Scotland appeared ready to renew the Border wars. This worrisome possibility, reported to Cromwell by his agent Ralph Sadler, provided additional justification for Norfolk's presence in the north.[56] Norfolk was well aware of the Scottish threat. In July the duke investigated an obscure plot by some disgruntled northerners to aid a Scottish invasion. Although no significant conspiracy could be uncovered, a priest, Robert Hodge, and two Yorkshire sailors were executed after Hodge confessed that he hoped to see James V invade and claim Henry VIII's throne. Hodge was unrepentant to the end, declaring that he wished he could see Norfolk and Cranmer, the authors of the north's misery, hanged on opposite sides of a tree![57]

Because of these unsettling events Norfolk inspected fortifications, including the castles at Wark, Berwick and Carlisle, sent reports on Scottish affairs to Cromwell, the council and Henry, and exchanged letters with Henry's sister Margaret and the archbishop of Glasgow, chancellor of Scotland. Norfolk steadfastly denied that there was any real threat of Scottish invasion, and although events proved him right, the unrest in Scotland was useful to Cromwell in keeping Norfolk out of the way.[58]

Meanwhile, Norfolk was left so far out of touch with events at court that when Henry met with Scottish ambassadors at Ampthill, Bedfordshire, in early August, the duke did not attend the meetings. In a letter to Cromwell on 8 August Norfolk complained that his valuable advice was ignored because "sore back frendes" at court poisoned Henry's mind against him. Ironically, Norfolk was forced to plead with Cromwell (surely the leading "back frende") to intercede with the king. "What is myne offence," Norfolk asked, "that I may not have license to see my Master, whom I love as intirely, and desire as moche to see, as any lyving man doth?" At the bottom of this letter the duke wrote a holograph note: "My gode Lord, I pray you think that the losse of one of my fyngers shuld not be so moche to my sorow, as to be in feare not to see my Maister at this tyme."[59] Most of Norfolk's surviving letters were written by clerks in neat secretary hand. Although Norfolk's handwriting was terrible and his spelling erratic, his holograph communications were usually like this one—pithy and deeply felt. It is in these occasional outbursts when Howard took pen in hand that we see the man's character most clearly.

Indeed, Norfolk had a point; the king could scarcely complain that the north remained in disorder or that Norfolk had failed in his duties. As early as 18 May, the duke was able to brag that "this cuntire, thanked be God, is, I think, at this houre, in as gode obedience, as any part of the realme." Henry had appointed a number of aristocrats sympathetic to the Pilgrimage of Grace to the northern council, which both demonstrated the breadth of the royal pardon and assured that a thorough job would be done in restoring the north to order. As Rachel Reid noted, "the government of the North could be safely entrusted to them, since there was none to whom they might look for help if they offended the king."[60] The ploy succeeded, for the lands north of Trent were reduced to uncharacteristic order in the spring of 1537. Yet Norfolk was far from satisfied with his reward for this accomplishment; by July he was again complaining of ill health and asking to be replaced. The good order of the north could surely now survive his recall, as he told Cromwell in a letter of 8 July:

> And, good my Lord, beleve not that, though the best were to have a Lieutenaunt here, but that, withowte any, and with a good Cownsail, and a good President, a good minister of justice, and so using hymself that men may be affrayed of hym, this countrey is nowe in that sorte, that none of the realm shalbe better governed than this. And, if that it shalbe thought at any tyme hereafter, so long as I shalbe hable to ryde, that by my sone commyng hither, I myght do His Highnes acceptable service, I shalbe, uppon three dayes warnyng, redy to lepe on horseback with 100 of my household servauntes at the lest, well horsed. Finallie, concernyng this matier, my good Lord, I require youe eftsones, if ye love my lyff, help me owte of this dawngier.[61]

As early as 12 June, Henry had hinted that Norfolk might be relieved, and had asked the duke's advice on a replacement. Norfolk nominated Cuthbert Tunstall, bishop of Durham, who had served on Richmond's council after 1525 and was an experienced northern hand. Despite his protests that he, too, was ill and could not afford the appointment, Tunstall was eventually named lord president of the council in the north, at the comforting salary of eight hundred pounds a year.[62]

It is not clear when Tunstall arrived at York to take up his duties, but a succession of letters through August and September reveal Norfolk still at his post, patience wearing thin. The onset of autumn found him ill with what sounds like influenza, so stricken that he was unable to ride for several days. Nonetheless, Norfolk begged Cromwell to hasten Tunstall northward. The duke's purse was long since bare, he said, and his aggravation grew daily that "my lorde of Duresme dothe make small haste hither."[63] The last letter that Norfolk wrote from the north, dated 7 October 1537, was written from Owlerton, Yorkshire, a town southwest of Doncaster. A week later, Tunstall had arrived in the north, and, in his first letter to Cromwell, noted that Norfolk had already departed. Tunstall had to forward several letters to Norfolk, who must have left Owlerton suddenly, for, despite his professed poor health, he was at Hampton Court by 15 October.[64]

Norfolk reached court just in time to join an elated Henry VIII in celebrating the birth of his long-awaited son and Tudor heir. On 12 October Jane Seymour gave birth to a boy named in honor of the feast of St. Edward the following day. Norfolk attended the christening on 15 October and along with Cranmer and Suffolk was named a godfather. Three days later, Norfolk was present for the ceremonies in which Edward Seymour was elevated to the earldom of Hertford, Sir William Fitzwilliam was made earl of Southampton, and Jane's brother Thomas and several others were knighted.[65] The significance of these creations was unmistakable; Norfolk's attendance as earl marshal could not disguise the fact that the party of Cromwell and the Seymours had taken firm command at court.

On 24 October, in the midst of the celebrations, Queen Jane died. She had been delivered of Edward by Caesarian section and had never left her childbed. Norfolk and Sir William Paulet were commissioned to conduct the funeral held on 12 November in the royal chapel at Hampton Court. Norfolk gave orders for twelve hundred masses to be sung for Jane's soul and presided over a week of vigils, masses and formal court mourning before Jane was laid to rest.[66]

The onset of winter found Norfolk again thrust aside. His ceremonial duties done, the duke was apparently unwelcome at court. Henry himself kept New Year's Day with Cromwell and Hertford at his elbow, but Norfolk is unmentioned in the records for the holiday except as a giver of the expected gifts to Henry and Edward.[67] Norfolk passed the winter at Kenninghall where, late in February, his first grandson was born. He wrote Cromwell to report the birth of this namesake, Thomas, and also to complain of his financial problems. The building of Kenninghall had doubtless cut deeply into the duke's reserves, for he wrote that he was two thousand pounds poorer than he had been a year before, noting somewhat resignedly that "a man can not have his cake and eat his cake."[68]

Through the winter, Norfolk remained isolated from affairs at court; on 25 March he wrote to Cromwell to ask how relations with Francis and Charles fared. A week later, Cromwell wrote to Sir Thomas Wyatt, the ambassador to the imperial court, noting that Norfolk, although named to a commission to treat with Chapuys and Mendoza, the imperial residents in London, would be absent from the talks. Only in May 1538 did Norfolk reappear at court, and then the French ambassador Castillon made the telling remark that Norfolk had been long absent because of the enmity of the lord privy seal, Cromwell. Henry and his agents were by now deeply enmeshed in the negotiations that would lead to the marriage to Anne of Cleves, so that Norfolk, with his French pension and pro-French politics, was "so snubbed and suspect for the affairs of France that for the present his advice is not much asked."[69]

From 1536 to 1538, Norfolk learned to his intense displeasure that Henry valued the talents of Cromwell more highly than the noble blood and servile loyalty of a duke. The suppression of the Pilgrimage of Grace had seemed a great opportunity for Norfolk. Perhaps Cromwell, the author of the policies being so forcefully protested, would fall from power; at the least, Norfolk hoped to regain favor with the king in return for his loyal service. Instead, he gained a prize he found he little desired as lieutenant of the north. Norfolk always had difficulty concealing his desire to be rewarded for his service; his family pride and greed for advancement were never far below the surface of his frequently self-proclaimed loyalty to the crown. Cromwell, like Wolsey, saw Norfolk as too dangerous to have about the king, and thus did all he could to keep Howard as far from Henry as possible.

The rise of the Seymours through Henry's marriage to Jane was unfortunate for Norfolk as well, for Cromwell's position was strengthened through the aid and support of the king's brother-in-law. Not until 1538–39, when Gardiner returned to court from diplomatic service, would Norfolk be able to build a conservative alliance strong enough to counter Cromwell and the progressives. Perhaps Norfolk learned a valuable lesson from the years following Anne's fall, that Cromwell's party at court could only be defeated by building a counter-party of his own, one equally able to serve the king. As events of the late 1530s would show, few at court were willing to risk their lives for the sake of political or religious policy, and Norfolk would benefit from the pliability of Audley, Southampton and others when he mounted his effort to topple Cromwell. During the years after Anne's fall, there could be little doubt that Cromwell and Norfolk would eventually come to open battle. By 1538, the issues of religious policy and diplomatic alliance over which the battle would be fought were becoming clear, the conservative, pro-French Norfolk versus the progressive Cromwell seeking alliance in Germany. It remained to be seen what issue would bring open battle, and whether Cromwell, despite his apparent power, could avoid Wolsey's fate if ever he faltered in serving the erratic Henry VIII.

CHAPTER 7

NORFOLK AND CROMWELL, 1538–1540

WITH THE DEATH OF JANE SEYMOUR in October 1537, Henry VIII paused for only the briefest period of official mourning before beginning the search for a new bride. Even before Jane's funeral Cromwell wrote to Gardiner and William Howard, the English residents in France, that the council had persuaded the king to marry again.[1] The prospects for a notable match seemed excellent; Charles V and Francis I were still at odds, and both had hopes of renewed alliance with England to tilt the balance of power. The imperial envoy, Don Diego Hurtado de Mendoza, had already raised the idea of an understanding based on yet another proposed marriage for the princess Mary; perhaps other arrangements might be made now that the king himself was free. Henry could also look to France, where over a dozen possible brides were available.[2] Despite these promising prospects, it would take Henry two years to find a new wife, and, after all the tortuous diplomacy involved, he would find himself saddled with a marvelously bad choice in Anne of Cleves.

In the Cleves alliance lay, at least in part, the seeds of Cromwell's destruction. The events of the later 1530s involving Norfolk's resurgence after the Pilgrimage of Grace and the fall of Cromwell are complex and have been subjected to widely varying interpretations. The problems of foreign policy, the religious settlement, and the making and unmaking of the king's marriages played a major role in the course of Norfolk's career in the years from 1538 to 1540. From Norfolk's perspective, the growing conflict with Cromwell for political dominance was the major focus and, like the period of the later 1520s and the fall of Wolsey, it was a perilous time; by 1540 the tension between conservatives and progressives at court was so great that someone would have to be destroyed to restore equilibrium. Norfolk did not singlehandedly destroy Cromwell, but as with the events of the fall of Wolsey, he was a major participant and, at least briefly, the main beneficiary. From the perspective of four and half centuries, the historian has a strange sense of *déjà vu* in reviewing the events of the 1530s; one wonders if Norfolk had the same feelings.

Norfolk found himself isolated from court for the first six months of Henry's latest search for a queen. The duke was able to reclaim some influence mainly through his diplomatic skills and his connections in France. When Norfolk returned to court in May 1538, Henry had already sent his court painter, Hans Holbein, to make portraits of several ladies. Cromwell, who much preferred an imperial alliance, urged Henry to consider Christina of Denmark, the emperor's niece, but the king was more intrigued by the French maidens. The result was Norfolk's recall to lead an embassy to France, and a sudden if temporary decline in Cromwell's influence. The French ambassador Castillon reported that on 14 May Henry publicly rebuked Cromwell, accusing him of being more in the emperor's service than his own. The king told Cromwell that he was a good manager, but not fit to meddle in the high affairs of kings. Through the month following this blowup, Castillon remained in high favor, receiving a shower of presents from Henry; Cromwell, Castillon wrote to Francis, absorbed Henry's lecture and took the hint, and began displaying more friendship to France.[3] Henry VIII was always a hard and capricious master; those like Norfolk who survived his reign had to be scrupulously loyal to the king, whatever his latest whims, and ever willing to follow the shifts and turns of royal policy. Cromwell ultimately fell into the same trap as Wolsey and came to believe that he knew better than the king what was best for the kingdom, but, at least for the moment in 1538, he learned his lesson and bent to the king's will.

As it turned out, Henry overplayed his hand with the French, demanding recognition of his title as supreme head of the church in England and unqualified support against any papal-imperial entente as part of any marital deal. Henry also insulted Francis by asking that several prospective brides be brought to Calais for his inspection.[4] Norfolk remained at court while all of this went on, actively pushing for a French match. As the negotiations foundered, however, the tone of the talks began to change. Henry's often-proclaimed love for Francis faded as his demands were refused. On 8 June, Norfolk lectured Castillon on Francis's duty to aid England against the emperor, warning that Henry would renounce France and join Charles in a war to wipe out the French gains in Italy.[5] This was a futile threat, as proved late in June when Francis and Charles agreed at Nice on a truce mediated by Pope Paul III. Norfolk's usefulness declined rapidly as the immediacy of the talks with France slackened, and by the first of August he was back at Kenninghall.[6] Although the failure of the French negotiations left Norfolk in political eclipse, his momentary importance while they went on foreshadowed the situation two years later. The making of the Cleves marriage was largely Cromwell's work; the blame would be laid on those who supported it, while Norfolk and those who had not would gain renewed influence and show their loyalty to the king by carrying out the latest judicial murder of an increasingly bloody reign.

Another episode in the summer of 1538 further weakened Norfolk's position. The birth of Prince Edward left the Seymours entrenched at court despite Jane's death. Norfolk, recognizing political necessity, was prepared to swallow his considerable dynastic pride and make alliance with the upstarts, and so he offered to wed his daughter Mary, widow of the duke of Richmond, to Hertford's younger brother Sir Thomas Seymour. Everyone involved—even, perhaps surprisingly, Cromwell—approved of the match. Norfolk averred gamely that, after all, there was much to be said for noble-commoner matches; "there ensueth no grete good by the conjunction of grete bloodes together."[7]

Early in June Henry consented to the marriage and ordered Cromwell to do everything necessary to further it. All that remained was the formality of Mary Howard's assent. To the surprise of everyone, and certainly to Norfolk's great chagrin, the dowager duchess of Richmond refused. Perhaps Mary was concerned that a new marriage would prevent her from obtaining her dower rights as Fitzroy's widow; although in January 1533 Cranmer had confirmed the marriage as lawfully contracted, she had never gained royal confirmation of her claims. Yet the real stumbling block to the match was placed by Mary's brother Henry, earl of Surrey. In July 1537, Surrey and Edward Seymour had almost come to blows at court; according to some accounts, Surrey actually struck Seymour—a serious offense against the king's peace. Seymour had provoked Surrey by repeating rumors of Norfolk's sympathy with the Pilgrimage of Grace. Surrey spent several months in confinement at Windsor, during which his resentment of the Seymours only grew. Apparently Surrey persuaded his sister to refuse Seymour's hand, for Mary left court in July determined not to wed Sir Thomas, and although Norfolk followed her to Kenninghall, he was unable to change her mind; the proposed match was ruined, and with it Norfolk's chances of an immediate return to a place of influence at court.[8]

The failure of the Howard-Seymour dynastic alliance had nothing to do with either political factions or religious positions, but with political expediency and personalities, a circumstance that raises interesting questions about the depth of either Norfolk's or Seymour's attachment to faction and faith. Survival at Henry's court demanded flexibility. The failure of the Thomas Seymour–Mary Howard match—and the hotheaded Surrey's central role in it—foreshadowed the fall of the Howards eight years later. Had Surrey not intervened and had Mary wed Sir Thomas, the politics of the 1540s might have taken a very different course.

Norfolk spent the late summer and autumn of 1538 in rustic isolation, busy with investigating troubles in East Anglia. On 9 August Norfolk and Sir Roger Townshend reported to Cromwell on rumors that the king intended to seize all unmarked cattle for his own use—a groundless but potentially seditious bruit which enjoyed wide circulation in Norfolk and Suffolk.[9] Norfolk also joined with the county justices of assize and the bishop of Norwich in examining a hermit who denied the royal supremacy. Anthony Browne, late a friar observant at Greenwich, proved to be a man "smally lerned and as little reasonable," but the county authorities nonetheless sent him to London for examination by the council before his execution.[10]

Norfolk had some contact with the court during these months; Thomas Audley, the chancellor, visited the duke at Framlingham in September "to kyll sum of his bukkes there"[11] and surely to talk politics as well. Norfolk's banishment was not without justification, for East Anglia was unusually unruly in 1538, and Howard was concerned to maintain order in his shires; the "good lordship" of a feudal magnate such as Norfolk required his frequent attention to local matters. Norfolk made a point of sitting with the quarter sessions in October, having first asked Cromwell for a letter to use during the court term, declaring the king's unhappiness with the unrest in the shire. Norfolk and the justices dealt with a number of local problems, including the surrender of the house of the White and Black Friars to the crown. Norfolk was careful to send the surrender petition, addressed to "the high and mighty prince Thomas duke of Norfolk," to Cromwell for approval.[12]

Rumors were abroad in the summer of 1538 that Paul III would finally promulgate Henry's sentence of excommunication. Reginald Pole, now a cardinal, was roaming the continent on a papal mission to bring Charles and Francis into an offensive alliance against Henry and to raise a Catholic rebellion in his realm. Being a cardinal was a perilous business in Henrician England. Thomas Wolsey had died in spite of his red hat, John Fisher in part because of his, and Reginald Pole would have as well had Henry been able to lay hands on him. Even with Pole out of reach, Henry was convinced that treason was in the air, and he responded by launching investigations into the dealings of Pole's friends and relatives. Sir Geoffrey Pole was sent to the Tower on 29 August 1538, and by October was providing a rambling series of statements that hinted of vague treasons committed or planned by the Catholic aristocracy. The net was soon cast wider to include most of the leading members of Pole's family and their sympathizers, the remnants of the "Aragonese" party at the time of Anne's fall and during the Pilgrimage of Grace. The leading victim of this sweep was Henry Courtenay, marquis of Exeter, whose most notable crime was great popularity in the west of the realm, which gave rise to rumors that he would assert his Plantagenet blood and claim the throne should the Tudor line falter. Stephen Gardiner, too, fell under investigation and nearly went to the Tower on charges preferred by Sir Ralph Sadler that Winchester wished to patch things up with Rome. The charges, in Gardiner's case, may have been true, but Gardiner had no royal blood and no obvious ties to the Poles and might prove useful in the future, so Henry spared him.[13]

Henry was always murderously suspicious of any threat to the succession—witness the deaths of Buckingham and More—and now he scented treason in the blood of the Poles and was determined to wipe out the family. Norfolk was in council on 1 December when the accused were examined, and served on the commissions that tried Henry Pole, lord Montague, Sir Geoffrey Pole and Sir Edward Neville—the latter a close friend of Cardinal Pole whose main crime was his overt Catholicism. By 9 December Montague, Exeter and Neville had been convicted and executed; Geoffrey was pardoned for his assistance in bringing the others to justice and was allowed to flee to the continent.[14]

The last of the Pole group to be destroyed was Sir Nicholas Carew, master of the horse and, like Neville, a member of Henry's household. Carew was found guilty of high treason on 14 February 1539 by a commission headed by Audley, Norfolk, Suffolk and Cromwell. Carew had been a member of the victorious faction in the court struggle surrounding the fall of Anne Boleyn, and his destruction along with that of Exeter and the Poles lends credence to the view that court politics played a role in the so-called Exeter conspiracy. Certainly the destruction of the Poles, Exeter, Neville and Carew was prompted in large part by Reginald Pole's threatening activities on the continent, but the choice of victims was also influenced by the factional politics of the previous several years. In destroying Neville, Exeter and Carew, Cromwell wiped out the remnant of the group that had tried to restore Mary Tudor to the succession in 1536. Whether or not a conspiracy to return England to Rome through a rebellion under Pole's leadership was a real threat in 1538, certainly it provided a convenient cover for Cromwell to finish off a struggle which had been going on since his own rise to power had ushered in a turn toward more progressive religious policies.[15]

For conservatives such as Norfolk and Gardiner—as well as Catholic Henricians such as Audley, Southampton and Russell who had been content to support Cromwell as long as he held Henry's favor—the object lesson from these proceedings must have been clear. Exeter and the Poles held political and religious positions beyond the allowable limits of the Henrician spectrum. Conservative Henricianism and support of a distinct line of political and religious policy were one thing; adherence to Roman Catholicism, if it meant even the faintest hint of support for alterations in the succession in favor of Mary or Henry Courtenay, was quite another. If Norfolk needed any reminder of the need for unquestioned loyalty to the king and his policies, surely the uncovering of the Exeter "conspiracy" was sufficient. There was a very serious difference between court politics and opposition to the crown. It was possible to contest Cromwell only on issues where Henry, the only one whose opinion ultimately mattered, had not made up his mind. Norfolk and Gardiner increasingly were becoming Cromwell's clearest opponents in council, but even while seeking the lord privy seal's ruin, they recognized the difference between political opposition and treason. The Exeter-Pole group had produced a clear traitor in Reginald Pole; the Gardiner-Howard party would not.

Just as the prosecution of Pole's followers was being completed, Rome published (but still did not promulgate) the bull for Henry's excommunication. This act was intended as the final step in bringing Catholic Europe together in a crusade against England and, indeed, for a while Henry seemed in real danger. The French were busy encouraging the Scots to invade—there were rumors of an army of twenty thousand men under the duke of Guise preparing to embark for Scotland—and the movements of Italian cavalry in French pay near Calais were anxiously watched.[16] Reginald Pole renewed his efforts to persuade Francis and Charles to take up arms against Henry; most alarmingly, on 12 January 1539 the emperor and the French king met at Toledo to sign a new pact by which each promised not to make any agreement with England without the consent of the other—a major step toward an offensive alliance against the heretical English.[17]

In fact, this all proved a false alarm. Charles was too preoccupied with problems in Germany and with the Turks to entertain the enterprise of England, and Francis, although willing to incite the Scots, could not afford war either. Yet the early months of 1539 looked perilous indeed from the perspective of London. The direct result for the Howards was an upsurge in influence. With the country in a frenzy of preparations for the feared invasion, Norfolk's military expertise became very valuable. In February 1539 he was appointed to oversee defense of the coasts and preparation of the border castles of Berwick and Carlisle.[18] The duke spent much of the spring in the north surveying defenses and reporting on the stirrings in Scotland. After several months of study, Norfolk wrote to Cromwell in April to offer his opinion that, although the Scots did not seek war, they would follow the lead of France, for they dared not break the Auld Alliance.[19]

Norfolk's mission in the north surely was Cromwell's idea, for the lord privy seal was anxious to keep the duke away from court. Demands of foreign affairs as well as Henry's desire to formulate a lasting doctrinal statement for the church were to work against Cromwell's plans. During early 1539 Norfolk began to see the tide turning in his favor in the struggle against Cromwell. In March Mary Howard's suit to obtain a share of Richmond's lands was finally granted by the king, and the same month Norfolk was given several parcels of monastic lands; as a mark of favor, the lands, buildings and possessions of the house of the Friars Minor of Norwich were granted to the duke without rent or fee.[20]

Norfolk returned to Kenninghall by 13 April, his northern mission complete, and by 27 April was in London for the opening of Parliament. Norfolk appears to have offered some assistance to Cromwell's efforts to insure the king a tractable House of Commons,[21] but the duke had a considerable bloc of supporters in that house, and Gardiner made his ambitions clear by attempting to have his own rather than Cromwell's nominees returned in the boroughs he controlled as bishop of Winchester.[22] If Norfolk's hostility to Cromwell was still masked by a show of deference, Gardiner, a bitter and arrogant man, made no secret of his resentment over his years of political isolation while Cromwell was supreme.

It was clear from the outset that this Parliament of 1539 would be a battleground between Cromwell and his conservative foes, and that Henry was inclined to side with Norfolk and Gardiner rather than his vicegerent. Cromwell, like Wolsey before him, was finding that those who shaped the king's policy bore the blame when events did not work out to Henry's entire satisfaction. The peril of a Catholic invasion of an increasingly Protestant England must have had something to do with Henry's sudden show of orthodoxy, but the impression remains that Cromwell's progressive policies of the 1530s had been tolerated more than enthusiastically supported by the king. Henry VIII was never himself a Protestant by any useful definition, a point that is sometimes blurred by the strength of Cromwell and Cranmer after the fall of Anne Boleyn. Henry's "Protestantism" arose out of political and diplomatic and not religious drives. Even the religious persecutions of the 1530s, such as the hanging of recalcitrant monks after the Pilgrimage of Grace, were motivated more by political and dynastic concerns than by any real rejection of Catholic dogma, as the events of the last years of Henry's reign would show.

Since the Ten Articles of 1536, several sets of injunctions and proclamations on matters of the faith had been issued. The last such, Henry's proclamation of November 1538, was an attack on the more radical sectaries and a warning that too much change could not be tolerated, although Cromwell was able to prevent any major changes in his rather Protestant policies at that time.[23] At the opening of Parliament in April, Cromwell was ill and missed the first several sittings, not attending until 10 May. By that time Nicholas Hare, a Norfolk client, had been elected Speaker. Hare was a conservative who served as the duke's understeward in the Court of Augmentations and eventually would be an executor of his will.

His selection as speaker, while indicative of royal favor, also showed the renewed influence of Norfolk and his allies. Another curious event may also be evidence of Cromwell's suddenly shaky position in early 1539. The opening speech, in which the causes of calling Parliament were explained to a joint session of both houses, was customarily given by the chancellor. Audley, who despite his conservatism was a Cromwell man, was perfectly healthy at the opening of the session, yet the address was given instead by Norfolk's in-law Robert Radcliff, earl of Sussex. If the roles of Hare and Sussex in the opening of Parliament are evidence, Norfolk and Gardiner had benefitted greatly from the foreign crisis and Henry's cooling zeal for radicalization of the English church in early 1539.[24]

The main business before Parliament was the drafting of a set of statutory articles of religion. The Ten Articles had been approved by Convocation alone and, although strictly orthodox as far as they went, mentioned only three sacraments, leaving out marriage, extreme unction, holy orders and confirmation. By their brevity the Ten Articles left many openings for either Catholic or Protestant interpretation. These articles were amplified and enforced by Cromwell's injunctions of 1536, which struck a more clearly Protestant tone than the articles themselves.[25] In 1537, another extraparliamentary statement was attempted in "The Godly and Pious Institutions of a Christian Man," better known as the "Bishops' Book." This was something of a conservative victory as the missing sacraments were explained and the observation of saints' days and other ancient customs were approved explicitly, although only as *adiophora* or indifferent things, not grounded in divine law. The Bishops' Book was never approved by Convocation or Parliament, and only received Henry's conditional approval. The Bishops' Book was published, however, and when Henry's proclamation of November 1538 is added to the balance, it is evident that the official theology of the English church had become a dangerously vague muddle in the face of a hostile Catholic Europe and amidst talk of a crusade against the heretical Henry VIII. Therefore the Parliament of 1539 was given the task of producing a statute to stand beside the act of supremacy and the other work of the Reformation Parliament; at last there was to be a clear and enforceable statement of Henrician doctrine.[26]

In the resultant Parliamentary debate, differences over religion and politics combined to produce at least the appearance of true parties arrayed in opposition. Gardiner and Norfolk, with the support of such as Tunstall, led the conservative faction against the progressive Cromwell and Cranmer; the conservatives hoped to use the struggle over religious policy for the political end of discrediting or destroying their progressive rivals.[27] Only as long as the king's mind was uncertain was opposition politics such as this possible. In 1539, the conservatives made the most of their opening; although Cromwell survived the challenge, the passage of the Act of Six Articles showed his vulnerability to attack.

The real peril for Cromwell and his enemies alike lay in the fact that in early 1539 Henry does not seem to have made up his mind on religious doctrine. When, on 5 May, the king asked the House of Lords to draft a new statement to safeguard the unity of the English church, a wide diversity of opinion was represented on the committee appointed. Cromwell as chairman along with Cranmer and Hugh Latimer led the progressives, while Edward Lee and Cuthbert Tunstall stood among the conservatives. Cromwell, although still absent from the house, won a partial victory when Gardiner was excluded from the committee.[28]

This move may have proved a costly mistake, for while the committee spent ten days wrangling, Henry was left to the counsel of Norfolk and Gardiner—and apparently reached a decision of his own on the form the new articles should take. On 16 May Norfolk offered six articles for discussion by the Lords. Since the committee had reached no conclusions, he suggested, these points might serve as a basis for debate in preparing a statutory definition of the faith. The questions offered showed the conservative genesis of the move:

1. Whether the elements of the Eucharist could truly be the body of Christ, except through transubstantiation
2. Whether the laity should receive the sacrament in both kinds
3. Whether vows of chastity made by men and women ought to be perpetually observed under divine law (i.e., by those formerly in religious houses dissolved since 1536)
4. Whether, by divine law, private masses should be celebrated
5. Whether divine law permitted priests to take wives
6. Whether auricular confession was necessary by divine law.[29]

While Cromwell had been sick, and then busy with the committee under his chairmanship, Henry gave in to the urging of Norfolk and Gardiner. The result was this set of conservatively leading questions. Contemporaries believed the articles to have been written by Gardiner, and the earliest draft bears corrections in Henry's hand. Norfolk's role in introducing the questions completes the picture of a conservative party encouraging Henry to push for a heavily Catholic statement of doctrine. Although Norfolk was not the author of the articles, the significance of the duke's sponsorship of the draft could not have been lost on Cromwell.[30]

None of this, perhaps, would have happened had Henry not already been inclined toward a strictly Catholic statement of doctrine. Yet he was still not prepared simply to ram a Catholic settlement through Parliament; what the king wanted was a show of unity in the face of a hostile Europe. The immediate response to Norfolk's articles was disappointing; Cranmer and several other progressive bishops voiced strenuous objections, and Cromwell, perhaps hoping to distract the king by raising other issues, stalled work on the articles while trying to push a subsidy bill through Commons. As a result Henry decided to pause long enough to poll the bishops on the proposed articles—and to persuade the recalcitrant to follow the conservatives' lead.[31] On 20 May Norfolk, still the king's spokesman in the House of Lords, rose to propose a week-long prorogation on the strange pretext that there was not enough time before the scheduled recess on Whitsunday, 25 May, for all the members to offer appropriate thanks to the king for his many efforts to defend the realm. Audley and Cromwell were clearly ordered to go along, for on 23 May Parliament was in fact prorogued for a week, although with the unusual stipulation that all bills already introduced would remain under consideration. This pause was used to pressure the bishops and higher clergy to accept the conservative statement of the faith. At the same time, the delay worked to Cromwell's advantage. There can be little doubt that Norfolk and Gardiner hoped to catch Cromwell in opposition to the articles, perhaps by rushing the king into supporting a strictly conservative statement that Cromwell would be unable to stomach. With any luck, open opposition to the articles by the lord privy seal could be used to trump up charges of treason (a year early) for the suspicious king. Instead, Cromwell had time to adjust and to accede to Henry's will. With the king's mind made up, Cromwell was quick to bend to political necessity.[32]

When Parliament reconvened, Cromwell and Audley were back in charge of the House of Lords. Nonetheless, the act for abolishing diversity of opinion that received royal assent on 28 June was a conservative triumph. Although several amendments weakened provisions of the act, on the whole Norfolk's questions were answered in an orthodox Catholic fashion. From Gardiner's viewpoint, the new statute must have been a great success, for two radical bishops, Hugh Latimer of Worcester and Nicholas Shaxton of Salisbury, resigned their sees rather than subscribe to the act. Nevertheless, and despite a considerable scare, Cromwell retained his authority apparently undiminished. The Act of Six Articles would not, under Cromwell as vicegerent, be strictly enforced; yet it remained the official doctrine of the English church for the rest of Henry's reign, and as such the act was a critical defeat for Cromwell, who learned the danger of pushing his personal beliefs against the king's desires. Perhaps as a result, Parliament, scheduled to resume in November 1539, was twice prorogued without sitting before finally meeting in April 1540 for the last time under Cromwell's management. Control of Parliament had been at the heart of Cromwell's power; shaken in his mastery of that institution, he was not anxious to give his opponents a chance to use it for further attacks.[33]

Cromwell's relations with Gardiner and Norfolk in later 1539 show the seriousness of his concern. Gardiner was busy in his diocese for much of the later half of the year, and Cromwell found no reason to summon him to court. Norfolk, however, remained at court and made his intentions toward Cromwell as clear as he dared. On 29 June Norfolk, Suffolk and Cromwell joined Henry for dinner at Cranmer's house. The conversation turned to Wolsey and those who had served him. Cromwell accused Norfolk of having plotted, had Wolsey become pope, to leave England to become his admiral. Norfolk hotly denied the charges, called Cromwell a liar, and apparently lost his temper altogether, leading to an exchange of recriminations. Cranmer did his best to soothe tempers, but the result was an open breach between Norfolk and Cromwell; for the last year of Cromwell's ministry, there would be no pretense of friendship between the two.[34]

The focus of the rivalry between Norfolk and Cromwell turned from religion to foreign affairs in the second half of 1539. The king was still without a bride and, after the initial hysteria of the campaign to arrange a new marriage had worn off and it became clear that no Catholic crusade was pending, diplomatic efforts to find a suitable match were resumed. The Six Articles mollified Charles and Francis but ruined the already floundering negotiations with the German Lutheran princes among whom

Cromwell had hoped to find an ally. Henry was left with the negotiations opened in 1538 with the duchy of Cleves as the only active prospect for a new marriage in the summer of 1539. Cleves was a small state on the Rhine ruled by a young Catholic of Erasmian leanings with two marriageable sisters. As an ally, Cleves was not without merits. Duke William had ties in Lutheran Germany (his brother-in-law was elector of Saxony), and was not entirely under Charles V's thumb, as the two were at odds over a complex inheritance case. Cleves, in brief, was Catholic but independent and strategically placed between France, Flanders, and the heartland of Germany.[35]

Norfolk had little to do with the diplomatic effort that tied Henry to Anne of Cleves, for which he was soon to be grateful. If anything, Norfolk opposed the match as much as he dared. Marillac, the new French envoy, continued to hope that Henry would listen to Norfolk and the pro-French councilors and resume negotiations for a French bride.[36] But Henry felt that he had been insulted by France, and was no longer looking for a wife there. Marillac's reports make it clear that Henry was not led into the Cleves marriage with his eyes closed. The king followed the negotiations closely and had Holbein's portrait of Anne to study; he could not have been completely surprised that Anne was not a stunning beauty. Further, the king's ambassadors in Germany gave all the hints they dared that Anne was not a lively Renaissance princess. Henry himself pushed the whole business forward. Cromwell was the main architect of the match, but even while he sought to avoid a French marriage which might have raised Norfolk's political stock, he was not fool enough purposely to tie Henry to a stupid or ugly woman. From the middle of the summer until he actually met Anne at Rochester in December, Henry was all enthusiasm for the match; only after the fact did he begin to mutter about the honesty of those who had carried out his will. In retrospect, Norfolk was fortunate to have had no role in the talks which led to the marriage treaty signed on 6 October, although Cromwell probably thought it a victory to have excluded the duke. After the marriage, when Henry's passions had cooled and his suspicions had been aroused, Norfolk was in an admirable position to profit from Cromwell's discomfiture.[37]

Norfolk was among those appointed to meet Anne's party at Rochester after a difficult winter journey from Cleves. Henry did not wait for Anne to come to him, but rushed to Rochester on New Year's Day, bearing gifts and expecting to "nourish love." Instead, after meeting Anne for the first time, Henry slunk back to London, the gifts left to be delivered by others. The king's heart had suddenly grown cold. Anne was nothing like he had hoped, but was a plain-visaged, quiet girl whom Henry knew at once he could never love. Had the international situation been less tense, had Henry been bold enough to risk a diplomatic crisis, Anne would have been sent home and the marriage forsaken. But Charles and Francis were meeting in Paris, and Henry, having been rebuffed by Lutheran Germany after the Six Articles had become law, needed an ally, no matter how small and hesitant. Thus the marriage took place as planned on 6 January after the frantic king had satisfied himself that he had no choice. Henry complained to Cromwell at the last minute, "My lord, if it were not to satisfy the world and my realm, I would not do that I must do this day for none earthly thing." Having married Anne, Henry immediately set his agents to work to find grounds for a divorce to be carried through as soon as the international crisis abated. Cromwell, although the author of the marriage, was not immediately in danger, for Henry needed him to help find a way out of the distasteful situation.[38]

Henry's determination to be rid of this tall, plain-faced maiden, who spoke only German and was given to embroidery rather than dancing, was the opening for which Norfolk had been waiting. Cromwell had won the struggle over foreign policy by matching Henry with a German princess rather than the French maiden Norfolk had favored; now the lord privy seal had to live with the consequences and with the knowledge that his rivals stood ready to pounce if he made any false move.

International affairs initially worked in Cromwell's favor. The Franco-Imperial friendship evidenced by the meeting at Paris late in 1539 was shallower than it appeared, for, among other things, control of Milan remained a divisive issue. Henry decided to send an embassy to France to undermine the shaky alliance between his rivals, and court politics in France seemed to offer promise of success. Anne de Montmorency, constable of France, was an avid supporter of the Franco-Imperial alliance and equally in favor of the pope's schemes to launch a crusade against England. Francis, however, was suspected to be more amenable to an English understanding of some sort. Since Marillac, the French resident in London, was Montmorency's man, any attempt to influence French politics would have to come from direct diplomacy. Thus in February 1540 Norfolk departed

London on a secret mission to the French court, commissioned to woo Francis away from Charles and into England's arms.[39] That anyone went to France at all was a blow to Cromwell, but that Thomas Howard was sent was doubly dangerous. A diplomatic revolution at Norfolk's hands might well signal the end of Cromwell's power.

Norfolk left London as quietly as possible by road around midnight on 13 February. Marillac was fooled; he thought Norfolk was on his way to meet the emperor, who was threatening Cleves, and not his own king. Norfolk's instructions were typical of Henry's diplomacy. In the course of his long, vague, but inflexible orders, Norfolk was commanded to convince Francis that all rumors of an Anglo-Imperial entente were false, and to assure the French king of Henry's most sincere love and respect. Mention was to be made of the pleasing prospects if Charles were to face an alliance of England, France, Cleves and Saxony; in the confusion, France could expect no problems in recovering Milan.[40] Even so, the impression left by Norfolk's instructions is that Henry needed Francis far more than France needed England.

And so it proved. Norfolk found the French court near Abbeville, on the Somme estuary midway between Paris and Calais. Francis received Norfolk on 17 February, accepting protestations of Henry's love warmly enough, but at the mention of Charles and hints that the emperor had ambitions to carve up France, the French king became visibly upset. Norfolk reported that Francis saw through Charles's motives in allying against England; the emperor only wished to keep all in flux while concentrating on Germany so that Milan could remain in his hands. If the purpose of English diplomacy was to sow distrust between Francis and Charles, Norfolk's mission was a success. Yet the broader objective of carrying out a diplomatic reversal failed. Francis would promise no more than to meet with Norfolk again later in the week after discussing affairs with his council.[41]

While waiting to resume talks with the king, Norfolk worked on the court. There he found a party that, if not pro-English, was at least anti-imperial. The most influential member of this faction, the king's mistress, Madame d'Estampes, was supported by his sister Marguerite of Navarre. During mid-February, Norfolk had several talks with Marguerite; there seemed some hope that Francis would consider a new English alliance.[42] At the same time, the duke discovered to his horror that the resident English ambassador in France seemed to be working to ruin any chance of agreement. In three letters of 17 February, including a private holograph note to Henry, Norfolk begged, "For God's sake, revoke the Bishop!" Edmund Bonner, bishop of London, had replaced Gardiner as ambassador to France but, unlike his predecessor, Bonner was a Cromwell man and a virulent enemy of pope and emperor alike, although not a reformer. Bonner's embassy, Castillon told Norfolk, had done more good for Charles V than the emperor, in person, had done the previous December. With Bonner sabre-rattling in France the chances of European peace and English safety were diminished every day. Only if Bonner returned to London was there any hope of Anglo-French alliance, or so Norfolk wrote.[43] Norfolk must have seen the hand of Cromwell behind Bonner, for the thwarting of the duke and his pro-French influence was a cornerstone of the lord privy seal's policy.

Not until 23 February did Norfolk meet again with Francis. In the meantime the duke pled his case with those at the French court who would listen, arguing that Milan would never return to French hands without Henry's aid. Norfolk suspected that Francis could not, for the moment, be brought to an open breach with Charles, but nonetheless the duke felt sure that neither would Francis attack Henry. Thus Norfolk urged gentle handling of the French rather than Bonner's vitriolic agitation. The pro-imperial faction led by Montmorency required special delicacy. "Faire wordes cost little," Norfolk wrote, "I mean towardes the Constable, who being irrytated may do more hurt at this tyme before the conclusion of these maters, than ever I trust it shalbe in his poure to do after."[44]

On 22 February Norfolk received amplified instructions approving his policy of placating Francis while seeking to poison Franco-Imperial relations.[45] As a result, when Francis and Norfolk met again on 23 February, their talk was brief but cordial. The French king was not ready to forsake Charles for Henry; in fact, he had reported Norfolk's veiled allegations of imperial perfidy to the emperor, who had smoothly assured Francis of his honorable intentions. Still, Norfolk did not believe his mission had been wasted, for he had found Marguerite and Madame d'Estampes eager to oppose the imperial influence at the French court. They would certainly keep the issue of Milan alive as a symbol of imperial treachery. In their final meeting Francis assured Norfolk that it would be much easier to come to peaceful terms with England if Cromwell and the Protestant party were

The Ebbs and Flows of Fortune

removed from power—a valuable but dangerous piece of ammunition for the duke in his campaign against the lord privy seal.[46]

Norfolk left Abbeville shortly after his last meeting with Francis, and was in London by 1 March. Norfolk met briefly with Henry to report on his mission, but Cromwell was careful to keep the duke from too much contact with the king. As long as Cromwell remained vulnerable over the unresolved Cleves divorce, Norfolk was too dangerous to allow at Henry's side. Therefore, while Cromwell and Henry went to Hampton Court to plan the opening of Parliament scheduled for April, Norfolk retired to his house in Hertfordshire—as close to London as possible, and not half as distant as Kenninghall. Yet his proximity to court was no guarantee of influence or even information. On 11 March Norfolk wrote Cromwell to ask what would be done concerning France. If his French pension were in danger of being cut off, he wished to know so that he might reduce expenses by lightening his household staff.[47] It seems incredible that Norfolk, just returned from France, would be so in the dark about the results of his diplomacy. Yet Cromwell had launched a counteroffensive against Norfolk and was determined to allow the duke as little influence as possible.

Perhaps in reply to this reminder of Norfolk's persistent interest in court affairs, Cromwell sent Norfolk further away. On 19 March Marillac reported that Howard had been sent north to dissolve an abbey at the vicegerent's orders. Nor did Cromwell make any secret of his feelings toward Norfolk, at least to those he thought loyal. In mid-April Cromwell warned Richard Pate, about to depart on a diplomatic mission to Germany, that association with Norfolk was dangerous. Pate ingratiated himself with Norfolk after Cromwell's arrest by revealing the conversation to the duke, calling Cromwell "him who does not love" Norfolk.[48]

Even while working to isolate Norfolk, Cromwell came under attack from another quarter. In February 1540 Robert Barnes preached a sermon at St. Paul's attacking Gardiner. Barnes, a former Austin friar, had recently been appointed to a benefice by Cromwell. There was nothing shy about Barnes, either in his Lutheran opinions or in his apparent confidence that Cromwell would protect him. Gardiner, armed with the Six Articles and strengthened by Henry's recent fears of Catholic assaults, proved stronger than Barnes had thought. The king ordered Barnes and Gardiner to air their views before the council, and ended up lecturing Barnes for his impertinence and ordering the friar to apologize to Gardiner and recant his forward views. This episode did not quiet Barnes; by 3 April he was in the Tower, having recanted his recantation and heaped further abuse on Gardiner. Marillac was shortly writing to Montmorency that Cromwell was "tottering." The lord privy seal's failure to save Barnes was widely seen as a sign that he was in grave trouble, perhaps soon to follow Barnes to the Tower. As further evidence that and the conservatives were gaining strength, Gardiner, Tunstall and John Clerk, bishop of Bath and Wells, were restored to the council in the spring.[49]

Gardiner's role in the fall of Cromwell remains uncertain. While Elton and Scarisbrick argued for a Norfolk-Gardiner *putsch* in which Henry was tricked into destroying Cromwell (and, by implication, held the progressive Cromwell the innocent victim of the reactionaries), Redworth is not so sure, seeing Gardiner as following Henry's lead rather than steering the king where would otherwise not have gone. Norfolk and Gardiner, Redworth writes, were "too divided over foreign policy to form a single conservative front at court. . . . Far from being a victim of Gardiner's manipulation of faction, Henry VIII had his own motives for removing the best servant he ever had." Whether Henry or Gardiner initiated the investigation of the radical preacher, Cromwell was careful to avoid any involvement with Barnes, and he tried to limit the damage as much as possible. Cromwell had a long and apparently friendly dinner with Gardiner on 30 March that resulted in at least an outward show of amity. Aware of the king's suspicions of heresy and of Barnes's unruly temper, Cromwell knew better than to press his luck. Marillac's optimistic hope of Cromwell's imminent fall was disappointed; Cromwell was able at least to delay disaster by sacrificing Barnes and placating Gardiner.[50]

Norfolk was a somewhat different problem. It was nearly impossible to exclude one of the great officers of state and one of the realm's two dukes from the coming Parliament, yet the passage of the Six Articles was proof of the danger posed by allowing Norfolk and Gardiner to work in concert. Cromwell grasped for any excuse to keep Norfolk from court, for late in March (while the Barnes fiasco was still going on), he apparently wrote to Norfolk ordering him to remain home on the pretext that contagious disease had arisen in his household. The situation is clear from Norfolk's reply of 1 April, in which he assured Cromwell that, although a servant of his had died, the man had not been at Kenninghall, but had been at Framlingham since Christmas. Besides, over a dozen other servants there had not sickened, so there could be no danger to the king in Norfolk's coming to court.[51] When Parliament assembled on 12 April, Thomas Howard took his seat among the lords; Cromwell's ploy had failed.[52]

The events of April 1540—crucial to understanding Cromwell's fall— are difficult to untangle. Early in the month Cromwell surrendered his post as king's secretary. The office was divided between two of his proteges, Ralph Sadler and Thomas Wriothesley. According to Sadler's biographer, A. J. Slavin, Cromwell engineered this move in order to retain supervision of the king's business while at the same time being freed to manage Parliament. Yet there seems some merit in the older view that the change was forced upon Cromwell by the king, and should be seen as evidence of Henry's eroding confidence in Cromwell and thus in the latter's power.[53] The real reasons remain obscure, but despite Sadler and Wroithesley's earlier ties to Cromwell, what may be more important is their subsequent politics. Neither fell from power with Cromwell but rather continued in royal service. Perhaps Cromwell was trying to solidify his position, but when Sadler and Wroithesley became the king's secretaries, they became the king's men. They may well have aided Cromwell as much as possible, but as with all Tudor officials, success and survival depended on loyalty to the monarch; neither proved willing to sacrifice a career, much less to die, for Cromwell.

Clearly Cromwell was becoming concerned with his position in April, for on the eighteenth of the month he finally accepted the earldom which Henry doubtless would have granted earlier had Cromwell thought it necessary. Taking advantage of two recent deaths, Cromwell was created earl of Essex and lord great chamberlain, the latter office a hereditary possession of the de Vere earls of Oxford. As Elton has noted, these creations were a thinly veiled insult to Norfolk, for both the Bourchier and de Vere families had Howard connections. Thus the choice of titles and offices made Cromwell's elevation all the more galling. Norfolk's opinion of Cromwell's elevation is not recorded, but it is not hard to guess that he found the ceremonies of creation and the dinner which followed in the council chamber extremely trying.[54]

Cromwell spelled out the main business of the new session of Parliament in his opening speech. The unity of church and state was to be preserved by the preparation of authoritative statements of doctrine and ceremonial; clearly, Cromwell did not consider the Six Articles the last word on the issue. Two committees of lords—mostly bishops—were selected to prepare draft bills, with Cromwell as vicegerent supervising their work. Unlike 1539 and the preliminaries to the Six Articles, a strong conservative voice was present on the committees with Gardiner, excluded a year before, now appointed; including Cranmer, there were only three genuine Protestants on the committees. Nevertheless, as the year before, little progress could be made and a recess was required. From 11 to 25 May Parliament was adjourned while work went on to prepare draft bills for the two houses to consider.[55]

It was during this recess that a new element in the power struggle between Cromwell and his conservative foes emerged. By the middle of April Henry had begun to be seen with a new maiden, Norfolk's niece Catherine Howard. This dark-haired beauty had come to court at the end of 1539 to serve in the household of Anne of Cleves—not as a replacement for Anne but simply as a Howard whose place in the queen's service was an expected mark of family favor. As Henry's distaste for Anne became apparent, however, Catherine became something much more, a rival for the throne, actively pushed forward by Norfolk and perhaps by Gardiner. Catherine began to dress sumptuously, and the dowager duchess of Norfolk offered advice on how to entertain the king. Soon Henry began to be seen at Norfolk's house at Lambeth for private dinners with Catherine and her family. On 24 April and again on 18 May, Catherine received royal gifts—the goods of two felons and a set of quilts from the royal wardrobe.[56]

Certainly Cromwell was aware of this romance, and it placed him in a considerable dilemma. Henry had already demanded a divorce from Anne of Cleves and had placed Cromwell in charge of obtaining it. As the amity between Francis and Charles faded, so did the diplomatic justification for the Cleves alliance. The divorce was certainly possible; Anne had a valid precontract to a son of the duke of Lorraine which was sufficient grounds for an annulment. Unfortunately for Cromwell, it was obvious that Henry was infatuated with Catherine and would marry her as soon as he was free of Anne. The ploy and its dangers must have been uncomfortably familiar to Cromwell, for he had seen it all before in the careers of Anne Boleyn and Jane Seymour. In the face of this potentially disastrous elevation of the Norfolk-Gardiner faction, Cromwell froze. By early June work on the divorce had ground to a halt, and Cromwell worriedly confessed to Wriothesley that "one thing rested in his head and . . . troubled him, that the King liked not the Queen" to whom Cromwell had bound him. Wriothesley, who understood exactly what was at stake, advised Cromwell: "For God's sake, devise for the release of the king; for, if he remains in this grief and trouble, we shall all [of the progressive party?] one day smart for it."[57]

Cromwell spent much of April and early May absorbed with Parliament. While he worked to obtain passage of a subsidy bill, the king kept company and counsel with Norfolk and Gardiner. When the king withdrew to Greenwich on 16 May, Cromwell stayed in London, remaining there for the next week until Parliament was prorogued.[58] Events had come to the point that either Cromwell or his enemies had to be destroyed. Cromwell knew this as well as Norfolk and Gardiner, and this must explain the sudden attack on Richard Sampson. An ally of Gardiner, Sampson was nominated in May to be first bishop of the newly created see of Westminster, a considerable promotion over his diocese of Chichester. To the bewilderment of foreign observers, on 1 June Sampson was invested at Westminster "with all solemnity," and two hours later was whisked to the Tower on Cromwell's orders. Accused of treason, on 7 June Sampson wrote a dazed letter to Cromwell that made it clear his arrest was connected in some way with a planned purge of the conservative episcopate. Indeed, Marillac saw Sampson's arrest as a first step against Gardiner, writing: "Things are brought to such a pass that either Cromwell's party or that of the Bishop of Winchester must succumb." Yet Marillac thought Cromwell held the upper hand, and even predicted that Robert Barnes would soon be freed as evidence of Cromwell's victory.[59]

Instead, it was Cromwell rather than Gardiner who joined Barnes in the Tower. Parliament met on the morning of Thursday, 10 June, with Norfolk and Cromwell both present. According to Marillac, Cromwell came to the council chamber for a meeting at three in the afternoon. Hardly had he entered when the captain of the guard, Norfolk's client Sir Anthony Wingfield, arrived to announce Cromwell's arrest on charges of high treason. The earl of Essex furiously snatched off his hat and threw it down, declaring to Norfolk and his assembled rivals that this was a fine reward for his service. Norfolk reproached Cromwell for his "many villainies," and snatched the Order of the Garter from around his neck. William Fitzwilliam, earl of Southampton, "to show himself as great an enemy in adversity as he had been thought a friend in prosperity," untied the Garter from Cromwell's knee. Essex was hustled out of a side door of Westminster palace and taken to the Tower by boat. Only when guards arrived to seize his house and goods did the fallen minister's fate become widely known; this peremptory confiscation was a sure sign that Cromwell was as good as dead.[60]

While Marillac may have been surprised by the events of 10 June, Cromwell certainly was not. Angry, yes, and deservedly bitter, he knew perfectly well that someone would be carted off to the Tower before court politics could resume any sort of stability. But Cromwell's attack, set in motion with the arrest of Sampson, never reached to the real targets, Norfolk and Gardiner. Instead, the conservatives were able to strike first. The problem in analyzing Cromwell's fall is not with the events of 1 June when Sampson was arrested, or of 10 June when Cromwell went to the Tower, but in unraveling what happened during the intervening days. Somehow Cromwell's enemies convinced the king that Essex was a traitor. It is easy to see that Henry was unhappy with the Cleves fiasco, but charges of treason were quite another thing. Certainly Henry let his infatuation with Catherine Howard color his perceptions, for Cromwell was stalling rather than promoting the divorce even as the king realized that the threatened Catholic crusade against the kingdom that had necessitated the Cleves marriage was no longer likely. Cromwell's foreign policy placed Henry in an uncomfortable position, and Essex's enemies were more than ready to urge the king to change policy by destroying the architect of the useless and distasteful German alliance. Surely Norfolk mentioned Francis's hints that Cromwell stood in the way of closer Anglo-French relations.[61] But Norfolk and Gardiner were not alone in opposing Cromwell. A large group of conservative courtiers and clerics, including Sir William Kingston, Sir Anthony Browne, Southampton, Tunstall, John Clerk, and even, possibly, Wriothesley and Audley, stood behind Norfolk and Gardiner, ready at least to cast their lots against Cromwell if he seemed likely to fall. The delay in parliamentary action on the new articles of religion in May showed both the strength of the conservative party and the paralysis of the progressives as Henry moved away from a Protestant settlement.[62]

The case against Cromwell must have been whispered into Henry's ear while the king was at Greenwich. The House of Lords had not sat on 9 June, and Gardiner was not present the next day. It cannot be proved, but it appears that Gardiner and Norfolk finally persuaded Henry to move against Cromwell during the recess; his arrest the day after Parliament reconvened seems more than a coincidence.[63] But what plausible case could be made against Cromwell? Religious accusations appear to have been at least as important as political ones in Cromwell's fall. The recent religious troubles at Calais—which Cromwell had tried to cover up, and then to blame on Lord Lisle—may have played a role. Certainly his ties to Barnes were stressed; as proof of the sinister Lutheran implications of this connection, Cromwell's efforts to make an alliance with Protestant Germany and Denmark during 1538 and 1539 must have been mentioned (and Henry's enthusiasm for the alliance and doctrinal unity passed over in silence). Other charges were raised as evidence of Essex's treasonable intentions. He was said to have set at liberty persons indicted for treason, to have sold licenses, passports and commissions without Henry's leave, to have usurped the king's power, and (shades of Wolsey!) to have grown sure of his master the king. Most of these charges appeared in Cromwell's attainder.[64]

Yet the decisive charges were accusations of heresy; here Henry's suspicions could really be aroused. The Supreme Head of the church in England had a violent fear and hatred of heresy. As Scarisbrick has argued, Cromwell's accusers did not stop with linking him to Luther, but improved the charge; they "ran howling to the king that his minister was a member of that rabid sect, denounced as violently by Lutherans as Catholics, that denied the Real Presence in the Eucharist." Cromwell himself, in a letter from the Tower, denied that he was a sacramentary. Yet his enemies provided the suspicious king with just the kind of evidence most likely to arouse his wrath. Had not Cromwell licensed heretics to preach— including Robert Barnes, a man personally obnoxious to the king, and who lay in the Tower at that moment? These charges were nebulous, to say the least, but a search of Cromwell's house happily turned up copies of letters he had written to religious radicals in Germany. Cromwell had, in fact, corresponded with Lutheran leaders, with Henry's knowledge and approval, but now this correspondence could be displayed to Henry as proof of Essex's vile intentions. Henry responded by declaring that Cromwell was the greatest wretch ever born in England; the king wished never to hear his name again.[65]

If the critical charge against Cromwell was heresy, the fate of Barnes provides further evidence. On 30 July, two days after Cromwell went to the block, Barnes and two others were burned at Smithfield as heretics. Barnes was certainly a Lutheran, but he was no sacramentary, as the sermon preached at his execution implied. Barnes had to die to give credibility to the charges against Cromwell; if support of Barnes's teachings was the crux of Cromwell's offenses, then Barnes had to die along with his patron.[66] As with the fall of Anne Boleyn, the executions of the accused's alleged henchmen could help give credence to shaky charges. To kill one person might smack of simple murder. To kill three or four or half a dozen could more plausibly be presented as proof of vile and treasonable conspiracy.

The victorious coalition led by Norfolk and Gardiner, as well as their newfound allies such as Southampton, were quick to adopt this charge of heresy as the official line; letters went out to John Wallop at the French court and to Richard Pate at Brussels instructing them so to explain events to Francis and Charles. Both rulers were pleased with Cromwell's destruction, although the emperor admitted some surprise at its suddenness. Evidently the heresy charges were not so outrageous that anyone openly questioned them. Even Cranmer, suddenly finding himself badly outnumbered on the council, could only express his sorrow that so loyal a servant had been found a traitor. The archbishop quickly added that he was glad the treason had been discovered, but where, he wondered, would the king find a councilor with Cromwell's many qualities to replace him?[67]

On balance, it would appear that the heresy charges were the excuse, and not the cause, of his destruction. Scarisbrick and Elton may have overstated the case, for Cromwell's death was certainly Henry's idea, with Norfolk and Gardiner the agents and not the instigators of the whole affair. Nonetheless, one cannot doubt their enthusiasm for the project. Had it been in his power to destroy Cromwell by his own volition, Norfolk would have done it, and Gardiner, for his own reasons, would not have been far behind.

By 29 June Cromwell's attainder had passed through Parliament, condemning him without the inconvenience of a trial which might have demonstrated the shaky evidence for his treason. Cromwell was not executed immediately, for his testimony was needed in the trial of Henry's marriage to Anne of Cleves. On 30 June Norfolk, Audley and Fitzwilliam visited Cromwell in his cell to take a statement. Cromwell faithfully told all he knew, even while begging for mercy and forgiveness—with faint hope of success as long as Norfolk and Gardiner held Henry's ear.[68] With Cromwell in the Tower, it fell to Norfolk and his party to carry through the divorce. The duke led a delegation which went through the formality of asking the king's consent to place the matter before Convocation. On 7 July Gardiner took charge of the deliberations of the clergy—despite the fact that Cranmer as archbishop of Canterbury was formally entitled to direct Convocation. Norfolk, Suffolk, Southampton, Tunstall and Cranmer gave their testimony that the ambassadors of Cleves had made false promises concerning Anne's freedom to marry, and by 10 July Gardiner read his decree that the marriage between Anne and Henry was void and both were free to marry, the laws of God and man happily coinciding in Henry's favor. The next day, a delegation led by Norfolk visited Anne, who readily agreed to the divorce and signed a letter to that effect to her "brother" Henry as "your majesty's most humble sister and servant Anne." Parliament quickly confirmed the nullity decree and gave legal bite to the proceedings by making it treason to assert that the marriage between Henry and Anne had ever been valid. Henry was a free man. Norfolk and Gardiner had delivered, with little difficulty, what Cromwell had feared to carry through.[69]

Cromwell was not executed for another two weeks. His death awaited the close of Parliament and Henry's formal assent to his attainder. Although executions had preceded attainders before, Cromwell's enemies took care to preserve legal niceties even while carrying out their political vendetta. On 28 July Cromwell was finally led out to Tyburn, and not to Tower Hill; this touch of disgrace seems to have been Norfolk's idea. Cromwell made a short speech expressing the customary regret that he had offended, knelt, and was beheaded, as befitted a peer; at least he was spared the more disgraceful parts of a common traitor's death.[70] The same day, with his usual lack of propriety, Henry wed Catherine Howard in a quiet private ceremony. Perhaps the king had had enough of gaudy state weddings; Catherine was, after all, his fifth bride. Even up to the last moment it was widely believed by some that she would be but his mistress, while other rumors hinted that she was pregnant.[71] Yet Henry took Catherine as his wife, and in doing so seemingly restored the Howards to social and political ascendancy.

Marillac certainly thought so. The day after Cromwell's execution and Catherine's marriage he wrote to Montmorency that Norfolk now had chief management of affairs.[72] Doubtless Norfolk would have wished it so, but the main result of Cromwell's destruction was to create a new political balance at court. On 10 August 1540, the king's council was reorganized, formally styled the "privy council" to emphasize its new compactness, and William Paget was appointed clerk. As Elton has demonstrated, the privy council in fact if not in name came into existence earlier, around 1536, but in 1540 the body was, for the first time, given formal recognition as an administrative body and, more important for its history, began to keep records that have survived. The newly reorganized privy council had nineteen members, including Norfolk, Gardiner, Tunstall, Cranmer, Suffolk, Audley, Hertford, Southampton, Sussex, Sadler, Wriothesley and Sir Anthony Wingfield, captain of the king's guard and a close supporter of Norfolk. This was an overwhelmingly secular body; only three clerics sat on the reorganized council. The membership also reflected the political realities of Henry VIII's later reign. Among the peers, all but Norfolk were "new men"; only Thomas Howard held a title that had been in his family before Henry's accession, and even the Howard dukedom was in reality a Tudor gift.[73] Obviously, all was not harmonious in this body of progressives and conservatives uneasily yoked together; on 6 August Marillac informed Montmorency that Henry's ministers "seek only to undo each other to gain credit, and under the color of their master's good each attends to his own. For all the fine words of which they are full, they will act only as necessity and self-interest compel them."[74]

Norfolk gained far less from the destruction of Cromwell than he had hoped. True, the king's foremost minister was removed, but Cranmer remained a progressive beacon; in Henry's final years, the archbishop, with the support of Hertford and others, would form an effective party at court. The continued tenure of Audley as chancellor, in which office he exercised little influence, left the council an open battlefield between conservatives and progressives with neither side dominant. Henry's gratitude to the men who had revealed Essex in his treasons was not so great as to place them in the fallen minister's stead. The king seemed determined to select no successor to Cromwell, but rather to take a greater personal role in policy-making, leaving the council to debate issues, deal with ambassadors, and execute policy. But the policy to be carried out was now, more than ever before, to be the king's.[75]

In the later summer of 1540 Norfolk had to be content to share power and prestige with the privy council and with his conservative ally Gardiner, whose administrative and legal skill rapidly made him the leading figure in the reconstructed council. Norfolk was hardly shunted aside; others could handle to day-to-day administration, for he held a position no other councilor could match. Once again a Howard was queen; the possibilities for family advancement seemed immense, and Norfolk was always a man with appetites and ambitions to match the loftiest aspiration. All things considered, Norfolk's prospects in mid-1540 were the brightest they had been since the fall of Wolsey. Alas that Catherine Howard's career would prove a greater family and personal disaster for Norfolk and the Howards than had been Anne Boleyn's.

CHAPTER 8

CATHERINE HOWARD: FROM TRIUMPH TO TREASON, 1540–1542

IN THE FALL OF 1539 Anne of Cleves arrived in England with an entourage of German maidens. Once in her new country, however, it was expected that she would accept the attentions of English servants. Anne's new household, appointed by the king, awaited her in London. Norfolk did particularly well in the struggle to place family members among Anne's servants. Mary Howard, duchess of Richmond, was named one of the "Great Ladies," and two other Howard women were among the six maidens attendant upon the queen-to-be. One was Mary Norris, the duke's cousin by marriage, and the other was his niece Catherine Howard.[1]

Catherine was a daughter of Norfolk's younger brother Edmund, a man whose career had been a series of misfortunes and disappointments. At Flodden, Edmund alone among the English commanders lost his personal engagement (and the army's baggage in the process). While his father and brother went on to careers at court and peerages, Edmund remained an obscure country gentleman with a talent for spending more money than he made, receiving notice only when he was in trouble for such things as interfering with "the good rule and execution of justice within the county of Surrey" in 1516 and 1519. Edmund died in 1539 after having mismanaged his only royal post of any consequence as comptroller of Calais, little loved or noticed by his brother or the king.[2]

If Edmund was something of an embarrassment to the duke of Norfolk, his eldest daughter was a more important person by far simply by virtue of her sex. Arranged marriages were an important element in obtaining and preserving influence and wealth in sixteenth century England, and it was no small part of Norfolk's success that he was well supplied with sisters, nieces and cousins with whom to bargain in this market. Catherine was born around 1521 and was raised in the household of her stepgrandmother Agnes, dowager duchess of Norfolk, where she was trained as a gentlewoman, learning courtesy and manners, sewing, singing and dancing and household management, all by the economical means of acting as a servant in the duchess's houses at Horsham and Lambeth.[3]

In the autumn of 1539 Catherine came to court—apparently for the first time despite the proximity of Lambeth to the capital—to take her place in Anne of Cleves's household. Since Catherine was appointed as one of Anne's maidens before Henry met and immediately developed a distaste for his new bride, Norfolk could not have intended Catherine as a replacement for Anne from the start. The duke's original purpose was no more than to place another Howard maiden near the king in the royal household; the course of events that raised Catherine from serving maid to queen was a welcome windfall.

Once it became obvious that Henry was unhappy with his new bride, Norfolk and Gardiner were quick to find a new career for their handsome young charge. It took little urging before the king came to prefer Catherine to his plain and all-too-German wife, and by April 1540 Henry and Catherine were keeping company. After Cromwell's arrest, Norfolk and Gardiner quickly carried through the divorce that freed the king to marry Catherine. On the day that Cromwell was executed, Henry and Norfolk's niece were wed. With Cromwell gone and with a Howard as queen to counterbalance the Seymours, Norfolk seemed to have achieved what had slipped from his grasp in the wake of Wolsey's fall—a combined political and dynastic ascendancy to assure a permanent place as Henry's leading councilor.

The king settled into married life with Catherine by going on progress among the royal residences around London. Norfolk spent a good part of August and September in his county but received frequent letters from the council informing him of the progress of affairs and soliciting his advice[4]— a practice unheard-of during Cromwell's dominance. By October, after supervising collection of the latest subsidy in Norfolk, the duke returned to court and rejoined the council as it followed Henry from Windsor to Westminster to Hampton Court. The new year found Norfolk still enmeshed in royal business in almost daily meetings of the privy council.[5]

There were other evidences of renewed Howard influence and favor at court. On 8 September 1540 the duke and his eldest son, Henry, were appointed stewards of Cambridge University, at least partially in recognition of Surrey's poetic accomplishments.[6] In January and April 1541, Norfolk was licensed to sell several parcels of monastic lands he had obtained in Shropshire and Cambridgeshire, making a tidy profit.[7] On 23 April 1541 Surrey was elected to the Order of the Garter, along with Sir John Gage and Sir Anthony Wingfield. The rise of the latter two attests to Norfolk's status after the fall of Cromwell, for both were longtime Howard clients. Wingfield was the captain of the guard who had arrested Cromwell and, like Gage, had a long career sitting in Parliament for Norfolk's boroughs. These two conservatives were among the new privy councilors prominent after Cromwell's fall as well; Wingfield was sworn of the council in August and Gage in October 1540.[8] In general, Norfolk must have found the rewards of having a niece as queen much as he had hoped. He hardly achieved the status of Wolsey in his prime, but Norfolk never really wanted more than the trappings of power. By early 1541, the duke had everything he had sought in his political career—wealth, influence and family aggrandizement.

The reformed council continued as a battleground between the Norfolk-Gardiner alliance and the remnants of Cromwell's faction. In October 1540 George Whelplay, who seems to have been trying to make a career out of informing on customs violators, appeared before the council to complain of rampant corruption in the customs collections in East Anglia.[9] Whelplay carefully chose to make his accusations on a day when neither Norfolk nor Gardiner was in council. The six councilors present were happy to encourage Whelplay's attack on Norfolk who, as treasurer, had charge of the king's customs. Led by the enigmatic Southampton, the council—which that day included Sir Ralph Sadler, Lord Russell and the earl of Hertford (none of them allies of Norfolk, all of them to take part in the assault on the Howards in 1546)—wrote to ask the duke for an explanation.[10] Norfolk replied on 16 October with a sweeping denial of any wrongdoing; in a scathing aside, he ridiculed Whelplay as a man of hardly spotless integrity himself. Perhaps, as Elton suggested, none of the councilors could have withstood a very stringent examination for official corruption; in any case, the investigation rapidly fizzled out.[11] Norfolk stood too high in the king's favor to risk an attack without unimpeachable evidence, but this episode demonstrated that the progressive faction was ready to strike against the duke if given the opportunity.

While the Whelplay affair was going on, although probably not in response to it, the conservatives launched an attempt of their own to purge the council of their enemies, beginning with an assault on one of the leading progressives, Sir Ralph Sadler. Early in September, apparently at Gardiner's instigation, an old investigation into the Heron family of Hackney, Middlesex, was resumed. Giles Heron had been sent to the Tower by Cromwell and eventually attainted as a sympathizer with his father-in-law Thomas More. Gardiner picked up the scent because the Herons had been clients of Sadler; especially after Giles's execution in August 1540, his family's ties to Sadler became a matter of great interest to the conservatives in council.[12]

The investigation also came to center on Lord Leonard Grey, an old Cromwellian who had the misfortune to preside over the collapse of English rule in Ireland in the later 1530s. Norfolk returned to court in October 1540 to find Grey under investigation and entered into the discussions with considerable zest, personally carrying charges preferred by Thomas Wyndham (a Howard cousin) from Windsor to London for further consideration.[13] Grey was finally executed for treason on 28 June 1541. By that time, the assault on the Cromwellian councilors was in full swing. Sir Thomas Wriothesley fell under scrutiny in June for alleged financial peculations during Cromwell's tenure; the charges were finally dropped in December, but Wriothesley nearly followed Grey to the block. The significance of the date lies in what followed. Wriothesley was able to make his peace with the conservatives and to disassociate himself from Sadler, his former fellow secretary, but probably at the cost of helping in the investigation. Gardiner and Norfolk took their time in preparing a case against Sadler; in the meantime several other Cromwellians were ruined, including William Grey, who was charged with the treason of having written the name of Philip Melanchthon, the German religious reformer, in one of his books![14]

By 16 January 1541 the conservatives were ready to strike. On that day Sadler and another courtier (usually identified as Sir Thomas Wyatt) were suddenly arrested and conducted to the Tower. The confused reports of the foreign ambassadors—almost the only source for the event—imply charges of treason, but even A. J. Slavin, Sadler's biographer, was unable to find evidence of exactly why Sadler was arrested or how he escaped. As with Cromwell, the charges likely had as much to do with heresy as treason, but unlike the case of the fallen earl of Essex, nothing could be made to stick against Sadler. With the memory of the loss of the efficient and industrious Cromwell still fresh, Henry may have been unwilling to destroy another useful servant upon the whim of his conservative councilors. By 20 January Sadler was out of the Tower and back in council, cleared of all charges; if there was a trial, it has left no records. Sadler's influence was reduced by the ordeal, but the king had finally made it clear that a balance was to be maintained in the council. Sadler was too useful to be sacrificed to Norfolk and Gardiner's ambitions, and Henry was unwilling to allow a general purge of the progressive faction in the aftermath of Cromwell's fall.[15]

In fact, the king took considerable care to balance the conservative influence. Gardiner was sent to observe the Imperial Diet in November 1540, and early the next year Norfolk was absent from court on a mission in the north.[16] But clearly Henry was leaning toward the conservatives. When the council was divided for the progress to York in 1541, Norfolk, Wriothesley, Southampton and Tunstall accompanied the king while Hertford, Cranmer, Audley and Sadler remained in London—a clear conservative-progressive division in which the former were guaranteed a monopoly on the king's attention.[17]

At least in part the conservative group owed its influence to the king's marriage. As long as Henry was content with Catherine, her family and friends prospered. The queen's household was, of course, filled with Howard relations and clients, but the favor did not end there. Catherine's brother George was named a gentleman of the king's privy chamber; another brother, Charles, received several grants of monastic land, and the pair shared a lucrative license to import wine and dyestuffs from France. The index to volume 16 of the *Letters and Papers* abounds with references to grants to Howards and their relatives. Even Norfolk's half-brother William, a man of limited talent, reaped the rewards of his name and was appointed ambassador to France in January 1541. Henry was pleased with Catherine, and was free with favors to her large and grasping family.

The Ebbs and Flows of Fortune

Unfortunately, Catherine was not very discriminating in sharing her good fortune, for she appointed a number of old friends and family from Duchess Agnes's household to her court. In doing so, she succeeded in supplying the fading progressive party with an opportunity to mount a counterattack that, before it had ended, would send Catherine to the block on Tower Hill and nearly wipe out the Howard ascendancy. Catherine took as a lady of her privy chamber the incompetent and bitter Jane, lady Rochford, widow of George Boleyn. Catherine also found a place for Mary Hall, whose brother John Lassells was a virulent Protestant anxious to do all in his power to overthrow the conservatives. Worst of all, Catherine appointed a former lover, Francis Dereham, as her private secretary and usher. The queen had not lived a chaste life before her sudden rise to the king's side. This was a matter of no importance when she was but a servant, and it is not clear if Norfolk knew the details of her life in Agnes Howard's household. By the time he found out it was too late, and Jane Boleyn, Mary Hall and Francis Dereham all would shortly take leading roles in the spectacular reversal of Howard fortunes.[18]

Henry believed Catherine had come to him a virgin, and certainly the king had no doubt of her fidelity to him after their marriage. It was a grave shock to discover otherwise. Although most of the evidence for Catherine's indiscretions came from the end of 1541 when the campaign against the Howards was in full swing, it seems clear that she had never been the paragon of virtue Henry supposed. At Lambeth and Horsham, Catherine had dallied with a number of young men, one of whom, Dereham, had been such a constant companion in bed and out that the ladies of the household considered him Catherine's common-law husband. Worse, Catherine's passions were not cooled by her marriage, and at least one man would testify to having shared Catherine's favors after she had become queen.[19] Similar charges had been used against Anne Boleyn in 1536, but Norfolk had disentangled himself from Anne by the time of her fall and escaped relatively unscathed from her destruction. In 1541, however, the attack on the queen was mounted in London by the progressive councilors left behind while the king went on progress. Norfolk had little inkling of Catherine's danger—and his own—until nearly the last moment. Although Norfolk escaped with his life and goods intact, it was a very near thing; the Howard ascendancy of 1540–41 owed a great deal to the rise of Catherine Howard, and in her fall she almost carried the whole clan down with her.

While Henry was on progress in the north, John Lassells came forward with what his sister had told him of Catherine's unchaste life before her marriage. Probably he was emboldened by the prospect of telling his story to the distinctly progressive council left in London. In telling his story, Lassells was setting greater events than he knew in train, for even while traveling to York with her husband, Catherine was committing acts that would make her youthful indiscretions pale by comparison. Yet despite having information likely to destroy Catherine in hand, Cranmer, Hertford and Audley hesitated to act; instead they waited for Henry to return from the north before revealing Lassells's accusations. On 2 November Cranmer carried a letter outlining the charges to Hampton Court. Finding Henry about to go to mass, the archbishop simply handed the king the note, begged him read it in private, and slipped away. Henry read the charges: how Catherine had given herself, first to Henry Manox, her music teacher, and then to Francis Dereham, and had concealed all from her husband, obviously with dark and treasonable intent. Curiously, at first Henry refused to believe the accusations, regarding them as slander. Nonetheless, during the next week the king ordered a quiet investigation—led, significantly, by Southampton, rather than by one of the London councilors who had heard Lassells's charges. Henry was completely shattered by Southampton's report that the story was true; both Manox and Dereham confessed their involvement with the queen, although both insisted that their liaisons had taken place before her marriage.[20]

Thus far, Catherine's only crime was fornication, or, if her intimacy with Dereham was held to constitute marriage, bigamy. In either case, the king's marriage could have been annulled and Catherine's life spared; her deeds, though felonies, were not treason. Norfolk had not come to Hampton Court with the king; thus he was absent when these early disclosures came to light. By 6 November he was summoned to court to meet with king and council. According to Marillac, Norfolk, not a man easily perturbed, was sorely vexed to find his niece at the center of a growing scandal; the now-sullied marriage had, after all, been his idea. The disturbing parallel of the collapse of the Cleves marriage and the fate of Cromwell must have occurred to Norfolk as he rode to London.[21]

The duke had no choice but to put up a brave front, and he sought to protect himself as much as possible by joining in the investigation of his niece's crimes. On 11 November Norfolk, Southampton and several other councilors ordered Catherine moved to the former monastic house at Syon under close watch.[22] Confronted with the evidence against her, the queen wrote a confession admitting her carnal relations with Manox and Dereham. Perhaps she hoped to escape without discovery of her other indiscretions, but meanwhile evidence was coming to light that would render her past dalliances inconsequential by comparison. In her confession Catherine swore that, since marriage, she had been "faithful and true unto your majesty."[23] In fact, as the council discovered in mid-November, she had saved her most flagrant dishonor to the king for the months of the northern excursion the previous summer.

Thomas Culpeper, a gentleman of the king's chamber, was a courtier of small means but great ambition. This distant cousin of the queen had paid flattering attention to Catherine—as many must have—through much of 1541. By 11 November rumors of Culpeper's real relationship with Catherine led Wriothesley to question her about him. The interview was inconclusive, but the rest of the council, including Norfolk, followed up with interrogations of the ladies of the queen's chamber, and soon the full story was pieced together. By 14 November Norfolk admitted to Marillac that Culpeper and Catherine had been closeted together to take their carnal pleasure "five or six times" during the northern progress.[24] The key to this sad knowledge was the examination of Lady Rochford. In an unsuccessful attempt to disentangle herself and place all responsibility on Catherine, Jane made the damning confession "that Culpeper hath known the queen carnally considering all the things that she hath heard and seen between them." These charges led to the detention of Culpeper, who promptly confessed his relations with Catherine. Worse, he added that in doing so "he intended and meant to do ill with the queen and that in like wise the queen so minded to do with him," a curious statement that hints that his examiners were fishing for evidence of an offense against the treason act of 1534, which made the "compassing and imagining" of harm to the king a crime punishable by death.[25]

Thus the evidence took shape. By 14 November Catherine was under armed guard at Syon, and Culpeper was in the Tower. On 22 November Catherine was declared to have forfeited her honor and was no longer to be called queen.[26] Norfolk dutifully sat in council as the investigation drew to a close and as commissions were sent out for grand juries to sit in the several counties where Catherine and Culpeper had committed their crimes. Ralph Sadler, almost the victim of a conservative plot in January, gained his revenge in directing much of the activity that led to the ruin of the queen. For good measure, the government also decided to prosecute Dereham, Catherine's first lover. Both Catherine and Dereham had denied that they considered themselves married by common law, making his worst crime fornication. Henry wanted no doubt to cloud his assertion that Catherine's indiscretions had rendered their marriage void from the outset, and so Dereham had to suffer along with Culpeper.[27] No trial was planned for Catherine herself. Instead, on 23 November writs went out for a Parliament to meet at Westminster on 16 January 1542. Catherine would go quietly by means of an act of attainder, a tool that had proved increasingly useful since Anne Boleyn's distasteful spectacle of a trial.[28]

On 1 December Dereham and Culpeper were brought to trial at the Guildhall in London before a commission headed by the lord mayor, Audley, Norfolk, Suffolk, Southampton, Sussex, Hertford, Russell, Sadler, Wriothesley, Wingfield and Gage. The charges against Culpeper were straightforward enough, that he had "falsely and traitorously held illicit meeting" with the queen; Anne's act of attainder in 1536 had generalized adultery with the queen as treason. For Dereham, the charges were more devious. He had admitted having sexual relations with Catherine before her marriage, but neither he nor the queen had confessed to intercourse after she became queen. Therefore Dereham was accused of having "falsely and traitorously" concealed a contract of marriage from Henry, thereby imperiling the succession by drawing suspicion upon Henry and Catherine's children. This certainly could be construed as treason under the act of 1534; as evidence of a plot to harm the king, the prosecution needed only to point to Dereham's employment in the queen's privy chamber. Initially both men pled not guilty, but after a jury was sworn and Catherine's confession read, they changed their pleas to guilty. The usual sentence for traitors not of noble blood was read out; Culpeper and Dereham were ordered taken to Tyburn, and there hung, cut down alive, disemboweled and their bowels burned before them, and finally beheaded and quartered. On 10 December the executions were carried out, although Culpeper, perhaps because he had been in the king's personal service, was spared all the horrors of the sentence and merely beheaded. Dereham, really the lesser offender, suffered the full pains.[29] Culpeper clearly was guilty at least of adultery within the royal family, but Dereham was innocent of anything worse than concealing his relationship with Catherine—one which, had it been revealed in time, would hardly have caused his death. Dereham had to die in order to justify the dissolution of the king's marriage. It is a little surprising that Henry Manox, the queen's other old lover, was spared; if Dereham deserved death for his dalliance with Catherine, so did Manox. The survival of the latter underscores the injustice done to the former.

Although he participated in the trial of Culpeper and Dereham, laughing during their examination "as if he had cause to rejoice," Norfolk was well aware that his troubles were far from over. Norfolk retired to Kenninghall around 5 December for, as Chapuys reported, the council had begun to look into the affairs of Catherine's relatives, and Norfolk's presence in council was not only unnecessary but inconvenient.[30] In fact the ruin of the Howards seemed at hand in mid-December. On 8 December Sir William Howard and his wife were sent to the Tower on charges of having concealed Catherine's treason, and the next day the dowager duchess of Norfolk followed after it was learned that she had burned a bundle of Dereham's letters to Catherine found in a chest at Lambeth. Norfolk's half-sister Catherine, lady Bridgewater, was likewise examined, imprisoned and her house searched.[31] By 15 December word of all this had reached Kenninghall, and Norfolk responded by writing an abject and cringing letter to the king in an effort to divorce himself from the crimes of his relatives. After assuring Henry that he had no doubt that all his kin were not imprisoned lightly, "but for som their fals and traytorous procedynges agaynst Your Royall Majestie," the duke, with the shadow of Traitors' Gate before him, reminded Henry that he had faithfully aided the investigation of Catherine's crimes. Finally, he wrote: "Eftsonys prostrate at your royall fete, most humble I beseche Your Majestie, that by suche, as it shall please you to comande, I may be advertised playnle, how Your Highnes doth way your favour towardes me; assewryng Your Highnes that onles I may knowe Your Majestie to contynew my gode and gracious Lord, as ye wer befor their offensys committed, I shall never desire to lyve in this world any lenger, but shortly to fynishe this transitory lyff, as God knoweth, who send Your Majestie the accomplishmentes of your most noble hartes desires."[32]

Henry's reply is unrecorded, but the investigations had apparently gone as far as the king would allow. As late as 16 December Marillac wrote to

Francis that Norfolk himself was likely to suffer for his family's sins. And indeed, on 22 December Sir William, his wife, and a number of Howard servants were convicted of misprision of treason and sentenced to perpetual imprisonment and loss of all goods.[33] Yet they were not charged with treason, a clear sign that there were limits to the king's wrath. On 30 December Chapuys noted that Norfolk had returned to his Lambeth house, presumably under orders to await the conclusion of Catherine's case before returning to court.[34]

As late as 1 January 1542 Marillac remained in doubt about Norfolk's fate, but by the opening of Parliament two weeks later, the duke had returned to court "apparently in his full former credit and authority."[35] The pressure from the progressives had not been enough. Henry had learned from Cromwell's destruction the danger of allowing any court faction too great a sway; luckily for Thomas Howard the aftermath of Catherine's arrest resulted in a balancing of forces. The progressives, seemingly reduced to small influence in mid-1541, made a considerable recovery by early 1542. The destruction of Norfolk was not permitted, any more than Henry had allowed the conservatives to ruin Sadler. Both sides were taught the lesson that the king alone would decide policy and choose his servants; for the moment, neither side was to be permitted a dominant share of power to the exclusion of the other.

Norfolk's return to court was made only at the cost of a considerable swallowing of family pride, for the major business of Parliament in Janaury was the attainder of Catherine and her accomplices. The draft of a bill of attainder was introduced in the upper house on 21 January but was not ready for final approval until 11 February. These three weeks witnessed something of a progressive victory, for the finished act also attainted Agnes Howard and Lady Bridgewater (both indicted, but neither convicted of misprision of treason) as well as William Howard, his wife, and the lesser folk convicted earlier of complicity in Catherine's crimes.[36] With the act approved by letters patent (sparing the king the pain of condemning his wife in person), on the morning of 13 February 1542 Catherine and Lady Jane Rochford were brought to the scaffold on Tower Hill. The fallen queen made a short speech confessing her crimes; a witness reported that the two women "made the most godly and Christians' end that ever was heard tell of."[37]

The spectacular rise and disastrous fall of Catherine Howard illustrate the turmoil that followed the fall of Cromwell, the factional struggles in court and council that led foreign ambassadors to comment on the viciousness of English politics. Norfolk and Gardiner emerged from the events of 1540 apparently supreme, and an attack on the remaining Cromwellians at court seemed under way by year's end. Yet Henry prevented a complete conservative triumph, and insured that the progressive element on the privy council led by Cranmer, Hertford, Audley and Sadler remained active. Neither did the king allow the fall of Catherine Howard to result in a general purge of her backers; the balance in council was not to be pushed to progressive extremes. Catherine's career and the events surrounding her rise and fall illustrate the political realities of the 1540s. More than ever, Henry VIII was king in fact as well as name; there would be no more Wolseys or Cromwells. Henry encouraged considerable political disagreement, which not only provided him with more than one viewpoint on issues, but also kept everyone at court in line. No one was so assured of favor that he dared to push extreme policies. The comments of E. W. Ives on Henrician factionalism are to the point for the 1540s as well as for the period surrounding the fall of Anne Boleyn. No permanent grand factions on the Elizabethan model existed. Norfolk and Cranmer attracted political followings, yet the main aim of every councilor was not factional triumph but to be on the right side of an issue when Henry made up his mind.[38] Hence Norfolk could not rely on Wingfield and Gage, much less on such as Southampton, to be more than fair-weather friends. Catherine's ascendancy, and Norfolk's consequent high esteem, were no guarantee of continued support, so Gage and Wingfield sensibly looked to their own interests in helping investigate the Howards in 1541.

Surely Norfolk recognized these realities, and in fact this system was well suited to a man of his character. Self-interest had always been one of Thomas Howard's highest priorities, and he was capable of considerable viciousness; he played the deadly game of court politics with cold-blooded relish in the later years of the reign. The triumph and tragedy of Catherine Howard provided a cautionary lesson in factional politics and the quest for royal favor, but it is doubtful that Norfolk learned anything he did not already know from the affair. His ability to recover so quickly from potential disaster—in part by abandoning his own relatives at the first hint of trouble—was an important lesson for his enemies. Thomas Howard was nearly seventy years old in 1542, but he had no plans to retire from public life. Instead, after Catherine's fall Norfolk entered into the most active political period of his career, his ambition and his personal and family pride all very much intact. The fall of Catherine Howard was a disappointment and a setback—albeit a temporary one—for Norfolk, but it did nothing to change his ambition or his willingness to use any means, fair or foul, to advance his interests.

CHAPTER 9

THE LAST YEARS OF HENRY VIII, 1540–1547

THE FINAL YEARS OF HENRY VIII'S REIGN brought a return to the policies of the 1510s and almost constant war. Thomas Howard, a man whose most distinguished service to the crown had always been as a soldier, played an important part in the politics and diplomacy of these years. Yet age was catching up with him, and the increasing strength of the progressive young men at court presented a difficult problem for the conservative Norfolk. Although he was able to maintain a position of influence, serving in campaigns in Scotland and France in the 1540s, the end of the reign brought disaster for Norfolk and his family. Some have detected a decline in the character of the king and the steadiness of policy in Henry's later years; whether this is true or not, certainly the period after 1540 witnessed increasing political infighting. In the realignment of 1547 Thomas Howard and his family were the greatest losers. A reign which began with the Howards as trusted councilors and the lauded victors of Flodden ended with Norfolk in the Tower and his son in a traitor's grave.

During the brief period of Catherine Howard's rise and fall, foreign policy as well as domestic politics remained in turmoil. Neither the destruction of Cromwell nor the divorce from Anne of Cleves brought immediate changes in English diplomacy. At the end of 1540, Henry remained a free agent in European affairs. To the king's satisfaction, the shaky entente between Charles V and Francis I was in trouble; in October, the emperor installed his son Philip as duke of Milan, an act Francis could not accept and a clear indication that Franco-Imperial accord would not long survive.[1] Despite the typically tortuous Henrician diplomacy of the early 1540s, in retrospect it is clear that when Henry reentered the continental fray, it would have to be on the side of Charles. Henry had nothing desirable to gain by joining Francis, while an alliance with the emperor offered an opportunity for renewal of the Hundred Years' War in quest of glory and territory in France. The French ambassador, Marillac, was slow to come to this realization, and through the spring of 1541 thought that Norfolk, with his French pension, would lead Henry to alliance with Francis.[2]

The direction of diplomacy was complicated by domestic politics. While Stephen Gardiner, bishop of Winchester, shared Norfolk's religious conservatism and played a major role in the fall of Cromwell and in the king's marriage to Catherine Howard, the two men were not in agreement on foreign policy. Gardiner shared Cromwell's pro-imperial leanings and wished to seek an alliance in Germany. Norfolk's pro-French stance was as much the result of his opposition to Cromwell as attributable to any real affection for the French, yet until Henry made a definite change of policy clear, and as long as his pension was paid, the duke would support the Anglo-French alliance of the 1530s. Henry's return to continental war was hindered by troubles in the north of the realm and with Scotland, the junior but troublesome partner in the Auld Alliance. While Gardiner was sent off to the Imperial Diet at Regensburg in November 1540, Norfolk too was employed away from court as Henry's agent in the north.[3]

In late January 1541 Norfolk was commissioned to inspect fortifications and take musters in the border shires. As Marillac reported, Norfolk's mission had two purposes. One, the official explanation, was to prepare for war against the Scots. Marillac suspected, however, that Henry was as much concerned with the good order of the north as with the threat of invasion.[4] The area was still in turmoil four years after the harsh suppression of the Pilgrimage of Grace. The situation was not improved by troubles with Scotland; during 1540 there had been an exchange of border raids across the Tweed and the Cheviot Hills. James V, who reached his majority in 1538, had launched on a distinctly pro-French policy, marrying a French princess in 1537 and, after she succumbed to the Scottish climate, replacing her with another. Catholic advisors, especially Cardinal David Beaton, archbishop of St. Andrews, cultivated James's deep suspicion of his uncle Henry VIII and the English religious innovations of the 1530s. The ruffians along the border needed little encouragement, and as a result conflict had become endemic in the years since Howard's last service as lieutenant in 1537. James was also harboring English Catholics and criminals and rebels wanted by English authorities for their parts in the northern risings of 1536–37.[5] Thus Anglo-Scottish relations presented serious problems at a time when Henry, anxious to turn his attention to the continent, could least afford to leave his northern flank unguarded.

Norfolk was a natural choice as lieutenant because of his long experience in the north and his familiarity with Scottish politics. In a letter to Cromwell in March 1538, Norfolk had warned of the growing power of Beaton, in whom the dangerous influences of the papacy and France were joined. "England hath no greter enemye to his powre," Norfolk wrote; "I thynke he wulde provoke all the hurt he can agaynst thys realme."[6] Yet Norfolk did not expect war in 1541, nor look upon his tasks as an exile from court; instead, as he informed Marillac early in February, he would need no more than two months to settle the affairs of the north. And in fact, by 18 March Norfolk's mission was complete, and he had returned to court.[7] The details of this short journey are obscure because none of Norfolk's reports to Henry survive, yet the main outlines are clear. On 20 February Norfolk wrote to James from Berwick, assuring the king that his mission was peaceful, and requesting the return of the English rebels and criminals harbored in Scotland. James replied smoothly that he would certainly return those true criminals at hand, but he was unaware of any rebels, and, as to religious persons, that would be up to his ecclesiastical officials. Further, James sent a list of his own, requesting custody of several errant Scots sheltered in England.[8] Nothing came of this exchange, and no rebels, criminals or heretics changed hands as a result. If James professed inability to tell rebels from loyal men, Henry could hardly be expected to return James's traitors.

Marillac's letters provide most of what is known of Norfolk's mission. The duke inspected fortifications and took musters, but the northerners were reluctant to turn out in arms; only three thousand men were arrayed, according to the ambassador's spies.[9] Norfolk had been a hero in the north after Flodden and the campaigns of the 1520s, but the suppression of the Pilgrimage of Grace and Bigod's rebellion had done a great deal to ruin his standing on the borders.

Henry's sudden interest in Scotland should have been a clear signal of his intention to reenter the continental fray on the side of the emperor. Yet during 1541 England and France engaged in an elaborate charade, each side trying to convince the other of peaceable intentions while preparing for war. Both Henry and Francis were spending heavily to repair and extend fortifications around the English pale at Calais. Norfolk assured Marillac of Henry's love for Francis and insisted that the work near Calais was purely defensive; England had no hostile intentions.[10] Marillac was not convinced; on 30 April he reported to Montmorency that, even with the apparently pro-French Norfolk as Henry's leading minister, the English protestations of friendship could only be explained by fear of troubles in the north, "or else they are trying to persuade us that they do not mean war in order the more easily to take us by surprise."[11]

Henry would have preferred that nothing distract him from continental war, but the north did not cooperate. Early in April, shortly after Norfolk's return to court, there was an abortive rising in Yorkshire which, though quickly quashed, added to Henry's apprehensions about the vulnerability of the northern shires. The rebels had planned to seize Pontefract Castle and begin a civil war in defense of the old faith, perhaps with the aid of James. This threat seems to have been the final spur to Henry; by the end of April, plans were begun for the long-promised and often-delayed royal progress to the north to tend the unhealed wounds left by the Pilgrimage of Grace. Henry was also anxious to come to an understanding with the Scots, and so efforts were begun to persuade James to come to York for a meeting with his uncle during the summer of 1541. If at all possible, Henry wished to avoid war with Scotland, or at the least to settle Anglo-Scottish affairs as quickly and painlessly as possible before turning to war in France.[12]

The court was to begin its northern progress in June. In the meantime Norfolk continued to offer Marillac protestations of Henry's affection. Marillac was hardly inclined to take these seriously. When in early June Norfolk began hinting at an Anglo-French marital alliance, Marillac scornfully assured Francis that the duke spoke sweet words to cover poison, for the English only wished to offer an alliance in order to raise their stock as a European power sought after by all sides in the Hapsburg-Valois conflict.[13] Francis, hoping at least to delay war, instructed Marillac to offer Norfolk a marriage between Princess Mary and Charles, duc d'Orleans, Francis's youngest son. Marillac was to deny any official authorization for such talks, but to try to entice the English into making the first offer. Probably neither Francis nor Henry was sincere in seeking peace, but the talks nonetheless went on for months. Marillac's offer, Norfolk said, could not be considered until it was made formally and openly; even when the French envoy hinted that such a move might be made, Norfolk countered by insisting that Mary could never be considered legitimate. When Norfolk left court in June, the talks were at a standstill. There was still no open breach between Henry and Francis, but prospects for lasting peace were far from bright.[14]

Norfolk was still at court as late as 16 June, sitting with the council at Greenwich, but shortly thereafter he left for Kenninghall to prepare for the royal progress. Norfolk went ahead to check roads and arrange housing, supplies and reception committees; Suffolk was given the full-time task of organizing the king's amusement at the hunt. In early July the court gathered at Enfield, twenty miles north of London, and on 5 July the procession headed north by the slowest possible stages. On 7 August Norfolk joined the royal entourage at Grimsthorpe in Lincolnshire, and thereafter remained with the court, meeting almost daily with the privy council for the remainder of the progress.[15] Henry was pleased with his new queen and with the enthusiastic reception he was given by his subjects and, despite miserable weather which impeded travel, enjoyed himself immensely. With Norfolk in close company, Henry made his way from Lincoln to York, hunting, dispensing justice, visiting castles and towns, and in general showing himself to a region that had never before seen him.

Marillac joined the progress in time to witness Henry's triumphant entry at Lincoln.[16] By 12 August Norfolk and Marillac reopened negotiations. Norfolk now suggested that Mary, although barred from the succession and bastardized, might yet be queen in default of male heirs. If need be, what had been done might be undone. Norfolk, perhaps unwittingly, revealed some of the tension in council by insisting that he could not discuss Princess Elizabeth for a French marriage. Not only was she too young to marry, and a bastard besides, but Elizabeth was his grandniece, and he dared not press her as a candidate for fear of suspicions that he sought only to promote his own family.[17]

Perhaps Francis really wanted peace more than did Henry, for in mid-August Marillac was sent formal authorization to treat for the marriage of Mary and Orleans. Marillac was instructed to show his accreditation only to Norfolk and to secure the duke's promise to keep the talks secret. Perhaps Francis hoped that Norfolk's avowed love of France would help keep Henry at peace, preventing an offensive alliance with the emperor. In fact, through the early autumn Norfolk proved extremely reluctant to serve as Francis's pawn, in large measure out of fear that the council would refuse to ratify anything he alone negotiated with the French. Thus the talks dragged on; Howard repeatedly attested to Henry's love for Francis and swore that his king desired to ensure its perpetuity by marriage, yet could not make firm promises or talk specifics on such things as a dowry until Marillac produced a full and open commission to negotiate with full powers. This Francis refused to do; both sides held back, each waiting for the other to make the first commitment. Finally on 31 October, after six months of talks, Norfolk gave up, writing to Henry that he saw no point in taking the French seriously on the matter since they regarded it so lightly themselves.[18]

A few days later, the first accusations against Catherine Howard were brought to Henry's attention. In the ensuing turmoil, Marillac saw little of Norfolk for several months and the negotiations remained stalemated. Norfolk was back at court in mid-January, the worst of his troubles behind him, and on 5 February Marillac reported that Henry was prepared to resume talks on the old condition of a full and open French commission to be displayed to king and council. Henry had meanwhile opened secret negotiations with Charles for an offensive alliance against France. Norfolk, hoping to goad Francis into action, reminded Marillac that continued French delays had kept Henry from giving fair hearing to Charles's offer of a marital alliance involving not one of the king's daughters but Henry himself.[19] This reminder of the threat of Anglo-Imperial alliance resulted, in March 1542, in Marillac being sent new instructions which, though broadening the area of discussion, were still not the full powers Henry demanded.[20]

By now the council had taken up the question of a possible assault on France, and the talks with Marillac became a matter for full discussions. Norfolk was almost alone in pushing for an accord with France. Gardiner as well as most of the progressives urged Henry toward the imperial alliance. Hertford and John Dudley, lord Lisle, were anxious to prove themselves in war and saw their most promising opportunity in the imperial alliance.[21] War was still, after all, the sport of kings and noblemen, and prowess in battle was held in high regard by king and peers alike. Norfolk, an old warhorse of nearly seventy years, himself had little to gain through war; he had long since won his spurs, and now was more interested in winning dominance at court as Wolsey had done by managing foreign policy. If so, he was rowing against an increasingly stiff current in pushing for the French alliance. Early in March Henry empowered Gardiner, Tunstall, Southampton and Wriothesley to join Norfolk in the negotiations with Marillac. French diplomacy was no longer to be the duke's private preserve and, worse, those with whom he was to share it all opposed the French alliance. Not surprisingly, Marillac made little progress with the new commissioners. At the same time, the talks with Chapuys became more serious, and by early April plans were being laid for a joint assault on France.[22] Henry made his determination to return to war clear by ordering a general naval mobilization that month and by demanding a loan from three hundred great men of the realm. Norfolk and Suffolk, with the highest assessments, were each to pay six thousand crowns into the royal warchest; Marillac estimated that a total of 600,000 crowns would be collected.[23]

Norfolk left court at the beginning of April, retiring to his county to raise his share of the loan. Gardiner and several other pro-imperial councilors were left to steer the talks with Marillac to ruin, while Southampton was given charge of completing a deal with Chapuys. In the process, Norfolk, the leading pro-French councilor, found himself unwelcome at court while the alliance with Charles took shape. Norfolk had staked his claim to replace Cromwell as Henry's leading minister by taking command of the French negotiations. Unfortunately, Henry's lust for continental glory was stronger than his desire for even the most favorable treaty with France; certainly marrying the bastard Mary to a French prince would have been a considerable coup. In leaving court, Norfolk let his pique spill out so far as to denounce Southampton to Chapuys. "See this little villain," the duke said, "he wants already to engross everything and do like Cromwell, but in the end he will pay for all."[24] This comment was more than sour grapes; the privy council was an open battleground, and Norfolk fully intended to continue the contest and settle scores with the young upstarts who had thwarted him.

Chapuys thought Norfolk would remain in exile until Parliament met again, but he underestimated Howard's resilience. Norfolk was absent when the Order of the Garter met on 23 April, but by early June he had reappeared at court. In his absence, talks with Chapuys had progressed to the point that an Anglo-Imperial accord of some kind seemed inevitable.[25] Norfolk lingered in his county until the direction of policy became clear; despite the misplaced hopes of Marillac that Norfolk would resurrect the Anglo-French talks, it soon became evident that the duke had managed an about-face. Norfolk had been severely wounded by the disgrace of Catherine Howard, but renewed war provided an opportunity for redemption. Now that it was clear that Henry would turn to the emperor, Norfolk threw himself into war preparations and dropped all francophile lobbying. Marillac ruefully noted that Norfolk had returned to court in high estate, so pampered and well received that his military service must soon be called upon. The duke's house at Lambeth was swamped with men hoping to serve under his command in the army against France.[26] Norfolk also began receiving reports from Sir John Wallop, Henry's agent in Calais and an old Howard client, on the situation in Flanders and northern France.[27] All signs pointed toward a continental invasion with Norfolk as commander.

In fact by late summer Norfolk was at the head of an English army and by early autumn was in battle, but the fighting was on the Anglo-Scottish borders rather than in the Low Countries. Henry had learned an enduring lesson from Flodden and the troubles of the 1520s; he wanted nothing now to stand in the way of the enterprise in France. James V had refused to come to England to meet with his uncle, even when Henry was at York in 1541. The Scots, far from seeking peace with England, appeared intransigent.[28] As a result, Henry was determined to secure his northern border before beginning the assault on France.[29]

Tensions had been running high along the borders, with English and Scots raiders engaging in hostilities at an increasing pace through the summer of 1542. At the end of July Sir Robert Bowes was sent north as warden of the East and Middle marches with orders to take musters and survey defenses in preparation for the coming of a lord deputy against the Scots. Initially Henry commissioned Thomas Manners, earl of Rutland, to oversee the north, but at the beginning of August Chapuys learned that Norfolk would be sent.[30] Howard had been in East Anglia since July raising forces for the French invasion, but early in August he was summoned to court.[31] On 10 August, Marillac reported that he and Chapuys had been called before a special meeting of the council. Norfolk, "as eldest and first in authority," made a long declaration of Henry's sadness that Francis and Charles were at war, with many protestations of England's intended neutrality. Marillac, fully aware of the ongoing Anglo-Imperial talks, was not impressed, and warned against the English plan to attack the Scots as a first step against France. Even Norfolk made no effort to preserve the fiction of English neutrality, privately admitting to Marillac that he would go to the north if needed.[32]

Henry initially intended nothing more than a few border raids to persuade the Scots to stay out of the coming war; at worst, the king anticipated a short punitive campaign across the Tweed to defuse the Scottish threat. Instead Henry found himself goaded into a full-scale assault on Scotland.[33] By mid-August Norfolk was gathering grain for shipment to Berwick and sending out orders for repairs to northern fortifications. On 24 August the duke was commissioned as king's lieutenant with full powers to lead an invasion of Scotland. The Scots still appeared willing to negotiate on the questions left unresolved since Norfolk's last mission in 1541, but at the end of August an event took place that convinced Henry that only a policy of forceful retribution would quell his unruly neighbors.[34]

On 24 August Sir Robert Bowes led three thousand men on a large-scale raid into the Scots' Middle Marches. At Haddon Ridge, near Kelso, Bowes was ambushed by an inferior Scottish force. After a sharp fight, Bowes, several of his lieutenants, and five hundred Englishmen were captured. The battle was on Scottish ground, and Bowes was the aggressor, but Henry chose to look upon Haddon Ridge as a provocation to war.[35] Norfolk was not at court when news of the battle reached the king, but Henry quickly ordered the duke to gather "all suche hable men" he could in East Anglia to supplement the border militia, and authorized sixty thousand pounds to pay and supply a northern army. The "insult" of Haddon Ridge convinced Henry that Scotland had to be punished before anything could be undertaken on the continent.[36] The privy council sent Norfolk instructions on dealing with the Scottish ambassadors James sent to York, but such was the thirst for battle that Southampton and several other councilors of a martial bent rushed to join Norfolk in the north. On 2 September Chapuys reported plans for a major offensive against the Scots, noting sadly that Charles could expect no aid until Henry was finished with James.[37]

Norfolk's campaign of 1542 had an almost comic opera air; although Henry was determined to punish the Scots, Norfolk was forced to go through the motions of negotiations with their ambassadors before launching an invasion. Henry wanted revenge, but he was pragmatic enough to accept a favorable settlement. As with the French, however, Henry's price was impossibly high, undermining any chance of an agreement. By the time it was clear than none was forthcoming, the season was well advanced, and the usual cold, wet weather of the north ruined stockpiled supplies and spread illness among the troops. Norfolk's eventual incursion was little more than an exceptionally large-scale border raid and did not result in a decisive battle. Under the circumstances of weather and supply and transportation problems, Norfolk's invasion was fairly successful, but the king had wanted much more; only English luck in the encounter at Solway Moss allowed Henry to forget how little Norfolk accomplished at such great cost.

The campaign of 1542 is richly documented in the state papers, which provide an opportunity for a detailed look at Norfolk as diplomat, administrator and soldier. Howard had to deal with a maddening array of problems—long supply lines, miserable weather, scanty equipment, and, perhaps worst, Henry's constant barrage of instructions and advice. While the final results were short of Henry's expectations, Norfolk displayed considerable industry in handling the endless details of the campaign. Numerous authors have judged Norfolk's service in 1542 a mismanaged failure,[38] but careful consideration of the events of September and October reveals that in fact he accomplished a good deal under adverse conditions.

Norfolk returned to London after word of Haddon Ridge reached court and spent several days in council before departing for the north on 30 August, passing through East Anglia to muster troops.[39] The threat from Scotland had the beneficial side effect of hastening his family's recovery from the fall of Catherine Howard, for Norfolk's half-brother William was pardoned and allowed to accompany him, and his eldest son Henry, earl of Surrey, was also sent along, the latter a mark of favor denied Norfolk during the Pilgrimage of Grace.[40]

Norfolk's main worry was supplies. He knew from past experience that there were not enough horses and wagons in the north to transport an army of any size and that special facilities would have to be constructed to brew beer and bake bread; otherwise, these supplies would have to be carried to Berwick by ship. By 6 September Norfolk had mustered two thousand men in Suffolk, armed and supplied for the march north. All seemed secure but the beer supply, Norfolk noting that "I feare the lack of nothing but that."[41] All armies march on their stomachs, but for sixteenth-century Englishmen beer was a staple as vital as bread. Norfolk left Kenninghall on the morning of 11 September and was in Lincoln three days later. Here he made musters revealing fewer men ready to serve from the Midlands than he had expected. Standing armies were unheard of in Tudor England; despite frequent musters, the government had only a general idea of the numbers able to serve in arms at any time. Norfolk wrote peevishly to the council that "surely I shall lacke a greate part of the nomber I shoulde have had."[42]

By 16 September Henry had already sent two sets of instructions for the talks with the Scots at York. The king struck a hard line intended to produce either a total surrender to English demands or else a *casus belli* should the Scots not live up to Henry's interpretations of the Anglo-Scottish treaties. Many of the demands echoed Norfolk's negotiations of March 1541, including return of English prisoners and an end to harboring of criminals and rebels. But Henry had raised the stakes, and instructed Norfolk to demand that all disputed lands between the two kingdoms be confirmed as English. The Scottish envoys were to agree to all these terms without consulting their home government, and, finally and most unlikely, the Scots were to provide hostages of the rank of earls and bishops as pledges for their promises. Henry recognized the slim chance that the Scots would yield to all of this, for in his second set of instructions he ordered Norfolk to continue repairing fortifications and gathering troops. Henry expected war, and relished the prospect, ordering Norfolk to prepare a sweeping invasion to seize the fortresses of the Scots Marches, as well as an amphibious assault on the Shetland and Orkney islands![43]

The meetings which began at York on 18 September proved a complete failure. Norfolk, Tunstall, Southampton and Sir Anthony Browne needed only two days of discussions to discover that the Scots had no power to treat for anything of weight, and were under orders to delay rather than negotiate—although the bishop of Orkney swore by the "blood, wounds, nails, body and passion of Christ . . . that they dissembled not." The Scots were given six days to communicate the English demands to James V. Norfolk warned Henry that no agreement could be expected, and began preparing to invade Scotland by the end of September. Little had yet been done to alleviate the shortages of beer, food, wagons, ships and ordnance in the north. Norfolk planned for the army to assemble in Newcastle on 27 September, but feared that food and drink would not arrive from the south in time or quantity enough to supply his men. Writing to the council, he lamented: "Thes matier [of supplies] is one of the greattest trobles to us all that can be possible, not doubtyng but that your lordshippes do well remember that I the Duc of Norffolk have often wryten to you myne opinion therin."[44]

While awaiting supplies from the south, Norfolk worked to collect what food and transport he could along the borders. Sir George Lawson was at Berwick baking bread and brewing beer, while Norfolk ordered every captain of one hundred men to bring two carts of drink and ten packhorses of food to Newcastle, not to be used until the army entered Scotland. Without such supplies, and without aid from the south which, thus far, had been forestalled by bad weather, the army would not be able to move beyond Newcastle.[45]

Henry sent further instructions on 22 September, demanding that James prove his peaceful intentions by promising to visit London before Christmas.[46] James had not come to York the year before; it must have been obvious that his advisors would not allow him to visit Henry's court. Indeed, the earl of Rutland reported to Norfolk from Alnwick that, although the Scots lords wanted peace, the pro-French churchmen desired war.[47] When the English and Scottish representatives met again on 27 September, no final agreement was reached but, surprisingly, the Scots produced James's pledge that, to preserve peace, he would meet Henry at York and perhaps journey to London with his uncle.[48]

Norfolk was so startled by this concession that initially he began planning to provide James a suitable escort from Berwick to York.[49] Henry was adamant, however, that nothing less than signed articles promising release of all English prisoners and laying out a schedule for James's journey to London would suffice. Rejecting the Scottish offer of 27 September, Henry ordered Norfolk to set forth to do "some notable exploit" against the Scots. At least the king had taken note of his commander's warnings about lack of supplies and transportation, for Henry conceded that a full-scale invasion might not be possible. Even so, he expected the devastation of the Scots Borders and Marches, as well as an invasion of the Shetlands and Orkneys, as minimum accomplishments for his expenses.[50]

Norfolk had planned to gather his forces at Newcastle on 27 September. This date was delayed twice while talks went on at York and the duke anxiously awaited the arrival of supplies. By 28 September, nineteen ships had made port at Berwick with the first of the long-delayed consignments of grain. Norfolk's personal effects were still missing, as was most of the artillery. Nonetheless, on 30 September Norfolk, Tunstall, Southampton and Browne reported that the army would be arrayed at Newcastle by 7 October, move immediately to Berwick and, unless a truce was made, begin the invasion.[51]

Norfolk had repeatedly told king and council of his problems in raising and supplying the army, and thought Henry would be satisfied with a punitive raid into Scotland. When the king's letters arrived, insisting on pillaging the Lowlands and looting the northern isles, the duke and his fellows were quite seriously concerned. In writing to the council, they delicately wondered if Henry had noted the lack of victual, the failure of the ships to arrive with supplies, the bad weather, all of which had been noted in their earlier letters? They went on:

> My lordes we desire you to consider, as yet we have nothing of the shippes of warre, ne others with ordnaunce, artillerie, munition, bere, Costerelles, hopes, twigges, ne other thinges belongyng to the Coupers craft that shold comme from London, saulve only one [ship] with CCC quarters wheate. Not doubtyng but your Lordships do also consider that when the same shalbe arrived, it is requisite that the Coupers have some convenient tyme to repayre, and put order to every thing thereonto apperteynyng, and the bred to be baken, and the bere brewed. And in case we shold set forwarde to Newcastle before tharrival of the premisses, we shold so fast consume the victualle there already, that we shold not be hable by any maners taccomplisshe that which we most desire.

As for the raid on the northern isles, such a venture was impossible so late in the year. There was little there anyway but oats and a few cattle, "so wyld as they can be taken noe otherwise, but by dogges." The assault "would not quicte the tenth part of the charge." Finally, Norfolk noted that the assembly at Newcastle would have to be delayed again, this time to 15 October, in hope that more of the long-delayed supply ships would arrive.[52]

Knowing that Henry would be displeased with this gloomy report, Norfolk wrote a private letter to Gardiner and Wriothesley, asking them to be his "bokler of defence" with the king. Since "it is not in our power to rule the wynde" that had kept his ships from Berwick, the duke argued that he could not be blamed if lack of provisions limited the invasion. To march on Edinburgh with the stores at hand would be folly; thus Norfolk begged Gardiner and Wriothesley to convince Henry that delay was necessary.[53]

In fact the king was not persuaded. Henry, who often displayed a magnificent disregard for inconvenient facts, ignored his commissioners' complaints; the royal will had been made clear, and the king was not interested in excuses. Henry did agree that the attack on the northern isles could be forsaken—but only because he now desired a naval assault on Edinburgh through the Firth of Forth! It mattered little to Henry that there were serious problems with supplies or weather in the north, and so, writing for the council, Wriothesley (who obviously had not been much of a "bokler" for Norfolk) admonished the duke not to give the king cause to think that his "greate charges" in mounting the expedition had not been employed to the fullest.[54]

The situation improved considerably in the next several days, to Norfolk's great relief. On 2 October thirty-two supply ships made port at Berwick bringing grain, cheese, ordnance, timber, tents and other supplies, while eight warships lay offshore for Norfolk's use.[55] Meanwhile, negotiations with the Scots continued, the talks mainly revolving around a meeting between Henry and James on English soil. On 5 October, Norfolk and his fellow commissioners concluded that James's advisors would never allow him to leave the country, no matter what the ambassadors at York promised on their own authority. Therefore, Norfolk and his colleagues wrote to Henry that "we shall procede in our Iorneye, and we shall assemble with all diligence, your hole Army" at Newcastle for a march on Scotland on 15 October.[56] There had never been much hope that James would give in to Henry's demands, yet a great deal of time, effort and money had been wasted while the two sides went through the motions of negotiating. If the Scots' objective had been to wear the English down and perhaps to prevent an invasion so late in the year, they accomplished a good bit by the talks at York. Norfolk, who had expected to resort to war all along, wrote with some relief to Gardiner and Wriothesley on 6 October, saying that "never men went forwarde with better will than we all shall do nor that more diligently shall procede in doing all that we may think to be most to his majesties contentacion and to the grettest hurt and displeasure to his adversarys."[57]

By 11 October Norfolk was in Newcastle preparing for the departure of the army; more good news had arrived from Berwick, for the rest of the supply ships had come into port safely. All seemed in readiness for the invasion.[58] Norfolk went to Berwick on 16 October while Tunstall, Southampton and Browne remained at Newcastle to supervise the ordering of the army. Yet with all the delays that had plagued the northern campaign since September, it is hardly surprising that further problems arose. In the first place, Southampton, Norfolk's second in command, fell ill early in October and was dead by the time Norfolk reached Berwick.[59] Armies required seasoned and titled commanders, and so Henry sent north Edward Seymour, earl of Hertford, as well as Norfolk's ally Sir John Gage. They did not reach Berwick until the night of 21 October, delaying the march into Scotland for several days.[60] The other problem Norfolk encountered was already familiar to everyone involved with the expedition. Arriving at Berwick, Norfolk found the supplies in great disorder. Somehow, only ten gross of bowstrings had been sent for an army of over ten thousand, and the provisions shipped from the south had dwindled away; only enough beer and bread remained for four days' march. None of the captains had obeyed Norfolk's orders to bring provisions; the two carts of drink and ten horses laden with food for each hundred men were nowhere in evidence as the troops arrived at Berwick around 19 October. Worse, many of the men had brought horses for which forage would have to be found each day. Still, Norfolk was encouraged by the enthusiasm of the men, and vowed to raise such a smoke in Scotland as had not been seen in a hundred years.[61]

Henry had ordered a full-scale invasion and a seaborne assault on Edinburgh; word that Norfolk could mount little more than a large-scale border raid led the king to remark acidly in a letter of 26 October that such a small exploit after months of preparation and enormous costs would be a victory for the Scots. Rather belatedly, Henry asked why his commanders complained of lack of transport, and offered the suggestion that, for so noble a purpose, they could have seized every cart and wagon north of the Trent in the king's name.[62] In fact, as C. S. L. Davies has noted, supply was always a grave problem for Tudor armies, and particularly so in the north. Provisioning by sea was the only feasible means of bringing an army of any size into the field for a Scottish campaign so late in the year.[63] Norfolk had chosen to supply his forces almost entirely with goods carried to Berwick by ship because he knew from past experience that there were not sufficient carriages and horses in the north to gather and move provisions for an army of ten thousand. Henry had never been in the wild country beyond York, and although as usual he was full of confident advice for his servants, it is doubtful that Norfolk's men could have been supplied for more than a few weeks' service by any means during a northern autumn.

By the time Henry's letter of 26 October reached him, Norfolk had already completed his assault. On Sunday afternoon, 22 October, the army crossed the Tweed near Berwick. Following a road which ran roughly parallel to the frontier, Norfolk moved southwestward and camped at Eccles on 24 October. Although reports out of Scotland indicated that James had ordered Robert Maxwell, warden of the West Marches, to stop Norfolk, no major Scottish force was encountered. After a few skirmishes around Eccles, Norfolk advanced on Kelso. Here, finally, something of a battle was waged. The Scots fell back, leaving the English to sack the town and burn the ancient abbey. But the army had by now covered twenty-five miles in five days on empty stomachs. According to Norfolk, most of the men had had nothing but water since leaving Berwick. Therefore, because of lack of victual rather than Scottish resistance, Norfolk turned back toward England from Kelso. The main result of the invasion, beside the largely symbolic value of burning Kelso (which Norfolk grandly called "the Edinburgh of the Marshe and Tevidale"), was the destruction of a string of villages and the burning of large quantities of grain on the march in and out of Scotland.[64]

By 28 October Norfolk was back in Berwick. Most of the men were sent home at once since there were no supplies left in the town. Although Norfolk's reports emphasized the destruction done to the rich farmlands along the Tweed, Henry was far from pleased with the results. The king asked pointedly why he had heard nothing of notable battles fought or of great castles thrown down.[65] Norfolk, reminding the king of his past exploits on the borders, replied that the Scottish fortresses still lay in ruins from his work of twenty years before. There had been no major battles because, although a Scottish army of ten to twelve thousand men had begun to assemble at Lawder to revenge the assault, it had been forced to disperse because "there was so great scarcitie of victaille, and suche honger among them by reason of the great wast done by us . . . that for lack of victailles they were constrayned to sparcle their army, and every one to go to his home."[66]

Henry was mollified, if not completely satisfied, by Norfolk's reports; the main purpose of the northern campaign had, after all, been accomplished if the Scots were unable to attack England while Henry turned toward war in France. Norfolk had by now fallen sick, and was anxious to avoid permanent appointment as lieutenant of the north, and so was grateful to hear from Wriothesley on 3 November that he could return to court as soon as northern defenses had been secured for the winter. "So extremely handled with my disease of the lax" (i.e., chronic dysentery) that he feared for his life if forced to endure another winter, Norfolk tarried little before setting out, for he was at York on 9 November when he received word of the appointment of John Dudley, lord Lisle, as warden. By 24 November, Norfolk had joined the council at Hampton Court, no doubt to his intense relief.[67]

Despite Norfolk's assertions to the contrary, the Scots did mount an invasion of England in November. To the surprise of all the border commanders (including Hertford, who had remained at Alnwick while awaiting the arrival of Lisle), an army of some eighteen thousand under Maxwell assembled near Carlisle and crossed into England, apparently without warning, on 24 November. A hastily assembled English force under Sir William Musgrave, numbering about three thousand, inexplicably routed the Scots at Solway Moss. In a disorderly retreat over the tidal estuary of the river Esk, the Scots lost few killed, but over a thousand were taken prisoner, and the English captured the horses, wagons, tents, and artillery of the invaders nearly intact, abandoned on the field.[68] The decisive victory Norfolk had failed to gain fell to the English almost by accident.

A month after the Solway Moss rout James V died, according to contemporaries of grief and shame over the ignominious defeat suffered by his favorite, Maxwell. A week-old girl, Mary, was left to rule Scotland. Henry, finding Scotland helpless before him, demonstrated none of the ambition for British monarchy that some writers have attributed to him. Ignoring the opportunity for a military conquest, he instead resorted to the old but inexpensive ploy of trying to build a loyal English party among the Scots lords in order to reduce Scotland to an English satellite. Following a round of Christmas celebrations in London, the prisoners of Solway Moss were sent home after swearing oaths to aid Henry's schemes: the infant Queen Mary was to be sent to England to wed Prince Edward, and the "assured lords" would rule Scotland in accordance with Henry's desires. Amidst the fierce rivalries and personal feuds of the northern kingdom, Henry's wildly optimistic plans came to nothing. James Hamilton, earl of Arran, a man long noted for his hatred of Henry VIII, was named governor of Scotland, and the assured lords quickly forgot their oaths. Through the spring of 1543, Henry gained little more than a truce for his efforts. The opportunity offered by Solway Moss was wasted because Henry was anxious to turn to continental war. Had Henry really been interested in obtaining the rule of Scotland, Solway Moss was surely his greatest opportunity. That he failed to do more than rely on the pledges of his unwilling Christmas guests is strong evidence that the king never wanted more than a tractable Scotland which could not interfere in his adventures across the Channel.[69]

Norfolk was at court in early 1543 while these events were played out, taking part in negotiations with the Scots and attending council meetings. Parliament was in session from 22 January to 12 May, with a break for Easter, and Norfolk was in frequent attendance. Plans for the French war were going forward, and so Norfolk took care to repair relations with the imperial envoy Eustace Chapuys in several long, friendly conversations.[70] In February Henry agreed to a new offensive alliance with Charles, and on 27 May the treaty was ratified with Norfolk and a host of other dignitaries witnessing Henry's signature. Yet Henry agreed only to invade France within two years, and military objectives were left purposefully vague.[71]

Norfolk accepted this commitment to war with particular eagerness. His northern campaign of 1542 had not gone well, and he could hardly claim credit for the lucky victory of Solway Moss. War against France gave Norfolk a chance to rebuild his tarnished reputation. As the council turned to preparations for war, Norfolk joined Cranmer and several others on a special council which remained in London to coordinate musters, prepare ordnance and supplies and arrange shipping to Calais. This group also took charge of talks with the Scots which resulted in a peace treaty signed on 1 July 1543. While the Scots refused to renounce France, they did agree to a marriage between Edward and Mary, with the stipulation that Mary was not to come to England until she was ten years old.[72]

Even with a commitment to war with France, and with a general mobilization under way, Henry continued to press Francis to come to terms without hostilities. Marillac was brought before the council in London on 22 June to hear Henry's ultimatim. Norfolk spoke first, warning that France must accept peace for the sake of Christendom so that all could do battle against the mutual enemy, the Turks. Chapuys also spoke, making a series of impossible demands on Francis and promising that the full might of Charles and Henry, "King of France and England," would be brought to bear should Francis refuse to admit his faults and accede to their claims.[73] Not surprisingly, since Francis could only satisfy Henry and Charles by agreeing to the dismemberment of his kingdom, Marillac could offer no assurances. The speeches of 22 June served as Henry's formal defiance of France and as a justification of the war for European consumption.

In the late months of 1543, England's relations with the Scots again foundered. The peace of July was not ratified in Edinburgh until August, and then with a dangerous air of hesitation. By year's end it was clear that Henry's efforts to erect a party in Scotland had failed and that the threat of war in the north was undiminished. Despite Norfolk's campaign of the previous year—or perhaps because of it—the Scots were unwilling to remain on the sidelines of a new Anglo-French war. The regency government of Arran took advantage of Henry's European preoccupation to revoke all Anglo-Scottish treaties on 15 December, and the Auld Alliance was formally reaffirmed. Henry threatened vengeance for this betrayal, but the Scots believed—wrongly, as it turned out—that Henry was too deeply committed to the French invasion to turn aside again. By year's end Henry's Scottish policy appeared an expensive failure; the king had gained nothing from Norfolk's invasion and the victory of Solway Moss.[74]

Norfolk meanwhile joined Gardiner, Hertford, Russell and several others in talks with Chapuys to settle details for the invasion of France. By 31 December arrangements were set. Henry would move through the Somme with thirty-five thousand foot and seven thousand horse while the emperor would invade through Champagne with a similar force. If all went well, Henry and Charles would meet in Paris in the autumn of 1544.[75]

As the new year began the English nation prepared for war. Norfolk and the London council continued to oversee arrangements for the army in France, with the duke taking a particularly active role in planning transportation across the Channel to Calais. Numerous memoranda on the subject in Norfolk's hand, dated in March 1544, survive along with other papers relating to war preparations which bear his emendations and additions.[76] As early as 18 February Chapuys heard rumors that Norfolk would command the vanguard, and in fact when the order of battle was established, Norfolk and Surrey were commissioned to lead a vanguard of ten thousand men. The Howards were to provide one hundred fifty horse and five hundred foot of their own and supervise musters in the east of the realm. The king's clerks produced the rather astonishing figure of nearly one hundred thousand men ready for service, with Norfolk's counties held able to provide over thirty thousand.[77]

Thomas Howard had several other matters to occupy him in the early months of 1544. Parliament met again from 14 January to 29 March, and while Norfolk attended most of the early meetings, by the end of the session he was present only about half the time. Norfolk and Audley seem to have shared duties managing the Lords as the session wore down. The main results were a new succession act (which tacitly recognized Mary and Elizabeth as legitimate by restoring them to the succession following Edward) and an act to cancel the king's obligation to repay the "loan" of 1542. On 29 March when Parliament was dissolved, Audley was too ill to attend, and Henry too was absent. Norfolk thus gave the concluding speech usually delivered by the chancellor and presided over Henry's consent by letters patent to the bills passed during the session. Then Norfolk announced that, with "the wars now breaking out on every side," the king thought it "a fit, if not a necessary opportunity, that every one of them should return to their homes."[78]

Norfolk also continued to follow Scottish affairs. Early in April Hertford reported from the borders that Henry's party in Edinburgh was in complete disarray. As a precaution against Scottish invasion while the French war was launched, Hertford suggested seizing several strategic border towns as well as Edinburgh's port of Leith. After consulting with the king, on 10 April Norfolk and the council ordered Hertford to march across the Scots East Marches and burn Edinburgh, Leith, St. Andrews, and the castles, villages and towns of the Lowlands. Although Hertford protested that such a policy would enrage rather than pacify the Scots, he obeyed the orders. Benefitting from better weather than Norfolk had faced in late 1542—but also displaying considerable skill in managing the operation—Hertford carried ten thousand men to Leith by sea while another four thousand marched overland from Berwick. By 16 May, the work was done; Edinburgh and much of the eastern coast of Scotland lay in ruins and Hertford was back in Berwick to receive Henry's congratulations. Scotland was thrown into turmoil, and Henry finally was freed to turn his attention to France, but at the cost of guaranteeing the Scots' lasting hatred. Scotland would remain a major problem (and Edward Seymour's special concern) for a decade to come.[79]

Norfolk was preparing to depart for France when word of Hertford's smashing success arrived at court. The comparison between Norfolk's disappointing campaign and Hertford's swift and decisive assault, and the resultant luster given to the king's brother-in-law's reputation, only added to Norfolk's worries over the political balance at court on the eve of his leave-taking. In July 1543 Henry had taken his sixth wife, Catherine Parr, a twice-widowed gentlewoman of Protestant persuasion who proved an ally and friend to Cranmer and the Seymours. At the same time, several other young men of progressive leanings were on the rise at court, including John Dudley, viscount Lisle, and Anthony Denny. Under the circumstances, it was something of a relief to the conservatives that when Thomas Audley was forced by ill health to resign the chancellorship during the spring (and died in April 1544), he was replaced by Thomas Wriothesley. A careerist of particularly pliable character even by Tudor standards, Wriothesley had served under Gardiner and Cromwell, surviving the fall of the latter by turning conservative when it became expedient to do so. When Henry named Catherine Parr as governor during his absence in France, the counterbalance of Wriothesley was especially welcome to the conservatives.[80]

Norfolk arrived in Calais by 8 June. He wrote a long series of letters supplying intelligence on French forces and fortifications, but also complaining about lack of transport, high food prices, and the generally difficult conditions under which he was forced to operate.[81] Under the terms of the Anglo-Imperial treaties, Norfolk was joined by a group of Flemish advisors led by Maximilian d'Egmont, count of Buren. On 22 June John, lord Russell arrived with a host that brought the total English forces to nearly thirty thousand. At the advice of the Flemings, Norfolk and Russell determined to lay siege to Montreuil, a fortified port town forty miles south of Calais. Norfolk had preferred an assault on Boulogne, which lay ten miles beyond the Calais pale, but the Flemings advised against an attack there on the grounds that the town could not be reduced quickly enough—a claim Suffolk would shortly disprove. Henry had long coveted Montreuil and heartily approved the plan. By early July Norfolk and Russell settled down to what quickly proved to be a hopeless task.[82] Located on the south bank of the Canche River about eight miles inland, Montreuil could not even be surrounded completely, while the flat lands along the river provided little shelter for the besiegers. The purpose of the Flemings was clear to Norfolk; they had no desire for an English victory, and were content to see the duke employed in a position convenient for defense of Flanders, but of little value for a drive toward Paris.

Henry arrived at Calais on 14 July. Despite promises to Charles that he would push at once toward Paris, Henry decided to extend the English pale by adding another fortified town, and ordered Suffolk to invest Boulogne. While Norfolk and Russell remained bogged down at Montrueil—complaining all the while of lack of supplies and the duplicity of the Flemings[83]—Suffolk was able to reduce Boulogne, and Henry entered the town in triumph on 18 September. The best news that Norfolk could send from Montreuil was that Surrey had looted and burned several small towns and captured a large number of cattle. This may have been welcome news to Norfolk's ill-supplied troops, but hardly matched the fall of Boulogne.[84]

Henry had not arrived in France until mid-July and then turned aside toward Boulogne. Charles was bogged down at St. Dizier and only began to move west in late August. By mid-September Charles's advance cavalry had ridden within thirty miles of Paris, but Henry gave no sign of moving from around Calais and Boulogne. Therefore, even while assuring Henry that he would make no separate peace with Francis, the emperor did exactly that, signing the Treaty of Crépy on 18 September, the day Henry entered Boulogne. Henry left Calais for Dover on 30 September, and close behind came news of Charles's abandonment. Henry had never held up his part of the Anglo-Imperial bargain, but at least he had resisted the French offers to talk peace, reporting the overtures to Charles even as the emperor accepted them in silence.[85] Now England was left alone to defend Calais and Boulogne against French forces fighting on their own ground without the distraction of a second front.

The effects of this turn were soon obvious as the French Dauphin Henry advanced north with an army of at least fifty thousand. Norfolk, abandoned by the Flemings (who had word of Charles's defection before Henry did), and denied reinforcements from Boulogne, had less than thirteen thousand men fit to fight. The English position at Montreuil was indefensible, and Norfolk was forced to lift his siege and retreat toward Boulogne and Calais by a series of forced marches. On the heels of the Scottish campaign of 1542, the siege of Montreuil must have appeared another ill-managed failure by an aged and incompetent Norfolk. Yet even after withdrawing to Boulogne Norfolk's troubles were not over, for the garrison there was hardly better supplied or healthier than the men who straggled in with him.[86]

Henry was determined to defend Boulogne at all costs; this, after thirty years of effort, was his greatest prize. Norfolk and Suffolk soon discovered that the dilapidated defenses of a city that had just fallen to one siege could not possibly resist another. Leaving a force of four thousand to hold the citadel, the dukes retreated from Boulogne to Calais with their disease-ridden and starving armies. Henry was enraged by this disobedience, and ordered an immediate return to Boulogne. The king marveled at his commanders' "too light coming away" from the town and accused them of being "too well-minded to come homeward." Norfolk, Suffolk, Russell and Gardiner, who made up the king's council in Calais, responded that, outnumbered five to one, they could not comply. If Henry saw the English musters, they wrote, he "would think the company very unmeet either to go to Boleyn or to tarry there." The situation was so grave in Calais, with no supplies for the troops and disease raging in the camps, that its commanders began evacuating troops to Dover—a practice the London council (with its progressive majority) greatly disliked. By sending home healthy men, they wrote, Norfolk and his fellows gave the king cause to think that they sought only "to enforce your own retire."[87]

Boulogne was indefensible, and Calais hardly more so unless reinforced, but to the great relief of Norfolk and his companions the dauphin made no attempt to capture either town. In the only major skirmish, the French were repelled in a night raid on Boulogne that convinced Henry Valois that the English were too dangerous to dislodge. By 10 October the situation was a bit more secure; Norfolk and the others wrote several letters to the king to explain the circumstances, begging for forgiveness if they had offended. Norfolk wrote that he thought it better to state things plainly rather than to attempt that which could not be done, and asked the councilors in London to intercede for their fellows in Calais. On 14 October Henry sent his reply. Considering the penitence of his servants in Calais, and that God had saved Boulogne, he accepted their submission and forgave them their errors. Nonetheless, the king ordered an immediate return to Boulogne and commanded that efforts be undertaken to repair the fortress there which Suffolk had blown up two months before. This done, and garrisons set in place, the army could be sent home for the winter.[88]

Even before coming to terms with Charles, the French had tried to reopen negotiations with Henry. Rebuffed by the king at Boulogne, Cardinal Jean du Bellay approached Norfolk in September at Montreuil, but the duke prudently reported the contact before any of his enemies discovered this potential treason. Now with autumn well advanced and the fighting season over, the French approached the council in Calais to renew the offer. Charles V nobly offered himself as a mediator; finally, on 13 October Norfolk, Suffolk, Gardiner and Russell were commissioned to open talks with du Bellay. Henry sent Hertford and William Paget to Calais with further instructions and to report on the situation in France to the king.[89]

The talks began on 18 October, but quickly foundered over Henry's refusal to give up Boulogne, for the French demanded surrender of the town as a precondition to any further talks. Likewise, the French rejected suggestions that the Auld Alliance with Scotland be abandoned, leading the English to view Francis as still determined to foment British war. By 24 October, Henry sent orders for Gardiner and Hertford to meet with Charles in Bruges to discuss his offer to mediate. In the meantime, Henry ordered that repairs to the fortifications at Boulogne be continued, and warned the Calais council to remain alert against attack.[90]

With the talks at an impasse, Norfolk managed to escape his disgraced isolation at Calais and arrived at court by 5 November. Although he attended council meetings, and his signature on a number of letters and grants issued during the winter indicates some political activity, it is clear that he had not won Henry's complete forgiveness. When Charles sent a new envoy, Francis van der Delft, to join Chapuys in England, letters of credence were sent to Norfolk as well as Henry, but it was clear to all observers that the king's business was no longer in the duke's hands. Gardiner, Hertford and Paget took charge of talks with Chapuys and van der Delft and, along with Cranmer and Wriothesley, were the leading figures at court. Despite his reduced status, Norfolk remained at court, exercising what influence he could as treasurer and councilor.[91] Perhaps Norfolk hoped to be called to service on the borders, as Scotland remained restive, but even though the pacification of the north had been a Howard task for fifty years, Norfolk remained in the south. After the Scots' victory at Ancrum Moor in February 1545, Hertford was sent north again.[92] Edward Seymour was rapidly building a reputation as the leading general in England while Thomas Howard, on the heels of disappointing performances in Scotland and France, found his services were not needed.

Norfolk remained at court through the spring of 1545, and on 23 April he took his place at the Garter dinner. Although he was named to commissions of the peace for the various shires in April and, the same month, commissioned to collect the latest of Henry's forced loans in Norfolk and Suffolk,[93] Norfolk's diminished status was demonstrated in May when the threat of renewed war began to warm with the onset of spring. While Paget, Henry's principal secretary, dominated council meetings, Norfolk was sent with Lisle and Sir Thomas Seymour to examine coastal defenses. Norfolk faithfully listed the state of town defenses, roads, bridges and beaches, as well as the status of local militias, concluding that a French invasion was unlikely owing to the dangers of the coasts and the strength of the navy.[94]

Negotiations with the French, even with Charles's mediation, had made no progress by the spring. The year 1545 seemed destined for further war, and Henry laid plans to mobilize the navy and to raise a new army to resist a French invasion. Norfolk took a major role in the latter project. After a brief visit to court in June, he returned to his county to supervise defensive preparations. Henry directed Norfolk, Suffolk and Russell to take musters and appoint captains to assure that each could raise a force of thirty thousand men if needed.[95]

Since March, Francis had been gathering forces for a three-pronged assault on England. Reports from spies in France told of plans for a siege of Boulogne, an attack from Scotland by a French army, and a seaborne move against the southern coast of England.[96] In mid-July Francis sent out a fleet of two hundred ships from the Seine estuary, personally reviewing the armada as it set sail from Rouen. While Henry was dining at Portsmouth on board his flagship *Great Harry* on 19 July, the French fleet appeared offshore. After two abortive landings—including a frightening twenty-four-hour occupation of the Isle of Wight—the French began to move eastward along the coast. Norfolk, busy mustering men in Essex, received warning from the council on 26 July to watch the coasts, but also to detach four thousand men to be sent to help defend Boulogne.[97]

Lisle finally sailed from Portsmouth with the English fleet on 9 August; after several days of fencing in the Channel, the two forces had not come to battle when the French suddenly slipped away eastward. Perhaps the French were discouraged by the strength of English coastal defenses; more likely an outbreak of pestilence in the fleet was a greater problem. But probably Francis had never intended more than a diversion, for Boulogne was the main prize he wanted to recover. To relieve the pressure on the English pale, Henry commissioned Suffolk to embark for Boulogne with an army of thirty thousand in August. Henry Howard, earl of Surrey, was given command of the vanguard of this enterprise. Misfortune plagued the king from the outset, however, for on 18 August Edward Poynings, commander of Boulogne, died, and a week later Suffolk died as well, leaving Henry without seasoned commanders in France. After these ill omens he decided not to send the full army of thirty thousand, but Surrey was sent with a force of eight thousand to strengthen defense of the pale. By 31 August the earl was named commander of Boulogne and captain general of the marches in France.[98] Thus by luck as much as in recognition of his ability Surrey won his first (and last) major command.

Whether Norfolk's influence was behind his son's elevation is unclear, but it is certain that while Surrey held command in France, Norfolk was in constant attendance in the privy council. With Hertford in Scotland and Lisle employed as admiral, the conservatives had a decided advantage in council, with Gardiner and Wriothesley, as well as Anthony Wingfield, John Gage and Anthony Browne frequently present.[99] With Henry's eager young warriors absent, the council strongly opposed taking any risks on the French front. Surrey proved a considerable problem, however, for he was anxious to prove himself by performing some "notable exploit" for Henry. The council advised Surrey to act cautiously, and on 27 September Norfolk wrote to remind Surrey of the perils of military command under Henry VIII: "Ye may be sure that I do not use my doings of any sort that may turn you to any displeasure. But have yourself in await that ye animate not the king too much for the keeping of Boleyne; for who doth so at length shall get small thank. I have so handled the matter that if any adventure be given to win the new [French] fortress at Boleyne ye shall have the charge thereof; and, therefore, look wisely what answer ye make to the letter from us of the Council concerning the enterprises contained in them."[100]

Surrey gave this advice little heed. Much to Henry's pleasure and Norfolk's disgust, Surrey sent home a stream of reports bragging of bold actions and promising defeat of the menacing French. Norfolk went so far as to try to bribe Surrey into agreeing with the council that Boulogne be abandoned as indefensible. The duke hinted that he would pay off the considerable debts of his high-living son (who was building a palatial mansion, Mount Surrey, near Norwich) if he would handle the situation at Boulogne more cautiously. Surrey ignored the hint, and continued his expensive French campaign—the defense of Boulogne cost Henry over thirteen thousand pounds a month—which led Norfolk to declare that "he would rather bury you [Surrey] and all the rest of his children before he would consent to the ruin of this realm."[101]

Norfolk spent much of November and December at court, following the king from Windsor to Westminster to Hampton Court. Surrey's continued success in defending Boulogne was a topic of frequent discussion in council. Meanwhile, peace talks languished. Gardiner was sent to Bruges in October to reopen discussions with the French under imperial mediation. Henry proposed sending Norfolk and Hertford as commissioners for the negotiations, but as the French seemed unwilling to counter with du Bellay or anyone else of sufficient rank, the plan was dropped. Thus 1545 ended with Scotland and France threatening England, and with peace talks making no progress. The coming year promised to be one of continued and expensive war.[102]

After the New Year Norfolk retired to Kenninghall for a rest from the cares of government and, probably, to escape the growing political tension. Hertford and Lisle had returned to court to resume leadership of the progressive faction, which was rapidly gaining control. Hertford could call upon the support of Anthony Denny of the privy chamber, Paget, the principal secretary, Queen Catherine and her brother William, earl of Essex, as well as Archbishop Thomas Cranmer, and the progressive party was further strengthened by the defection of Chancellor Wriothesley from the conservative ranks sometime during 1546. After Norfolk and Gardiner (who had not really formed a cohesive party since just after the fall of Cromwell), the conservatives could not match Hertford's faction in prestige, talent or influence.[103] Norfolk's New Year's respite was extended by several minor tasks given him during his absence, for on 27 January the council acknowledged a report on corn shortages from the duke and asked him to muster five hundred men for the army, which kept him in the country another week.[104]

When Norfolk returned to Greenwich on 2 February he found Henry's attention still focused on Boulogne. Surrey had finally suffered defeat in a skirmish on 7 January, and the loss of two hundred lives had upset the council greatly. Perhaps this failure by Surrey, whom Henry had seen as the young, dashing leader who would lead England to glory on the continent, finally awakened the king to the necessity of coming to terms with France. Although Hertford was sent to Calais with thirty thousand men in March, at the same time Henry finally agreed to talk with the French without setting impossible preconditions.[105]

The first step toward peace was to get the hotheaded Surrey out of France. On the pretext that plans for modifications to the defenses of Boulogne required Surrey to meet with king and council, the earl was called to court on 21 March. Norfolk was especially happy to see his son home, not only because he desired an Anglo-French peace, but because he feared Surrey would come to grief in France as commander of a position that Norfolk knew from firsthand experience to be indefensible. By 28 March Surrey was in London, and two days later he met with the king. Henry was kindly, assuring Surrey that he would have a place in any future campaign in France.[106] With Surrey out of the way, on 17 April Paget, Hertford and Lisle were commissioned to meet with French envoys at Calais or some "indifferent ground." Talks began on 24 April and, after considerable bargaining, resulted in the Treaty of Campe signed on 7 June 1546. England and France swore the usual perpetual peace and amity; Henry agreed not to make war on the Scots unless the latter broke the peace; Boulogne was to be returned to France after eight years and payment of an indemnity of eight million crowns. Nothing was said of dynastic marriages to seal the treaty, but after three long, expensive years of war, peace was finally restored.[107]

While these negotiations went on, Norfolk spent much of his time in the country, only returning to court in early June. In the spring of 1546 Gardiner led a counterattack against the growing progressive ascendancy, an assault made possible by the absence of Hertford, Paget and Lisle in France. Gardiner obviously had political motives, but the focus of the attack was religious. Using the Six Articles as a tool, the bishop began investigations of a number of minor figures at court on charges of Protestant heresies, hoping to do to Hertford what had been done to Cromwell if another Robert Barnes could be turned up. Norfolk was involved in interrogation of some of the small fry hauled before the council, but the main attack was carried out by Gardiner. Several individuals with ties to Hertford or Queen Catherine were examined in May and June, including George Blage, a former Howard client who had gone over to the Seymours, and Dr. Edward Crome, a popular court preacher of questionable views. The most promising suspect turned up was Anne Askew, who was accused of being a sacramentary—the same heresy involved, however falsely, in the fall of Cromwell and Barnes. Gardiner hoped to tie Anne to the ladies of the progressive faction at court, including the wives of Hertford and Denny and even the queen herself. Although racked by Wriothesley and Richard Rich, Anne refused to crack. On 16 July she was burned at Smithfield; several days later Hertford returned to court, forcing Gardiner to call off the witch-hunt without having reached the victims he most desired to lay low.[108]

Norfolk was not actively involved in Gardiner's attack, for at the peak of the investigations the duke had reached his own conclusions on dealing with the progressives. Norfolk had sought once before to make a dynastic alliance with the Seymours. Now, in the dangerous days of mid-1546, he tried again. At worst Norfolk was hedging his bets, admitting that Hertford's position as the uncle of Prince Edward was impregnable. Yet it is also possible that Norfolk, despite his personal religious conservatism, was prepared to shift with the prevailing winds and become as Protestant as Henry's leading servants. Norfolk proposed a series of marriages to bind together the Howards and Seymours. Norfolk's daughter Mary, duchess of Richmond, was to wed Sir Thomas Seymour, and Howard grandchildren were proposed as mates for three of Hertford's offspring. On 10 June, Henry gave his approval to the proposal. The main difficulty, as before, was with Norfolk's tempestuous son, Surrey.[109]

Henry Howard—who had himself been in trouble for eating meat in Lent and had been a friend of George Blage, then under investigation as a sacramentary—could hardly object to the Seymours on religious grounds. His opposition arose from enormous pride in his noble and royal lineage; as the grandson of the duke of Buckingham, Surrey had the blood of Edward III flowing in his veins. When Surrey arrived at court in mid-June and found plans for the marriages well advanced, he began making trouble.

Surrey was irritated to find that his sister and his children had been espoused without his approval, but the idea of Thomas Seymour marrying into the family was the greatest insult to his dignity. Mary Howard had balked at wedding Seymour earlier, but now seemed willing to go through with the marriage. Determined to prevent a disgrace to the family, Surrey confronted Mary in an anteroom at court and berated her for even considering the match, cruelly suggesting that, if Mary wanted power, she ought to follow the French example by becoming the king's mistress.[110] This spectacle, played out before a fascinated court audience, effectively ruined the budding Seymour-Howard alliance. Henry Howard had inherited all of his father's pride and ambition, but none of his prudence. Norfolk had long before realized the virtue of making peace with an enemy too strong to destroy, but Surrey's rashness and overbearing dynastic pride, besides ruining Norfolk's plans, led directly to his family's destruction. Surely Hertford concluded that Surrey was too hotheaded and dangerous to let live, while the earl's pride in his royal blood provided just the point of attack needed to arouse the suspicions of a king whose own royal ancestry was none too impressive.

The fall of the Howards was closely tied to and may have been made possible by Henry's worsening health. In the scramble for the spoils of a minor king's reign, Hertford and his allies took risks that a younger Henry VIII would have pounced upon as treason. In the process Hertford had to be certain that the Howards would not stand in his way. Had Henry Howard been more cautious, perhaps nothing more would have happened than the exclusion of Norfolk and his son from the council of regency established by Henry's will; certainly Norfolk was careful in Henry's final months to do nothing to call attention to himself. But Henry Howard refused to keep a low profile. Thus the fall of the Howards was almost entirely owing to Surrey.

In the summer of 1546, Norfolk was in frequent attendance in council and maintained his position of ceremonial precedence as earl marshal, taking a prominent place in the reception of Claude d'Annebaut, admiral of France, who arrived in July to ratify the Treaty of Campe. On 31 July d'Annebaut was received by the privy council and heard Norfolk deliver an address praising the peace, but admonishing France to stay out of Scottish affairs.[111] As summer turned to autumn Henry VIII's health failed noticeably, and the Hertford faction moved to cement their control. While

Hertford and Lisle dominated the council, Paget as principal secretary commanded the king's ear as well as the machinery of government. Perhaps more important, Hertford's ally Sir Anthony Denny of the privy chamber controlled the dry stamp used to affix the king's signature to routine documents. In August 1546 Denny and two of his servants were granted exclusive control of the dry stamp, giving the progressive faction a firm hold over patronage and politics, since all royal acts thus signed had to pass through Denny's office.[112]

Seeing the trend of events, by the first of November Norfolk decided to withdraw to the country to ride out the period of transition as quietly as possible. Surrey, too, spent early autumn away from court, and seems to have been unaware of the king's rapidly failing health. At the beginning of November, however, Surrey came to court in hope of obtaining title to a piece of monastic property in Norwich, and in doing so, fell into the hornets' nest that Norfolk had taken such pains to avoid.[113]

Surrey was firm in his conviction that his father, as the leading peer of the realm, ought to be named regent for Edward. Hertford and his friends were upstarts, and Surrey did not hesitate to express his views. Perhaps he was correct in considering Norfolk, at least in terms of formal precedence, most deserving of the Edwardian regency, but Surrey spoke his prideful words to a court dominated by enemies of his family, his father and himself. Words alone were not enough to ruin the Howards, but Surrey's words provoked a sharp investigation into his conduct in the hope that something more substantive could be turned up. And it was. Surrey had expressed his arrogant self-assurance by commissioning heraldic decorations for Mount Surrey blending the arms of Howard, Mowbray and Plantagenet.[114] This genealogically correct but foolish display provided the opening his enemies would exploit.

During November, while Henry was gravely ill, Surrey fell into an argument with Sir George Blage over the earl's pretensions and, though Surrey was wise enough to hold his temper while at court, where the striking of another was a serious offense, he did not let the matter rest. Surrey made an evening visit to Blage's house but was denied entry. To ensure that Blage knew of his wrath, in case he had not heard his enraged pounding at the door, Surrey sent Blage a letter threatening dire consequences should a mere knight ever insult his comital dignity again.[115]

Blage delivered this missive to his patron Hertford. By 1 December

Henry was well enough to be shown the letter, no doubt at the same time being given a detailed report on Surrey's provocative words and deeds. That evening Surrey was detained after dinner at Westminster and taken into custody at Wriothesley's house. Hertford took advantage of Surrey's indiscretion to launch a full inquiry into the affairs of the Howards with the aim of convincing the king that a dire plot was afoot, with the Howards planning to murder their rivals and seize the person of Edward without waiting for Henry's demise. The charges should have been preposterous to any who knew Norfolk and had witnessed his long and loyal service to the Tudors. But Henry was not well in body or spirit, and was willing to listen when Richard Southwell, another Howard servant who had turned to the Seymours, came forward to offer substantiation.[116]

Southwell revealed to the king that Surrey had, in preparing his armorial bearings for Mount Surrey, placed the arms of England in the first quarter, signifying royal blood and, presumably, royal ambitions. This charge was pointless, for Surrey descended from kings through both of his grandfathers; his quartering of the royal arms was no different from that of the last Mowbray duke of Norfolk. More pertinent, however, Southwell charged that Surrey had employed the arms of Edward the Confessor in his escutcheon, differentiated only by three labels of silver—the rightful arms of Prince Edward. These charges were, at best, evidence of Surrey's brashness, but hardly the stuff of treason. The importance of the evidence lay in what Henry's suspicious mind could be led to make of it, and the king's annotations of the charges and the notes from interrogations of witnesses with many queries ("what it importeth?") show the success with which indiscretion was promoted to treason. The annotations also show that, as with the falls of Wolsey, Anne Boleyn and Cromwell, the king was an active party to the destruction of the Howards. Even at the end, Henry might be swayed, but he could seldom be duped outright. Henry would not have destroyed the Howards had it not been for Surrey's foolish indiscretions, but even with the earl's follies, Seymour and his clique could not have harmed the Howards had Henry not decided to dispatch them. As much help as his ministers often gave him, most of the ample blood shed in the reign must rest on Henry's hands, not least of it Henry Howard's.[117]

Surrey contributed to his own destruction by continued arrogance. Brought before Hertford and the council to hear Southwell's charges on 2 December, Surrey attacked Southwell as a dishonorable liar and offered to defend himself in a trial by combat. Norfolk was at Kenninghall when word of his son's arrest arrived, and he immediately wrote several letters to friends at court, including Gardiner, who was in near exile at Southwark. Norfolk was only trying to find out what had happened, but Hertford intercepted several of the letters and chose to interpret them as evidence of Norfolk's complicity in his son's treason; hence the duke was summoned to London. On the morning of 12 December, Surrey was escorted through the streets to the Tower. He had given his accusers further fuel by swearing that "there were some who make no great account of him whom he trusted one day to make very small," and this seeming boast that a mere earl would someday rule seems to have been the final straw in convincing Henry of a plot to seize power. That afternoon, Norfolk arrived in London and was seized, stripped of his Garter and staffs of office and taken to join his son in the Tower.[118]

The sudden arrest of the Howards took the courts of Europe by surprise. Thomas Thirlby, bishop of Westminster and ambassador to Charles V, wrote that the emperor had taken the news gravely, with gladness that Henry had discovered the plot in time. Thirlby himself wrote an almost hysterical postscript to Paget, excoriating Norfolk, "whom I confess I did love, for that I supposed him a true servaunte to his master," but now giving thanks that the duke's crimes were revealed.[119] Francis I took the news more skeptically, puzzled that Norfolk would have planned treason. "Having found hym verye earnest yn your Majesties causes, He sayd he never wold have thought enye such thing yn hym," as Nicholas Wooten reported it. Indeed, as far as Wooten, Henry's envoy in France, could see, Norfolk "had ever so dissimulid the mater, that he had decyvid menye mennes expectacions who had better opinion of hym."[120] These comments reflect the reality that Norfolk's crimes were as much the imagination of his accusers as had been Cromwell's—as well as the truth that the Howards were as good as dead no matter what the merit of the charges.

Surrey wrote to the council when he learned of his father's arrest, saying he much sorrowed to see "the long approved truth of mine old father brought into question by any stir between Southwell and me." Norfolk had a clearer idea of the situation. In a letter to the king on 13 December, Norfolk wrote, "I am sure that some great enemy of mine hath informed your Majestie of some untrue matter against me. . . . And certainly, if I knew that I had offended your Majestie in any point of untruth, I would declare the same to your Highness." Norfolk asked to know the specific charges against him, and sought to confront his accusers in council. Remembering the persecutions of the past summer and suspecting that the attack was on religious grounds, Norfolk protested that, in matters of faith, "Whatsoever laws you have in past time made, or hereafter shall make, I shall to the extremity of my powers stick to them as long as my life shall last." Finally, perhaps hoping to escape the full penalties for the treasons with which he was charged, Norfolk offered the king all of his lands and goods as a gift and token of his loyalty.[121]

Although Norfolk's offer to surrender his lands was taken up at once—the king saw that the Howard lands would be a fine endowment for Edward's creation as Prince of Wales—Hertford and his allies never considered giving Norfolk a hearing. The charges against Surrey were weak, but those against the duke were based on little more than guilt by association. Nevertheless, with Henry nearing the end of his life, Hertford could not afford to risk Norfolk and his grasping son escaping to threaten the arrangements being made for Edward's regency government. The Howards had to be destroyed. Once father and son were in custody, Richard Southwell and two others were sent to Norfolk to search the residences of the Howards for evidence of their treasons while the council interrogated the prisoners and their servants. Southwell found sumptuous furnishings, considerable jewelry, several thousand pounds in cash, but no trace of the alleged escutcheons bearing the arms of the prince and no documents of any use.[122] Surrey meanwhile steadfastly refused to admit any act which could be construed as treason; the only charge he admitted was the heraldic abuse of quartering his arms with those of St. Edward, which Surrey claimed as his right because his Mowbray predecessors had done so.[123]

Examination of the Howard servants provided little of use. Richard Fulmerston, the duke's steward, swore he knew of no disloyalty by his master—probably a prudent course, since his closeness to Norfolk would have exposed him to charges of misprision of treason had he acknowledged any crimes.[124] Norfolk was questioned at length by Paget and William Paulet, lord St. John. The interrogation ranged over a number of points, most of them dealing with Norfolk's relationships with foreign ambassadors, perhaps in hopes of turning up evidence that Norfolk had thwarted royal policy or illegally opened the king's counsels. Surrey's crimes were not mentioned, perhaps because it was evident that Norfolk could not plausibly be tarred with the same brush; other treasons had to be sought out.[125]

Henry Howard was earl of Surrey by courtesy as son of a duke; by law he was a commoner, a point he may not have realized when he demanded a trial by his peers. Therefore when Surrey was brought to trial on 13 January he faced, not a panel of lords, but a jury of East Anglian gentlemen who could be overawed by the powerful prosecutors. Surrey was charged under the succession act of 1536, which made any act that imperiled the succession treason.[126] The trial lasted eight hours, and Surrey put up a spirited defense, arguing that as a true nobleman, he would never lie, but that low-born churls such as Paget, Lisle and Seymour would do anything, however dishonorable, for money and power. The most damning piece of evidence presented may have been that Surrey had tried to escape from the Tower before his trial. Even so, the verdict was slow in coming; the jury deliberated for five hours without result before Paget entered their chamber to demand a verdict in the king's name. Shortly thereafter the panel reached the desired decision, and Surrey was pronounced guilty and sentenced to suffer the full pains of a common traitor's death. Nonetheless, he was allowed a more honorable execution, and on 19 January was quietly beheaded on Tower Hill.[127]

Norfolk, as a peer, was entitled to trial by the House of Lords or a special commission under the lord high steward. In fact, Howard was never brought to trial. The charges against him—that he had planned, with Surrey, to murder the council, depose the king and take over rule of the realm, and that he had had secret and treasonable dealings with foreign ambassadors with the aim of betraying Henry—were shaky at best, but were cleverly designed to arouse the deepest doubts and most dangerous suspicions of Henry VIII. Norfolk saw the handwriting on the wall, and on 12 January, the day before Surrey went to trial, capitulated by signing a confession that gave his enemies all that they could have wished.

Norfolk admitted having opened Henry's "previe and Secrete Counselles at diuerse and sondreye tymes to sondreye persones," to the peril of the realm and the disappointment of Henry's affairs. Further, Norfolk confessed the central "treason" of which the Howards stood accused by admitting that he had known of and concealed Surrey's treasonous presumption in displaying the arms of England in the principal quarter of his own arms. For these crimes, Norfolk admitted that he deserved condemnation as a traitor with all due punishments, including forfeiture of goods. Yet perhaps the point of the confession is made most clear by its concluding abject plea for mercy: "Although I bee not worthie to haue or enioye any parte of the kinges maiesties Clemencie and mercy, . . . yet I most homblye and with moste sorowful and Repentant harte beseeche his highnes to haue mercy pittie and compassyon vppon me, and I shall moste devoutedlye and hartellye make my dayle prayers to gode for the preservation of his most noble successyon as long as I live or brethe shall continewe in mee."[128]

Norfolk's confession, witnessed by Wriothesley, Paget, Hertford, and several other councilors (but not, interestingly enough, by his former allies Gage and Wingfield), cleared the way for an act of attainder to seal his condemnation. Yet if the case against him was so weak that his enemies hesitated to try him, why did Norfolk make things easy for them? Thomas Howard was not, as some have suggested, either a coward or a fool.[129] He had spent a lifetime in the service of the Tudors, his loyalty often tested but never found wanting. Surely Henry would now have mercy on one who had sacrificed so much for his prince, or so Norfolk must have thought. He had been in danger many times before and had always managed not only to wriggle free, but to return to Henry's confidence. Others, most recently including Catherine Parr, had escaped the king's wrath by similarly abject submissions. Norfolk's confession was a small price to pay for freedom and an opportunity to revenge himself upon his enemies once he had explained all to the king. Alas for Thomas Howard that his enemies were far stronger than he imagined, and that Henry's final and painful illness left the king little interested in anyone else's fate.

The Parliament of 1545 had last sat in December of that year. A new session began on 14 January 1547. Thus on the heels of Norfolk's confession and Surrey's conviction, the final ruin of the Howards could be worked. On 18 January a bill to attaint them both was introduced in the Lords as a petition addressed to the king. This charged that the Howards had "most falsely, malycyously and treytourously" committed high treason, "to the great perill and slander of your most Royall person and to the disturbance and interupcion of your most Iust and undoubted title to your Croune in this your Realme." Thus the key charge remained tied to the succession act, the unproved assertion that Norfolk and his son had plotted to overthrow Henry's council and seize Prince Edward pending the king's death. Specific evidence was not mentioned; Norfolk's confession was cited, but the bill was based largely on Surrey's conviction and the principle of guilt by association.[130]

For some reason, the bill took a week to pass both houses, although it does not appear to have been amended. Probably Henry's worsening illness delayed things, but by 27 January the formalities were concluded, and Wriothesley presided over a joint session which, although not the closing ceremony (Parliament met twice more after Henry died), was held for the specific purpose of giving royal assent to the attainder. As with Catherine Howard's statutory condemnation, the king's assent was given by letters patent produced by Wriothesley. All was prepared for Norfolk to follow Surrey to the block.[131]

Knowing that Henry was dying, Hertford and his allies had rushed to complete the attainder before the session was ended by the sovereign's death. This they accomplished, but during the night of 27–28 January Henry died, holding Cranmer's hand, with Denny at his bedside and Paget, Wriothesley and Hertford waiting outside the chamber door. Norfolk's execution had been planned, probably for the 28th; Odet de Selve wrote Francis I on 31 January to report Norfolk's secret beheading the day before. But this proved a rumor. For three days, during which Norfolk could have been executed, the king's death was kept secret while Hertford prepared to seize power in Edward's name. Norfolk remained in the Tower, perhaps wondering when he would go to his death. Instead, the king's demise brought Norfolk an unexpected reprieve. Hertford, busy with more pressing affairs, was satisfied to leave the seventy-three-year-old Howard to die of natural causes rather than begin the new reign with an act of gratuitous bloodshed. By the accident and ironic good fortune of Henry's death, Norfolk, who had served that king long and well, lived.[132]

Norfolk's survival underlines the point that Henry was the main source of the reign's bloodshed. Nothing in law prevented Hertford from sending Norfolk to the block. Henry always pursued his real and imagined enemies to the death, yet the Catholic duke of Norfolk was spared by the Protestant party of Edward Seymour.[133] Had Henry lived another day or two, Norfolk would surely have died, yet Hertford was content to leave Norfolk safely out of the way in the Tower. It was an act of mercy which granted Howard another seven years of life, more than twice the remaining span for Hertford, the apparent victor of the struggle at the end of Henry's reign. For the Catholic and conservative Thomas Howard, the Tower may have been the safest place to spend Edward's reign, although it was not a choice he would willingly have made.

CHAPTER 10

THE FINAL YEARS, 1547–1554

THE DEATH OF HENRY VIII spared the life of Thomas Howard but left him a prisoner in the Tower of London for the duration of Edward VI's reign, only a spectator to the events of the Edwardian regency, with what emotions we do not know, for the material which remains gives little information about his thoughts. Yet survive he did, and that in itself is a testimony to the toughness of Thomas Howard, for a term of over six years in the damp of the Tower should have been enough to finish off most men in their seventies. Howard not only outlived Edward VI, but returned to a place of influence under Mary to cap off a career of service to the Tudors.

By the terms of his attainder, Howard was stripped of all titles and offices and his lands and goods were forfeited to the crown. Now made regents by the terms of Henry's will, the fallen duke's enemies were quick to begin a division of the spoils. On 10 February 1547, Edward Seymour was made lord treasurer. A week later, following his creation as duke of Somerset and appointment as the young king's protector, Seymour was granted Norfolk's former office of earl marshal as well.[1]

With a few exceptions the regency government, though taking an increasingly Protestant religious direction, was drawn from the privy council of Henry VIII's last months. While Somerset dominated affairs, some conservatives such as Cuthbert Tunstall, Anthony Browne and Richard Rich continued in public life. Stephen Gardiner, excluded by Henry's will from the regency council as a man only a strong king could control, was the most notable figure to fall from power at Edward's accession. Gardiner was persecuted intermittently until being sent to the Tower in June 1548 and deprived of his bishopric in 1551. Thomas Wriothesley likewise did not long survive Henry's death as a leading figure; although elevated to the earldom of Southampton in February, he was too conservative in religious matters for Somerset's taste, and was forced to resign the chancellorship and his place on the council by the first week of March.[2]

These adjustments took time. Perhaps encouraged that there was no immediate assault on all the conservatives in council, Howard made a concerted effort in the early months of his imprisonment to win his freedom. According to the imperial ambassador, at Edward's coronation on 20 February "all those who had offended the king were pardoned except the duke of Norfolk, who was excluded by name, and also Cardinal Pole, and the son of the marquis of Exeter," Edward Courtenay, resident in the Tower since 1538. Thomas Howard, brother of the earl of Surrey and Norfolk's eldest surviving son, was given a general pardon and restored to the rank of baron in mid-April; the rest of the Howards, including the duke's half-brother William, were untouched by the family's crimes and left unmolested.[3] This leniency gave Norfolk reason to hope for his own restoration, and so in April he asked Thomas Cranmer to visit him in the Tower. Howard knew Cranmer well, and hoped to win his freedom through an emotional appeal to the politically naïve archbishop. In the course of a two-hour conversation, in which they shared tears and lamentations, Howard persuaded Cranmer to lobby for his release. Unfortunately, Cranmer did not have sufficient influence; Somerset was unwilling to release a potential opponent, and the attainted duke remained in the Tower.[4]

A fair amount of evidence remains concerning Howard's imprisonment. He was probably held in Beauchamp Tower, the residence of many noble prisoners, including Anne Boleyn, and later the prison of Guildford Dudley, husband of Lady Jane Grey. During Henry VIII's last days, when his execution seemed imminent, Howard was deprived of all comforts, including books, sheets for his bed, and hangings for the damp stone walls above the west moat. Further, he was confined to a narrow cell on the upper floor and forbidden exercise in the outer chambers of the tower.[5]

These conditions were improved early in Edward's reign when it became clear that Norfolk would remain a prisoner. On 3 March 1547 Sir John Markham, lieutenant of the Tower, was ordered to provide Norfolk with clothing and personal furnishings befitting his station. A list sur-

The Final Years

vives, noting that Norfolk received a gown of damask with a fur collar, doublets and jackets of satin, hose and shoes, linens for the table, towels, gloves, and even a pair of "furred buskins of Spanish leather," all to be replaced yearly. Norfolk was permitted a featherbed, bolsters and blankets for himself and another set for a servant. Later, in February 1549, the council approved a warrant for six pieces of hangings for Norfolk's chamber, although whether these were new items or replacements for old is not clear. As early as February 1547 Norfolk began to be allowed family visitors; Mary, duchess of Richmond, and Elizabeth, duchess of Norfolk, were permitted to visit Howard "at tymes and with traynes convenient, the Lieutenant [Markham] being present." Further, a bit of personal freedom was now allowed: "the said Duke may have libertye to walke in the gardein and gallery when the Lieutenant shall think good."[6]

Several documents record the expenses of Norfolk's imprisonment. An undated draft warrant issued to Markham authorized annual expenditures of £73 5s. 4d. for apparel and £80 "for the spending money of the seid late Duke."[7] Another document[8] records the money allocated Norfolk for servants' wages and "other necessities in his chamber." Norfolk was allowed £5 a week for food and drink, board for five servants at 6s. 8d. a week each, and 8s. a week for fuel and light. Norfolk's imprisonment cost the crown over £450 a year, making his continued life an expensive investment.[9]

Political turmoil in the Edwardian regency was reflected in the conditions of Norfolk's incarceration. After three years of increasingly inept and insensitive rule, and following rebellions in Cornwall and Norfolk, Somerset was forced from power at the end of 1549, and by early 1550 John Dudley, earl of Warwick, had emerged as his successor.[10] Howard and Dudley had never been personal enemies, and so after his rise to power Norfolk enjoyed greater liberty, although not his freedom.[11] In July 1550 Norfolk was given leave to walk or ride within the precincts of the Tower, accompanied by a guard, and in April 1551 was permitted a visit from his son Thomas. Although the conversation was held in the presence of Markham, such a meeting between a traitor and his son was very unusual.[12]

There were rumors from time to time that Dudley, now made duke of Northumberland, would release Norfolk, and after Somerset's execution an imperial envoy reported in February 1552 that Norfolk was no longer in danger and would soon be freed. Norfolk was given permission to write a letter to the council (perhaps petitioning for his liberty; the letter has not survived),[13] but remained a prisoner until Mary Tudor arrived in London in August 1553. The most reasonable explanation for Norfolk's not being freed is that certainly Somerset and probably Northumberland had no good reason for releasing a former rival who, despite his age, was still a potential threat if given his liberty.

But just as important to the Edwardian junto were their considerable financial gains from the redistribution of Norfolk's forfeited lands and goods. Most of the progressive faction had profited from Norfolk's fall; they were little inclined to see the attainted duke freed, much less restored to his titles and property, at their expense.

After his arrest, Norfolk's land and personal property at Kenninghall and elsewhere were inventoried by crown agents. Robert Holdiche, Norfolk's receiver of land revenues, turned over £1,480 in cash at the duke's arrest, and eventually completed a detailed survey of lands in Norfolk, Suffolk, Essex, Cambridgeshire and Lincolnshire. Not until January 1549, when Holdiche delivered a final £47 2s. 3 1/4d. to the council, was he freed of his responsibilities.[14] On 6 February 1547 Paget presented a memorandum to the council in which he claimed that Henry, before his death, had directed the division of Norfolk's land among the leaders of the Hertford faction. The new king, Paget said, had ratified his father's wishes, and so the plunder of the Howards' wealth began.[15] Somerset and Warwick were both granted large blocs of Howard lands "without fee or fine," many of which they sold for ready money. Somerset, granted the possessions of the dissolved Cluniac priory of Thetford, sold the property to Norfolk's former steward Richard Fulmerston in August 1547;[16] Warwick was granted lands including the manor of Romburgh, Suffolk, on 22 December, and obtained a license to alienate the property three days later.[17] In another case, Warwick sold the reversion of a Suffolk manor from the Howard estates one day after receiving letters patent for the land.[18] Deals of this nature cannot have been made casually, but were straight profit-making ventures, financial exploitation by the highest-ranking servants of the crown.

Several others of Seymour's faction received Howard lands. Thomas Seymour, on his elevation to the baronage in August 1547, received a group of properties in Sussex, all of them former Howard lands, to an annual value of well over £500. William Parr, when made marquis of Northampton, was given Norfolk's house at Lambeth.[19] Anthony Denny obtained lands in Norfolk and Suffolk, including about nine hundred acres of pasture that had come to Howard with the dissolved monastery at Sibton.[20] William Paget had his own modest reward, obtaining the manor of Willington, Kent, in May 1547 and selling it in October, presumably for more than the £3 13s. 4d. he paid for the license to alienate.[21] Later in Edward's reign, Howard lands were granted to Thomas Darcy, the lord chamberlain, when he was made a baron, and in May 1551 John Cheke, the king's tutor, was given a group of Howard manors in Suffolk and Lincolnshire.[22] Norfolk's palace at Kenninghall went to the king's sister Mary on 17 May 1548 as part of a group of manors worth nearly £4,000 a year, including several Howard properties in East Anglia.[23]

In addition to outright grants or sales at bargain prices to the Edwardian regents, other Howard properties were alienated at more normal market values. Between April 1549 and May 1553 lands of a yearly value of around £200 were sold at twenty years' purchase, bringing almost £4,000 to the crown.[24] Yet a large portion of Norfolk's estates were still in crown hands, with royal officials collecting the rents, in 1553.[25] In 1545, Norfolk had assessed himself at 5,000 marks (£3,333 6s. 8d.—£67,000 at twenty years' purchase) in landed income for the parliamentary subsidy. When the known value of gifts and sales of Howard lands by 1553 is computed, less than half of this income is accounted for.[26] Still, enough land went to the Edwardian regents that it is not hard to understand their reluctance to free Norfolk and face the possibility of legal actions to recover his property.

The fate of Norfolk's personal property is even better documented, for the inventories drawn up at the time of his arrest were annotated as goods were sold or given away.[27] Norfolk's apparel—ranging from satin gowns and velvet coats to petticoats, doublets and hose, and including his parliamentary robes and Garter regalia—went to Edward Seymour, who also obtained Surrey's parliamentary robes and several gilt rapiers and daggers from the earl's estate. Elizabeth Holland, Norfolk's mistress, and Mary, duchess of Richmond, were allowed to keep their personal clothing, no small favor considering the mass of satins, velvets, rich embroidery and cloth of gold and silver. Bess Holland also kept her personal jewels—which included a number of rich pieces such as a gold cross set with six diamonds, four rubies and three pearls, and a set of red, white and gold enameled beads. With the exception of a collar of gold with the medallion of St. George and a Garter set with rubies, both of which went to

Paget, Somerset received most of Norfolk's personal jewelry, including another St. George, a French Order of St. Michael, gold chains, and rings, broaches and badges set with precious stones. The pillage included Norfolk's household goods, from which Somerset obtained carpets, hangings and cushions as well as featherbeds, bolsters, quilts, blankets, sheets and pillows from twenty beds (ten for "gentlemen," ten for "yeomen"). From the hall and chapel at Kenninghall came a number of rich items, including several salt cellars and the finest plate and service books. Finally, Somerset took his pick of the 200 horses, 88 oxen, 115 steers, 420 hogs and 407 sheep found at Kenninghall. The duchess of Richmond and the countess of Surrey divided what remained of the household goods after Somerset was sated.[28]

This redistribution of wealth among the victors of the power struggle at the close of Henry's reign was not confined to Howard possessions. W. K. Jordan estimates that some £20,000 annual value (£400,000 at twenty years' purchase) in lands was parceled out during Somerset's ascendancy alone. Some was Howard land, but most came from existing crown estates and property from dissolved monastic houses and chantries.[29] In the midst of a general orgy of self-enrichment at the expense of a minor king, the forfeited Howard estates were a small part of the spoils.

Edward VI's regents continued the factional politics that had marked the later stages of Henry VIII's reign. In 1550 Somerset was thrust from power in a palace coup, as several key councilors shifted sides or remained neutral in his time of crisis—a situation reminiscent of the fall of Cromwell a decade before.[30] Somerset was executed on 22 January 1552, but Dudley, as duke of Northumberland, became effective ruler of England from 1550 onward. Perhaps in an effort to win the support of Edward, who was thirteen in 1550 and had grown into a devout and bigoted Protestant, Northumberland and Cranmer continued the radicalization of the English church with the Act of Uniformity and Prayer Book of 1552. By the close of Edward's reign, the official state church, whatever the feelings of the populace as a whole, was solidly Protestant.[31]

The English Reformation and its champions were hardly secure, however, for all hung on the slender thread of the young king's life. And by the end of 1552, Edward's never very robust health began a decline which, with increasing rapidity and certainty, led to his death in mid-1553. The succession became a question of vital importance because, by

The Final Years

Henry's will, the next heir to the throne was Mary, daughter of Catherine of Aragon and a devout Catholic. This threat drove Northumberland to a desperate attempt to insure his own power by tampering with the succession. On 21 May 1553 Northumberland's son Guildford was married to Jane Grey, whose claim to the throne was through Henry's younger sister Mary. By the terms of Henry's will, this line would succeed only in default of Henry's own children. Edward was induced to draft a "device" in his own hand disinheriting his sisters, thus establishing the Grey line and the Dudleys as paramount, in fact alone, in upholding the succession.

Probably Northumberland hoped for a son from the marriage; any male in the Tudor line could have been put forward as heir to the throne with a certain plausibility. Unfortunately Edward faded rapidly, forcing Northumberland to further expedients and alterations in Edward's plans for the succession. The final version of Edward's device passed over the actual heir in the Grey line, Frances, the daughter of Mary Tudor and Charles Brandon, and named Jane Grey as heir. The council reluctantly accepted this arrangement, so clearly designed to elevate the Dudleys, but when Edward died on 6 July the scheme quickly collapsed. Jane was proclaimed in London, but Mary, forewarned, fled to Framlingham, the old ducal castle of the Mowbrays and Howards in Suffolk. Northumberland's failure to secure the person of Mary proved his undoing. Armed forces flocked to her side; the councilors supported Northumberland only as long as he remained in London. When the duke ventured to Cambridge to face Mary, he found that Jane had no support in the countryside. Far from capturing Mary, Dudley was forced to surrender without a fight, his scheme in ruins.[32]

On the day of Jane's elevation (10 July) there were rumors that the prisoners in the Tower—Norfolk, Gardiner and Courtenay—would be executed, but as Northumberland's attempted coup collapsed, their fate changed dramatically. Simon Reynard, the imperial ambassador, reported on 22 July that Gardiner had been offered his liberty but had refused, wishing only to be released by his queen. Norfolk, too, remained in the Tower, but hardly as a prisoner; everyone who wished to see him, Reynard said, was able to do so.[33]

On 3 August Mary entered London in triumph, with Northumberland a prisoner in her train. To the accompaniment of "a great peal of ordnance" Mary proceeded to the Tower and found Howard, Gardiner and

Courtenay kneeling at the gateway. Mary stooped to kiss the three and bade them rise, declaring them her men.[34] On 4 August, they were granted pardons, and Howard, now again recognized as duke of Norfolk, was restored to the council along with Gardiner.[35] Lady Jane Grey and the rest of the Dudleys joined Northumberland in the Tower, and the fallen duke was examined several times by Norfolk and the council early in August. On the tenth, Norfolk left the Tower and was restored as earl marshal and lord high steward to preside over Mary's coronation. The office of treasurer, ably performed by William Paulet, marquis of Winchester, was not returned to Norfolk. Gardiner, however, recovered his bishopric of Winchester and was also made chancellor, an act that did much to set the tone of Mary's reign, for Gardiner was a bitter man with political and religious grudges to settle. Although Gardiner would be a major figure in the first half of Mary's reign, Norfolk, nearly eighty years old, was reserved mainly for ceremonial purposes. Mary wisely retained much of Edward's council, and there was no real place for Norfolk among these professionals of a younger generation; still, the duke attended a majority of the council meetings through January 1554.[36]

Norfolk's first important service to the new queen was to preside over the trial of Northumberland. The fates of the Howards and Dudleys had been intertwined for almost fifty years under the Tudors. Norfolk's father had conducted the trial of Northumberland's father, Edmund Dudley, in 1509, and in 1546 John Dudley had been active in the fall of the third duke, examining him in the Tower and helping direct passage of the attainder of the Howards in the House of Lords. Norfolk took his revenge in condemning John Dudley, but this score would be evened by Dudley's sons, who, as earls of Leicester and Warwick, were among those who found Norfolk's grandson and heir, the fourth duke, guilty of treason in 1572.

On 18 August, Northumberland, his eldest son Ambrose, earl of Warwick, and William Parr, marquis of Northampton (the latter almost the only peer to have stood by Northumberland to the end) were tried in Westminster Hall before the court of the lord high steward.[37] Northumberland protested that he had committed no crime, having only supported his sovereign queen, Jane Grey, but Norfolk quashed the objection and declared the court lawful and the charges just. After the indictment was read, Northumberland declared his repentance, confessed his guilt, and "mooved the duke of Norfolke to be a meane unto the queene for mercie."

Norfolk, having spent almost seven years in the Tower, was hardly moved by the plea. According to Simon Reynard, Norfolk did not bother to consult the judges before sentencing Dudley to the full horrors of a traitor's death, as he was ordered hanged, his heart to be drawn from his body and flung against his face, and quartered.[38]

Warwick and Northampton escaped death, but Mary insisted on Dudley's execution. The duke begged for the more honorable death by decapitation to which his estate entitled him, but Mary relented only after Dudley made a gratifying and cowardly last-minute conversion to Catholicism. This failed to save his life but gave Mary an important propaganda victory. On 22 August Northumberland was beheaded, with Norfolk among the official witnesses. Only two others—Sir Thomas Palmer and Sir John Gates—died with him, perhaps demonstrating how little support there had been for Jane Grey and her father-in-law.[39] Norfolk gained a final measure of revenge against Northumberland, for on 22 September he recovered his gold ducal coronet, a collar and badge of the Garter, as well as other jewels and plate from the late duke's estate; these items had probably passed from Somerset's hands in 1550.[40]

With a Catholic now on the throne, the Edwardian religious innovations required immediate attention in the early days of Mary's reign. On 14 September Archbishop Cranmer was examined before the council, with Gardiner, Norfolk, Tunstall and several other conservatives in attendance. Cranmer was ordered to the Tower for the crimes of having circulated seditious literature attacking the mass and supporting the errors of the previous reign—this despite the fact that the Edwardian religious settlement had been established by statute and, having not yet been repealed, was not only legal but still in force. On 13 November Cranmer was brought to trial on charges with more substance, that he had committed treason in declaring Jane Grey queen on 10 July. Norfolk presided as Cranmer, Jane Grey and her husband Guildford Dudley were convicted of the treason of seeking to usurp the succession and were sentenced to death. Cranmer was returned to the Tower where he waited almost three years before meeting his fate, finally being burned as a heretic in 1556.[41]

Norfolk served as earl marshal for Mary's coronation, riding before the queen's carriage in the procession through London on 30 September and, at the banquet at Westminster Hall, riding among the guests on horseback along with the earl of Arundel, the queen's champion.[42] The coronation itself was held at Westminster Abbey, with Gardiner presiding over a long ceremony replete with all the medieval trappings. Even Norfolk's fee for his services was traditional; the duke claimed Mary's horse and "all of the furnyturre that is on the horse," as well as the cloth of state hung behind her chair.[43]

Norfolk had been pardoned and restored to his peerage and offices by Mary in August, but the embarrassment of the act of attainder and the legal problem of his lands and possessions remained. In August, writs went out for Mary's first Parliament, which assembled on 5 October. Just as with Norfolk's father who, as earl of Surrey, sat in the Parliament of 1489 which reversed his own attainder, no one seems to have complained about the attainted Thomas Howard taking his place among the Lords in 1553. Norfolk's attainder was duly reversed by statute, and he was restored to the dukedom and his grandson Thomas made earl of Surrey. The bill was cast as a petition, in which the act of attainder was recited and declared invalid on the grounds of the irregularity of Henry's assent by letters patent. The bill glossed over the confessed treasons for which Norfolk had been condemned, noting only the heraldic offense of having borne the royal arms on the Howard shield—which, the reversal act asserted, was the Howards' lawful right.[44]

Although restoration in blood and titles was easy enough to obtain, the Howard lands were a more difficult matter. Norfolk expected at first to have all the lands he had held in 1547 returned, for Reynard wrote to Charles V on 29 November that Parliament had been delayed for several days because Norfolk had insisted that lands sold or granted by Edward be repurchased or seized by the crown. The act, as passed, shows that Norfolk backed down, for several clauses were inserted to protect the rights of those who had purchased or been granted Howard lands. Only those lands still in the hands of the crown, with all profits due since the death of Edward, were restored immediately. Even with perhaps a third of his estates lost, Norfolk reclaimed lands worth upwards of sixteen hundred pounds clear.[45]

At Mary's accession, Thomas Howard was an old man, and the years in the Tower had done much to ruin his health. His military prowess, once reputed the greatest in England, had not been tested since the disappointing French campaign of 1544. Yet when rebellion broke out in the winter of 1554, Mary turned to Norfolk to face Sir Thomas Wyatt and his followers. The reasons behind this nearly disastrous decision must be sought in the tense balance at court and in council. Many of Mary's leading advisors were among the most vocal opponents of her proposed marriage to Philip, son and heir presumptive to Charles V. Gardiner had urged Mary to wed Edward Courtenay, the bishop's fellow prisoner in the Tower for five years, who had recently been restored as earl of Devon. There were other candidates, including Cardinal Reginald Pole who, his red hat notwithstanding, was still a deacon and thus eligible to wed. Probably a large majority of the ruling class was opposed to a foreign match or a return to Roman obedience (or both). Yet Mary insisted on following her heart, and in January 1554 the queen was formally betrothed, sight unseen, to Philip.

The French ambassador, de Noailles, had done all in his power to prevent an Anglo-Imperial match; now he turned to fomenting rebellion to replace Mary with her sister Elizabeth. Several areas were supposed to rise at once to overwhelm the monarchy, but Wales, Lancaster and Cornwall were all unready when hints of the plot began to reach the council. Only Wyatt was able to mount an armed rising, and the near success of his effort hints strongly that Mary would have been driven from the throne had the conspirators been able to coordinate their efforts. As it was, the queen received frightening proof of the weakness of her hold on the crown.[46]

On 25 January word reached London that Wyatt and three hundred men in arms had risen in rebellion at Maidstone, Kent, where Wyatt published a manifesto calling for the queen to be freed from her evil councilors. Gardiner and probably Paget had known for several days of the planned risings. Mary, aware of the disaffection with the Spanish match, rightly suspected that the leaders of the council had not revealed all that they knew about the threatened rebellion; Gardiner, with his close ties to Courtenay, was especially suspect. Mary turned to Norfolk to suppress Wyatt's rebellion largely because he had not been involved in the political battles in council. Despite his age, Norfolk's recent service in presiding over the trials of Northumberland and Cranmer showed that he was fit enough. He had the unquestioned loyalty that Mary could not find in most of her ministers, and, having spent the reign of Edward in the Tower, Norfolk bore no taint of the Protestantism that Mary feared in many of her councilors.[47]

At the first word of Wyatt's rising, Mary had tried to open negotiations with the rebels, but by Saturday, 27 January 1554, it was clear that these efforts were doomed; Sir Thomas would have nothing to do with

Mary's envoy. Thus Wyatt and his followers were declared traitors, and in preparation for a military confrontation a force of about six hundred Londoners was scraped together under Norfolk's command.[48] On the morning of 28 January Norfolk led his company out to Gravesend. There he met Sir Henry Jerningham, who brought about three hundred men from Kent, as well as George Brooke, lord Cobham who, despite being Wyatt's uncle, was to be Norfolk's second in command. With this force of less than a thousand men, Norfolk set out against Wyatt, who by now had entered Rochester with an army swollen to several thousand men and had fortified the city bridge with artillery.[49]

Most of Norfolk's Londoners were members of a city militia company, the White Coats, led by several captains including Alexander Brett. Even before Norfolk left the city, the White Coats had been subverted by an agent of the French ambassador.[50] On the morning of the 28th, Norfolk's herald rode to Rochester Bridge to read Mary's proclamation, offering free pardon to all who would lay down their arms and submit to royal authority. Ostensibly in response to this offer, Sir George Harper left the rebel camp and "ran to the Duke of Norfolk. To whom he seemed greatly to lament his treason, that the Duke, pitying his case, the rather for the long acquaintance between them in times past, received him to grace."[51]

Norfolk's acquaintance with Harper is a bit obscure; the duke probably knew him from court, but perhaps from connections in Kent as well. Harper, from Chart Sutton, Kent, had been an esquire of the body in Henry VIII's last years and a member of Commons in 1545 and 1547, and continued a courtier's career under Edward, serving on several royal commissions and as sheriff of Kent, being licensed to retain thirty men besides household servants in 1553. In May of that year, Harper was involved in a land deal with John Dudley, and may have been expected to rise in support of Jane Grey if this, and his license to keep retainers, is evidence of his political ties. Yet Harper stayed neutral when Jane Grey was proclaimed, and he was not in any notable trouble until Wyatt's rebellion broke out.[52]

Once in Norfolk's camp, Harper contacted Brett and the other captains of the White Coats to arrange their desertion to Wyatt. Norfolk meanwhile accepted Harper's story of disaffection in Wyatt's camp and prepared to move on Rochester. On the afternoon of 28 January Cobham wrote Norfolk to warn that the Londoners were untrustworthy, but Norfolk chose not to believe him. Cobham was, after all, Wyatt's uncle, and the duke had firsthand intelligence from Harper on the unrest in Rochester. Therefore Norfolk wrote to the council on the morning of the 29th that he would attack Rochester Bridge, and asked Henry Neville, lord Abergavenny, to mount a simultaneous assault on Wyatt's rear.[53]

By about four o'clock in the afternoon Norfolk, Jerningham, and Thomas Butler, earl of Ormond, led combined forces of about twelve hundred men to a position overlooking Rochester Bridge. Wyatt's men, far from looking despondent and ready to capitulate, as Harper had said, hung their banners impudently over the walls of the bridge. The White Coats assembled in the rear while Norfolk rode forward to place his artillery. Seeing the apparent resolution of Wyatt's men, the duke commanded his artillery to open fire.[54] In the meantime, Brett was making a speech to the White Coats, reminding them that the men down the hill were English, too, and that they stood in the field only for the sake of the detestable Spanish. Therefore, he called upon his men to follow him into the camp of "this wourthy captain, maister Wyat," the only true Englishman who dared resist the enslavement threatened by the Spanish match.[55]

Brett's words had the desired effect, and before Norfolk's gunners could open fire the White Coats broke ranks, crying, "We are all Englishmen! We are all Englishmen! A Wyatt! A Wyatt!" and charged forward toward Norfolk. Finding himself outflanked, Norfolk began to order the guns turned on the White Coats, but realizing the futility of any attempt to hold the field, "the Duke's grace, with the Captain of the Guard Sir Henry Jerningham, considering (not without bleeding hearts) their chief strength turned upon them, so that they were now environed both behind and before with traitorous enemies, shifted themselves away, as did also their company."[56]

Leaving behind eight brass cannon and their munitions and supplies, Norfolk, Jerningham, Ormond and a few loyal officers retreated toward London, leaving the field to Wyatt and the road to the capital open. The few Londoners who did not go over to Wyatt straggled home, "ther cotes tourned, all ruyned, without arowes or stringe in their bowe, in a very strange wyse, which discomfiture, lyke as it was a hart-sore and very displeasing to the queen and counsayll, even so yt was almost no lesse joyous to the Londoners and most parte of all others."[57]

The disaster at Rochester signaled the end of Norfolk's military career. Command of the army passed to other hands (including Mary's admiral, the duke's half-brother Sir William), and Norfolk withdrew into his home shire. On 30 January Cobham surrendered Cowling Castle to Wyatt after only token resistance (confirming Norfolk's suspicions of his loyalty), and the remaining royal forces in Kent fell back toward London.[58] In the face of a rebel assault on the capital, with the citizens of such uncertain loyalty, Gardiner urged Mary to withdraw to Windsor. The queen rejected the advice, and in doing so probably saved her throne. Meeting little resistance to his advance, Wyatt circled to the west of London by 7 February and found William Herbert, earl of Pembroke, waiting with a small force. Had Wyatt awaited support from other disaffected elements which might have gathered to his banner, had he been more patient, the city might still have fallen to him. Instead, he advanced through the outskirts, past Charing Cross and down Fleet Street, while Pembroke followed warily and the Londoners looked on; each side seemed afraid to start the battle, knowing that the uncertain allegiance of the city would really decide the issue. Finally Wyatt came to Ludgate, held against him by William Howard. With the cryptic remark, "I have kept towche"—an acknowledgment that he had done all that he had promised?—Wyatt turned back, and the spell was broken. With scattered fighting, the rebels were dispersed and Wyatt taken prisoner.[59]

Wyatt and about a hundred others were executed for their parts in the rebellion; Mary would probably have done away with Elizabeth as well had Paget not pled for her and Charles V not cautioned mercy for fear of further upsetting an already troubled realm. The rebellion should have warned Mary how weakly she held her throne and how little her subjects trusted her. Instead, disgusted with bickering among her already distrusted councilors, and by the failure of Norfolk, as loyal a Catholic as she could find, Mary seems to have been driven to rely on her own counsel and the advice of Reynard. Parliament met for five weeks beginning on 2 April to arrange for the marriage to Philip of Spain which had spurred Wyatt's rebellion in the first place. Norfolk attended the sessions and took part in ceremonial functions but, his health beginning to fail, he withdrew increasingly to Kenninghall in the spring of 1554.[60]

In his own East Anglia, Norfolk was treated as a hero despite the disgrace at Rochester—or perhaps with the cautious deference of an area which had long experienced Howard's strict lordship. On 14 February 1554, the city court of Norwich voted to send him a hogshead of white wine, one of red, two of claret, six ten-pound sugar loaves, and two dozen wax torches "as a remembrance of their old value for him and to welcome him home after his deliverance."[61] Ket's Rebellion in 1549 had demonstrated the dangerous social instability in the county after the fall of the Howards; perhaps the city fathers really were relieved that a Howard was again in residence. Norfolk also began the slow process of regaining control of the lands recovered from the crown; early in 1554 he held a manorial court for his tenants at Framlingham in Suffolk.[62]

Norfolk's last appearance in council was on 7 May. Two weeks later Reynard reported that, although the court was busy with preparations for the marriage of the duke's grandson and heir Thomas to Mary Fitzalan, daughter of the earl of Arundel, Norfolk was too ill to come to London.[63] In June the council wrote to the duke asking for aid in enforcing regulations against the export of foodstuffs from the realm. Norfolk replied in early July by asking that his cousin Sir Edward Wyndham be allowed to remain in the shire with him to help keep order.[64] The duke was too weak to lend anything more than his name to his duties.

These were Norfolk's last recorded official acts. Thomas Howard knew his end was near as the summer wore on, for on 21 July he called George Holland, his secretary, and seven other trusted servants into the great chamber at Kenninghall. Here he dictated a will, beginning:

> Calling nowe unto Remembrance the greate age I am nowe grown unto, and feling my self therebye to be fallen into greate weaknes of my body, albeit thanks be unto almightye god, having my full, hole and perfitt memory, [I] do herefore declare, my last will and testament in forme followinge:
> First, I bequeath my soule, to almightie god, having sure trust and confidence, that through and by the merittes of Christes death and passion, to have that remyssion and forgevenes of my synnes and trespaces and to be a partaker and one of the inheritoures of the kingdome of god.

Norfolk's grandson Thomas was named heir to "all and singular, my mannors, Landes, tenementes, possessions, hereditamentes, Whatsoever, which I have within the Realm of England, and whereof I do stand seised in possession or reversion of an estate or an inheritance in fee simple." Bequests were made to others: five hundred pounds to Mary, duchess of Richmond, for her pains in bringing up her brother's children and "her greate costes and charges in making Sute for my delyveraunce out of my ymprisonment"; one thousand pounds to each of Surrey's three daughters upon their marriage or attainment of the age of twenty-one; one hundred pounds for the bringing up of "the child which [is] in my housse nowe comenly called Jane Goodman"—evidently a bastard daughter of the duke. Norfolk left his collar of the Order of the Garter and his jeweled St. George to his grandson—perhaps in hopes that he would shortly be elected to the order. Stephen Gardiner, Nicholas Heath, bishop of Worcester, Richard Rich, Nicholas Hare, Robert Southwell and several others were named as executors, and Queen Mary was named supervisor with a gift of one hundred pounds.[65]

Norfolk's health continued to fail; finally, on 25 August 1554, he died in his bed at Kenninghall. A Howard servant, Bassingbourne Gawdy, rode to London with the news. The new duke was still a minor, and so for the moment he became the ward of the crown, although he inherited the titles and duties of duke of Norfolk and earl marshal at once. Details of the funeral of the third duke are not extant; Norfolk willed "my bodie to be buried, in such place and order as shall be thought moste convenyent to my executoures," and he was laid to rest at St. Michael's church, Framlingham, just outside the castle walls. The family tombs had been moved from Thetford when the Cluniac priory was dissolved, and Norfolk had begun enlarging the chancel at Framlingham as a new resting place, but the alterations were not completed until after his arrest in 1547. The tomb of the third duke and his wife today lies alongside those of Henry Fitzroy, duke of Richmond, Henry Howard, earl of Surrey, and of the wives of the fourth duke of Norfolk.[66]

Norfolk's tomb cannot have been completed until after 1558, when his wife Elizabeth died. Estranged from her husband for many years, Elizabeth was reunited with Norfolk after his release from the Tower in 1553. The two effigies lie side by side, hands folded in prayer, atop an Italianate sarcophagus. Norfolk's monument is a curious blend of medieval and Renaissance styles—a fitting tribute, in many ways, to his life. The sarcophagus is adorned with neoclassical figures of the apostles in niches along the sides. At each corner stand lions rampant holding the Howard arms. Norfolk's figure, dressed in armor, with elongated hands and feet, a spade beard, and long hair topped by a ducal coronet, is characteristic of much earlier monuments. His helmet is under his head, and, in testimony

The Final Years

to his love of the hunt, a stag lies at his feet. Around the neck of the duke's effigy is a collar of twelve medallions, with the Latin motto "Gracia Dei sum quod sum"—by the Grace of God, I am what I am. Norfolk adopted this motto after his miraculous escape because of Henry's death.[67]

Immediately after Norfolk's death, an inquest was held at Norwich to survey his fifty-six manors, thirty-seven advowsons, "and many other considerable estates." The resultant inquisition *post mortem* is mutilated and largely impossible to read, but Neville Williams, biographer of the fourth duke, computed the yearly value of the lands passed with the ducal title at about £2,500. Even after the depredations of the Edwardian regents, Thomas Howard left a handsome estate to his heir. The inquisition bears no legible date, but Norfolk's will was proved 23 November 1554 at Canterbury.[68] With this event, the church gave its sanction to Norfolk's final wishes, and a formal capstone was placed on a long and tumultuous life.

CHAPTER 11

AN ENGLISH DUKE,
1524–1554

THE KEYS TO POLITICAL POWER, WEALTH AND INFLUENCE in early Tudor England were land, family connections, and the links of clientage and patronage at court and in his country that placed a man such as Norfolk atop the social hierarchy. Thomas Howard owed a large part of his wealth and power to the titles, lands and offices he inherited. His use of these resources played a vital role in his political successes and failures.

In considering Howard as duke of Norfolk, several areas merit consideration. The first and perhaps most important is family. Tudor England was a small place, and personal connections often played an important role in politics. Beyond the family circle, the lines of clientage and patronage, no less personal, were likewise vital to success. A network of "well-willers" loyal to one such as Norfolk were sources of information and doers of favors who extended his personal and political reach. Personal wealth, much of it from land, provided the lubrication of Tudor politics and enabled Norfolk to pay salaries and fees and to offer good lordship in his houses. This all translated, finally, into power at court and in East Anglia.

To understand Norfolk and his career, one must do a certain amount of reading between the lines. There is nothing from Howard's pen that explicitly says what his goals were. From the perspective of surveying his actions and recorded thoughts over more than thirty years, however, it would seem clear that Thomas Howard was no different from men and women of any age in that he sought wealth and power at least in part for the sake of their material rewards, but also in part for their own sake, as a means of making his mark in the world. And he succeeded on both counts. There is no point in writing the biography of a total failure, after all. Thomas Howard is intrinsically far more interesting than his brother Edmund, and Thomas Winter has attracted little attention and would merit none at all had he not been Thomas Wolsey's son. Family, patronage, land and wealth were both cause and effect of Howard's success and were all part and parcel of what it meant to be a sixteenth-century English duke.

Norfolk and His Family

In the England of Henry VIII, wealth and power did not depend on offices of state or nobles titles alone. Family connections were of paramount importance, for the Tudor ruling class was closely interrelated. With a very high attrition rate—about twenty-five percent of noble families failed to produce a male heir in each generation[1]—the continuation of a family line was a delicate and uncertain proposition. Thomas Howard presided over a large and unruly family which was a valuable source of influence, wealth and political connections, but also a constant danger. The siblings, offspring, cousins and in-laws who made up the Howard clan could be the duke's allies and agents, but every family crisis was also potentially a personal crisis for Norfolk. Thomas Howard was thus often preoccupied with the needs and problems of his family.

The second Howard duke of Norfolk married twice, producing five sons and six daughters who married within the peerage. As a result, the third duke was related by marriage and his siblings' descent to many of the Tudor noble families. The third duke's marriages were rather less successful in the long term, despite the high status of his two wives. Thomas Howard first wed Anne Plantagenet, daughter of Edward IV and Elizabeth Woodville. Anne bore Howard four children, but none of them lived to maturity. A son, Thomas, born in 1497, was the last to die in 1508, leaving Howard childless at Anne's death in 1512.[2] By his second wife, Elizabeth Stafford, daughter of the third duke of Buckingham, Howard gained prestige, wealth (in the form of a dowry of 2,500 marks, a guaranteed income for his wife, and a parcel of lands, goods and jewels), and political connections. His brothers-in-law soon included Henry, lord Stafford; Ralph Neville, fourth earl of Westmorland; and George Neville, lord Abergavenny. Elizabeth bore three children who lived to maturity—Henry in 1517, Mary in 1519 and Thomas in 1520.³ It is doubtful that Norfolk would have considered any of his children a great political asset had he pondered the matter while sitting in Beauchamp Tower from 1546 to 1553; both his daughter and elder son brought Norfolk more trouble than help in his political career.

In seeking marriages for their kinfolk, the dukes of Norfolk had two separate but related aims. Perhaps foremost was their quest for status through marriages within the peerage for children and relatives, and in this the Howards were quite successful in the early 1500s as they forged ties with the earls of Derby, Oxford, Sussex, Bridgewater and Wiltshire and the lords Lisle and Dacre. Yet financial elements were also important. Many of the Howard marriages arranged by the second duke brought wealth and new blood into the family through matches with well-to-do gentry families.[4] The third duke was usually able to obtain wealth and social status alike for his relatives. For this purpose, wardships were especially attractive, for the guardian often was able to obtain the right of marriage along with possession of the goods and person of his ward.[5] Norfolk unsuccessfully sought the wardship of Lord Monteagle in 1523, but he was luckier with several others, perhaps because he virtually sat by the deathbeds of Lord Marney in April 1525 and the earl of Oxford the next year in order to win guardianship of their heirs.[6] In both cases, Norfolk was particularly interested in the outcome because he had designs on the wards as mates for his own children.

Norfolk obtained the wardship of Elizabeth Marney at the end of May 1526 and purchased the right of her marriage from the master of the king's wards in April 1529 for one thousand pounds.[7] Although Norfolk had an elder son, Henry, who was then thirteen, the duke was planning a better match for his heir, and so Elizabeth was espoused to the duke's second son, Thomas, who was ten, in December 1530. The marriage was performed on 14 May 1533 at Norfolk House in Lambeth. Thomas and Elizabeth Marney eventually had four children, but Thomas, created Viscount Bindon in 1559, remained an obscure figure. Norfolk apparently considered Thomas to be sufficiently provided for by his marriage, for by the terms of the third duke's will Thomas got nothing but the unlikely prospect of inheriting the dukedom and lands should none of his brother Henry's children survive or leave issue.[8]

In matching his elder son and heir Henry, styled earl of Surrey, Norfolk turned to the de Vere earls of Oxford. There had been numerous Howard–de Vere matches in the past, and the fourteenth earl, John (1499–1526) had been married to Norfolk's half-sister Anne. They had no children, and the title passed to a second cousin. This John de Vere, fifteenth earl of Oxford, had a daughter, Frances, born around 1517.[9] Rumors began circulating in 1529 that Norfolk, to assure Howard blood in the succession, would wed Surrey to Princess Mary.[10] It was partially to forestall this dangerous notion that Norfolk arranged his heir's marriage to Frances de Vere. On 15 January 1532, Norfolk and Oxford drew up an indenture whereby the duke agreed to settle lands worth three hundred pounds a year on Surrey; Oxford settled four thousand marks on his daughter to be paid in installments of two hundred marks on the day of the marriage and one hundred every six months thereafter. Each father was to provide for his child's personal clothing.[11] The marriage took place by 16 April, but the two sixteen-year-olds were considered too young to live together, and remained under parental control for several years. In 1535 or 1536, Henry and Frances began married life at Kenninghall. Their first child, Jane, was born there in 1537, and Thomas, eventual fourth duke of Norfolk, followed in 1538.[12]

Norfolk may have matched Surrey with Frances de Vere to allay suspicions of Howard dynastic ambitions, but he had not abandoned hope of a place for his family in the succession. In 1533 Howard arranged for his daughter Mary to wed Henry Fitzroy, duke of Richmond, the king's illegitimate son by Elizabeth Blount. Mary and Richmond were related within prohibited degrees of consanguinity, but were granted a dispensation in November 1533.[13] Married shortly after, they were also too young to live together, both having been born in 1519. Their marriage was never consummated, and when Richmond died in 1536, Mary (who never remarried and persisted in calling herself duchess of Richmond to her death in 1557) had considerable difficulty in gaining recognition of her claims as Fitzroy's survivor, much less obtaining title to his estates. In January 1538 Cranmer finally ruled that the contract between Mary and Richmond constituted matrimony, but only in March 1539 was Mary granted the manor of Swaffenham as token of her rights as Richmond's widow. The lands granted Fitzroy at his creation as duke of Richmond reverted to the crown, leaving Mary with the empty dignity of her title. Norfolk provided for her in later years, while twice trying to marry her to Thomas Seymour, brother of the earl of Hertford. At Norfolk's arrest in 1546, Mary was still living at Kenninghall.[14]

In seeking marriages for other family members, Norfolk managed several times to come to grief. The two Howard nieces who wed Henry VIII —Anne Boleyn and Catherine Howard—both ended on the executioner's block and brought considerable disgrace to the family. Several other Howard liaisons and marriages ended in executions. In 1531, Sir Rhys ap Griffith, husband of Norfolk's half-sister Catherine, was sent to the Tower for his part in a bungled Irish-Welsh plot to invade England in the service of Charles V and the pope, presumably because of Henry's efforts to divorce Catherine of Aragon.[15] Norfolk so obviously had nothing to do with this adventure that little damage to the family resulted. Catherine was left at the mercy of her family when Rhys was attainted and executed and his goods and lands forfeited to the crown, but she recovered by marrying Henry Daubeney, later earl of Bridgewater, a match which was doubtless more useful to the family than one with a Welsh knight.[16]

In 1530, Norfolk found himself in trouble over what he must have considered a mere formality, the requirement for the king's assent to all marriages within the peerage. Norfolk arranged for his half-sister Dorothy to wed Edward Stanley, earl of Derby, whose family had long held considerable influence in the north of the realm. Henry chose to view the arrangement as an abduction of the twenty-year-old Derby, who was still legally a minor. Norfolk was forced to sue for pardon and post a bond with the king, but was still allowed to carry the marriage to conclusion.[17]

Unfortunately, not all of the Howards learned their lesson from the Derby marriage. In 1536, Thomas Howard, another of Norfolk's half-brothers, made the serious mistake of attempting to elope with Lady Margaret Douglas, Henry's niece. Margaret, daughter of the king's sister Margaret, was the highest ranking woman of her generation in the realm if Mary and Elizabeth Tudor were held illegitimate. Besides being a valuable pawn in the international marriage market, Margaret held a important place in the succession. Henry suspected that Howard aspired to the crown itself by means of such a marriage, and clapped the young man in the Tower. Lord Howard was attainted for his presumption in meddling in the succession. The act went on to make any marriage within the royal family without the king's assent treason in all future cases. Thomas Howard died

An English Duke

in the Tower in October 1537; Norfolk dared not sue for his pardon at the height of Cromwell's power.[18] Lady Margaret was freed after a short imprisonment, but was again in disgrace in 1541 for having an affair with another of Norfolk's relations, Catherine Howard's brother Charles. Margaret eventually married Matthew Stewart, fourth earl of Lennox, begat Henry, lord Darnley, and so played a vital role in the succession of James I in 1603.[19]

If Howard family marriages were a source of danger as well as political advantage, the duke's own marriage and his relations with his children were constant problems in the later part of Henry's reign. Thomas Howard and Elizabeth Stafford were wed in 1513. From the beginning there were problems. Elizabeth later claimed that she had been in love with Ralph Neville, heir to the earldom of Westmorland; whether this is true or not, Thomas was forty to Elizabeth's seventeen, and she surely had no choice in being married to him.[20] In the early years of the marriage Howard was often away from home, at sea, on the borders, or in Ireland. The resentment Elizabeth may have felt against her often-absent husband was surely made much worse by the trial and execution of her father on treason charges in 1521. The second duke of Norfolk presided over Buckingham's trial, and Howard, in Ireland, raised no word of protest. The next year, the Howards accepted a parcel of lands forfeited by their attainted in-law. Whatever the political wisdom of this action, Elizabeth understandably was deeply hurt, and her estrangement from her husband may date from this time.

By 1526 Howard, now duke of Norfolk, began a liaison with Elizabeth Holland that lasted until his arrest in 1546. Although Duchess Elizabeth scornfully called Bess Holland "a churl's daughter," and "a drab who was but a washer of my nursery," in fact Elizabeth Holland was the daughter of John Holland, Norfolk's household treasurer and chief steward, and was related to Sir John Hussey (later Lord Hussey), a Lincolnshire man sometimes a client of the duke.[21] Bess Holland likely entered Norfolk's household as a servant, but when she reached maturity the duke raised her to other duties. By May 1533 the situation in Norfolk's household had become impossible for Duchess Elizabeth to bear. From their letters, neither duke nor duchess appears to have been very well tempered, and if any of the scenes Elizabeth described took place—such as being held down by Norfolk's servants until her fingers bled and, in her rage, she spit blood—a separation may have been the only solution, since Norfolk obviously was determined to keep Bess Holland as his mistress. Initially, Norfolk tried to convince his brother-in-law Henry Stafford to take in Elizabeth, but Stafford knew his sister's temper well enough to refuse. Having her in his house, Stafford said, "shuld be my utter undoing. Whiche is to put your Grace in remembrance of her acustomed wild langiage whiche lyeth not in my power to stope, wherebye so greate daunger myght insue to me and all myne."[22]

After Stafford's refusal, Norfolk set up a household for his wife at Redbourne, Hertfordshire. Elizabeth was far from content with her allowance of two hundred pounds a year, and by August 1534 she was writing letters to Cromwell, bemoaning her poor estate and complaining of mistreatment at Norfolk's hands. The duke, she said, "came riding all night, and locked me up in a chamber, and took away all my jewels and apparel." Shortly thereafter, "he sent his two chaplains, Master Burley and Sir Thomas Seymer, [to offer that] if I would be divorced, he would give me all my jewels and my apparel, and a great part of his plate, and of his stuff of household; and I rebuked his priests."[23]

Not only did Elizabeth refuse to accept a divorce, but she continued to pour out her complaints to Cromwell. By 1539, Cromwell tired of the harangue, and advised her to return to her husband and live in peace. Perhaps understandably, she was unwilling to submit herself to Norfolk again, for she wrote: "I will never come at my Lord my husband for no fair promises nor cruel handling. I had rather be kept in the Tower of London during my life, for I am so well used to imprisonment I care not for it; for he will suffer no gentlemen to come at me . . . and very few gentlewomen."[24]

Some authors have seen Elizabeth's complaints as exaggerations, but in an undated letter to Cromwell (doubtless in response to one of Elizabeth's vitriolics), the duke showed that he was probably capable of all Elizabeth had accused him of doing. Although he denied that he had, as she said, dragged her out of her childbed by the hair and pulled her around the house, wounding her in the head with a dagger, Norfolk closed this letter with an open threat: "Finally my lord I require you to send her in no wise to come where I am. For the same should not only put me to more trouble than I now have (whereof I have no need) but might give me occasion to handle her otherwise than I have done yet."[25]

At the time of his arrest in 1546, Norfolk—then over seventy—was making arrangements for Bess Holland's long-term security. When Kenninghall was searched, not only did Henry's agents find Bess laden with jewelry, but they reported that Norfolk had recently established a house for her, "newly made in Suffolk, which is thought to be well furnished with stuff." Bess Holland was evidently permitted to remain in this house after Norfolk's arrest, for when her personal jewels were returned to her in February 1547, she was described as living at Mendham, Suffolk.[26]

Norfolk's estrangement from his wife was an embarrassment, but one which he was able to deal with in his own rough manner. The duke's elder son Henry, earl of Surrey, became a more dangerous liability as he became older. Unlike his father or grandfather, had been raised as the heir to a peerage and had never known the imprisonments and attainders that they had suffered. Surrey had more than his share of his father's dynastic pride, but far too little caution and self-restraint for his own good. Thus his brief adult life brought a succession of crises and misadventures born out of this dangerous pride and ambition, to the exasperation of his father.

Surrey was examined before the council several times in the later 1530s and 1540s before his final commitment to the Tower in 1546. In 1537 Surrey was involved in a fray at court in which he struck Edward Seymour, Viscount Beauchamp and brother of Henry's third wife Jane. Surrey was confined to the grounds of Windsor Castle briefly, but was free by the end of the year.[27] In 1542 he was examined and sent to the Fleet for having challenged another courtier (a sympathizer with Reginald Pole?) to a duel; the details of this episode are obscure, but again Surrey was freed after a short time.[28]

What Surrey seems to have learned from these incidents was that, as a Howard, he was above the law, for early in 1543 he was in trouble again, this time for leading a pack of young men, including his steward, Thomas Clere, and Norfolk's treasurer, Thomas Hussey, through the streets of London, breaking windows and threatening the citizens. The examination which resulted turned up evidence of other misdemeanors, such as eating meat in Lent, but also charges that Surrey considered himself a prince, and his family fit to rule should Henry die before Edward reached his majority. Although these accusations were passed over at the time, they played a large role when the Howards fell from power with such spectacular suddenness three years later.[29] It is no wonder that Surrey, despite his talents as a poet, was thought "the most foolish proud boy that is in

The Ebbs and Flows of Fortune

England."[30] Even Norfolk despaired of bringing his son under control. In 1545 when the earl was commander of Boulogne and seemed determined to ruin his father and the conservatives in council by his costly and dangerous military adventures, Norfolk was forced to write several (unheeded) letters to his son, pleading for caution. It is no great surprise that Surrey finally came to grief. Unfortunately Norfolk was never able to tame his unruly son or to distance himself from Surrey's actions, and thus fell from grace and almost lost his life with his son.

Mary, duchess of Richmond, was another problem for Norfolk, not only for her insistence upon being recognized as Fitzroy's widow, but also because she twice refused to marry Thomas Seymour (in 1538 and 1546) when her father most needed to neutralize the influence of Hertford and his family.[31] After Surrey and Norfolk were arrested, Mary made no attempt to defend them, but made a full confession of family crimes that might charitably be considered an act of fear, or less charitably of malice, for she readily offered substantiation of the charges against Surrey. Perhaps Mary deserves the benefit of the doubt, for she was made guardian of Surrey's children during Norfolk's imprisonment, and was recognized as a loving and loyal daughter in the duke's will, being left a bequest of five hundred pounds for her pains in bringing up Surrey's children and her efforts to win her father's freedom.[32]

All things considered—estranged from a wife who never ceased to vilify him, and with two elder children who proved as much a hindrance as a help to him—Norfolk had a difficult family life. When the various disasters of his brothers, sisters, nieces, nephews, aunts and uncles are considered, it is clear that the duke's position as head of the Howard clan was neither easy nor comfortable. Some of his problems were attributable to his own personality; there is little evidence of kindness in his relations with family and associates, and a great deal to suggest that Norfolk was a thoroughly unpleasant man, and one capable of vicious cruelty when he felt his honor or his ambitions threatened.

Nonetheless, Thomas Howard's place at the head of a large family, with many marriageable relatives and a wide web of connections with other noble families, was an important part of his power. Maintaining the influence of the Howards probably was second only to the quest for personal wealth and power in Norfolk's priorities. Like most aspects of Norfolk's career, his family affairs were at best a mixed achievement. Few of Norfolk's contemporaries played the game of family politics with as much success—certainly none could brag of having had two nieces made queen—but few suffered as much from the attendant dangers. The Tudor nobility suffered repeatedly from Henry VIII's vicious suspicions and shifting whims.[33] Perhaps no noble family gained as much from service to the Tudors, yet suffered as much for their family failures as did the Howards. It is a telling commentary on Thomas Howard's character that he managed to suffer some of his most disastrous failures as a consequence of what had seemed his greatest successes.

Patronage and Politics

In addition to finding suitable marriages and political favors for his immediate family, Norfolk was constantly at work building up a network of clientage and patronage in his home shires and at court. Throughout the reign of Henry VIII, Norfolk was first and foremost a politician who constantly looked to Henry and the court as the focus of all worth having. The real power of a nobleman, as D. M. Loades notes, "did not lay in his hosts of tenants or retainers, but much more in his influence at court and the number of his servants and 'well-willers' who were strategically deployed in the central administration." Power in Tudor England not was measured solely in men at arms ready to answer one's call. In 1516, Wolsey had launched a successful campaign to limit abuses of livery and maintenance at court, and Thomas Howard, then earl of Surrey, was one of those punished. Although as duke of Norfolk Howard continued to be served by a large retinue, and was licensed, as late as November 1546, to retain ten gentlemen and twelve yeomen in his livery, he operated in a system based increasingly on grants of land, control of local offices, and the ability to influence the granting of other royal gifts. Patronage, and not livery and maintenance, stood at the heart of Norfolk's power. The offices of treasurer and earl marshal, beside their handsome salaries, were of great value to Norfolk as a source of jobs, grants and other gifts to his clients, present and potential.[34]

The measure of Norfolk's success is to be found in part in names on sheriff rolls, commissions of the peace, appointment fiats for customs offices, and every other type of royal grant and license, as well as in placement of family members and clients in the households of the king, his wives and his children. Early in Henry VIII's reign, certain names appeared on East Anglian commissions of the peace—Boleyns, Pastons, Knevets, Wingfields, Wyndhams, Tylneys, LeStranges, Cleres and Townshends[35]—and these names recur throughout the reign in other appointments. Not every grant is proof of allegiance to the Howards, of course; the Wingfields, for example, were involved in the Paston-Howard rivalry of the fifteenth century, and during Henry VIII's reign were as often clients of the duke of Suffolk as of Norfolk's. The Southwells, too, were rising gentry not always loyal to the Howards.[36] It would appear that, while Norfolk was largely Howard country, in other shires in which the Howards held land they competed for patronage with other peers. In 1537, for example, the dukes of Norfolk and Suffolk both influenced appointments to commissions of the peace for Suffolk and Kent; Norfolk's clients Anthony Rouse, John Jerningham and several Wingfields appear along with Willoughbys and Southwells for Suffolk, while Anthony St. Leger, a Howard man, was named for Kent.[37]

The names connected with the Howards remained fairly constant during the reign, although new families appeared and some became more prominent, such as Bedingfields, Jermyns, Greshams and Heydons.[38] Norfolk himself was frequently named to commissions of the peace for many or all of the shires, which served as a mark of status but also probably broadened his general influence. Obviously, the duke did not attend courts across the countryside, but as a justice of the peace in any given shire, Norfolk held legal powers which made him all the more useful to the crown in carrying out inspections and investigations. It is difficult to know the nature of the political ties between Norfolk and the other men named to these commissions for lack of evidence linking them to the Howards. Other than such as Husseys in Lincolnshire, St. Legers in Kent, and several families in Surrey and Sussex, Norfolk's local patronage throughout the rest of the realm remains shadowy.[39]

One important area of patronage is clear from records of grants of office that lay within Norfolk's province as treasurer. As L. B. Smith has noted concerning Catherine Howard's family, "it was essential to the duke's control of his family and his status at court . . . that Bryans, Westons, Leghs, and Howards, Holdens and Knevets, all members of the duke's dynasty, should be listed in the treasury reports of 1539–41 as having received money for services rendered the government."[40] The point is valid throughout Henry VIII's reign. Although a few treasury receipts and records of assays of the mint survive from the mid-1520s onward,[41] only from the 1540s do large numbers of letters of appointment and grants of customs licenses appear in the published state papers. Many of these offices and grants were given to men of importance in the localities involved, and may have had little to do with Norfolk's direct patronage, but in at least a few cases recognizable names appear. In May 1544, Thomas Legh, related to Norfolk through his brother Edmund Howard's marriage, was appointed comptroller of the customs in London, and in November 1546 Thomas Wingfield and George Blage received grants. The latter would shortly be one of the leading figures in the fall of the Howards and subsequently a Seymour man; perhaps this grant was an unsuccessful effort to retain the support of a client known to be slipping into the following of a rival. In Blage's case, the effort may have been doomed to failure because of his religious views. A radical protestant, Blage had been a companion to Henry Howard, earl of Surrey, in some of the latter's escapades in the 1540s, but once it was clear that Surrey supported his father's conservative religious and political program, Blage turned to the Seymours instead.[42]

The mechanics of political clientage can be illustrated by looking at a few Howard followers in detail. One of the best documented for the latter part of Henry VIII's reign is Anthony Rouse of Denington, Suffolk, a man who began as a Howard servant and ended up as a respected midlevel Tudor official. In August 1538, Norfolk referred to Rouse as "treasurer of my house," a post he entered sometime after 1524. But as a leading servant of the duke, Rouse already had wider duties, representing Norfolk's interests in various businesses. In January 1536 Rouse aided Sir Richard Southwell in inventorying the goods of Richard Nix, deceased bishop of Norwich, and during 1538–39 Rouse began to be named a commissioner of the peace for Suffolk. Service to the Howards tended, because of Norfolk's status, to blend into service to the crown. As Norfolk's treasurer, Rouse commanded considerable respect; although he was not knighted at the time, several commissions of the peace called him "Sir Ant. Rouse."[43] Rouse gained other duties outside of Norfolk's household. In 1539 he was named one of the victualers for Calais and Guisnes and was paid twenty pounds for his services, and named among the squires attending the reception of Anne of Cleves that year.[44]

Rouse began seeking Cromwell's support while Norfolk was in eclipse in 1539; as a result, the duke and his treasurer had a falling out when Rouse successfully sued Cromwell for the marriage right to a daughter of Sir Edward Ichingham, a squire worth fifty pounds a year. Norfolk's steward, Robert Holdiche, abducted one of Ichingham's daughters, planning to marry her to one of his sons, probably with Norfolk's consent. Through Cromwell's intervention, Rouse obtained the girl, leaving Norfolk upset at Rouse's independence and that his local patronage had been interfered with.[45] In March 1540 Rouse was granted part of the lands from the dissolved monastery of Bury St. Edmunds, Suffolk, and the next month obtained a license to alienate part of the property.[46] Although Norfolk shared in the spoils from Bury, it is not clear which of Rouse's patrons helped him in this deal. In any case, Rouse managed to avoid any role in Cromwell's fall. By April 1541 he received another post away from Norfolk's household when he was appointed treasurer of the king's works at Guisnes, a job which entailed transporting stores to France as well as aiding the investigation into the finances of Arthur Plantagenet, lord Lisle, who was recalled as deputy of Calais in May 1540. Norfolk's hand cannot be directly traced in Rouse's appointment, but as treasurer and leader of the newly constituted privy council, the duke was in a position to deliver such a promotion. Rouse served in France for several years, later acting as comptroller of Calais. In May 1544, Rouse was recalled and given the honorific office of keeper of the crown jewels at a salary of fifty pounds, although he continued intermittent service in France; several warrants for war expenses were addressed to him at Calais in 1545.[47] Sometime before 1545 Rouse was replaced as Norfolk's treasurer by Thomas Hussey, and Rouse himself was dead by September 1546.[48] His career is evidence that service in a noble household could pave the way to advancement in royal service; those who served Norfolk had much to gain.

Sir Richard Southwell (1504–64) provides a more clear-cut case of a man who began his career under the Howards but successfully established an independent career. Southwell's early years were spent as a ward of Sir Thomas Wyndham, a Howard brother-in-law. In 1532 Southwell showed his perhaps overzealous loyalty to the Howards by leading a band of men (including his brother Robert and a cousin, Anthony Southwell) who murdered Sir William Pennington, a leading gentleman of the duke of Suffolk and a rival in East Anglia for the preferments due clients of the great men of the realm. Richard Southwell paid a fine of a thousand pounds for this crime, and obviously was not impeded in his career, for in 1534 he was appointed sheriff of Norfolk.[49] By 1535 Southwell had begun shifting his allegiance to Cromwell; he was appointed tutor to the latter's son Gregory in that year. Besides engaging in such tasks as the inventory of Bishop Nix's goods in 1536, Southwell became one of Cromwell's agents in the dissolution of the monasteries.[50]

In 1539, Southwell was one of the principals in a curious affray which demonstrates how much damage Cromwell's rise had done to Norfolk's patronage in his own shire. Cromwell had already arranged that Southwell and Edmund Wyndham would be returned as knights of the shire for the Parliament which was to meet on 28 April, seemingly with Norfolk's full, if somewhat reluctant, approval, for both men had family connections to the duke. At almost the last moment, Norfolk's nephew Sir Edmund Knevet asked Cromwell for a place in Parliament for the county. Cromwell denied the request, saying the Henry desired Southwell and Wyndham. Despite Knevet's attempt to disrupt the proceedings, the election went as Cromwell had planned. Unfortunately, Knevet felt that he had been cheated, and publicly pronounced that he could "never love Southwell, calling him false gentleman, knave and many other opprobrious words."[51]

Norfolk proved unable to effect a reconciliation after this unseemly squabble, and Knevet and Southwell were ordered before the council. Knevet ended up assaulting Surrey's squire, John Clere, who had conducted him to court, and almost lost his hand for the offense. It is tempting to guess that the whole affair was stage-managed by the duke, arising out of his anger at Southwell for defecting to Cromwell, but if so, Norfolk gained no immediate satisfaction. Southwell avoided further difficulty and sat undisturbed in Commons until the next elections in 1542, when, following Cromwell's fall, he was replaced by Norfolk's friend Sir Roger Townshend.[52] Southwell survived Cromwell's fall without further damage, however, and made some effort to patch things up with the Howards. Knighted in 1542, Sir Richard served in France under Surrey in 1545–46. Upon returning to court and discovering the strength of the Seymour faction, Southwell shifted sides again. It was Southwell who first came forward with charges of treason against Surrey, and he was sent to Kenninghall to inventory the duke's possessions after Norfolk's arrest. Southwell's reward for this was a post on Edward VI's privy council until 1549, when he was imprisoned briefly on suspicion of Catholic sympathies. This supposition was well founded, for Southwell returned to favor under Mary and helped suppress Wyatt's rebellion (although not serving directly with Norfolk). By 1554 Southwell had returned to Norfolk's good graces, for he was named an executor of the duke's will. At Elizabeth's accession, Southwell retired because of his Catholic faith and died in 1564.[53]

Southwell illustrates the kind of career possible in Tudor England, as well as the perils. Beginning as a minor client of a great lord, Southwell succeeded in obtaining wealth and position through service to the crown and its ministers; he was able to abandon the Howards because he had secured the patronage of others, but twice returned to the fold after the ruin of Cromwell and the Seymours. Only a handful of men could play an independent role in Tudor politics, and such as Southwell never found themselves in a position to do so; the support of one of the great men of the realm was necessary for advancement.

Robert Holdiche, Norfolk's steward at the time of his fall, represents another type of Howard client. Holdiche was evidently of yeoman stock, and remained a loyal servant throughout his long service to the Howards. In 1519 Holdiche was treasurer of the Howard castle of Framlingham, the main residence of the second duke.[54] By 1523, Holdiche was part of the younger Thomas Howard's staff at his houses at Stoke and Hunsdon, and over the next several years appeared on assorted commissions—of the peace, oyer and terminer and jail delivery, and to collect the subsidy for Norfolk—evidence, no doubt, of his closeness to the Howards, and a reflection of the status he more or less automatically attained as a result.[55] In 1539, as noted above, Holdiche unsuccessfully tried to abduct a ward sought by Anthony Rouse. Perhaps Holdiche resented Rouse's desertion of the Howards, but unlike Rouse, Holdiche made no move to break away from Norfolk in the later years of Henry's reign. During the 1540s, Holdiche was mentioned repeatedly in letters as Norfolk's steward, but at the time of Norfolk's arrest, he does not seem to have been examined before the council as were many other Howard clients and servants.[56] During the reign of Edward VI Holdiche continued as steward for the Howard lands seized by the crown, delivering yearly accounts of the revenues collected, and late in 1547 served as the crown's agent in returning to Bess Holland the jewelry Norfolk's mistress had been found to possess (and had tried to hide) when Kenninghall was first searched in January of the year. His reward for all this was to be named to several royal commissions and

An English Duke

to be allowed a few valuable land deals.[57] Holdiche returned to Norfolk's service upon Mary's accession and was one of the witnesses to the duke's will. Later, in the reign of Elizabeth, Holdiche served from 1556 to 1559 as treasurer at wars, vice-treasurer and general receiver for Ireland under Henry Sidney, lord deputy of Ireland, and was also apparently Sidney's household steward. Holdiche is last mentioned in the state papers in 1562, and probably died shortly thereafter. He must have lived to be well over sixty, and spent much of his life in the service of the Howards.[58]

One last Howard client has left sufficient traces in the records to bear examination. Like Robert Holdiche, Richard Fulmerston began as a yeoman servant to the Howards, but unlike his fellow household officer, Fulmerston managed to amass a considerable fortune before Norfolk's attainder and even to add to his estate in the years following. Fulmerston first appears carrying letters between Kenninghall and the court for Norfolk in the later 1530s; he is mentioned as "my servant Fulmerston" in May 1537. As late as 1539, Fulmerston was still carrying the duke's mail.[59] Unlike many of Norfolk's servants, Fulmerston was not named to the usual variety of commissions; perhaps his status in Norfolk's household did not warrant such recognition. Although Norfolk finally did reward Fulmerston with appointment to a customs post at Ipswich in May 1545, the duke's most valuable gifts to Fulmerston may have come indirectly. Beginning in 1537, Fulmerston's name began to appear on deeds for grants of former monastic lands. In that year he obtained the house, site and immediate possessions of Thetford Priory, worth about £150, while Norfolk obtained the more valuable manor lands from the establishment. Fulmerston acquired several other dissolved religious sites including, in 1545, the lands, site and possessions of Brundish Chantry, Suffolk, which his own family had founded.[60]

By 1538, among his other duties Fulmerston became steward to Norfolk's son Henry, earl of Surrey. Surrey, with a wife and family of his own, began an extensive building program, centering on a palatial house in Norwich, Mount Surrey. Fulmerston's personal finances became thoroughly entangled with Surrey, through bills paid or advances made with Fulmerston's own money. Surrey's excessive pride seems to have extended to an unwillingness to recognize the limits of his finances—Norfolk had to pay debts for his son on more than one occasion—and Fulmerston must have tired of the situation. As a result, in October 1545, while Surrey was in France, Fulmerston began a lawsuit to recover £140 he claimed was owed him.[61] The dispute must have been settled to his satisfaction, for when Fulmerston was examined after his patrons' arrests, he refused to make any charges against them, declaring that Norfolk and Surrey were, as far as he knew, true and faithful subjects.[62]

Fulmerston continued collecting land during Edward's reign, and appears to have served with Holdiche as a steward for the seized Howard lands, since a number of grants note him being "in possession" of properties sold by Edward's regents. Several parcels of Norfolk's lands were granted to Fulmerston, perhaps as a reward for his duties. In May 1547, Fulmerston was pardoned for all offenses committed prior to Edward's accession, clearing the way for his appointment to the commission to collect the subsidy of 1550.[63] In 1554 Fulmerston's daughter married a son of Sir John Clere (the latter a Howard client in his own right), and at an unknown date Fulmerston was knighted, for his will, proved in January 1567, refers to him as "Sir Richard Fulmerston." He retained ties to the Howards after the third duke's death, serving in Parliament for Horsham in 1558 and Thetford in 1559 and 1563.[64] It would appear that Fulmerston died a fairly wealthy man; as with Anthony Rouse and Robert Holdiche, service to the Howards enabled Fulmerston to become a man of some substance within the lower levels of the Tudor gentry.

An important area of Norfolk's patronage, one which fits in with the more old-fashioned aspects of his character, was the "good lordship" demonstrated through hospitality at his houses. A great lord was expected to provide lodging and entertainment to visiting friends, relatives and clients, as well as jobs and charity for the common people of the shire. Evidence of all of this is to be found in the two surviving Howard household books. The first covers the period from 18 April 1523 to 17 January 1524 (while he was earl of Surrey), recording events and household expenses at Stoke-by-Neyland, Suffolk, and Hunsdon, Hertfordshire. The second runs from 1 October 1526 to 30 September 1527 at Stoke and Framlingham early in Howard's tenure as duke.[65] Both give evidence of hospitality to a number of visitors: his parents, brothers and sisters, in-laws and cousins, local knights and gentlemen and clients and servants, and, occasionally, other nobles and their families. Just as important to Norfolk's position are the frequent notations of hospitality extended to travelers. The first Howard household book includes notations of meals and lodging given to "a priest of London," "ii persons of town," "iv of my lord's servants," and "a man of the town." In addition, it was common practice to feed the poor with the leavings from meals served to the household, extending noble largess down the social scale. Thus Howard's household served as a center of local hospitality and charity—an acknowledgment of Norfolk's place as the leader of local society.[66]

At Christmas 1526 Norfolk's household at Framlingham was the center of local celebrations. The "strangers" who stayed at Framlingham through 30 December included Sir Anthony and Humphrey Wingfield, Sir Philip Tylney, Sir John Willoughby, Sir Thomas Wentworth and about a dozen others, as well as thirty of their servants. Meals were served on Christmas day to sixty visitors who ate at the first table with Norfolk, his lady, and the household officers and servants; another two hundred "persons of the Country" were fed outside the manor house itself, perhaps in outbuildings of the castle.[67] Even when no feast was being celebrated, and with the duke himself absent, meals were prepared for a household of twenty-five or thirty. Clearly Norfolk was important simply as an employer for the people of the shire; at his arrest in 1546, there was a staff of 150 gentlemen, yeomen, chaplains, grooms and other servants at Norfolk's mansion of Kenninghall.[68]

Yet another area of Norfolk's patronage deserves notice for the light it sheds on his intellectual attainments and his ideas about religion and the new learning. Although little is known of Norfolk's own education, it is clear that he was no illiterate medieval baron. Howard was fairly fluent in French and knew more than a bit of Latin. Norfolk was a man of action, however, and hardly fit the model of a Renaissance courtier. In outlook and sympathies he was decidedly old-fashioned; in 1540 he declared that he had never read the Scriptures, nor ever would, and thought that England had been a far merrier place before "all this new learning came up." Nevertheless, when in Beauchamp Tower awaiting death in 1546–47, he asked for books to read, saying that for the past dozen years he had not been able to fall asleep without reading. The books he requested were Augustine's *City of God* and several works of Josephus and Sabellius—classical authors then fashionable for their seeming support of the Henrician reformation.[69]

Considering his own beliefs, it is interesting to note that, while Norfolk patronized Catholic writers, he was also willing to support at least the more Erasmian of the reformers. It was once believed that the poet John

Skelton was a client of the third duke and his wife, an attribution which would seem to fit in with the more traditional and aristocratic aspects of his character, but recent work has demonstrated that Skelton was in fact supported by the duke's stepmother Agnes Tylney, dowager duchess of Norfolk.[70] Most of the writers known to have been Norfolk's clients were of a more modern stripe than Skelton.

Shortly after succeeding as duke, Howard employed John Clerk as secretary and tutor to his children. Clerk was a Catholic humanist proficient in Latin, French and Italian, who dedicated several works to the Howards. Clerk's 1543 *Treatise on Nobility*, a translation from the French, and a 1546 pamphlet defending a Catholic interpretation of the faith, were dedicated to Norfolk, while a 1545 tract on the resurrection and last judgment was dedicated to Surrey. Clerk was arrested in 1546 along with Norfolk, and he hanged himself in the Tower in May 1552.[71] Clerk was the most obviously conservative of Norfolk's clients, but the duke did not limit his patronage to Catholics. In 1532, at Cromwell's request, Norfolk granted a pension to Richard Tavener, a writer who translated Erasmus into English and wrote defenses of Lutheranism.[72] Roger Ascham, an Erasmian reformer, was sponsored at court by Norfolk and William Paget when he presented his 1545 treatise *Toxophilus (The Art of Shooting)* to the king. Ascham later helped Norfolk find a tutor for his grandchildren.[73] At various times Norfolk had several illustrious men in his service, including John Leland, the antiquarian, who was tutor to the duke's second son Thomas in the 1520s, and Hadrian Junius, a Dutch scholar and physician who entered Norfolk's service in the 1540s; a number of Junius's Latin letters were written at Kenninghall.[74]

The most radical individual connected to Norfolk was Richard Grafton, who dedicated his 1543 edition of Hardyng's *Chronicle* to the duke in a poem of fulsome praise. Grafton was a wholehearted Protestant who had printed an English Bible and would later see Cranmer's English Prayer Books through the press. The main reason for the dedication to Norfolk seems to be that Hardyng gave great attention to Anglo-Scottish relations, and Norfolk had returned recently from his latest service in the north in 1543. There seems otherwise no connection between Grafton and Norfolk, although presumably the duke gave his consent for the dedication.[75] In his patronage of men of letters, the duke generally lent his support to conservatives or, at best, Erasmians. Yet it is important to note that

Norfolk was touched enough by the Renaissance currents at Henry VIII's court to employ and support scholars alongside stewards and household treasurers.

One of the privileges of the Tudor nobility which Howard exercised was the appointment of priests to benefices within his gift. Most of the churches on Howard manor lands were under Norfolk's control, and while the livings were usually not luxurious, dispensations for plurality could be obtained. At least six such dispensations appear in the archbishop of Canterbury's faculty office registers from 1538 to 1545, with the beneficiaries invariably listed as chaplains to the duke of Norfolk in addition to their other (usually absentee) church livings. The most famous, perhaps, of Norfolk's ecclesiastical preferments came in March 1529, when he presented Stephen Gardiner as archdeacon of Norwich upon the resignation of Thomas Winter, Wolsey's natural son. Gardiner held the post until March 1531, when he became bishop of Winchester as his reward for his part in bringing down Wolsey.[76] Few of Norfolk's ecclesiastical appointments went to men who attained the stature of Gardiner, but like customs licenses and household offices, control of benefices which were often little more than sinecures formed a small but important part of Norfolk's ability to reward his followers and maintain ties of clientage and patronage.

The arena in which Norfolk's influence can most graphically be seen translated into political power is in control of elections to Parliament. Full returns do not exist for any of the elections from 1524 to 1545, but enough information remains to give a good idea of Norfolk's influence.[77]

In 1529 elections were held for what would become the Reformation Parliament, which met on 3 November. The elections were held on short notice; although writs were enrolled in Chancery on 9 August, they were not sent out until early October, a delay caused by Wolsey's impending fall from power. New channels of patronage were opening for local men to obtain seats formerly controlled by Wolsey. In Norfolk, the knights of the shire were Roger Townshend and James Boleyn, the former a lawyer and minor administrator, the latter an uncle of Anne. Norfolk had ties to both, and probably helped secure their election. Norfolk was given the writs for Derby and Nottinghamshire to execute, but beyond assuring the election of men favorable to the king, the duke's role there is unclear.[78] In other areas, however, Norfolk had a considerable voice in elections. In Sussex, he boasted, he could control ten seats for the boroughs of

Horsham, Shoreham, Stening, Lewes and Gatton, the latter a classic "rotten borough" with only one house "where Sir Roger Copley dwelleth."[79] William Roper, Thomas More's future son-in-law and biographer, was returned for Bramber, Sussex, along with a fellow student at Lincoln's Inn, Henry See. Thetford, on the Norfolk-Suffolk border, home of the Cluniac priory patronized by the dukes of Norfolk, was newly enfranchised in 1529—doubtless by Norfolk's influence—and although the borough elections were controlled by the duchy of Lancaster, Norfolk's hand can probably be seen in the return of William Dauntsey and Giles Heron, both sons-in-law of More. Cooperation in the elections of 1529 between Norfolk and More helped to secure a House of Commons willing to acquiesce in the destruction of Wolsey—and in the subsequent dismantling of Roman authority in England, with consequences Norfolk and More alike came to regret.[80]

Elections in 1536 and 1539 were heavily influenced by Cromwell. In both years Norfolk was in political eclipse to varying degrees and probably had to give way to Cromwell in controlling elections. Cromwell must have conceded Norfolk his Sussex boroughs in 1536, for Howard clients seem to have occupied these seats. In addition, a Norfolk retainer, George Gifford, who had sat for Maidhurst, Kent, in the Reformation Parliament, was returned for Buckinghamshire in 1536. Sir Anthony Wingfield was one of the knights of the shire for Suffolk, doubtless welcome to Norfolk as a fellow conservative and sometime ally, and Sir Roger Townshend, a Howard man, was returned for Norfolk.[81]

In 1539 the election dispute between Richard Southwell and Edmund Wyndham took place. Southwell and Wyndham, despite their attachment to Cromwell, were from families with long ties to the Howards; even at the height of his power, Cromwell had to defer somewhat to the Howards in their own shire. In fact the elections of 1539 went rather better for Norfolk than had those of 1536. Sir Anthony Browne in Surrey was Norfolk's man, Sir Anthony Wingfield remained for Suffolk, and Sir Robert Southwell sat for King's Lynn. In Sussex Sir John Gage had a place, and Nicholas Hare, a lawyer and a Cambridge man who had been Norfolk's understeward in the court of augmentations and would later serve as an executor of the duke's will, was returned from an uncertain constituency, perhaps in Wiltshire.[82] Although none of these men was squarely under Norfolk's thumb, and several, such as the Southwells, had ties to Cromwell as well, they formed part of a distinctly conservative bloc in Commons that was of crucial importance to Norfolk, Gardiner, and the conservative party that steered the Act of Six Articles through this session despite Cromwell's opposition.

Cromwell was ill at the opening of this session on 28 April, leaving the field open to the conservatives. The election of Hare as Speaker, and the earl of Sussex's role in delivering the government's opening address, must be seen as evidence of the strength of the Howard-Gardiner coalition. The session of 1539 was a battleground between Cromwell and his opponents, and was the beginning of open conflict between the lord privy seal and the Howard-Gardiner faction which would lead to the former's fall the next year, an event made possible in no small degree by the strength of the conservatives in the lower house.[83]

In 1542, Cromwell was gone, and court politics and local ambitions had a strong influence upon elections. Men such as Gage, Wingfield and Thomas Wriothesley continued a strong conservative presence in Commons, while Norfolk's cousin Sir Francis Bryan was returned from Buckinghamshire, where he owned land. Roger Townshend, Anthony Browne, Robert Southwell and Humphrey Wingfield continued to hold seats and formed part of a group of men well known to Norfolk. The duke's personal patronage was again strong in Sussex and East Anglia; at least one complete interloper with no local ties, Sir John Clere, was returned at Bramber through Norfolk's influence.[84] Clere was probably the older brother of Thomas Clere, and both were household retainers of the Howards and companions of the earl of Surrey. The Cleres were connected by marriage to the Boleyns, and thus were part of the Howard clientage in several ways.[85] Norfolk's clients and friends were well represented in Parliament in 1542, although since the major purpose of the session was the attainder of Catherine Howard the strength of his party was little comfort to the duke. The house elected that year also met in 1543 and 1544, and in each of these sessions private acts were passed confirming land exchanges between Norfolk and the king.[86]

The elections in 1545 for the final Parliament of Henry VIII returned a house well supplied with friends and supporters of Norfolk—even if this Parliament, in later session, passed the attainder of the Howards. Sir John Clere sat again at Bramber; Thomas Hussey, the duke's treasurer, was at Grimsby; Edward Bellingham, who had served with Surrey in France, sat for Gatton. Thomas Gawdy, a witness to Norfolk's will and later a retainer of the fourth duke, sat for Salisbury after a by-election in 1545; Thomas Arundel, married to a sister of Catherine Howard, was a knight of the shire for Dorset; Sir Nicholas Hare had a seat for Lancaster; and John Steward, Norfolk's understeward in augmentations, was at Colchester, Essex. Sir John Baker, chancellor of the exchequer and Speaker in 1545, had been an ally in the abortive conservative assault on Cranmer in 1544, and now sat for Lancaster along with Hare. In Sussex, Sir Francis Knollys (married to a Howard niece), Sir John Gates and Henry Gates were returned, along with Sir Anthony Browne's son and namesake, while Anthony Wingfield and John Gage, both of the privy council and Norfolk's allies, had seats as well. These last were elected at least in part because of their positions at court and held first loyalty to the king (and their own careers, as events would show), but they should be seen as part of Norfolk's party until the final disaster in 1546.[87]

A few others elected in 1545 had Howard connections but were not returned through the duke's direct patronage. Richard Morgan, a member for Gloucester, was imprisoned during Edward's reign, but was made chief justice of the Common Pleas by Mary and was an executor of the duke's will.[88] Anthony Rouse, elected in Suffolk, was a former Howard client, and Sir Thomas Legh, a distant connection by marriage, was returned at Wilton. At Grimsby, the second member was Richard Goodrich, attorney to the court of augmentations. Sir Richard Rich also found a seat. Rich, chancellor of augmentations, was a slippery politician who betrayed Thomas More, survived Cromwell's fall, and lived on to serve Mary and be appointed an executor of Norfolk's will. Goodrich and Rich cannot be ignored as at least potential Howard allies. Finally, among the knights of the shires are found Sir Francis Bryan, the senior Anthony Browne, and George Harper (later a supporter of Wyatt's rebellion), all friendly to the duke.[89] The returns for the elections of 1545 are unusually full, and so allow a very clear view of Norfolk's influence in Commons, both in direct patronage and through other political and family connections. It is hard to believe that Sir Thomas Paston and Christopher Heydon, for example, the knights of the shire for Norfolk, were not among the duke's "well-willers" even if they cannot be shown to be direct clients, for both had long-standing family ties to the Howards.[90]

Nonetheless, the limits of political patronage in Parliament are clearly shown by the fact that Norfolk's attainder was passed by these men; the subjects of Henry VIII knew where first loyalties lay. Interestingly, the bill took four days to get through Commons, even with the determined support of the Hertford faction, the leaders of which knew the king was near death. Perhaps this is evidence of one last protest against the fall of the Howards before the Commons gave in and assented to the inevitable.[91]

Elections to Parliament were an important element of Norfolk's patronage and a foundation of power in court and country. Even at the height of Cromwell's power in 1536, Norfolk had some influence; after Cromwell's fall, the duke's patronage is quite clear. As Stanford Lehmberg has shown, Norfolk was not alone in trying to influence elections; Gardiner certainly worked to build a following in 1539 and after, and there is some evidence that men such as William Fitzwilliam, earl of Southampton, had clients elected at boroughs under their control. Lehmberg identifies several members who owed their election in 1545 to Hertford, to a coalition headed by relatives of Queen Catherine Parr, to Gardiner, or to Norfolk. Much more so than in earlier Henrician parliaments, the sessions of 1545 and afterward were real political battlegrounds. Although Wolsey and Cromwell had made concerted efforts to manage elections, it was only after the latter's fall that the conservative-progressive polarity at court reached the point that parties approaching those on the Elizabethan model appeared in Commons. Even so, throughout Henry's reign the foremost party in any session was not Wolsey's, Cromwell's, Norfolk's or Hertford's; the confidence of the king was always the main criterion for election to the Henrician House of Commons.[92]

The one area of political patronage where Howard had little success was in infiltrating the king's inner circle. Thomas Howard was too old to become one of Henry's close companions. At the beginning of the reign, Howard's younger brother Edward and brother-in-law Thomas Knevet were among the king's inner circle, but both were dead by 1513. Although others with Howard connections appeared among the gentlemen of the privy chamber later in the reign, except for the brief period of Catherine Howard's reign none of Henry's minions seem to have been more than fair-weather friends of the Howards. Lord Thomas Howard, Norfolk's younger son, for example, was a hanger-on at court and never the king's intimate in the 1540s. In the long run, the lack of access to Henry's bedchamber may have been a decisive factor in the fall of the Howards in 1546, for there were none there who wished—or dared?—to speak on behalf of the duke and his son when the crisis came. Inability to gain control of or at least a voice in Henry's chamber may have been Norfolk's greatest failure in the game of factional politics.[93]

Clientage and patronage lay at the heart of Norfolk's effectiveness as head of a widespread system of family, friends and followers. His ability to deliver favors—government posts, grants of land and licenses of various kinds—was fundamental to his political success, while hospitality, charity and employment all added to his social and political prestige. Ket's Rebellion in Norfolk in 1549, the result as much of the power vacuum caused by the fall of the Howards as of economic distress, serves as evidence of the extent of Norfolk's influence as much as does recitation of members of Parliament elected through his patronage.[94] Thomas Howard was a politician who spent a long career seeking power and prestige from the hands of the king, but he never forgot the necessity of being a good lord to his well-willers. In the highly personal government of Tudor England, attention to followers and friends was expected of men of status, and Thomas Howard both sought and granted favor through this intensely personal system.

Land and Income

Land was the basis of personal wealth and a considerable source of power for the ruling class in sixteenth-century England, and therefore was vitally important to Thomas Howard. Income from rents, leases, fees and fines made landholding a source of cash income, while payments in kind and labor services from tenants added to the value of real property. Men such as Norfolk did not generally exploit their lands directly (except, perhaps, for the estates surrounding principal residences), and therefore employed large staffs of stewards, receivers and auditors to collect and account for landed revenues. Norfolk was noted by contemporaries as an unusually oppressive landlord, one of the last to retain villenage on his East Anglian estates. Dairmaid MacCullough has suggested that the violence of Ket's Rebellion was in part owing to the "extremitie" of Norfolk's methods and relief at his overthrow.[95] Records of land values, estate accounts and deeds and other evidences of land transactions are, as classes of documents, difficult to use and interpret, especially since records for any individual or family are seldom complete. Landed income is therefore an elusive subject.

This is particularly true for Thomas Howard. Few documents provide more than partial surveys of his income at any point in his life. His inquisition *post mortem*, which might have been a major source of information, is badly mutilated and therefore of limited use. His will mentions only one manor by name. Reports of landed income survive for two points a dozen years apart during his tenure as duke, giving some idea of his wealth.[96] The most comprehensive document available is the land survey prepared after his arrest in 1546. This lists all the properties in Norfolk, Suffolk, Essex, Cambridgeshire and Lincolnshire that passed into the hands of the crown in 1546. It is also, unfortunately, badly mutilated. A second volume, which records rents collected and sales and alienations of lands for 5 and 6 Edward VI and 1 Mary, is in better condition, but less useful, as many Howard properties had by then passed out of the crown's hands.[97] In any case, neither book listed all of Norfolk's lands since he is known to have entered into a group of manors in Sussex and elsewhere after his stepmother's death in 1544, none of which were included in the surveys.

Despite these shortcomings, the general outline of Norfolk's landed estate can be seen. A great deal can be learned from the many grants and land transactions involving Norfolk during his lifetime, since many list locations and values. Particularly at the time of the dissolution of the monasteries, Norfolk made dozens of land deals. Using all of these sources, what emerges is an incomplete but revealing picture of the widespread properties—castles, manors, rents and other rights—which were the foundation of Norfolk's wealth.

By his first marriage Howard obtained rights to an assortment of lands granted to his wife Anne, as well as the use of several manors with an annual value of £120 given to the couple by Howard's father.[98] Howard was initially debarred from holding any Plantagenet lands in his own right, but before Anne died in 1512, he made a deal with Henry VIII that gave him a life estate in some of her lands not derived from crown estates. In addition, Howard obtained other lands in his own right which continued in his hands. In March 1510, Howard and Anne were jointly granted in tail "a messaunge and garden in Stepenhithe, Middlesex, late of John Hert, brewer in London"; this was sold to the crown by Howard in 1520. In other exchanges involving Anne's lands in 1510 and 1511, Howard obtained in his own right the manors of Claxton in Norfolk and Fyndon in Suffolk.[99] These he sold to the crown in 1514 shortly after becoming earl of Surrey, in order to settle a loan of £2,000 made to him as admiral. In 1538 Norfolk noted that these manors had been worth £70 a year (£1,400 at twenty years' purchase), making this settlement an excellent bargain.[100]

By his second marriage, to Elizabeth Stafford, Howard gained a dowry but little real property. Until his creation as earl of Surrey, he had little land in his own right. The basis of his personal estate was a collection of lands granted him by the king in February 1514 with a gross value of £1,037 16s. 10d. The grant was originally made for life, at an annual rent of one red rose to be delivered on the feast of John the Baptist, but in 1525 the grant was improved to tail male at a service of two knights' fees.[101] Until the death of the second duke of Norfolk in 1524 there were few changes in Surrey's landholdings. One transaction concerned the lands of his father-in-law Edward Stafford, duke of Buckingham. Following Buckingham's attainder Surrey and his father received several former Stafford manors worth about £40 a year.[102]

With the death of his father, Howard took possession of lands that more than doubled his income; only at the age of fifty-one did he become a really wealthy man. The second duke's total income, not all of which passed to his son, can only be estimated. In 1519 the Venetian ambassador reported the second duke's income at 12,000 ducats, or about £4,500. This may be too high, for Buckingham's lands, valued in this report at £11,250, were, according to a recent student of the family, worth about half that sum.[103] Yet clearly the second duke had accumulated a considerable estate since his attainder in 1485, for the commissioners for the subsidy in 1523 valued his goods at £4,000 and his son's at £1,000, presumably because these were higher than landed income; the subsidy was collected on the value of lands or goods, whichever was greater. A large part of the second duke's lands were Mowbray and Howard estates, granted back piecemeal by Henry VII and Henry VIII, but he also received thirty manors worth almost £400 at his creation as duke in 1514.[104] At his death in 1524, the second duke's widow, Agnes Tylney, retained a considerable jointure, including twelve manors in Suffolk, Surrey, Essex and Lincoln and more than a dozen others in Sussex. These lands returned to the dukedom only at her death in 1544, and not until July 1546 was the third duke confirmed in possession of Agnes's holdings.[105] The second duke's estates were valued at £2,241 net at his death; although not all of this passed to his son, the third duke also received the income from several offices held by his father.

An English Duke

The treasurership, which the second duke had resigned in his son's favor in December 1522, carried a fee of £365 per annum.[106] Adding fees from offices and land inherited from his father to his own landed income of about £1,000, the third duke probably had a gross income of £3,500 to £4,000 from all sources.

After 1524, and especially after the dissolution of the monasteries began in 1536, Norfolk constantly sought to increase and centralize his landholdings. The effect of these transactions is clear from two documents recording his net landed income, first in 1525–26, shortly after becoming duke of Norfolk, and again a dozen years later. In the receiver general's accounts for 1525–26, Norfolk's gross income was listed as £2,800, with a net cash income of about £1,900. By 1538, when Norfolk drew up a memorandum listing a number of sales and exchanges, he concluded that, after paying all charges, "there remaineth to me clear, £2,638."[107] It appears that Norfolk had realized almost a fifty percent increase in landed income since succeeding to the title. From the transactions listed in the 1538 memorandum and other records, the nature and scale of the activities in the land market that resulted in such a striking rise in Norfolk's wealth can be seen in some detail.

Between 1524 and 1538, Norfolk purchased lands with an annual value of at least £331, and sold other properties worth about £550 per annum.[108] While the lands sold were scattered across the realm, most of those acquired were in East Anglia, where Norfolk was building his mansion at Kenninghall; the difference in values between lands sold and purchased probably produced several thousand pounds in cash for the building of Kenninghall. This manor had been a Mowbray hunting lodge, but it came into Howard hands when Norfolk's great-grandfather married Margaret, daughter of the first Mowbray duke. The name came from the Old English "cyning hall," or king's palace, as the site was near the ancient capital of the kingdom of East Anglia. Originally a park of seven hundred acres had surrounded the old house, but Norfolk wanted a larger expanse. In 1533 he acquired the manor of Fersfield adjacent to Kenninghall and attempted to enclose forty-four acres of Fersfield commons, ejecting the tenants. This led to a lawsuit which Norfolk lost, for, at the time of his arrest, he was surveying land in the nearby manor of Lopham to compensate the tenants of Fersfield.[109] Good lordship obviously had its limits; Norfolk was not above dispossessing his tenants if it would improve the hunting at Kenninghall.

With Kenninghall completed, Norfolk alienated several former residences. Hunsdon, Hertfordshire, where Howard had lived before becoming duke of Norfolk, was sold to the king in 1538, the yearly value then being given as fifty pounds.[110] In 1540, by means of a private act of Parliament, Norfolk disposed of one of his London houses. Since the fourteenth century a house at Broken Wharf, St. Mary's parish, Surrey, had served the earls and dukes of Norfolk. Howard House, Lambeth, was sufficient for the duke's London business; amidst the tensions of Cromwell's fall and attainder, Parliament passed a bill ratifying Norfolk's sale of Broken Wharf to Sir Richard Gresham, the financier, for an unstated price.[111]

After the crown began seizing monastic property in 1536, Norfolk became very active in the land market. Although many individuals purchased or were granted monastic lands, those with court connections and capital were best able to take advantage of the dissolutions. Among the peerage, Norfolk and Francis Talbot, earl of Shrewsbury, were the leading recipients of monastic lands. Doctrinal beliefs obviously did not blunt their willingness to accept these spoils, for both these men were religious conservatives.[112] In Norfolk's case, simple greed was certainly a motive, but it also appears that the duke, with the support of his Catholic neighbors, sought church lands in part to prevent them falling into the hands of outsiders who might be enemies to the old faith. Norfolk was quite successful in his pursuit of former monastic property in East Anglia, and while much of this was exploited for profit, at least part of Norfolk's income from these lands went toward the support of the displaced clergy. In his 1538 memorandum, Norfolk noted that he was spending seventy-two pounds a year to support former monks. Other expenditures were added later. Thomas Manning, for example, abbot of the dissolved Butley priory, Suffolk, which Norfolk acquired in 1540, was given a life estate in a Warwickshire manor.[113]

Most of Norfolk's monastic lands were in East Anglia. This was part of a general pattern of concentrating his estates, but it also shows his interest in protecting his home shires from the worst effects of the dissolutions. As early as 1536 Norfolk began trying to shelter Thetford priory, a Cluniac house long patronized by the dukes of Norfolk and the burial place of his father. By an act of Parliament (27 Hen. VIII, c. 33), Norfolk, the prior of Thetford and the king agreed to an exchange of properties. Norfolk received a group of advowsons and tithe rights from the prior of Thetford at a rent of 26s. 8d. to the king, and granted the manor of Imworth, Surrey to the king, who was expanding the park at Hampton Court. In exchange, Thetford was left unmolested, at least for the moment.[114] In 1539, when the dissolution of the larger monasteries was ordered, Norfolk petitioned to have the priory converted to a church of secular canons. Henry agreed, and Norfolk was in the process of drawing up articles giving the Howards the right to nominate the dean of this new foundation when the king changed his mind. On 16 February 1540, Prior William Ixworth signed a deed of surrender, but within two weeks Norfolk had begun a series of sales and exchanges that led, on 9 July, to a royal grant of the site, manors, advowsons and other appurtenances and rights of the former Priory of St. Mary, Thetford, to Norfolk. The duke exchanged a group of manors in Wiltshire and Oxfordshire for the rights to Thetford, and in addition paid a settlement of £1,000 and made indenture to pay an annual rent of £59 5s. 1d. to the court of augmentations. In return, Norfolk acquired properties worth nearly £350 a year clear, including the lands of the priory of Wangford, Suffolk, a dependent house dissolved along with that at Thetford.[115] This deal shows how Henry's disposal of monastic lands worked to the financial advantage of such as Norfolk, for the king accepted ready cash, rents and property worth less than half the value of the Thetford property when figured at the usual twenty-years' purchase of almost £7,000.

Norfolk acquired several other East Anglian monastic properties, most of them resulting in the kind of handsome profits he enjoyed from the Thetford arrangement. In May 1537, he was granted the lands and rights of Coxford priory, Norfolk, with an annual rent of £230. The house itself, with a lead roof worth £100, was dismantled and sold, and Richard Southwell, who carried out the dissolution, received about 70s. worth of plate.[116] Later in 1537 Norfolk acquired the lands of Castle Acre priory in Norfolk with its dependent house, Normansburgh priory, and over a dozen manors and a group of advowsons worth more than £300 a year; the rent to the crown was £44 19s. 3/4d.[117] In 1540 the duke purchased the lands of a fourth major East Anglian house when he paid £1,239 0s. 10d. and a yearly rent of £14 15s. 12d. for a group of manors connected with Butley priory, an Augustinian house in Suffolk. In 1541 Norfolk granted a manor house, rectory and advowson which had come from this exchange to his mistress, Elizabeth Holland; these properties, in Lincolnshire, had been owned by Thorney Abbey, Cambridge, a dependent house of Butley.[118]

Finally, in 1539 Norfolk was confirmed in ownership of the possessions of the monastery of Sibton, Suffolk. In 1537 Norfolk had negotiated the surrender of Sibton, and by the second act for the dissolution of the monasteries (31 Hen. VIII, c. 13), Henry made a gift of all the possessions of Sibton to the duke, a handsome prize yielding a net annual value of around £250. This transfer demonstrated the thoroughness of the process of dissolution, as Norfolk was made the legal successor of the last abbot of Sibton, retaining all rights but also all obligations for debts, rents and services.[119] In this way, the crown sought to minimize the legal disruption caused by the dissolutions and the transfer of vast tracts of land with complicated attendant rights and obligations.

In addition to these large houses, Norfolk obtained property from a number of other monastic establishments. In December 1537 he was granted possessions of Bungay priory, Suffolk, worth £62 2s. 1 1/2d., at a rent of just over £16. During the next several years, the duke obtained the site of the priory of St. Leonard, Norwich; the church of the Grey Friars, Norwich (paying the friars forty shillings each to buy secular dress); the house of the Austin Friars, Norwich; the collegiate church of Rushworth, Norfolk; a manor from Lewes priory, Sussex; and at least some of the possessions of the great house at Bury St. Edmunds, Suffolk. The annual values and rents paid for most of these are not clear, although Rushworth appears to have been worth about £85 a year, to judge from a license to alienate the property granted the duke in 1545.[120] In many cases, manors from these smaller houses, and at least some of the properties from the larger houses as well, did not remain in Norfolk's hands, but were sold for ready cash. Many individual transactions appear in the state papers, with Howard clients receiving a good bit of the land sold. Other properties were still in Howard's hands at his attainder and were alienated during the Edwardian regency.[121]

Norfolk seems to have had two goals in mind in his many land deals in the later reign of Henry VIII. The first and probably paramount aim was to enlarge and concentrate the landholdings that would pass on to later Howard dukes of Norfolk; this quest for family enrichment was one of Norfolk's most notable characteristics. Many other land deals seem to have been made for immediate profit; the cost of building and furnishing Kenninghall was met largely through profits from sales and leases of lands Norfolk received as a consequence of the monastic dissolutions.

Howard's income rose steadily during his tenure as duke of Norfolk, although pinpointing a figure for any date is a difficult problem. The most valuable evidence is Norfolk's own statement in 1538 that his "clear" or net income totaled £2,638. The monastic lands obtained after 1538 presumably boosted this figure substantially, even after taking into account rents paid, sales and exchanges. Figures for the subsidy of 1545 (for which Norfolk served as a commissioner and provided his own valuation) placed his income at 5,000 marks (£3,333 6s. 8d.), the highest assessed income for that year and a sum nearly four times the average figure of £873 for all the peerage. This figure must be judged a minimum, even taking into account the enforced honesty compelled by Henry's scrutiny; it is unlikely that Norfolk would have overestimated his income when facing a tax of one-sixth of his revenue.[122]

Land was not Norfolk's only source of income. He also collected pensions, annuities, and fees from office, although in any given year all or part of these might have been in arrears. At Norfolk's arrest in 1546, a list of such cash receipts showed a total of £672 a year, despite several blanks where Hertford's agents were unsure of amounts. On top of this, until his death in 1545 Charles Brandon, duke of Suffolk, paid Norfolk an annuity of £413 6s. 8d. as a result of land exchanges in Lincolnshire.[123] Thus an average income figure for Norfolk during the 1540s would include perhaps £1,000 in excess of landed income. From the scattered evidence we have, it seems likely that Norfolk enjoyed a gross income of between £5,000 and £6,000 at the end of Henry's reign. In 1554, even after the losses during the reign of Edward VI (and not including fees from office or other annuities), the fourth duke inherited lands worth £2,489 net; a gross figure would be perhaps one-third higher.[124]

Compared with the rest of the Henrician peerage, Norfolk was certainly one of the wealthiest men in England. In 1545, fourteen peers were assessed at incomes over £1,000. Among these were Hertford, who admitted revenues of £1,700 but more likely was worth something like £4,400, according to Helen Miller. Others with over £1,000 a year included: John deVere, earl of Oxford, with £1,500; John Dudley, viscount Lisle, at £1,360; John, lord Russell, with about £1,600; and Thomas Wriothesley, with £1,500. After Norfolk's fall, when the second payment of the subsidy was assessed in 1547, the highest recorded income was that of Edward Stanley, earl of Derby, with £2,900.[125] From these figures alone, it is evident that Norfolk stood at the top of the lay peerage in wealth at the end of the reign of Henry VIII.

Norfolk's wealth was used in large part to maintain the lifestyle his rank demanded. The lavish furnishings at Kenninghall recorded at his arrest attest in part to the luxury in which he lived,[126] but his wealth was employed in other ways as well. Money had to be paid to servants, gifts had to be made to the king, friends and fellow courtiers, and any transaction within the bureaucracy required the payment of fees, if not what would today be considered bribes, in order to obtain warrants, licenses, deeds of grant and other legal documents for Norfolk and his well-willers. Money, in the sixteenth century just as today, provided the grease for the machinery of business and government. Men such as Norfolk who had ample wealth were able to lubricate the machinery and make things happen to the advantage of themselves and others, and Norfolk, his allies and his enemies knew it. Thus the constant quest for income was a part and parcel of the game of Tudor politics; Norfolk's importance and success as a player was tied, in no small measure, to his financial position as one of the richest men in the realm.

Administration, Politics and Power

Thomas Howard's ultimate goal was to attain primacy in court and council, to achieve the kind of position held in turn by Wolsey and Cromwell as master of Tudor government. Except for brief interludes in the early 1530s and again a decade later, Howard never reached this goal. Yet the quest for administrative primacy, with the wealth and power that went with it, was one constant which helps to explain much about Norfolk's career and his character. To understand the man, we must understand what he sought and why he sought it.

For all their differences of personality, Henry VII and his son had this much in common: each demanded loyal and useful service from those about him, and each was more inclined to employ and reward the able and devoted servant than to rely on those whose only claim to power was noble birth. Thomas Howard understood this, for in a long career under the Tudors he saw the rise and fall of many men of ambition and talent, and came to recognize that Henry VIII was a hard master who demanded his servants' unquestioned loyalty and harshly punished those who fell short.

Howard began his career under the Tudors primarily as a soldier, and mainly under his father's command. Not until around the age of forty did he begin to receive independent commands, and only after his father's death in 1524 did he move into the highest circles of the king's service. Thomas Howard was something of a late bloomer, and his frustration with his slow advancement sometimes showed. By his own account, often repeated in plaintive letters to court, Howard's health and purse alike suffered considerable damage from his service to the crown. The Howards eventually gained great wealth and power under the Tudors, and these rewards were earned, for a family that first confronted the Tudor dynasty as enemies at Bosworth field could never afford to give less than undivided loyalty and their fullest, even self-sacrificing, efforts. The disaster of 1485 cast the Howards into disgrace; only by hard work and faithful service could they ever hope to recapture the status that had, so fleetingly, been theirs under Richard III.

Although the elder Thomas Howard regained the earldom of Surrey, the treasurership, and a seat on the council under Henry VII, his son was only a minor figure until after 1509. The career of Thomas Howard the younger began, for all practical purposes, with the accession of Henry VIII, when a new prince provided new opportunities to seek honor and rewards. From 1509 to 1513, Howard served Henry VIII in several military capacities and, perhaps more important, found a place at court on the fringes of Henry's personal circle. Even after the triumph at Flodden, Howard, newly created earl of Surrey, played a distinct second fiddle to his father, who, as duke of Norfolk, reaped the lion's share of the family's rewards. From 1513 to 1524, Surrey served at sea against the French, in Ireland, and in the north against the Scots. While building an independent career and reputation, however, he paid the heavy price of being away from court almost constantly. From January 1520 to December 1524, at the peak of his military career, Surrey spent at least forty out of sixty months in the field.

Surrey's first really independent command was as admiral, an office he gained after the untimely death of his brother Edward in 1513.[127] He remained busy with the admiralty until peace was made with the sealing of the Treaty of London in 1518. As admiral, Howard was responsible not only for leading the Tudor navy against the French, but for organizing coastal defenses, arranging supplies for the fleet, and appointing and supervising officials who did such things as inspecting ships in the Thames estuary and other ports.[128] The admiralty provided Surrey considerable administrative experience. His first surviving letters come from this period, and they not only reveal his personality but also show the difficulties of pleasing Henry, a king who seldom concerned himself with the real world problems of command which plagued such as Howard. Still, as a letter of 1513 shows, Surrey had fully absorbed the Howard creed of faithful, even obsequious, service to the king, for he wrote: "It hath pleased the king's grace to give [me] this great room and authority, more meet for a wise expert man than me. But since it hath pleased his Grace to admit me thereunto, as far as my poor wit can extend, I shall endeavor myself from time to time to do all manner of service where I shall think to deserve his most desired favor."[129]

Howard continued to hold the office of admiral after becoming duke of Norfolk, although he ceased active command of the fleet and left it to his deputy, Sir Christopher Middleton. This illustrates the pattern of having more interest in status and its rewards than in being burdened with administrative details, a pattern that would continue to manifest itself throughout his career. In 1525 Norfolk yielded the office to Henry's bastard son Richmond with a show of great reluctance. The admiralty, an office of unmatched military preeminence, was important to Norfolk for the prestige and patronage involved even when he had little interest in actually exercising the office.[130]

As admiral, and later as lord lieutenant of Ireland and lieutenant of the north, Howard gained further administrative experience along with a reputation as Henry's most able soldier. Yet this service kept Howard away from court far too much and, after becoming duke, he seems to have resolved to remain at court, the "center of social and political life," as Elton described it, as much as possible.[131] Diplomatic and military missions often took Norfolk away from court in later years, and more than once Wolsey or Cromwell was able to banish him, at least temporarily, to the countryside, but Norfolk could seldom be kept away for long, for Henry continued to find him a useful man. The years of toil at sea, in Ireland and in the north might not appear at first a very promising foundation for a career at court as a councilor and adminstrator, but Howard's early career under Henry VIII served the very significant purpose of assuring the king of his unswerving loyalty and his willingness, as he put it in 1521, "to serve your grace in what ever place so ever your pleasure shall be to command me." Yet Howard knew very well the goal toward which he was working, for he continued with the plea that "once, ere I die, I do your highness service in such business in your own presence."[132] The paradox of Howard's later career is that, having earned his reputation as a soldier, he found himself trapped in that role even when he might have preferred to remain at court and shape policy.

With the death of his father, Howard became a major political player. It might be argued that Norfolk's position at court was unearned and unmerited; without the dukedom and the other trappings of wealth and power which his father had earned, Howard might never have been much of a political force. Yet the family rewards had at least in part been won by the younger Thomas Howard's efforts and, furthermore, titles alone did not a major Tudor figure make; the careers of men such as Buckingham and Dorset show that Henry VIII was little impressed by noble rank alone. The Howards, for all their pride, were as much new men as was Charles Brandon. Even with his recently obtained noble rank, in one respect Norfolk was very much an old-fashioned baron in that he expected to hold primacy in politics as a matter of right, and he saw high office largely for the financial, political and personal rewards. Norfolk embraced the medieval notion of the nobility as literally the king's peers and therefore his rightful companions and advisors. The drudge work of day-to-day administration could be left to clerics, lawyers and other such mean sorts once the lines of policy had been set by those fit to rule. Henry VIII was not, fortunately for Norfolk, an administrator-king like his father. Yet Henry was aware enough of what went on in his name to demand more of his councilors than prowess in the lists. This may explain why Charles Brandon, Henry's close friend, was seldom given anything of weight to do. Thomas Howard's great frustration was that he was fit enough to be among Henry's councilors but neither clever nor hardworking enough to be first among them.

There are two reasons for Howard's ultimate political failure. One was his incapacity or disinclination to do the routine work that Wolsey and Cromwell relished. Part of this may have been lack of ability, or at least of the self-discipline of the bureaucrat, but a large part was pride, the sense of self-importance and expectation of deference, which Henry evidently detected and disliked in Howard. For the second cause of his failure was that he was never able to command Henry's personal friendship. This was hardly due to unwillingness to serve the king; if anything, Howard's career demonstrates an almost self-destructive devotion to the king's causes, and a disdain for those who were not so dedicated. Some of this may have been rooted in Howard's personal or family insecurity which manifested itself in unpleasant whining and fawning, as if in an effort to convince himself as well as the king of the value of his service. This attitude was made clear in an impassioned passage from a letter of 1523, written when Howard was in the north facing the dangerous threat of the duke of Albany's invasion with a force two or three times the size of Howard's:

> God knoweth, if the poorest gentleman in the king's house were here, and I at London, and were advertised of this news, I would not fail to kneel upon my knees before the king's grace to have license to come hither in post to be at the day of battle. And if young noblemen and gentlemen be not desirous and willing to be at such journeys and to take pain and give the adventure, and the king's highness well contented with those that will do so, and not regarding others that will be but dancers, dicers and carders, his grace will not be well served when he would be. For men without experience shall do small service, and experience of war will not be had without it be sought for and the adventure given.[133]

Thomas Howard was a proud man—proud of his noble blood, proud of the service he and his family had given to their kings, and determined that neither should be overlooked or left unrewarded. He had a striking deficit of *noblesse oblige*. By the 1520s, Howard was in his fifties, and he had a developed a strong and easily disliked personality. Unlike rivals such as Wolsey and Cromwell, Norfolk was neither deep nor subtle; he was a man of action rather than of contemplation, one who was prone to threats—as to tear Wolsey with his teeth when he was too slow to head to York—rather than sweet reason. Several times Howard servants complained of his haughty manner. John Stile, his Irish treasurer in 1520–21, complained that Howard "was sometimes more hasty than needith," and Thomas Magnus, his treasurer on the borders several years later, wrote that his master "was in some deal suspicious and will conjecture far enough, and soon will move to be hasty."[134] These were not the qualities of a leading minister. Henry VIII, having seen this side of Howard's personality, never warmed to him and may not have trusted him fully. In the personal world of the Tudor court, the resultant lack of the king's confidence played a role in Norfolk's political failure.

For all that, Norfolk managed to accumulate an impressive collection of offices of state under Henry VIII, and from his succession to the dukedom until Henry's final illness, Norfolk usually played a major and sometimes a dominant role in politics. The most important office was that of treasurer, which not only paid a handsome salary of £365 a year, but provided enormous opportunites for patronage. Norfolk devoted little attention to mundane Exchequer matters beyond occasional attendance at assays of the mint.[135] However, from almost the beginning of his tenure, Norfolk actively exploited the political and financial possibilities of the office. The treasurer had charge of a variety of financial officers—surveyors, receivers and escheators—as well as the all-important customs service which was the major source of royal revenue. Norfolk held dozens of profitable offices in his gift, and also controlled the grant of licenses to import and export goods outside of normal regulations.

The state papers are peppered with traces of Norfolk's patronage as treasurer, from January 1525, when Robert Beaumond and William Halse received license to export five hundred quarters of wheat, to October 1546, when Norfolk signed a fiat of office for a new collector of customs for London.[136] Exactly what Norfolk gained from these transactions is difficult to say. Sale of offices was technically illegal,[137] but even if Norfolk did not collect outright bribes, political clients could be expected to give their masters New Year's gifts and, just as important, those who benefitted from Norfolk's patronage could usually be counted upon as friends when the duke needed them. A considerable degree of what would today be considered official corruption flourished in Tudor England, and Norfolk's control of the Exchequer provided ample opportunity to profit from the practice.

On at least one occasion Norfolk found his conduct as treasurer called into question. In October 1540, in the wake of Cromwell's fall, Norfolk was accused before the council of accepting improper gifts from customs officials in East Anglia and allowing corruption to run rampant. The charges may well have been true, but probably none of the privy councilors could have withstood a careful scrutiny of their own semiofficial business, and as a result, when Norfolk vehemently denied everything, the charges were dropped without a serious investigation.[138]

The treasurership was financially and politically Norfolk's most rewarding office of state. His second great office, as earl marshal, was also of considerable value for patronage and for the ceremonial precedence conferred on its holder. The salary was only twenty pounds a year,[139] but as earl marshal Norfolk had charge of many state ceremonials which played an important role in Tudor politics and statecraft.[140] Throughout the Tudor period, Howard earls marshal presided over marriages, baptisms, and funerals too numerous to list. The third duke did not receive this office directly from his father, for Charles Brandon, duke of Suffolk, had been granted its reversion in 1523. Eventually, in 1533, Norfolk was able to force Suffolk to yield the office back to him, in return for which Suffolk was given the justiceship of the forests south of Trent for life—a more rewarding office financially, but far less significant in court politics.[141]

The direct political value of serving as earl marshal was twofold. In the first place, Norfolk headed the College of Heralds and could appoint, with royal approval, the heralds and pursuivants who researched and recorded (and sometimes simply invented) the arms of Tudor gentlemen. These men also played an important role in diplomacy by arranging details of meetings between the noble councilors of European kings.[142] The heralds and pursuivants were valuable sources of diplomatic news and gossip for Norfolk even when he was not directly involved in their missions. In 1540 Gilbert Dethicke, Hammes pursuivant, served as Norfolk's advance man on a diplomatic mission to France and accompanied him to Abbeville to meet with Francis I. As well as being an official courier, Dethicke, described by Richard Pate as Norfolk's servant, remained at Calais to aid in the ongoing Anglo-French negotiations as Norfolk's private eyes and ears.[143]

The office of earl marshal was valuable in another respect, however, for Norfolk's presence at court on occasions of state was virtually a necessity, even when Cromwell would rather have had him as far away as possible. At the birth and christening of Prince Edward and the funeral of Jane Seymour in October 1537, for example, Norfolk was by Henry's side at Hampton Court while Cromwell tended to administration at Westminster. As it developed, Henry spent little enough time weeping on Norfolk's or any other's shoulder at Jane's death, so pleased was he to have a son, but the duke enjoyed ten days by Henry's side, while Cromwell and the other London councilors were kept from the king for fear of bringing the infection that had scattered the court in early autumn. Cromwell got news of Jane's death at second hand, and was reduced to fuming that she had been the victim of enemies about her who had "suffered her to take great cold and to eat things that her fancy called for."[144] Probably the office of earl marshal added little to Norfolk's purse, but for prestige, patronage and access to the center of power it proved of significant value.

Another office which Norfolk obtained in the 1530s proved of more obvious financial value. At the dissolution of the monasteries in 1536, the court of augmentations was established to receive, administer and alienate the new crown lands. Norfolk, seeing the opportunity to profit from this business, immediately petitioned to be made chief steward of augmentations, writing to Cromwell, "and if I may have it wholly, so much the better; if not, at least on this side Trent."[145] In fact the office was divided, with Cromwell made steward north of Trent and Norfolk gaining the half he most coveted. The salary for the post was a hundred pounds, but its real value was that it placed Norfolk at the center of the monastic land market, a position from which, as shown above, he profited greatly. Norfolk did not bother to attend routine sessions of the court of augmentations, but as his client Nicholas Hare was made his deputy, there is little doubt that Howard family interests received great attention in the court's deliberations.[146]

In the later years of Henry's reign, Norfolk's most important administrative position was as a member, and often the leader, of the reformed privy council.[147] This body came into being some time after 1536, and by 1540 had taken distinctive form and, more important for historians, had begun keeping a register which has survived. With only about a dozen active members, the privy council was small enough to serve as an executive board of sorts, and, as the later chapters of this study have shown, Norfolk was a major figure in council business and the factional infighting among its members. The compact council was ideally constituted for Norfolk's talents. Never an active hands-on administrator in the mold of Wolsey or Cromwell, Norfolk was nonetheless very capable of dominating government from the vantage of a council which served as a clearinghouse for all manner of business. Routine matters could be left to others as long as Norfolk had access to the flow of information through the council and could influence the direction of policy.

By the later 1530s, court politics had become a complex and dangerous game, but an intoxicating one as well. Norfolk seldom sought refuge from court, and always demanded to return when any business kept him away for long. The infighting at court could be bewildering to outsiders; as one observer wrote, "but what the matter is, God knoweth; for all things here are kept secret. . . . here go so many lies and tales that a man knoweth not whereunto to trust."[148] The fall of the Howards in 1546 was, ironically, a testimony to Norfolk's abilities and to the importance of controlling the council in order to control government. Had Howard not been a dangerously effective political player, the Seymour faction would not have needed to force him from power. After the proposed Mary Howard–Thomas Seymour marriage collapsed, Norfolk was left isolated as court and council alike fell into hostile hands. Norfolk's removal from power was a necessary step in the consolidation of Seymour's power. Even in his seventies, Norfolk remained a formidable rival, and one the Seymours did not want to face on the council of a minor king.

As all of this makes clear, Thomas Howard was more than a soldier and a landed magnate; he was actively involved in administration during the reign of Henry VIII and, through his varied offices, had access to multiple paths of power. It would be difficult to argue convincingly that Norfolk was an administrator of the first rank, but that argument would miss the important point that Norfolk never sought the responsibility and bureaucratic drudgery of such a position. Perhaps Norfolk is best understood as an old-fashioned baron, the companion and giver of good council to his king. Norfolk was by nature and experience a man of action, and always looked down on mere clerks such as Cromwell, no matter how valuable their paper-shuffling duties. This explains both his quest for high office and his evident disdain for the routine duties involved. Thomas Howard prized ceremonial and administrative posts for their direct rewards—prestige, access to patronage and wealth, and the honor and deference due great officers of state. This attitude contributed to his ultimate political failure, for he sought primacy at court largely for the trappings and not the substance of power. In doing so, he forgot the lessons his family had learned with such pain since 1485. It was by loyal and self-sacrificing service that the Howards won the trust of the Tudors. Once at the center of power, Norfolk proved unable or unwilling to keep up the hard work and, when he rested on his laurels, found himself shoved aside time and again by men of greater talent and industry.

CONCLUSION

Thomas Howard lived a long and tumultuous life by the standards of any age. Born in 1473 while Edward IV was king, he lived under five more monarchs, "tossed to and fro betweene the reciprocall ebbes and flowes of fortune," before his death in the reign of Mary Tudor.[1] Norfolk experienced a succession of near disasters in his career, barely avoiding disgrace when two nieces lost their heads for crimes as queens to Henry VIII, and surviving almost seven years of imprisonment to die in his bed at Kenninghall. Yet he also achieved considerable success in a long political and military career. Norfolk survived because he was a pliable man who was willing to follow whatever path the king chose. Despite a few outbursts and occasional grumbling as the Henrician Reformation moved forward, Norfolk was able to rationalize his loyal support to the crown in the same way that his father had: the second Howard duke of Norfolk defended his support for Richard III by saying that, if the crown were placed on a post, he would fight to the death to defend it.

Considering Howard's pliability, most students of the period have judged Norfolk's character harshly. Elton called the duke "one of the most unpleasant characters in an age which abounded in them,"[2] a fair enough appraisal, especially when the second half of the quotation is noted. Norfolk was, as L. B. Smith has said, a man of "few inhibitions and inordinate ambition," but even so "he was a realist, and though his instincts were feudal both in politics and religion, he realized the expedience of compromise with the powers that be."[3] Norfolk was, after all, a successful politician and diplomat, and thus a master of the charm and deceit, as well as the viciousness, necessary for survival in the harsh world of Tudor England.

Any judgment of Norfolk must be made with reference to the realities of Tudor politics and society. Norfolk was indeed cruel and vindictive at times, for he was ambitious for himself and his family and greedy for wealth and power. None of this was unusual in the least for the age. The volatile and self-indulgent Henry VIII set the pattern for his court, and, at least from the 1520s onward, seems to have encouraged a certain degree of partisan politics, much in the manner of his daughter Elizabeth. The court of Henry VIII lacked some of the veneer of Renaissance refinement that masked the crass, self-serving competition of Elizabeth's, but Elizabeth's favorite Essex would not have been out of place in Henry's day, and had Henry Howard, earl of Surrey, survived, he would have been a model Elizabethan courtier.

Thomas Howard was a conservative in his religious and social views and in his political concepts, yet he was hardly Garrett Mattingly's "ponderous, cold-hearted, chicken-brained Duke, moving sluggishly in the mists of the feudal past like some obsolete armoured saurian."[4] The feudal age disparaged by Mattingly was, in many respects, not yet past. Although Norfolk's political impact was often negative, his success in toppling Wolsey and Cromwell underlines his fitness for his environment; no one who served the crown as long and in so many roles as did Norfolk can be considered obsolete. The very style of Henrician politics had an unsavory air about it, with courtiers seeking advantage by playing upon the king's suspicions, offering obsequious flattery and self-serving suggestions in the place of disinterested advice. Yet no Tudor creature should be criticized for playing the game by the prevailing rules. In the months leading up to his fall, Cromwell himself was trying to destroy Norfolk and Gardiner as actively as they were seeking his ruin. Norfolk was not so much an obsolete holdover from a passing age as living evidence of the persistence of medieval ideas into the reign of Henry VIII. Norfolk's success is a measure of the character of his age; amidst the "new men" of Tudor government, there was still an important place for the old landed nobility as long as its members were capable and willing servants to the crown. If Norfolk was in any respect a "feudal wolf," as Smith called him, he was to a considerable degree "tamed" by the demands of loyalty to Henry VIII.[5]

Yet Norfolk deserves no great praise for fitness for his age. Thomas Howard's loyalty to the crown was seldom more than a thin veil over his own deeper motives of self-interest, greed, ambition and pride. There was nothing very noble about his reasons for serving the Tudors. If he had ideals, they were reactionary ones: adherence to a social system that placed him and his family at the pinnacle, and to a religious faith that offered little spiritual warmth, but was conventional, comfortable and hardly a bridle to his ambitions. In short, Norfolk saw no reason to change a system of government, a social order, or a religious faith that tended to benefit his family and himself. It is no wonder that Howard was disdainful of "new

Conclusion

men" from obscure backgrounds; he had little to gain, and much to lose, from the advancement of men such as Wolsey and Cromwell.

The politics of reaction might seem to have little place in an age that some have identified as a progressive one, and there is no denying that Norfolk's family pride and resistance to change sometimes made it difficult for him to follow the king's will. The progress of the Henrician Reformation is a case in point. Howard had little objection to curbing the power of the pope—or even the native higher clergy—in England. He hesitated when real doctrinal change seemed possible, as during the later years of Cromwell's ascendancy. Like Stephen Gardiner, Norfolk preferred a Catholic religious orthodoxy and a God who could be appeased by the endowment of chantries and the building of chapels. He did not quail at the looting of the monasteries, perhaps because he stood to gain so much by their destruction. Only when Cromwell seemed bent on real doctrinal change, and perhaps alliance with German Lutherans, did Norfolk really draw the line—although perhaps as much out of a xenophobic nationalism as from theological scruples.

Norfolk was most successful in politics when self-interest coincided with the king's will. Thus in the fall of Wolsey and rise of Anne Boleyn, and again with the fall of Cromwell and rise of Catherine Howard, Norfolk was able to convince the king to take a new wife while dispensing with an old minister. If lies and flattery were needed to accomplish his aims, Norfolk was perfectly willing to use them. The duke's ultimate failure to obtain political predominance, ironically, arose from his very successes, for finally Henry recognized that Norfolk, despite his crafty subservience, was bankrupt of original ideas. The duke was well equipped to work the ruin of Henry's most powerful ministers but unfit to take their place. Norfolk's career, in the end, was a shallow and futile mockery, for he contributed little or nothing positive to the development of Tudor government.

As a politician, Norfolk relied to a large degree on allies at court to achieve his ends. This is not to say that there was a long-term faction at court tying together the Howards and a stable array of allies and supporters. Rather, a pattern of shifting factional alliance can be traced through the reign. Norfolk and the Boleyns were joined by Suffolk in convincing Henry of what he already suspected in the 1520s, that Wolsey had outlived his usefulness. Norfolk abandoned the Boleyns even before Anne became queen and by the late 1530s had become Suffolk's rival for influence in the north, where both sought to build a power base on the ruins of the Percys and Nevilles. In the same way, the Norfolk-Gardiner alliance of the late 1530s, which produced the Act of Six Articles and toppled Cromwell, was shortly dissolved over the issue of foreign policy. Norfolk and Gardiner continued to work together in the 1540s, opposing the Protestant pressures of Cranmer and the Seymours, but their ties were much looser than they had been a few years earlier. Gardiner opposed Norfolk's effort to arrange an marital alliance with France in 1542–43, and Norfolk was not an active partner in most of Gardiner's religious persecutions in the later years of the reign. Indeed, in 1546 Norfolk was trying to make an alliance with the Seymours almost at the moment that Gardiner was attempting, through Anne Askew, to destroy the earl of Hertford and his supporters. This disarray in the conservative camp certainly was a factor in the fall of the Howards in 1546 and the exclusion of Gardiner from the Edwardian council of regency. Nor was the Hertford-Wriothesley-Paget-Lisle faction of Henry's last years very solid. Wriothesley was out of the council within months, and the dissentions among the rest of the Edwardian councilors are too well known to require comment here.

All of this points to the conclusion that Henrician politics was not based on ideology and solid factional alliances so much as upon the changing whims of the king and the self-interested efforts of his minsters to mold policy or benefit from its shifts. For longevity if nothing else, Thomas Howard is notable among early Tudor politicians. He joined Henry VIII's council in 1516 at the latest, although he was already prominent for his military exploits. Almost forty years later Norfolk was still called upon as a councilor and warrior by Mary. Perhaps only Cuthbert Tunstall, bishop of London and Durham, had a career rivaling Norfolk's in length, but while both were councilors, administrators and diplomats, Norfolk's military service gives him an importance that overshadows Tunstall's. Despite the criticisms leveled at Norfolk of servility, pedestrian intelligence, and anachronistic social and religious views, his long service to the Tudors and his ability to survive the many twists and turns of politics remain Thomas Howard's greatest claims as an important early Tudor figure. Wolsey and Cromwell achieved greater prominence than Norfolk, but neither could adapt politically as Norfolk could to preserve their careers and lives. That Henry VIII was still fighting in France with such as Norfolk and Suffolk as his commmanders in the 1540s says much for the essential continuity of the reign, and underlines Norfolk's fitness for the service Henry demanded.

Conclusion

The veneer of Renaissance and Reformation had begun to be laid upon the England of the 1530s and 1540s, but deep undercurrents of the ideas and traditions of the medieval world remained.[6] Thomas Howard was decidedly more comfortable with the age that was passing than that which was coming into being; perhaps it was fitting that he died in the reign of Mary amidst England's abortive return to Catholicism. The third duke of Norfolk was one of the last of the great Tudor figures who was, first and foremost, a nobleman—one who had inherited wealth and position and used these, rather than extraordinary talent, for entry into court and council. Norfolk fashioned a career as much out of his inherited titles and family position as from industry and talent. Had Thomas Howard been born a butcher's son at Ipswich or an innkeeper's son at Putney, it is hard to imagine that he would have matched the achievements of Wolsey or Cromwell. The life and career of the third duke of Norfolk stand as a monument to the importance of nobility in early Tudor England, even when the relatively recent origin of the family titles is noted. Howard was not, after all, born an earl nor his father a duke. Their nobility was a fifteenth century gift, based on service to the crown by John Howard and Thomas the elder. Henry VII and Henry VIII confirmed the Howard titles and granted them new ones and new favors only after receiving proof of their loyalty and usefulness. Yet it is one of the most striking features of Norfolk's life that he was able to claim a place as a representative of the traditional nobility when his own title dated only to 1514—and that he was in fact treated with the deference he claimed. Noble titles remained vitally important in Tudor England, a point underlined by the fact that Thomas Cromwell was made a baron and, in 1540, earl of Essex, and that the Edwardian regents thought it necessary to augment their knighthoods with baronies, earldoms and dukedoms of their own.

Thus the character of the age in which he lived cannot be underestimated in assessing Norfolk's life and career. The reign of Henry VIII was a mixture of medieval and modern, with Renaissance and Reformation meeting bastard feudalism, perpendicular Gothic architecture, decadent Catholicism and lay piety. Thomas Howard was an exemplar of this age, a man whose long royal service argues against giving too modern a gloss to the period.

NOTES

The following abbreviations are used in the notes. For full citations, see the bibliography.

BIHR	*Bulletin of the Institute of Historical Research*
BL	British Library
CCR	*Calendar of the Close Rolls, Henry VII, 1485–1500*
CChR	*Calendar of the Charter Rolls, 5 Hen. V–8 Hen. VIII, 1427–1516*
CPR	*Calendar of the Patent Rolls*
DNB	*Dictionary of National Biography*
LP	*Letters and Papers, Foreign and Domestic, of the Reign of Henry VIII*
HMC	Historical Manuscripts Commission
Paston Letters	*The Paston Letters, A.D. 1422–1509*
PRO	Public Record Office
Rot. Parl.	*Rotuli Parliamentorum, ut et Petitiones et Placita in Parliamento*
Sp. Cal.	*Calendar of Letters, Dispatches . . . Spain*
S.P. Hen. VIII	*State Papers, King Henry the Eighth*
TRHS	*Transactions of the Royal Historical Society*
VCH	*Victoria County Histories*
Ven. Cal.	*Calendar of State Papers . . . Venice and . . . Northern Italy*

Citations to *LP* and *Ven. Cal.* are to document numbers; all other citations are to page or folio numbers unless otherwise noted. In citing manuscript material, I have used the most recent or most accurate of the often multiple foliations of Public Record Office and British Library materials. In cases of older published collections (especially *LP*), my foliations may not coincide with those cited.

Quotations have not been modernized, although in quoting unpublished manuscripts I have extended abbreviation and added modern punctuation where necessary to make the sense clear. In dating, adjustments have been made to conform to modern usage, with the year beginning on 1 January. Likewise, regnal dating (that is, based on the accession of a monarch—in Henry VIII's case, 21 April 1509) and dating by festivals of the church have been modernized where necessary.

INTRODUCTION

1. *Ven. Cal.* 4: 694.

2. E. W. Ives, *Anne Boleyn* (Oxford: Basil Blackwell, 1986), p. 159.

3. William Camden, *Britainia, or a Chorographicall Description of the Most Flourishing Kingdomes, England, Scotland, and Ireland* (London, 1637), p. 483.

4. See L. B. Smith, *A Tudor Tragedy: The Life and Times of Catherine Howard* (New York: Pantheon Books, 1961); Ives, *Anne Boleyn*; Retha M. Warnicke, *The Rise and Fall of Anne Boleyn* (Cambridge: Cambridge University Press, 1989); Melvin J. Tucker, *The Life of Thomas Howard, Earl of Surrey and Second Duke of Norfolk* (London: Mouton and Co., 1964); Edwin Casady, *Henry Howard, Earl of Surrey* (New York: Modern Language Association of America, 1938); Neville Williams, *Thomas Howard, Fourth Duke of Norfolk* (New York: E. P. Dutton and Co., 1964).

5. G. R. Elton, *England, 1200–1640: The Sources of History*, Studies in the Use of Historical Evidence, general editor G. R. Elton (Ithaca and London: Cornell University Press, 1969), pp. 243–44.

6. E. W. Ives, *Faction in Tudor England* (London: The Historical Association, 1979), pp. 1–2.

7. G. R. Elton, "Tudor Government: The Points of Contact: III. The Court," *TRHS* 5th series, 26 (1976): 223.

8. E. W. Ives, "Faction at the Court of Henry VIII: The Fall of Anne Boleyn," *History* 57 (1972): 169–88; Ives, *Faction in Tudor England*, pp. 12–20. This argument is developed in greater depth in his *Anne Boleyn*.

9. Warnicke, *Anne Boleyn*, passim.

10. Glyn Redworth, *In Defense of the Church Catholic: The Life of Stephen Gardiner* (Oxford: Basil Blackwell, 1990), pp. 40–41, 109, and elsewhere.

11. Lacey Baldwin Smith, *Henry VIII: The Mask of Royalty* (Chicago: Academy Chicago, 1982), esp. chapter 4, pp. 83–110.

12. S. J. Gunn, *Charles Brandon, Duke of Suffolk, c. 1484–1545* (Oxford: Basil Blackwell, 1988), pp. 90, 197, and elsewhere.

13. *Sp. Cal.* 5(2): 269.

14. T. H. Swales, "The Redistribution of the Monastic Lands in Norfolk at the Dissolution," *Norfolk Archaeology* 34 (1966): 20–22.

15. The most important study, still unpublished, is David Starkey, "The King's

Privy Chamber, 1485–1547" (Cambridge Ph.D. diss., 1973). Some of his findings are in his *The Reign of Henry VIII: Personalities and Politics* (New York: Franklin Watts, 1986). See also D. M. Loades, *The Tudor Court* (Totowa, N.J.: Barnes and Noble, 1987), and Helen Miller, *Henry VIII and the English Nobility* (Oxford: Basil Blackwell, 1986), for discussions of factionalism and court politics.

16. G. W. Bernard, *The Power of the Early Tudor Nobility: A Study of the Fourth and Fifth Earls of Shrewsbury* (Brighton, Sussex: Harvester Press, 1985), pp. 1–3.

17. Ibid., pp. 199–200.

18. C. E. Moreton, *The Townshends and Their World: Gentry, Law and Land in Norfolk, c. 1450–1551* (Oxford: Clarendon Press, 1992), is a recent study of one such East Anglian family which produced a number of sometime Howard servants.

19. See Kate Mertes, *The English Noble Household, 1250–1600: Good Governance and Politic Rule* (Oxford: Basil Blackwell, 1988).

20. J. J. Scarisbrick, *Henry VIII* (Berkeley and Los Angeles: University of California Press, 1968), pp. 11–12, 32.

21. Bernard, *Early Tudor Nobility*, pp. 20–22.

22. Miller, *Henry VIII and the English Nobility*, p. 158.

CHAPTER 1 The Howard Family and Early Life to 1509

1. See Sir George Buck, *History of Richard III* (1619), ed Arthur Noel Kinkaid (Gloucester: Alan Sutton, 1979), pp. 110–11; John Martin Robinson, *The Dukes of Norfolk: A Quincentennial History* (Oxford: Oxford University Press, 1982), pp. 1–9.

2. G. E. Cokayne, *The Complete Peerage, or a History of the House of Lords and all of its Members from the Earliest Times*, 13 vols. (London: St. Catherine's Press, 1910–40), 9, *s.v.* "Norfolk."

3. *VCH Norfolk*, 2: 492; *Paston Letters*, 3: 34–36, 303; Tucker, *Thomas Howard*, pp. 17–20; George Smith, *The Coronation of Elizabeth Wydeville, Queen Consort of Edward IV, on May 26th, 1465. A Contemporary Account Now First Set Forth from a XV Century Manuscript* (London: Ellis, 1935), p. 19.

4. *CPR*, 1461–67, pp. 111, 187, 277–78, 348; *CCR*, 1461–68, p. 114.

5. There seems little doubt that John Howard was born around 1420–22; he certainly died in 1485. Nonetheless, the dates of his life and of his wives' and childrens' have been muddled thoroughly. Even Smith, *Tudor Tragedy*, includes a genealogical table showing John Howard born in 1435 and his son Thomas in 1443! See also Tucker, *Thomas Howard*, pp. 27–30.

6. Tucker, *Thomas Howard*, p. 29. See also *Paston Letters*, 5: 109–11.

7. Tucker, *Thomas Howard*, p. 31; *Paston Letters*, 2: 331; 3: 303; 5: 111, 137.

8. Tucker, *Thomas Howard*, p. 30. Thomas was last noted as an esquire for the body on 22 May 1477; see *CPR*, 1476–85, p. 37.

9. *CPR*, 1467–77, pp. 605, 622–23; *CPR*, 1476–85, pp. 49, 108–11, 566–67.

Notes to Pages 14–16

10. *The Household Books of John, duke of Norfolk, and Thomas, earl of Surrey, Temp. 1481–1490,* ed. John Payne Collier (London: Roxburghe Club, 1844), passim.

11. *CPR,* 1476–85, pp. 112, 137, 219; E. F. Jacob, *The Fifteenth Century, 1399–1485* (Oxford: Clarendon Press, 1961), p. 585. John Howard was granted reversion of the constableship for life on the death of its holders, John Sutton and Sir Richard Fiennes, but there is no evidence that Howard ever entered the office. It was granted by Richard III on 17 July 1483 to Robert Brakenbury, without notice of Howard's resignation. See *CPR,* 1476–85, p. 364 and note 14, below.

12. Cokayne, *Complete Peerage,* 9, *s.v.* "Norfolk"; *Rot. Parl.,* 6: 167–70. Charles Ross, *Richard III* (London: Eyre Methuen, 1981), p. 37, notes that Berkeley "agreed to surrender his share of the reversion of [Anne's] estates if she died without male issue . . . allegedly because he owed the crown debts of £34,000 which the crown forgave."

13. *Letters and Papers Illustrative of the Reigns of Richard III and Henry VII,* ed. James Gairdner, 2 vols. (London, 1861–63), 1: 4–10.

14. See Ross, *Richard III,* and P. M. Kendall, *Richard the Third* (New York: W. W. Norton, 1955), for details.

15. Tucker, *Thomas Howard,* pp. 37–45. In an appendix, Kendall, *Richard the Third,* reviews the murder of the princes and, while suspecting Richard of the deed, makes no mention of the Howards.

16. Gerald Brenan and E. P. Statham, *The House of Howard,* 2 vols., pagination consecutive (London, 1907), pp. 43–46.

17. Kendall, *Richard the Third,* p. 251, and Tucker, *Thomas Howard,* p. 40, note John Howard's role. The earliest source for this seems to be *The Chronicle of Iohn Harding, Together the Continuation by Richard Grafton, to the Thirty-Fourth Year of King Henry VIII,* ed. Henry Ellis (London, 1812), p. 488, but as earlier chronicles make no mention of Howard in this regard, Grafton's attribution may be wrong. Mancini, the earliest of the contemporary writers, as well as most of the city chronicles, give Thomas Bourchier, archbishop of Canterbury, credit for persuading Elizabeth to place Richard of York and Norfolk in Gloucester's care. See C. A. Armstrong, ed., *The Usurpation of Richard the Third: Dominicus Mancini ad Angelum Catonem de Occupatione Regni Anglie per Ricardum Tertium Libellus,* second edition (Oxford: Clarendon Press, 1969), pp. 88–89, and note 74.

18. Edward Hall, *Hall's Chronicle; Containing the History of England During the Reign of King Henry the Fourth, and the Succeeding Monarchs, to the end of the Reign of Henry the Eighth,* ed. Henry Ellis (London, 1809), pp. 36–61. Thomas More, in his *History of King Richard III,* does not give the name of the knight who escorted Hastings, but on this see A. F. Pollard, "The Making of Sir Thomas More's Richard III," in *Historical Essays in Honor of James Tait,* ed. J. G. Edward, V. H. Galbraith, and E. F. Jacob (Manchester: Printed for the Subscribers, 1933), pp.

223–38. Pollard suggests that More's source for this episode was an Exchequer underling who answered to the Howard treasurers. More therefore remained silent out of prudence. A recent exchange in the *English Historical Review* and *Bulletin of the Institute of Historical Research* has argued the chronology of Hastings's murder, shedding a bit of light but mostly generating heat in the already warm atmosphere of Ricardian studies.

19. *CPR*, 1476–85, p. 385; *CChR*, 1427–1516, p. 258.

20. Tucker, *Thomas Howard*, p. 42, n. 28; Cokayne, *Complete Peerage*, 9: 611; *CPR*, 1476–85, pp. 359, 363, 365; Ross, *Richard III*, pp. 164–65.

21. J. R. Lander, *Government and Community: England, 1450–1509* (Cambridge, Mass.: Harvard University Press, 1980), p. 318.

22. Jacob, *The Fifteenth Century*, pp. 625–26.

23. *CPR*, 1476–85, pp. 479, 501.

24. *The Household of Edward IV; The Black Book and Ordinances of 1478*, ed. A. R. Myers (Manchester, 1959), p. 278; *CPR*, 1476–85, pp. 370, 400, 465, 489–90, 519, 553, 566–80.

25. Kendall, *Richard the Third*, pp. 414–15; *Paston Letters*, 3: 320; S. B. Chrimes, *Henry VII* (Berkeley and Los Angeles: University of California Press, 1972), pp. 40–45.

26. Kendall, *Richard the Third*, pp. 428–44; Tucker, *Thomas Howard*, p. 46. For the battle itself, see Michael Bennett, *The Battle of Bosworth* (Gloucester: Alan Sutton, 1985).

27. *Paston Letters*, 6: 87–93; Tucker, *Thomas Howard*, pp. 47–49.

28. *Rot. Parl.*, 6: 275–78.

29. *Materials for a History of the Reign of Henry VII*, ed. William Campbell, 2 vols. (London, 1873–77), 1: 309, 319; 2: 40, 53, 138, 199, 319, etc.; *CPR*, 1485–94, pp. 74, 128, 196.

30. *CPR*, 1485–94, p. 86.

31. Campbell, *Materials*, 1: 208. Most of these prisoners were not earls, even attainted ones. "Sir Thomas Dalalund, knight" was allowed ten shillings a week and no servants. Sixty years later, the third duke of Norfolk was allowed five pounds a week board, plus 6s. 8d. a week each for five servants. See PRO, E. 101/60/22, fol. 2r.

32. *Rot. Parl.*, 6: 410, 426; J. R. Lander, "Attainder and Forfeiture, 1453–1509," *Historical Journal* 6 (1961): 136–43.

33. J. D. Mackie, *The Earlier Tudors, 1485–1558* (Oxford: Clarendon Press, 1952), pp. 90–91; *CPR*, 1485–94, pp. 285, 314; *Rot. Parl.*, 6: 426–28; Lander, "Attainder and Forfeiture," pp. 136–43; *CCR*, 1485–1500, nos. 781, 824, 939.

34. *Household Books*, introduction, xvii–xxix, and p. 227; Tucker, *Thomas Howard*, p. 23. On the literacy of the late medieval aristocracy, see K. B. McFarlane,

The Nobility of Later Medieval England: The Ford Lectures for 1953 and Related Studies (Oxford: Clarendon Press, 1973), pp. 228–47, where he takes issue with J. H. Hexter, "The Education of the Aristocracy in the Renaissance," in his *Reappraisals in History* (New York: Harper and Row, 1963), pp. 45–70.

35. *DNB*, s.v. "John Bourchier."
36. Tucker, *Thomas Howard*, pp. 22–25.
37. Buck, *History of Richard III*, p. 212.
38. Tucker, *Thomas Howard*, p. 72; *Rot. Parl.*, 6: 479; [Sylvanus Urban], "Anne Lady Howard," *Gentleman's Magazine*, n.s. 23 (1845): 147–52; George F. Nott, ed., *The Works of Henry Howard, Earl of Surrey, and of Sir Thomas Wyatt the Elder*, 2 vols. (London, 1815–16; New York: AMS Reprint, 1965), 1: v–vi.
39. Tucker, *Thomas Howard*, pp. 67–68; Chrimes, *Henry VII*, pp. 89–90; Denys Hays, ed. and trans., *The Anglica Historia of Polydore Vergil* (London: The Camden Society, 1950), p. 94 and note.
40. Chrimes, *Henry VII*, pp. 88–89.
41. Tucker, *Thomas Howard*, pp. 89–90.
42. *Letters and Papers of Richard III and Henry VII*, 1: 388–404, 404–17; *CPR*, 1494–1509, pp. 479, 484, 486.
43. Nott, *Henry Howard*, p. vii; Urban, "Anne Lady Howard," pp. 151–52.
44. Fox was also bishop of Winchester, Warham bishop of London, 1502–1503, and archbishop of Canterbury, 1503–32. See *CPR*, 1494–1509, p. 239; Tucker, *Thomas Howard*, pp. 75–83; G. R. Elton, *The Tudor Revolution in Government: Administrative Changes in the Reign of Henry VIII* (Cambridge: Cambridge University Press, 1953), p. 22.
45. Chrimes, *Henry VII*, pp. 305–309.
46. Edward Hall, *The Triumphant Reign of King Henry VIII*, 2 vols. (London, 1904), 1: 3; *LP* 1: 20.

CHAPTER 2 The Resurgence of the Howards, 1509–1513

1. J. D. Mackie, *The Earlier Tudors, 1485–1558* (Oxford: Clarendon Press, 1952), p. 233.
2. Tucker, *Thomas Howard*, pp. 94–95; David Starkey, *The Reign of Henry VIII: Personalities and Politics* (New York: Franklin Watts, 1986), pp. 40–47.
3. The Venetian ambassador fully expected Henry VIII to go to war with France; see *LP* 1: 5, Andrea Badoer to the Signory, 26 April 1509.
4. On 27 May 1509; see *LP* 1: 51.
5. Polydore Vergil, *The Anglica Historia of Polydore Vergil*, ed. and trans. Denys Hay (London: Camden Society, 1950), pp. 150–51; Hall, *Henry VIII*, 1: 4.
6. *LP* 1: 94 (43, 88).

7. Ibid., 2, p. 1441, "The King's Book of Payments, 1–10 Henry VIII." Carre was one of Henry's sewers of the body, appointed 18 May 1509 (Ibid., 1: 54 [76]), and a frequent royal companion in the early years. See also Hall, *Henry VIII*, 1: 5–12, 16, 21. A mark is two-thirds of a pound sterling and was an archaic form of money of account in the early sixteenth century. Thus 500 marks would be £333 6s. 8d.

8. *The Great Tournament Roll of Westminster*, ed. Sydney Anglo, 2 vols. (Oxford: Clarendon Press, 1968), 1: 46–48. See also *The Great Chronicle of London*, ed. A. H. Thomas and I. D. Thornley (London, 1938), pp. 341–42, and Hall, *Henry VIII*, 1: 4–12.

9. *Great Tournament Roll*, 1: 48–49; *Great Chronicle of London*, pp. 342–43; Hall, *Henry VIII*, 1: 13–14.

10. *LP* 1: 54 (42).

11. Ibid., 37, 442.

12. Ibid., 414, 520. See also *A Descriptive Catalogue of Ancient Deeds Preserved in the Public Record Office*, 6 vols. (London, 1890–1915), 4, A 4551; 5, A 13566; Francis Blomefield, *An Essay Towards a Topographical History of the County of Norfolk*, 11 vols. (London, 1805–10), 2: 410–11; PRO SC 11/837 (General Surveyor's roll of the king's estates, Michaelmas 1515).

13. *LP* 1: 257 (40).

14. Sydney Anglo, *Spectacle, Pageantry and Early Tudor Policy* (Oxford: Clarendon Press, 1969), pp. 108–23.

15. Hall, *Henry VIII*, 1: 22–23; Anglo, *Spectacle, Pageantry*, pp. 111–12; *Great Tournament Roll*, 1: 55, 98, 104, 111, 113–15; 2; plate 21; *Great Chronicle of London*, pp. 370–73.

16. *LP* 1: 689, 707.

17. Hall, *Henry VIII*, 1: 28–29.

18. Tucker, *Thomas Howard*, pp. 97–98; A. F. Pollard, *Wolsey* (London: Longmans, Green and Co., 1929), pp. 11–13.

19. *Sp. Cal.* 2: 36; Scarisbrick, *Henry VIII*, pp. 25–26.

20. Pollard, *Wolsey*, pp. 12–14.

21. Scarisbrick, *Henry VIII*, pp. 26–27.

22. Richard Glen Eaves, *Henry VIII's Scottish Diplomacy, 1513–1524: England's Relations with the Regency Government of James V* (New York: Exposition Press, 1971), pp. 27–28; Edward Herbert, Lord Herbert of Cherbury, *The Life and Raigne of King Henry the Eighth* (London, 1649), p. 16; Hall, *Henry VIII*, 1: 37–39; *LP* 1: 885.

23. Herbert, *Henry the Eighth*, p. 16; Eaves, *Henry VIII's Scottish Diplomacy*, pp. 27–28; Tucker, *Thomas Howard*, p. 98; *LP* 1: 880.

24. Scarisbrick, *Henry VIII*, p. 28.

25. *LP* 1: 969 (29); *Sp. Cal.* 2: 59; Thomas Rymer, *Foedera, Conventiones, Litterae*

et cujuscunque Acta Publica . . . , Second ed., with additional material edited by Robert Sanderson, 20 vols. (London, 1727–35), 13: 323.

26. In March, Thomas made indenture to borrow 2,000 marks to support himself honorably in the war; see *LP* 1: 1103, 1156.

27. Hall, *Henry VIII*, 1: 42–44.

28. Scarisbrick, *Henry VIII*, pp. 28–31.

29. Hall, *Henry VIII*, 1: 44; Scarisbrick, *Henry VIII*, p. 29; *LP* 1: 1286, 1326.

30. Hall, *Henry VIII*, 1: 49–51; Scarisbrick, *Henry VIII*, pp. 28–30; *LP* 1: 1326, 1327, 1442, 1458.

31. For Buckingham, see Carole Rawcliffe, *The Staffords, Earls of Stafford and Dukes of Buckingham, 1394–1521* (Cambridge: Cambridge University Press, 1978), and Barbara J. Harris, *Edward Stafford, Third Duke of Buckingham, 1478–1521* (Stanford: Stanford University Press, 1986).

32. *LP* 1: 82; Garrett Mattingly, *Catherine of Aragon* (Boston: Houghton Mifflin Co., 1941), pp. 145–46; Barbara J. Harris, "Marriage Sixteenth Century Style: Elizabeth Stafford and the Third Duke of Norfolk," *Journal of Social History* 15 (1982): 371–82.

33. Hall, *Henry VIII*, 1: 55–56, 59–60; Tucker, *Thomas Howard*, pp. 101–2. Rymer, *Foedera*, 13: 326–42, 402, records the Howard commissions as admiral.

34. Howard to Wolsey, [7 May 1513], BL Cott. Cal. D vi, ff. 104–5; Howard to Henry VIII, ibid., ff. 106–7. Both of these letters are holograph, burned and torn along the bottom and right side of the leaves. They are calendared as *LP* 1: 1851–2.

35. *LP* 1: 1858, 1869; Scarisbrick, *Henry VIII*, pp. 34–35.

36. *LP* 1: 1870, 1875, 1876, 1886, 1894, 1948.

37. Ibid., 1907; Henry Ellis, *Original Letters Illustrative of English History*, 11 vols. (London, 1824–46), ser. 3, vol. 1, no. 63.

38. *LP* 1: 1978, 1992.

39. Tucker, *Thomas Howard*, p. 103; Mattingly, *Catherine of Aragon*, p. 155; Scarisbrick, *Henry VIII*, pp. 34–35. See also Gunn, *Charles Brandon*, pp. 14–16.

40. Hall, *Henry VIII*, 1: 95; J. D. Mackie, "Henry VIII and Scotland," *TRHS* 4th series, 29 (1947): 95–96.

41. John Hall Burton, *The History of Scotland*, 8 vols. (Edinburgh: William Blackwood and Sons, 1899), 3: 73.

42. Mackie, "Henry VIII and Scotland," pp. 103–6; Tucker, *Thomas Howard*, pp. 103–6; John McEwen, "The Battle of Floddon, September 9th 1513," *History Today* 8 (1958): 340–41. For Henry's dynastic pretensions, see *Statutes of the Realm*, ed. A. Luders et al., 11 vols (London, 1810–28), 3: 74–89 (3 Hen. VIII, c. 23) and David M. Head, "Henry VIII's Scottish Policy: A Reassessment," *Scottish Historical Review* 61 (1982): 1–24.

Notes to Pages 34–36

43. *LP* 1: 1960, 2026; Hall, *Henry VIII*, 1: 76; Tucker, *Thomas Howard*, p. 108; Charles W. C. Oman, *A History of the Art of War in the Sixteenth Century* (New York: E. P. Dutton and Co., 1937), pp. 302–3; Cadwallader John Bates, *Flodden Field: A Collection of Some of the Earliest Evidence Concerning the Battle of Branxton Moor, 9th September 1513* (Newcastle upon Tyne, 1894), p. 5. The account in Hall is an almost verbatim transcription of BL Add. Ms., 29,506, "Thordre and behauvoure of the . . . Erle of Surrey . . . ayenst the Kynge of Scottes . . . at the Batayle of Brankston." This manuscript, on paper bound in vellum and illustrated with the arms of the earl of Surrey, appears to be a presentation copy for Surrey; the account was printed late in 1513 by Richard Pynson, printer to the king, perhaps from this manuscript, for there are signature marks on the corners of the pages. The manuscript gives no author's name, but an introduction states that the account was written by a member of Surrey's household who was an eyewitness to the battle.

44. *LP* 1: 2260; Tucker, *Thomas Howard*, p. 109–10.

45. "Thordre and behauvoure of the . . . Erle of Surrey," BL Add. Ms., 29,506, f. 6v, reports the English army as 26,000 men when the battle was joined. Herbert thought the English numbered 25,000 and the Scots 50,000 before desertions began to thin the ranks. Oman estimated the sides at 26,000 English and 28,000–30,000 Scots. Pay warrants for 18,699 men under Surrey were approved 18 February 1514; although this does not include the admiral's men, the figure is probably the most reliable source for the English side. Exaggeration, even in early accounts of the battle, has been common. Brian Tuke, Wolsey's secretary, numbered the English as 40,000 and the Scots as 60,000 on 22 September, from what source we can only guess. See on this problem Bates, *Flodden Field*, p. 6; Herbert, *Henry the Eighth*, p. 42; Oman, *War in the Sixteenth Century*, pp. 305–11; *LP* 1: 2651: *Ven. Cal.* 2: 134.

46. Bates, *Flodden Field*, pp. 7–8; Hall, *Henry VIII*, 1: 99–102; P. Hume Brown, *The History of Scotland: Volume I, to the Accession of Mary Stewart* (Cambridge: Cambridge University Press, 1909), pp. 335–36.

47. Bates, *Flodden Field*, pp. 8–9; Hall, *Henry VIII*, 1: 102–5; Tucker, *Thomas Howard*, pp. 110–11; Ellis, *Original Letters*, ser. 1, vol. 1, no. 31; *LP* 1: 2246.

48. Bates, *Flodden Field*, pp. 9–10; Tucker, *Thomas Howard*, pp. 110–11.

49. Raphael Holinshed, *Holinshed's Chronicles of England, Scotland and Ireland*, 6 vols. (London, 1808), 3: 595.

50. Hall, *Henry VIII*, 1: 106; Tucker, *Thomas Howard*, p. 112 and note 24; McEwen, "Floddon," pp. 342–43.

51. Bates, "Flodden Field," pp. 10–11; McEwen, "Floddon," pp. 342–43; Hall, *Henry VIII*, 1: 106; *LP* 1: 2246; Tucker, *Thomas Howard*, pp. 112–13. According to

Oman, *War in the Sixteenth Century*, p. 307, the admiral had the artillery with him; this is not unlikely, since seamen might have been expected to be more suitable as gunners, but other sources do not support Oman on this point.

52. Bates, *Flodden Field*, pp. 13–15; McEwen, "Floddon," pp. 344–45; Brown, *History of Scotland*, p. 337.

53. Bates, *Flodden Field*, p. 16; *LP* 1: 2246; Tucker, *Thomas Howard*, p. 113; Hall, *Henry VIII*, 1: 107–8.

54. McEwen, "Floddon," p. 344–45; Hall, *Henry VIII*, 1: 108–9; Bates, *Flodden Field*, pp. 16–17.

55. McEwen, "Floddon," p. 345; Hall, *Henry VIII*, 1: 109.

56. C. W. C. Oman, *The Art of War in the Middle Ages*, A.D. *387–1515*, revised and edited by John H. Beeler (Ithaca: Cornell University Press, 1953), pp. 120–22; Tucker, *Thomas Howard*, p. 115; McEwen, "Floddon," pp. 345–46.

57. *LP* 1: 2246; Hall, *Henry VIII*, 1: 110–13; Oman, *War in the Sixteenth Century*, p. 315.

58. Bates, *Flodden Field*, p. 19; McEwen, "Floddon," pp. 337–38; John Riddell, *Inquiry into the Law and Practice in Scottish Peerages*, 2 volumes, pagination consecutive (Edinburgh, 1842), p. 1001. See also Hall, *Henry VIII*, 1: 111 and *LP* 1: 2246, 2651.

59. Oman, *War in the Sixteenth Century*, pp. 318–19.

60. Tucker, *Thomas Howard*, pp. 117–19.

61. *LP* 1: 2246.

62. Ibid., 1: 2268, 2269, 2284.

63. Tucker, *Thomas Howard*, p. 122; Scarisbrick, *Henry VIII*, pp. 39–40.

CHAPTER 3   The Making of the Duke of Norfolk, 1514–1524

1. *LP* 1: 2590, 2629, 2684 (1–5). Rymer, *Foedera*, 14: 43–45. The properties granted Surrey were given "pro termino vitae suae, per servitum unius Rosae Rubae solvendae ad festum Sancti Johannis Baptistae."

2. Scarisbrick, *Henry VIII*, pp. 41–42; Tucker, *Thomas Howard*, pp. 125–26; *LP* 1: 2629; 2: 1959.

3. *LP* 1: 2478, 2479, 2652, 2669, 2686, etc.

4. Ibid., 2863 (2), 2946, 2959.

5. *Ven. Cal.* 2: 445; *LP* 1: 2900, 2974. James Gairdner, "On a Contemporary Drawing of the Burning of Brighton in the Time of Henry VIII," *TRHS* 3rd series, 1 (1901): 19–31, corrected the misapprehension that Brighton was burned in 1545, as claimed by most of the chronicles. The exact date of the French attack remains unclear, for Gairdner placed it in July, which is certainly too late. Surrey's letters in June refer to the late burning of "Brighthelmstone" and the Venetian ambassador also mentioned the raid in a letter of 17 June. See on this *LP* 1: 2974, 3000, 3009.

6. Surrey to the Council, 27 May [1514], BL Cott. Cal. D vi, f. 108. See also *LP* 1: 2946, 2959, 3000, 3001.
7. *LP* 1: 2888, 2912, 2995.
8. Ibid., 3108; Scarisbrick, *Henry VIII*, pp. 54–55, and G. R. Elton, *Reform and Reformation: England 1509–1558* (Cambridge, Mass.: Harvard University Press, 1977), pp. 40–41.
9. *LP* 1: 3101, 3129–31; *Sp. Cal.* 1: 230–33.
10. *LP* 1: 3146, 3161, 3226(6, 24), 3294, 3324(33), 3325, 3326; Scarisbrick, *Henry VIII*, pp. 51–53.
11. *LP* 1: 3348.
12. Ibid., 3355–57, 3376.
13. Ibid., 3240.
14. Ibid., 3424, 3430, 3449, 3477.
15. Scarisbrick, *Henry VIII*, pp. 56–57; Hall, *Henry VIII*, 1: 146; *LP* 2: 367. See also Walter C. Richardson, *Mary Tudor: The White Queen* (Seattle and London: University of Washington Press, 1970), pp. 170–72; R. J. Knecht, *Francis I* (Cambridge: Cambridge University Press, 1982), pp. 11–12, and Gunn, *Charles Brandon*, pp. 32–38.
16. See Gunn, *Charles Brandon*, pp. 38–54; Dairmaid MacCullough, *Suffolk and the Tudors: Politics and Religion in an English County, 1500–1600* (Oxford: Clarendon Press, 1986), pp. 57ff.
17. Neither the list of those summoned in *LP* 1: 3464 nor an Elizabethan copy, PRO SP 12/2/78r., coincides with the lists of those summoned and attending in the *Journals of the House of Lords, Beginning Anno Primo Henrici Octavi*, vol. 1 (London, 1808), pp. 18ff. For the difficulties with records of the House of Lords in this period, see G. R. Elton, "The Early Journals of the House of Lords," *English Historical Review* 352 (1974): 481–512.
18. Hall, *Henry VIII*, 1: 144; Elton, *Tudor Revolution* pp. 46–47; *LP* 2: 119, 300, 301; Elton, *Reform and Reformation*, pp. 50–51.
19. *Journals of the House of Lords*, 1: 18–23; *LP* 2: 119.
20. J. A. Guy, "Wolsey, the Council and the Council Courts," *EHR* 91 (1976): 482–83; Scarisbrick, *Henry VIII*, pp. 57–59.
21. *LP* 2: 207, 789, 1152; the letter to Wolsey was written from "Halyngbury" (Hollinbury), Sussex, a village north of Brighton.
22. *LP* 2: 1153; Hall, *Henry VIII*, 1: 148–49.
23. A. F. Pollard, *Wolsey* (London: Longmans, Green and Co., 1929), p. 70.
24. *LP* 2: 1573.
25. *Ven. Cal.* 2: 691.
26. Hall, *Henry VIII*, 1: 150–52.
27. Huntington Library, San Marino, California, Ellesmere Manuscript 2655,

"Minutes of proceedings from 8 Henry VII to 18 Henry VIII . . . Court of Star Chamber," f. 10r; Guy, "Wolsey, the Council and the Council Courts," p. 482.

28. Pollard, *Wolsey*, p. 76; *Illustrations of British History, Biography and Manners*, ed. E. Lodge, 3 vols. (London, 1791), 1: 13, 16, 23, 27–28. Several others—Lord Hastings, Sir Richard Sacheverell and Sir Edward Guildford among them—were also punished at the end of May for keeping retainers. See Hall, *Henry VIII*, 1: 152–53, for Wolsey's punishment of "ryottes, bearyng and maintenaunce." The size of Surrey's band of retainers is not clear from these sources, nor from those cited in note 27, above.

29. Polydore Vergil, *The Anglica Historia of Polydore Vergil, A.D. 1485–1547*, Denys Hay, ed. and trans., (London: Camden Society, 1950), p. 265.

30. Ellesmere Ms. 2655, f. 10v.

31. *LP* 2: 2459; 3: 272. Middleton was Surrey's vice-admiral and commissary in 1515; see *LP* 2: 235.

32. Hall, *Henry VIII*, 1: 161. Surrey's movements before May Day are uncertain. He was at court, sitting in Star Chamber, on 20 February, but his whereabouts for the next six weeks have left no trace. See Ellesmere Ms. 2655, f. 10v.

33. Vergil, *Anglica Historia*, pp. 243–45; *Ven. Cal.* 2: 887. The Londoners may have had good reason to fear a Howard's wrath. According to Hall, *Henry VIII*, 1: 161, "The Citie thought that the duke [of Norfolk] bare them grudge for a lewde priest of his, which the yere before was slain in Chepe, in so much the duke then in his fury sayd, I pray God I may once have the citezens in my daungier, and the duke also thought that they bare him no good wil, wherefore he came into the citie with xiii C men in harneys to keep the Oyer and determiner." The size of Norfolk's private army provides a glimpse of the feudal power still exercised by Tudor nobles, and may be a hint of the kind of retinue for which Surrey was punished the previous year.

34. Hall, *Henry VIII*, 1: 161; *Ven. Cal.* 2: 887; Scarisbrick, *Henry VIII*, p. 67.

35. *LP* 2: 3437, 3571, 3603; Scarisbrick, *Henry VIII*, pp. 64–68. See also Elton, *Reform and Reformation*, pp. 69–70.

36. Ellesmere Ms. 2655, f. 11v; Scarisbrick, *Henry VIII*, p. 68.

37. Sebastian Guistiani to the Doge of Venice, 16 June 1518, *LP* 2: 4232. Surrey apparently accompanied Henry back to court, for on 25 June he was among those hearing a case in Star Chamber. See Ellesmere Ms. 2655, f. 12r.

38. Scarisbrick, *Henry VIII*, pp. 69–73; *LP* 2: 4348; Hall, *Henry VIII*, 1: 166; Pollard, *Wolsey*, pp. 165–73, has an excellent discussion of Wolsey's legatine commission.

39. *LP* 2: 4467–71, 4475–77, 4480–81, 4564; Elton, *Reform and Reformation*, pp. 70–71; Scarisbrick, *Henry VIII*, pp. 72–73; Guy, "Wolsey, Council and Council Courts," p. 484.

40. *LP* 3: 128; Elton, *Reform and Reformation*, pp. 58–59, 71–72; Mackie, *The Earlier Tudors*, p. 308.

41. Edwin Casady, *Henry Howard, Earl of Surrey* (New York: Modern Language Association of America, 1938), pp. 21–24; George F. Nott, *Henry Howard*, 1: ix–xi and note; appendix, no. 30 (Elizabeth, duchess of Norfolk, to Thomas Cromwell, 24 October 1537).

42. Nott, *Henry Howard*, 1, appendix, no. 2, pp. ix–xv.

43. Ellesmere Ms. 2655, f. 14v–15r.

44. See Brendan Bradshaw, *The Irish Constitutional Revolution of the Sixteenth Century* (Cambridge: Cambridge University Press, 1979), pp. 3–57, and Steven G. Ellis, *Tudor Ireland: Crown, Community and the Conflict of Cultures, 1470–1603* (Harlow: Longman, 1985), pp. 19–109, for the background to Surrey's Irish mission.

45. *LP* 1: 632 (22). Kildare was given power to appoint all officials except the chancellor and chief justice, to receive and dispose of all revenues, and to pardon all offenses saving treason touching the king's person and false coinage. Ellis, *Tudor Ireland*, pp. 85–107, provides an excellent account of Kildare's rule of Ireland.

46. *LP* 1: 2535.

47. Ellis, *Tudor Ireland*, pp. 104–5.

48. Ellis, *Tudor Ireland*, argues (pp. 104–5 and 108) that Kildare was recalled not so much because the quality of his rule had decayed, but out of increased royal interest in the good order of Ireland. Thus Surrey's lieutenancy had its origins in "one of Henry VIII's spasmodic fits of reforming energy," but was at heart "an expedition mounted without any clear aims or adequate consideration of the consequences."

49. PRO SP 60/1/12–34.

50. Ibid.

51. Hall, *Henry VIII*, 1: 182; Vergil, *Anglica Historia*, pp. 262–65; Pollard, *Wolsey*, p. 107.

52. Mortimer Levine, "The Fall of Edward, Duke of Buckingham," in A. J. Slavin, ed., *Tudor Men and Institutions: Studies in English Law and Government* (Baton Rouge: Louisiana State University Press, 1972), pp. 32–48, argues that Henry and not Wolsey was responsible for Buckingham's destruction and that Surrey's Irish mission had no part in it.

53. *LP* 3: 1287–88, 2382.

54. Levine, "Fall of Buckingham," pp. 34–36. There was suspicion at the time of Buckingham's arrest that the net would be cast wider. Sir John Pechy, sent to Ireland in May 1521 to bring order to royal finances there, was thought by the Venetian ambassador to have gone to recall Surrey, who would then be accused of plotting with his father-in-law to depose the king. This proved a false alarm, but one purpose of Pechy's mission was to see how Surrey took the news of Bucking-

ham's fall. Barbara J. Harris, "Landlords and Tenants in the Later Middle Ages: The Buckingham Estates," *Past and Present* 43 (1969): 146–50, estimates Buckingham's annual rents at £6,000. One wonders how much Henry was tempted by this rich prize in seeking the duke's destruction.

55. PRO SP 60/1/69–72; *LP* 3: 669.

56. PRO SP 1/20/112 (memo of 30 June 1520); see also BL Cott. Titus B i, f. 419, Sir John Stile to Wolsey, 30 July 1521, on Irish finances.

57. A draft of royal instructions for Surrey (PRO SP 60/1/36–39) must never have led to a final version which arrived in Dublin. Surrey's report of 23 July (*S.P. Hen. VIII*, 2: 35–38) makes it clear that no instructions had yet arrived from London, and as late as 6 September (*S.P. Hen. VIII*, 2: 43) the earl had received no letters from the king—a state of affairs Surrey blamed on ill winds in the Irish sea.

58. *S.P. Hen. VIII*, 2: 35–38, 42–45.

59. Ibid., 2: 37.

60. PRO SP 60/1/40–41.

61. Surrey to Wolsey, 25 August 1520, PRO SP 60/1/42.

62. Henry VIII to Surrey, [September?] 1520, *S.P. Hen. VIII*, 2: 51–57.

63. *S.P. Hen. VIII*, 2: 42–45. In undated instructions probably sent in late September or early October (Ibid., pp. 51–58), Henry gave Surrey the desired authority to put all but men of noble rank to death for due cause. Piracy was already rampant in the Irish Sea, as Surrey knew. When, on 29 July 1521, the earl captured Richard Peper, an English rover out of Calais, Surrey admitted that there were many other pirates who used Ireland as a base to raid English shipping. See *S.P. Hen. VIII*, 2: 76–77.

64. BL Cott. Titus B i, f. 415; PRO SP 60/1/40–41, 47–48, 49. The last, Surrey to Wolsey, 3 October [1520] is miscatalogued as *LP* 3: 1628, for 1521. Context makes the earlier date clear.

65. *S.P. Hen. VIII*, 2: 51–57.

66. BL Cott. Titus B ii, f. 385; B i, f. 411. This manuscript, a draft of a letter presumably sent to Ireland, does not name its recipient. Henry may have sent such a letter to several Irish lords; this copy is incomplete and separated in two volumes of the Cottonian collection.

67. *S.P. Hen. VIII*, 2: 62.

68. PRO SP 60/1/51.

69. PRO SP 60/1/53.

70. *S.P. Hen. VIII*, 2: 63 (note).

71. Instructions to Sir John Pechy, April 1521, PRO SP 60/1/54–63.

72. BL Cott. Titus B ii, f. 627.

73. *S.P. Hen. VIII*, 2: 72–75.

74. Ibid.

75. Stile to Wolsey, 30 July 1521, BL Cott. Titus B i, f. 419.
76. Surrey to Henry VIII and Stile to Wolsey, July 1521, *S.P. Hen. VIII*, 2: 75–82.
77. Surrey to Henry VIII, 14 September 1521, *S.P. Hen. VIII*, 2: 82–84.
78. Surrey to Henry VIII, 16 September 1521, PRO SP 60/1/65.
79. Wolsey to Henry VIII, 14 October 1521, *S.P. Hen. VIII*, 1: 72.
80. Henry VIII to Surrey, 30 October 1521, *S.P. Hen. VIII*, 2: 88–91.
81. PRO SP 60/1/68, 73–74.
82. *S.P. Hen. VIII*, 2: 93; *LP* 4: 4302.
83. *LP* 3: 1493, 1802, 1816, 2296; Scarisbrick, *Henry VIII*, pp. 88–89.
84. *LP* 3: 2304, 2308, 2315, 2320, 2329, 2336, 2337; *Ven. Cal.*, 3: 463, 474.
85. *LP* 3: 2355, 2362; Hall, *Henry VIII*, 1: 258–61.
86. Hall, *Henry VIII*, 1: 261–62, 266–67; *LP* 3: 2431.
87. Hall, *Henry VIII*, 1: 266–71; *LP* 3: 2451 ff.
88. At 6d. per day per man, Surrey's 3,000 troops cost Henry £75 a day for wages alone for nearly seventy days. To this must be added £5,000 for the costs of coats (40d. each) and transport to Calais (40d. a man), as well as weapons and other equipment. Surrey was paid 12s. a day, while his lieutenants were paid various rates, the 30 captains 4s. a day each, and 30 petty captains 2s. a day each. It is no wonder that Surrey was sent £10,000 on 3 September and was still short of funds on 15 October, able to pay his troops only eight days' wages for the month. See *LP* 2: 2500, 2549, 2592, 2614, 2745, and Scarisbrick, *Henry VIII*, pp. 125–27.
89. Scarisbrick, *Henry VIII*, pp. 125–26.
90. Norfolk's poor health also compelled him to give up the office of treasurer. On 2 December he resigned and the office—surely by prior arrangement, although Surrey had to go through the formality of making supplication to the king and Wolsey—was granted to his son. See *LP* 1, addenda, 365. For the background of Scottish affairs, see David M. Head, "Henry VIII's Scottish Policy: A Reassessment," *Scottish Historical Review* 61 (1982): 5–7.
91. PRO SP 1/27/123.
92. PRO SP 49/2/9. Much of the manuscript material for the period is in SP 49/2 and in BL Additional Manuscripts, 24,965, the latter Dacre's letter book, 2 June 1523–24 September 1524, which includes copies of Dacre's letters to others and many originals received. Part of Thomas Howard's letter book for the period is preserved as BL Cott. Cal. B vi, ff. 375ff.
93. PRO SP 49/2/4 and 5–6, Surrey to Margaret, 25 March [1523] and Margaret to Surrey, an undated holograph letter presumably in answer and probably before 10 April. These are catalogued as *LP* 3: 2912 (1,2). See also BL Cott. Vesp. F iii, f. 155, Surrey to Wolsey, 11 April [1523], miscatalogued as LP 4: 236 [1524].
94. PRO SP 49/2/4, 5–6, 8, 11–12; *LP* 3: 2937, 2944, 3096; Wolsey granted

Monteagle to neither claimant, still in August 1523 holding the wardship himself. Finally the boy went to Surrey's client Sir John Hussey, who sold the marriage rights to the duke of Suffolk. See *LP* 3: 3234; 4: 113, and Gunn, *Charles Brandon*, pp. 93–94.

95. Surrey's report to Wolsey is PRO SP 49/2/15–16; see also *LP* 3: 2974, 2995, 3039.

96. Surrey's warrant appointing Dacre as deputy, dated 3 June 15 Henry VIII, is in BL Add. Ms., 24,965, f. 9. This warrant, on vellum, bears an unusually fine impression of Surrey's seal in red wax—a lion rampant, facing left, surrounded with the legend "THOME+COMITZ+ZURREY+."

97. A household book, "The Catorer's Book of the Household and Expenses in Provisions and Beer of Thomas, Earl of Surrey . . . 18 April 1523 to 17 January 1524," University of California at Berkeley, HF 5616 E5 N6 (formerly Ms. Ac 523), helps account for Surrey's movements during this period. While in London, Surrey does not seem to have taken his seat in Parliament, which had been in session since April and was at work on a new subsidy for the war in France, which he presumably would have favored. It is likely that the attainder of Buckingham kept Surrey away, for he wanted no part in the statutory disgrace of his father-in-law.

98. *LP* 3: 3098, 3116, 3120, 3128, 3134, 3158, 3172, 3173, 3198–3200, 3233.

99. *S.P. Hen. VIII*, 4: 6–11.

100. Surrey wrote so many detailed letters to Henry and Wolsey that on 4 September he apologized, "for the paeyne shall be onely to your Grace in reding and to me in writing, for the chardges of the poostes bee all one, riding or lying still." See PRO SP 49/2/23v., as well as *S.P. Hen. VIII*, 4: 10–11, 13–14, 25 and *LP* 3: 3300.

101. BL Cott. Cal. B vi, ff. 341–43; *S.P. Hen. VIII*, 4: 11–12, 20–30; Ellis, *Original Letters*, ser. 1 vol. 1, nos. 72–73; *LP* 3: 3321.

102. BL Cott. Cal. B i, f. 192.

103. BL Cott. Cal. B ii, ff. 33–34.

104. BL Cott. Cal. B vi, ff. 331–33, 337–38; *S.P. Hen. VIII*, 4: 37–39; *LP* 3: 3362; Ellis, *Original Letters*, ser. 1, vol. 1, no. 76.

105. *LP* 3: 3123, 3225, 3346, 3371, 3659.

106. Surrey to Wolsey, 1 October 1523, BL Cott. Cal. B vi, ff. 331–33; *LP* 3: 3368, 3369, 3379.

107. BL Add. Ms., 24,965, ff. 51–67, includes copies of Dacre and Surrey's correspondence; see also *LP* 3: 3401, 3404, 3409, 3421, and *S.P. Hen. VIII*, 4: 44–49.

108. BL Cott. Cal. B vi, f. 330. How much money Surrey received is not clear, but on 5 November the earl thanked Wolsey for £2,000 in emergency funds; see PRO SP 49/2/47–48. By late October, Northumberland, Clifford, Latimer, Scrope

and Darcy, as well as Dorset, had joined Surrey, bringing a considerable number of men. See BL Cott. Cal. B vi, ff. 337–38.

109. Surrey to Wolsey, 1 October and 19 October 1523, PRO SP 49/2/32–33, 39–40. See also *LP* 3: 3400, 3445 and Hall, *Henry VIII*, 1: 304–5. As Wolsey wrote Surrey, "and no little comfort it is to the kinges highnes, to perceyve that His Grace hath so hardy a captain as ye be, against such a coward as the duke of Albany is known to be, so discreet and sober a servant, against so furious and wilful a fool." See Ellis, *Original Letters*, ser. 1, vol. 1, introduction to number 85.

110. *LP* 3: 3438, 3447, 3449, 3491.

111. BL Cott. Cal. B vi, ff. 337–38.

112. BL Add. Ms., 24,965, ff. 60–65; PRO SP 49/2/42–43; BL Cott. Cal. B vi, ff. 362, 364–65. BL Cott. Cal. B ii, ff. 31–32, Surrey to Wolsey, 28 October 1523, bears Wolsey's marginal note. See also *LP* 3: 3460, 3469, 3491.

113. Hall, *Henry VIII*, 1: 302–4; *LP* 3: 3477, 3481, 3489.

114. BL Cott. Cal. B vi, ff. 356, 360, 354–55 (this volume, Wolsey's Scottish file, is in considerable disorder, with many items out of chronological sequence); PRO SP 49/2/47–48; *LP* 3: 3499, 3507, 3508. For other accounts of Albany's attack, see Vergil, *Anglica Historia*, p. 317 and Holinshed, *Chronicles*, 3: 692.

115. PRO SP 49/2/49–50 (Surrey to Wolsey, 7 November 1523); *S.P. Hen. VIII*, 4: 51–56; *LP* 3: 3508, 3520.

116. BL Cott. Cal. B i, f. 324; *S.P. Hen. VIII*, 4: 60–63.

117. PRO SP 49/2/67–68, 69–70; *LP* 3: 3551–55.

118. *LP* 3: 3608, 3623; 4: 10, 47. "The Catorer's Book" (see note 97 above), f. 139r., provides evidence of Surrey's arrival and departure at his home.

119. On 27 January, Thomas Walsh was appointed remembrancer of the exchequer, succeeding Robert Blage, patriarch of a family that also produced George Blage as a Howard servant. See *LP* 4: 86 (27). For evidence of Surrey's activities in court and council, see also PRO SP 49/2/69–70; BL Add. Ms., 24,965, f. 77 and several letters at f. 152 and following; see also *LP* 4: 10, 25, 28, 47.

120. Gerald Brenan and E. P. Statham, *The House of Howard*, 2 vols., pagination consecutive (London, 1907), p. 109.

121. "The Catorer's Book," ff. 138r–172v.

122. Scarisbrick, *Henry VIII*, pp. 131–34.

123. Brewer placed several letters—Surrey to Henry VIII, dated 8 March, PRO SP 1/30/234 [*LP* 4: 149], and Surrey to Wolsey, dated 11 April, BL Cott. Vesp. F xiii, f. 81 [*LP* 4: 236]—in 1524 rather than 1523, resulting in some confusion about the movements of Surrey and several other people during the spring of 1524, among them the king's favorite Sir William Compton. Neither of the manuscripts cited above includes a year in the contemporary date, but every dated paper from

the first half of 1524 makes it clear that Surrey did not return north until after his father's funeral; further, Hall, *Henry VIII*, 1: 319, places Surrey at court on 10 March 1524, assisting Henry and Suffolk in a joust to test a new set of royal armor. These papers, misdated by Brewer, were placed in the wrong volume of the *Letters and Papers* (and, in the case of the former, miscatalogued in the PRO).

124. Tucker, *Thomas Howard*, pp. 141–42; *LP* 2: 1363; 4: 546 (15); *Ven. Cal.*, 2: 1287. For the value of the Howard lands, see Arundel Castle Ms. G.1/4 and Pembroke College (Cambridge) Ms. B.5, cited in R. Virgoe, "The Recovery of the Howards in East Anglia, 1485–1529," in E. W. Ives, R. J. Knecht and J. J. Scarisbrick, eds., *Wealth and Power in Tudor England: Essays Presented to S. T. Bindoff* (London: Athlone Press of the University of London, 1978), p. 18.

CHAPTER 4 The Peer and the Prelate: Norfolk and Wolsey, 1524–1530

1. Scarisbrick, *Henry VIII*, pp. 131–33; *LP* 4: 255.
2. *LP* 4: 278, 474.
3. *S.P. Hen. VIII*, 4: 84–85, 104–8.
4. Ibid., 96–110.
5. Ibid., 119, 126–28; *LP* 4: 601, 613, 615.
6. *S.P. Hen. VIII*, 4: 119; Rymer, *Foedera* 14: 21–23; *LP* 4: 601ff.
7. *S.P. Hen. VIII*, 4: 126–34, 167–68; *LP* 4: 651. See also BL Cott. Cal. B vi, f. 404, Margaret to Norfolk, 6 October 1524, rehearsing the queen's objections. Margaret's eccentric spelling is one of the special joys of this correspondence; fortunately, she wrote a clear hand.
8. BL Cott. Cal. B iii, f. 124.
9. *S.P. Hen. VIII*, 4: 146–49, 167–72, 183–84, 188–90, 201–5; *LP* 4: 745 (Arran to Norfolk, 18 October 1524).
10. BL Cott. Cal. B i, ff. 334–36, Wolsey to Norfolk, 3 October 1524.
11. *S.P. Hen. VIII*, 4: 149–56, 159–65, 169–72, 174–82.
12. Ibid., 169–72, 183–84. The latter letter has appended a four-page holograph postscript added by a worried Norfolk in response to Wolsey's latest letter; see BL Cott. Cal. B i, ff. 329–31.
13. BL Cott. Cal. B iii, ff. 118–20; *S.P. Hen. VIII*, 4: 188–90, 201–5.
14. BL Cott. Cal. B i, ff. 337–38; *S.P. Hen. VIII*, 4: 190–91.
15. BL Cott. Cal. B iii, f. 76.
16. *S.P. Hen. VIII*, 4: 205, 218–23.
17. For a particularly telling example of Wolsey's impatience, see Wolsey to Norfolk, 11 November 1524, BL Cott. Cal. B iii, ff. 129–31.
18. *S.P. Hen. VIII*, 4: 138–45.
19. Ibid., 223–24, 227–30, 243–48.

20. Ibid., 256–68.

21. John Hill Burton, *The History of Scotland*, 8 vols. (Edinburgh: William Blackwood and Sons, 1899), 3: 130–39.

22. *S.P. Hen. VIII*, 4: 149, 205, 248–49.

23. Rymer, *Foedera*, 14: 28; *S.P. Hen. VIII*, 4: 271–72.

24. Rymer, *Foedera*, 14: 30–31. The truce was again extended on 23 March, but the talks made no progress.

25. *LP* 4: 1097. In addition, as a mark of status, between November 1524 and August 1525 Norfolk was named to commissions of the peace for twenty-seven shires—the beginning of a long tradition of such appointments. See *LP* 4: 895, 961, 1049, 1136, 1377, 1610.

26. Gunn, *Charles Brandon*, p. 98.

27. Scarisbrick, *Henry VIII*, pp. 136–37; *Sp. Cal.* 3: 87; Knecht, *Francis I*, pp. 161–75.

28. *LP* 4: 1379, 1380; *Sp. Cal.* 3: 51–65; G.W. Bernard, *War, Taxation and Rebellion in Tudor England: Henry VIII, Wolsey and the Amicable Grant of 1525* (Brighton, Sussex: Harvester Press, 1986), pp. 3–45.

29. Hall, *Henry VIII*, 2: 32; *LP* 4: 547, 1235; Bernard, *Amicable Grant*, pp. 55–58.

30. Ellis, *Original Letters*, ser. 3, vol. 1, p. 379. Henry VII coined dandiprats (worth about 2d. each) for his French army in 1492. See Pollard, *Wolsey*, p. 141 and note 1.

31. Ellis, *Original Letters*, ser. 3, vol. 1, p. 379; BL Cott. Cleo. F vi, f. 323; PRO SP 1/34/162, 165. Norfolk's original instructions are not extant, so much of what is known of them is based on his letters and Wolsey's answers. Warham's instructions, surely similar to Norfolk's, are in *LP* 4, appendix, no. 34.

32. Hall, *Henry VIII*, 2: 36; *LP* 4: 1249.

33. BL Cott Cleo. F iv, ff. 323–24; Robert Woods, "The Amicable Grant: Some Aspects of Thomas Wolsey's rule in England, 1522–26 (Ph.D. dissertation, University of California at Los Angeles, 1974), p. 154. Norfolk reported that those who had paid £20 in the last subsidy were now paying £33 6s. 8d., or 66 percent more. See *LP* 4, appendix, no. 36.

34. *LP* 4: 1261.

35. Hall, *Henry VIII*, 2: 36, 42.

36. *LP* 4: 1243, 1263, 1266, 1267. 1272, 1306, 1311, 1321, 1330.

37. Woods, "Amicable Grant," pp. 154–56; Hall, *Henry VIII*, 2: 36–40. The statute is 1 Ric. III, c. 2 (in *Statutes of the Realm*, 2: 478).

38. *LP* 4: 1319.

39. Hall, *Henry VIII*, 2: 42–43.

40. *LP* 4: 1318, 1319; Ellis, *Original Letters*, ser. 1. vol. 1, pp. 369–75.

41. Ellis, *Original Letters*, ser. 3, vol. 2, p. 2; Hall, *Henry VIII*, 2: 43.

42. *LP* 4: 1329. For the troubles in Cambridge and at the university, see *LP* 4: 1212 (Nicholas West, bishop of Ely, to Wolsey, 19 April) and for Essex, *LP* 4: 1325 (Henry Bourchier, earl of Essex, to Wolsey, 9 May).

43. *LP* 4: 1343; Hall, *Henry VIII*, 2: 44-45.

44. Hall, *Henry VIII*, 2: 38; *LP* 4: 1318 (Henry VIII to Norfolk and Suffolk, 8 May 1525); Scarisbrick, *Henry VIII*, p. 139.

45. Scarisbrick, *Henry VIII*, pp. 139-40.

46. *LP* 4: 1578, 1600, 1601, 1617.

47. Ibid., 1963.

48. Ibid., 3: 3161; 4: 578 (50), 1431, 1500, 1510, 1540, 1576. At the time of Richmond's elevation, Henry made several other noble creations. Henry Clifford (1493-1542) was made earl of Cumberland; Henry Brandon (1516-34), son of the duke of Suffolk, was made earl of Lincoln; Thomas Manners, lord Roos (1492-1543), was made earl of Rutland; and Thomas Boleyn (d. 1539) was made viscount Rochford. See on these men Cokayne, *Complete Peerage* and *DNB*, s.v.

49. As on 10 February 1526, discussing Francis's release from captivity with the Venetian envoys, and on 4 May 1526, when he was among those in council who ratified Wolsey's arrangements for his college at Oxford. In October 1527, Norfolk surrendered the monastery of Dodnes to Cardinal College; as its patron, he listed the value of the house as 53s. 4d. in spiritualities and £40 5s. 4½ d. in temporalities. Norfolk was also in Star Chamber on at least three occasions; see Huntington Library, San Marino, California, Ellesmere Ms. 2655, f. 18.

50. Details of the furnishings of Kenninghall come from PRO LR 2/113-17 (Auditors of the Land Revenues, Misc. Books), the surveys made at the time of Norfolk's arrest. Only a fragment of the palace remains. See Robinson, *The Dukes of Norfolk*, p. 37, for a photograph.

51. *LP* 4: 2002.

52. Ibid., 1503; Rymer, *Foedera*, 14: 43-45 (the Latin text).

53. *LP* 4: 1533 (12), 3211, 2427; Cokayne, *Complete Peerage*, s.v. "Oxford"; Casady, *Henry Howard*, p. 36.

54. *LP* 4: 2203; Edmond Bapst, *Deux Gentilshommes-poètes de la Cour de Henry VIII* (Paris, 1891), p. 173. In 1527, Norfolk obtained custody of Marney's possessions during the minority of his daughters; see *LP* 4: 3324 (2).

55. John Smyth, *The Berkeley Manuscripts: The Lives of the Berkeleys, Lords of the Honor, Castle and Manor of Berkeley in the County of Gloucester, from 1066 to 1618*, ed. John MacLean (Gloucester, 1883-85), pp. 224, 252, 284. Catherine subsequently wed the earl of Derby.

56. *LP* 4: 2241.

57. *Sp. Cal.* 3 (1): 34, 152, 201; *LP* 4: 1410, 1408, 1819, 1987.

58. For these developments, see Knecht, *Francis I*, pp. 209–13; Scarisbrick, *Henry VIII*, pp. 142–45; Elton, *Reform and Reformation*, pp. 101–2; *LP* 4: 3105.

59. *LP* 4: 3140, 3147; Scarisbrick, *Henry VIII*, pp. 153–55; Henry A. Kelly, *The Matrimonial Trials of Henry VIII* (Stanford, Calif.: Stanford University Press, 1976), pp. 21ff. See also Geoffrey DeC. Parmiter, *The King's Great Matter: Anglo-Papal Relations, 1527–1534* (New York: Barnes and Noble, 1967), passim, and Warnicke, *Anne Boleyn*, pp. 48–49, 54–56.

60. Scarisbrick, *Henry VIII*, pp. 147–48, 163; Ives, *Anne Boleyn*, pp. 2–58.

61. Scarisbrick, *Henry VIII*, p. 145; *Sp. Cal.* 3 (2): 107, 190–93. On Tunstall, see Charles Sturge, *Cuthbert Tunstall, Churchman, Scholar, Statesman, Administrator* (London: Longmans, Green and Co., 1938).

62. Scarisbrick, *Henry VIII*, pp. 156–57; *LP* 4: 3279; Ludwig von Pastor, *The History of the Popes, From the Close of the Middle Ages*, trans. and ed. Antrobus, Kerr, Graf and Peeler, 40 vols. (St. Louis: B. Herder, 1889–1953), 9: 436–43. See also D. S. Chambers, "Cardinal Wolsey and the Papal Tiara," *BIHR* 38 (1965): 20–30.

63. *LP* 4: 3318, 3360; Scarisbrick, *Henry VIII*, p. 158.

64. *S.P. Hen. VIII*, 7: 1, 3; Scarisbrick, *Henry VIII*, pp. 157–62; Parmiter, *The King's Great Matter*, pp. 20–24; Hall, *Henry VIII*, 2: 105; *Sp. Cal.* 3 (2): 224. See also Warnicke, *Anne Boleyn*, pp. 61–64, where it is argued that Henry "had begun seriously to consider marrying Anne" only in the summer of 1527, but that by 23 July "his decision to marry Anne was virtually irrevocable."

65. Ives, *Anne Boleyn*, pp. 132–35.

66. *LP* 4: 3625, 3663, 3664, 3703.

67. *LP* 4: 3890, 3893, 4012, 4045, 4162. These three were all related to Norfolk by marriage; if he was sincerely concerned with troubles in the east, they were trustworthy allies to have close at hand.

68. Ibid., 4162, 4192.

69. Norfolk to Wolsey, 17 May [1528], PRO SP 60/1/114; *LP* 4: 4239, 4320; *S.P. Hen. VIII*, 2: 134. Norfolk had already begun his journey to London and was at Evesham in Kent when word arrived that an outbreak of sweating sickness had caused the term to be broken up, so he returned to Kenninghall.

70. PRO SP 60/1/122, 127–28; *S.P. Hen. VIII*, 2: 129–30; Ellis, *Tudor Ireland*, pp. 145, 318.

71. *Sp. Cal.* 3 (2): 790.

72. Scarisbrick, *Henry VIII*, pp. 204–16.

73. On 14 November, Norfolk signed a treasury receipt with More; on 28 November Lord Hastings wrote to his wife, mentioning that Norfolk had been at court for "some time." See *LP* 4: 4931; *HMC Reports*, vol. 78, p. 2.

74. Mendoza to Charles V, 2 December 1528, *Sp. Cal.* 3 (2): 861.

75. *Ven. Cal.* 4: 385; *LP* 4: 5048.
76. *LP* 4: 5210, 5403, 5415, 5458.
77. Ibid., 5255.
78. Ibid., 5403.
79. George Cavendish, *The Life and Death of Cardinal Wolsey* in *Two Early Tudor Lives*, ed. R. S. Sylvester and D. P. Harding (New Haven and London: Yale University Press, 1962), pp. 43ff. Cavendish, a hearty supporter of Wolsey, put most of the blame for his fall on the wicked machinations of an "aristocratic" group.
80. *LP* 4: 5581.
81. Ibid., 5635.
82. Scarisbrick, *Henry VIII*, pp. 224–26; Hall, *Henry VIII*, 2: 150–53; *LP* 4: 5751, 5759, 5773, 5916. There is some dispute about the chronology of these events; I follow here Scarisbrick, who differs somewhat from Pollard and Hall.
83. *LP* 4: 5571, 5583, 5599, 5710, 5744, 4829; Scarisbrick, *Henry VIII*, pp. 232–33; Elton, *Reform and Reformation*, pp. 110–11.
84. Cavendish, *Wolsey*, p. 98; *LP* 4: 5885, 5911; *Sp. Cal.* 4 (1): 195. Elton, *Reform and Reformation*, pp. 111–15, insists that Wolsey was not destroyed by an "Aristocratic faction." This is essentially true. What did persuade Henry to dump Wolsey was the unanimous opposition of lay and clerical councilors, as well as the common lawyers and the members of Commons. Norfolk and his faction were not solely responsible for Wolsey's fall, but their persistent attacks were certainly a major factor in the cardinal's ruin. In the end, the decision to jettison Wolsey was Henry's alone.
85. Pollard, *Wolsey*, pp. 236–37; Cavendish, *Wolsey*, pp. 97:98; Scarisbrick, *Henry VIII*, p. 234; Ellis, *Original Letters*, ser. 1, vol. 1, p. 307.
86. Cavendish, *Wolsey*, pp. 98–100; Scarisbrick, *Henry VIII*, p. 234. Ives, *Anne Boleyn*, pp. 149–50, argues from the evidence of Thomas Alward—an eyewitness—that Henry and Wolsey met again on 20 September and parted cordially. In any case, the discussions at Grafton were the last time Henry and Wolsey saw each other.
87. Elton, *Reform and Reformation*, p. 111; Stanford E. Lehmberg, *The Reformation Parliament, 1529–1536* (Cambridge: Cambridge University Press, 1970), pp. 1–3; Pollard, *Wolsey*, pp. 239–40. Gardiner was sworn as Henry's secretary on 28 July; on 1 March he had been installed as archdeacon of Norfolk on the resignation of Thomas Winter, Wolsey's natural son. Norfolk held the advowson for this grant, and by appointing Gardiner may have helped to bring him into the anti-Wolsey coalition. See Francis Blomefield, *An Essay Towards a Topographical History of the County of Norfolk*, 11 vols. (London, 1805–10), 3: 644. Glyn Redworth, *In Defense of the Church Catholic: The Life of Stephen Gardiner* (Oxford: Basil Blackwell, 1990),

pp. 16–17, says that as late as 1528 "Gardiner was unswervingly loyal to the cardinal." Exactly when he switched sides cannot be known, but it must have been in mid-1529 as the odds against Wolsey lengthened.

88. *LP* 4: 5993. Pollard, *Wolsey*, p. 239, dates this letter to 29 September, which may be more reasonable.

89. *LP* 4: 5945, 5983; Pollard, *Wolsey*, p. 239 and notes. J. A. Guy, *The Public Career of Thomas More* (Brighton, Sussex: Harvester Press, 1980), pp. 30–32, maintains that More "was not involved in these high politics" leading to Wolsey's fall, but even a passive role in failing to come to Wolsey's defense would have been obvious enough.

90. *LP* 4: 6035.

91. Cavendish, *Wolsey*, pp. 101–2; Rymer, *Foedera*, 14: 349–50; *LP* 4: 6025. The dating of the surrender has been thoroughly muddled, but Guy, *Thomas More*, notes that the Chancery Close Roll dates the formal surrender as 17 October (PRO C. 54/398/19).

92. *Sp. Cal.* 4 (1): 295.

93. *LP* 4: 6011, 6019. Guy, *Thomas More*, pp. 107–9 and elsewhere, argues that Suffolk was especially determined to take advantage of Wolsey's fall to urge the king "to strip the clergy bare and return to the ideals of the primitive church." Gunn, *Charles Brandon*, pp. 104–5, disagrees with Guy, arguing that, although Suffolk supported Henry's divorce and the subsequent work of the Reformation Parliament, he did so, like Norfolk, for political reasons. As for Suffolk's personal religious views, Gunn notes that "the most that can be said is that Brandon seems to have been tolerant of unorthodoxy" and that he "showed little sign of theological commitment," either Catholic or Protestant.

94. *LP* 4: 6164, 6461.

95. *Sp. Cal.* 4 (1): 292–303.

96. J. J. Scarisbrick, "Thomas More: The King's Good Servant," *Thought: The Fordham University Quarterly* 52 (1977): 249–59; G. R. Elton, "Sir Thomas More and the Opposition to Henry VIII," in *Studies in Tudor Politics and Government*, 2 vols. (Cambridge: Cambridge University Press, 1974), 1: 129–56; William Roper, *The Life of Sir Thomas More*, in *Two Early Tudor Lives*, pp. 217–18; *Sp. Cal.* 4 (1): 326; *LP* 4: 6125.

97. Pollard, *Wolsey*, pp. 242–45; Cavendish, *Wolsey*, pp. 105, 114.

98. *LP* 4: 5749, 6075; Scarisbrick, "The King's Good Servant," p. 258; John M. Headley, "The New Debate on More's Political Career," *Thought: The Fordham University Quarterly* 52 (1977): 271; Pollard, *Wolsey*, pp. 259–60; Hall, *Henry VIII*, 2: 164–65.

99. Cavendish, *Wolsey*, pp. 104, 120–22. A number of royal grants for Decem-

ber 1529 were signed at York Place; see *LP* 4: 6135. The seizure of York Place was ratified in February 1530 by More, Norfolk, Fitzwilliam and others; see Rymer, *Foedera*, 14: 365–66.

100. Cavendish, *Wolsey*, pp. 117–22 and 119, note. The Howard coat of arms featured a prominent rampant lion.

101. Lehmberg, *The Reformation Parliament*, pp. 89–90. The act was enrolled as 21 Hen. VIII, c. 24 (*Statutes of the Realm*, 3: 315–16). See also Hall, *Henry VIII*, 2: 169.

102. *Sp. Cal.* 4 (1): 275–77, 331, 367.

103. Ibid., 416; *LP* 4: 6199.

104. Ellis, *Original Letters*, ser. 1, vol. 2, pp. 1–7; *Sp. Cal.* 4 (1): 449–50; *LP* 4: 6080. Wolsey had no real hope of aid from the nobility, so he aimed at lesser men— Henry Norris, William Fitzwilliam and John Russell, all of Henry's household, as well as his own secretary Thomas Cromwell. The latter's loyalty even at this late date has been asserted by A. J. Slavin, *Politics and Profit: A Study of Sir Ralph Sadler, 1507–1547* (Cambridge: Cambridge University Press, 1966), pp. 17–23, who concludes that Cromwell remained loyal to Wolsey mainly for lack of a better and more palatable patron.

105. *LP* 4: 6210, 6213; HMC *Reports*, vol. 9, p. 7.

106. *Sp. Cal.* 4 (1): 460. 469.

107. *LP* 4: 6248 (21).

108. Cavendish, *Wolsey*, pp. 127–28; see also Pollard, *Wolsey*, pp. 268–71.

109. Cavendish, *Wolsey*, pp. 128–35; *LP* 4: 6295.

110. *LP* 4: 6310, 6320, 6455, 6459, 6461; *S.P. Hen. VIII*, 7: 232–34; *Ven. Cal.* 4: 601; Rymer, *Foedera*, 14: 392–99. Gardiner and Rochford were also active in pursuing the university decrees; the latter stopped in Paris to prod the faculties while on his way back from a mission to Rome in June.

111. *Sp. Cal.* 4 (1): 510–11.

112. *LP* 4: 6513. Guy, *Thomas More*, pp. 127–31, argues that More was pushed out of the inner circle by Norfolk, who did not trust More on the divorce question— as it turned out, with good reason.

113. *Sp. Cal.* 4 (1): 719, 762. Norfolk also asked the nuncio to obtain a dispensation to clear up the questions involved in the marriage of the earl of Derby to a Howard; one wonders if the inconsistency of this piece of personal politics occurred to Norfolk, or if this is evidence of his basic loyalty to Rome and his inability to envision the radical course of English Reformation to be undertaken by Cromwell.

114. Scarisbrick, *Henry VIII*, pp. 287–95. The most forceful view of Cromwell's role is G.R. Elton, "King or Minister? The Man Behind the Henrician Reformation," *History*, new series, 39 (1954): 216–32.

115. *The Life and Letters of Thomas Cromwell*, ed. R. B. Merriman, 2 vols. (Oxford: Clarendon Press, 1902), 1: 327.
116. *LP* 4: 6582, 6688.
117. Ibid., 5985, 6330, 6579; introduction, dlxxxvii–dlxxxviii.
118. Pollard, *Wolsey*, pp. 279ff.
119. Rachel Reid, *The King's Council in the North* (London: Longmans, Green and Co., 1921), p. 113–15; Hall, *Henry VIII*, 2: 180–81; Pollard, *Wolsey*, pp. 292–95.
120. *LP* 4: 6679, 6687; *Sp. Cal.* 4 (1): 832.
121. *LP* 4, introduction, dxcix–dc; 6738, 6773; *Ven. Cal.* 4: 637. See also E. A. Hammond, "Doctor Augustine, Physician to Cardinal Wolsey and King Henry VIII," *Medical History* 19 (1975): 215–49.
122. *Ven. Cal.* 4: 629, 637.
123. *Sp. Cal.* 4 (1): 819; *LP* 4: 6720. Ives, *Anne Boleyn*, pp. 157–58, gives Anne most of the credit for Wolsey's arrest, arguing that Norfolk, fearing Wolsey's return, had begun "to alternate between vindicative fright and sycophantic self-preservation" when faced with Henry's complaints that "everyday I miss the cardinal of York."
124. Cavendish, *Wolsey*, pp. 156ff; *LP* 4: 6720.
125. *Sp. Cal.* 4 (2): 41.

CHAPTER 5 The King's Great Matter and the Rise of Cromwell, 1530–1536

1. *Sp. Cal.* 4(2): 22ff.; *Ven. Cal.* 4: 694 (pp. 294–95). Chapuys's reports are a major source of information on politics and personalities in the later 1520s and 1530s. Despite his obvious biases, Chapuys cannot be ignored, for he talked to everyone and reported his conversations at great length. Warnicke, *Anne Boleyn*, pp. 2–3 and 93–98, attacks Chapuys as entirely unreliable. Read with care, though, Chapuys's reports remain, I think, both generally credible and really essential to understanding events of the period.
2. For Cromwell's life, see *DNB*, s.v.; Merriman, *Thomas Cromwell*, 1: 27–44; B. W. Beckingsale, *Thomas Cromwell, Tudor Minister* (Totowa, N.J.: Rowan and Littlefield, 1978). G. R. Elton, "Thomas Cromwell Redivivus," *Archiv für Reformationsgeschichte* 68 (1977): 192–208, is only a sketch.
3. Merriman, *Thomas Cromwell*, 1: 67–68; Slavin, *Politics and Profit*, pp. 17–23.
4. Lehmberg, *The Reformation Parliament*, p. 27.
5. Cavendish, *Wolsey*, p. 116.
6. Elton, *Tudor Revolution*, p. 97; Scarisbrick, *Henry VIII*, p. 303.
7. Guy, *Thomas More*, pp. 128, 145. Several of these, including Darcy and Hussey, either were or would become supporters of the "Aragonese" faction.

8. *LP* 5: 419, 423. Ives, *Anne Boleyn*, pp. 302–31, makes a strong case for Anne as at least a patron of Christian humanism, if not a real evangelical reformer. Warnicke, *Anne Boleyn*, pp. 107–13, concurs in general with Ives, saying that Anne was very interested in religion and, if not entirely orthodox, influenced by French humanism and the *Devotio moderna* of the Netherlands. Neither accepts Anne as anything resembling a Lutheran. On Gardiner and his pro-imperial stance, see Redworth, *Stephen Gardiner*, p. 56 and elsewhere.

9. Guy, *Thomas More*, p. 141; Elton, *Reform and Reformation*, pp. 103ff.

10. Elton, *Reform and Reformation*, pp. 132–38. Dr. Virginia Murphy, an Elton student, is now working on the fragments of the companion theological collection supporting the divorce; she presented some of her findings in a paper read at the American Historical Association meeting in December 1985 in New York City.

11. *Sp. Cal.* 4(2): 22–23.

12. Ibid., 95–96.

13. *LP* 5: 171; Lehmberg, *The Reformation Parliament*, p. 128–29; G.R. Elton, "More and the Opposition to Henry VIII," pp. 129–56.

14. *Sp. Cal.* 4(2): 171–72, 177. Catherine was justified in her accusation, for one of the major purposes of the visit was to coerce the queen into confessing that her marriage to Arthur had been consummated—an admission that would have simplified Henry's case considerably. Since Norfolk and Suffolk had both testified earlier that they had been present during the days following the marriage and had heard Arthur brag of having known Catherine carnally, they were hardly disinterested parties. See Kelly, *Matrimonial Trials*, pp. 190–92, and Herbert, *Henry the Eighth*, pp. 243–44.

15. Chapuys to Charles V, 24 June and 17 July 1531, *Sp. Cal.* 4(2): 199, 213. Norfolk and other English political leaders were commonly given pensions by foreign rulers in connection with treaties. Just which such pension Chapuys had in mind is not clear, although between 1522 and at least December 1529 Norfolk had been paid one thousand ducats as Charles's captain general of English forces on land and sea. See *Sp. Cal.* 4(1): 355.

16. *LP* 5: 390, 432, 536, 683. Rhys's act of attainder is 23 Hen. VIII, c.34; he was eventually executed.

17. Ibid., 564.

18. Ibid., 599.

19. Ibid., 805; Lehmberg, *Reformation Parliament*, p. 134, where unpublished Chapuys manuscripts are cited for these incidents. Darcy was friendly to Chapuys throughout this period, to the extent of a possibly treasonous correspondence during the Pilgrimage of Grace; he was probably Chapuys's source for this report and for other inside information which makes Chapuys's correspondence an extremely

valuable source for the period, even considering his obvious biases. See also Guy, *Thomas More*, p. 181.

20. *Ven. Cal.* 4: 726, 733, 744.

21. *LP* 5: 824.

22. *S.P. Hen. VIII*, 7: 349–50.

23. *Sp. Cal.* 4(2): 377–78.

24. Ibid., pp. 391, 411–12; *LP* 5: 869.

25. *LP* 5: 283.

26. *LP* 4: 4835, 4912, 5952, 6803; 5: 166 (12); *Ven. Cal.* 4: 761. See also Gunn, *Charles Brandon*, pp. 123–27.

27. PRO SP 1/70/186 (cited in Gunn, *Charles Brandon*, p. 125, n. 78); *Ven. Cal.* 4: 761; *LP* 5: 1193 (11); *DNB*, s.v. "Sir Richard Southwell." Southwell and seven others were eventually given statutory confirmation of their pardons for Pennington's murder. See *Statutes of the Realm*, 3: 489 (25 Hen. VIII, c. 32).

28. On this view of Henry's dilemma, see especially Franklin L. Baumer, *The Early Tudor Theory of Kingship* (New Haven: Yale University Press, 1940), p. 26; see also Scarisbrick, *Henry VIII*, pp. 250–81.

29. Lehmberg, *Reformation Parliament*, pp. 132–33; Guy, *Thomas More*, p. 145; Redworth, *Stephen Gardiner*, pp. 40–41.

30. Lehmberg, *Reformation Parliament*, p. 137.

31. *S.P. Hen. VIII*, 7: 349–50. The act is 23 Hen. VIII, c. 20.

32. *Sp. Cal.* 4(2): 417.

33. Guy, *Thomas More*, pp. 116ff.

34. Scarisbrick, *Henry VIII*, pp. 297–98; Hall, *Henry VIII*, 2: 209.

35. *LP* 5: 1013.

36. Michael Kelly, "The Submission of the Clergy," *TRHS* 5th ser., 15 (1965): 115; Guy, *Thomas More*, pp. 185–93. Redworth, *Stephen Gardiner*, p. 51, argues that Gardiner's foot-dragging over the Supplication in Convocation, despite his eventual acquiescence, allowed Cranmer to outstrip him as the rising Henrician church leader, winning Cranmer the see of Canterbury which might have been Gardiner's. Winchester never hid his bitterness very well, and Henry took due note: "In Henry's mind, too, a doubt had been set over Gardiner's loyalty." If this interpretation is correct, Gardiner's career was early doomed to frustration.

37. Chapuys to Charles V, 22 May 1532, *Sp. Cal.* 4(2): 447.

38. *LP* 5: 1059.

39. Roper, *Life of Sir Thomas More*, p. 225. Roper, pp. 49–50, recounts a story that, if true, tells a great deal about More and Norfolk's relationship. Norfolk "coming upon a time to Chelsea to dine with him, fortuned to find him at the Church, in the choir, with a surplice on his back, singing. To whom, after the

service, as they went homeward together arm in arm, the Duke said, 'Godsbody! Godsbody! My Lord Chancellor a parish clerk—a parish clerk! You do dishonor the King and his office!'

"'Nay,' quoth Sir Thomas More, smiling on the Duke: 'Your Grace may not think that the King, your master and mine, will be with me for serving of God his master offended, or thereby account his office dishonored!'" Norfolk held More in affection, but it is unlikely that he ever understood More's religious devotion.

40. *LP* 5: 1075; Rymer, *Foedera*, 14: 433–34; Elton, "More and the Opposition to Henry VIII," pp. 129–56.

41. Recent work has stressed the resignation of More as a decisive turning point. Guy, *Thomas More*, p. 201, argues that now, "directed by Cromwell, the radical group had won the factional battle for control," while Elton, *Reform and Reformation*, p. 156, says almost the same: "Guided by Cromwell, the radical faction had won; the day, and the next eight years, were theirs and his."

42. *Sp. Cal.* 4(2): 475–77; *LP* 5: 1165, 1306.

43. *LP* 5: 1187, 1294, 1308ff.; *Sp. Cal.* 4(2): 494–96, 506–7; Scarisbrick, *Henry VIII*, pp. 305–6. Norfolk had a considerable hand in papal politics as well, exchanging a long series of letters with Benet; see *S.P. Hen. VIII*, 7: 379–86, and *LP* 5: 1379, 1431.

44. *LP* 5: 1373, 1484–85; Hall, *Henry VIII*, 2: 213–14; "The Manner of the Triumph at Calais, 1532," in *An English Garner: Tudor Tracts, 1532–1588*, ed. Thomas Seccombe (Westminster: Archibald Constable, 1903), pp. 4–8.

45. Scarisbrick, *Henry VIII*, pp. 307–9.

46. *LP* 5: 1274 (3,4), 1292.

47. Scarisbrick, *Henry VIII*, p. 309; Kelly, *Matrimonial Trials*, pp. 195–96. Redworth, *Stephen Gardiner*, pp. 48–49, argues that Henry had not decided to break with Rome at this point. Even while in dispute with the pope, Henry always thought himself a true Catholic and maintained an essentially orthodox theology throughout his reign.

48. See, for example, *Sp. Cal.* 4(2): 580–84; *LP* 6: 110, 111, 159.

49. DuBellay to Francis I, 26 February 1533, *LP* 6: 184.

50. *LP* 6: 390, 392; Scarisbrick, *Henry VIII*, pp. 310–11.

51. *Sp. Cal.* 4(2): 625.

52. Lehmberg, *Reformation Parliament*, pp. 163–75. The act is 24 Hen. VIII, c. 12.

53. *Sp. Cal.* 4(2): 642; Scarisbrick, *Henry VIII*, p. 312.

54. *LP* 6: 495, 525, 529.

55. *Sp. Cal.* 4(2): 691–700.

56. *LP* 6: 444, 454; *S.P. Hen. VIII*, 7: 455–56.

57. *LP* 6: 502, 542.

58. Ibid., 476, 555, 558, 641.

59. Ibid., 721.

60. Ibid., 642, 669, 687, 774, 807, 811, 891; Scarisbrick, *Henry VIII*, p. 318. Anthony Browne wrote to Cromwell of a strange omen that preceded Norfolk's arrival in Lyons. A tree under which Norfolk and his party had lunched was struck by lightning a half hour later, killing one of Francis's archers. One wonders if this was interpreted as God's judgment on English diplomacy! See *LP* 6: 891.

61. Henry VIII to Norfolk and others, 8 August 1533, *LP* 6: 954.

62. *LP* 6: 996, 1030, 1038, 1070. Norfolk passed through Calais in such haste that he hardly paused, having written ahead to Lord Lisle to arrange for a boat. The whole trip, from Montpellier (just west of Marseilles) to Calais and then to London, took eight days, which must have been near-record time for a sixty-year-old man on horseback. See *The Lisle Letters*, ed. Muriel St. Clair Byrne, 6 vols. (Chicago and London: University of Chicago Press, 1981), 1: 550–52 and letters 45, 45a.

63. *LP* 6: 1042, 1078, 1426, 1427; *Ven. Cal.* 4: 977; Scarisbrick, *Henry VIII*, pp. 318–20; Redworth, *Stephen Gardiner*, pp. 55–56. Gardiner's confrontation with Francis ruined his credit with the French and, Redworth argues, drove him to a pro-imperial diplomatic stance for the rest of the reign. Given Norfolk's generally pro-French politics in the 1530s and 1540s, this diplomatic difference drove a further wedge between Gardiner and Norfolk, undermining the strength of the conservatives later in the reign. One wonders also how much personalities had to do with the lack of warmth between Norfolk and Winchester. Neither was an easygoing man, and they seem to have shared a certain prickliness that brought them few real friends.

64. Hall, *Henry VIII*, 2: 242–43; *LP* 6: 1089, 1111.

65. *LP* 6: 1479; Scarisbrick, *Henry VIII*, pp. 318–21.

66. *Sp. Cal.* 4(2): 794, 875–76.

67. Ibid., 881–82; *LP* 6: 1542.

68. *LP* 7: 111.

69. Ibid., 6: 1550; 7: 86, 87.

70. Ibid., 7: 296. This report may have been wishful thinking on Chapuys's part, since he tended to see Catholic conspiracies behind every turn of English politics.

71. Lehmberg, *Reformation Parliament*, pp. 258–59. Only ten of forty-four peers summoned were present more often.

72. Ibid., pp. 190–99; *Statutes of the Realm*, 3: 460–74, 484–86.

73. *LP* 7: 232, 391; *Journals of the House of Lords, Beginning Anno Primo Henrici Octavi*, vol. 1 (London, 1808), p. 82.

74. See on this Elton, *Reform and Reformation*, pp. 180–87, 250–72. Warnicke,

Anne Boleyn, dismisses the concept of an "Aragonese" faction as a result of taking Chapuys's reports too much at face value.

75. Lehmberg, *The Reformation Parliament*, p. 195; Scarisbrick, *Henry VIII*, pp. 321–23; Redworth, *Stephen Gardiner*, pp. 58–59.

76. *LP* 8: 474; Roper, *Life of Sir Thomas More*, p. 237.

77. Scarisbrick, *Henry VIII*, p. 334; see also Roland Bayne, ed., *The Life of Fisher*, The Early English Text Society Extra Series, 117 (London: Oxford University Press, 1921), pp. 114–19, 126.

78. *LP* 7: 962, 1029; Hall, *Henry VIII*, 2: 261; Penry Williams, *The Tudor Regime* (Oxford: Clarendon Press, 1979), pp. 381–82.

79. *LP* 7: 1003; G. R. Elton, *Star Chamber Stories* (London: Methuen and Co., 1958), pp. 52–77, deals with this dispute in detail.

80. *LP* 7: 1031; Rymer, *Foedera*, 14: 529–37, 540–43. Audley, Cromwell and Edward Fox, the king's almoner, led the English commission.

81. *Sp. Cal.* 5(1): 254.

82. Ibid., 279; *LP* 7: 1255; *S.P. Hen. VIII*, 7: 573. The Roman report was from Norfolk's old confidant Gregory Casale.

83. *LP* 7: 1416, 1427.

84. Knecht, *Francis I*, pp. 234–35.

85. *Sp. Cal.* 5(1): 355.

86. *LP* 8: 263.

87. Ibid., 341, 342.

88. Ibid., 666, 673; *Sp. Cal.* 5(1): 453.

89. *LP* 8: 793.

90. *S.P. Hen.VIII*, 7: 608–615.

91. *LP* 8: 876.

92. Chapuys to Charles V, 5 June 1535, *LP* 8: 826. Warnicke, *Anne Boleyn*, pp. 101–7 and 135, argues that no alliance between Anne and Cromwell ever existed and that Chapuys's version of events was often born of wishful thinking or spite.

93. *S.P. Hen. VIII*, 2: 276–78.

94. *LP* 9: 398, 420.

95. Ibid., 156; Lehmberg, *Reformation Parliament*, p. 217.

96. *LP* 10: 282; *Sp. Cal.* 5(2): 67; Scarisbrick, *Henry VIII*, p. 348.

97. *LP* 10: 351, 494, 575.

98. Ibid., 410.

99. E. W. Ives, "Faction at the Court of Henry VIII: The Fall of Anne Boleyn," *History* 57 (1972): 169–88, has been supplanted by his much more detailed account in *Anne Boleyn*, pp. 335–82. In line with Elton's account in *Reform and Reformation*, pp. 250–56, Ives has come to emphasize the role of faction, and Cromwell's adroit manipulation of the battle to cement his own position while simultaneously

Notes to Pages 127–131

crushing two sets of rivals—the progressive Boleyn and the conservative Aragonese factions. Ives also ties diplomacy into the affair, arguing that Cromwell's desire to ally with Charles V played a major role in the destruction of the pro-French Boleyns, while also requiring the disarming of the Aragonese group. Warnicke, *Anne Boleyn*, pp. 75–76, 189–90 and 207, discounts the role of faction, accusing Elton and Ives of taking the ambassadorial reports too much at face value. Anne, Warnicke says, was firmly in Henry's good graces throughout 1533–35; only her miscarriage, with all the doubts it raised about her fitness as a Tudor broodmare, turned Henry against her.

100. *Sp. Cal.* 5(2): 108; Ives, *Anne Boleyn*, pp. 358–61.

101. Ives, "Fall of Anne Boleyn," pp. 176, 182; *Sp. Cal.* 5(2): 81–85.

102. Ives, *Anne Boleyn*, pp. 347–49.

103. *Sp. Cal.* 5(2): 106.

104. Ives, "Fall of Anne Boleyn," p. 170; Elton, *Reform and Reformation*, p. 253.

105. Ives, "Fall of Anne Boleyn," p. 170; idem, *Anne Boleyn*, pp. 365–76. Warnicke, *Anne Boleyn*, pp. 191–94, disagrees, arguing that those who died with Anne were not victims of Cromwell's purge of the privy chamber but died as a result of their reputations as sexual libertines and perhaps even homosexuals. Henry's horror of sexual irregularity, and not Cromwell's political vendetta, led to the choice of victims.

106. See Gilbert Burnet, *The History of the Reformation of the Church of England*, revised with a preface by E. Nares, 3 vols. (New York, 1843), 1: 320.

107. *LP* 10: 848; Ives, "Fall of Anne Boleyn," pp. 170–71. Smeaton alone pled guilty (and only to adultery), but had been "grevously racked."

108. *LP* 10: 876; Ives, "Fall of Anne Boleyn," pp. 171–72; idem, *Anne Boleyn*, pp. 367–70.

109. Scarisbrick, p. 349; Ives, "Fall of Anne Boleyn," p. 179; *LP* 10: 792, 915.

110. *LP* 10: 1000; Elton, *Reform and Reformation*, pp. 253–54.

111. *LP* 10: 816; Stanford E. Lehmberg, *The Later Parliaments of Henry VIII, 1536–1547* (Cambridge: Cambridge University Press, 1977), p. 4.

112. See, for example, *LP* 10: 1069, 1212; 11: 7, 8, 40; *Sp. Cal.* 5(2): 190.

CHAPTER 6   The Pilgrimage of Grace, 1536–1537

1. Elton, *Reform and Reformation*, pp. 253–54. For Norfolk as courtier and councilor, see *LP* 10: 1069, 1212; 11: 7, 8, 40; *Sp. Cal.* 5(2): 190. For the duke in Parliament, see *Journals of the House of Lords*, pp. 84ff.

2. *LP* 10: 1021; Elton, *Reform and Reformation*, p. 254; Lehmberg, *Later Parliaments*, pp. 20–25. The act is 28 Hen. VIII, c. 7.

3. I avoid the terms "Protestant" or "radical" to describe Cromwell and Cranmer's party; both are rather misleading in the context of English politics and society in the 1530s. "Progressive" more adequately embraces the religious and political aspirations of this group, which was reformist in a broad sense. G. R. Elton regards Cromwell as a social and political reformer of sweeping vision, a view argued at length in *Policy and Police: The Enforcement of the Reformation in the Age of Thomas Cromwell* (Cambridge: Cambridge University Press, 1972) and *Reform and Renewal: Thomas Cromwell and the Commonweal* (Cambridge: Cambridge University Press, 1973). I do not believe that Henry VIII, despite his vacillations, was ever close to adopting a continental Protestant program for the English church. "Radicals" there had been in the early 1530s, pushing the *Collectanea satis copiosa*, but practical Henrician politics were never radical in any modern sense. Thus "progressive" and "conservative" serve as useful descriptive terms, suggestive of the political polarity of the later part of Henry's reign.

4. For details, see David M. Head, "'Beyng Ledde and Seduced by the Devyll': The Attainder of Lord Thomas Howard and the Tudor Law of Treason," *Sixteenth Century Journal* 13 (1982), 1–16.

5. Casady, *Henry Howard*, pp. 48–49, 56–57.

6. *LP* 11: 40, 228.

7. Ibid., 233, 236, 404, 434.

8. Dom David Knowles, *The Religious Orders in England, Volume 3: Henry VIII, The Tudor Age* (Cambridge: Cambridge University Press, 1959), pp. 291–93.

9. *LP* 10: 601.

10. C. S. L. Davies, "The Pilgrimage of Grace Reconsidered," *Past and Present* 41 (1968): 54–76; see also Christopher Haigh, *The Last Days of the Lancashire Monasteries and the Pilgrimage of Grace* (Manchester: Chetham Society, 1969), pp. 50ff; Reid, *King's Council in the North*, pp. 121–25; Knowles, *The Religious Orders in England*, 3: 320–28; J. J. Scarisbrick, *The Reformation and the English People* (Oxford: Basil Blackwell, 1984), p. 82 and FN 38; Bernard, *Early Tudor Nobility*, pp. 30–58.

11. B. W. Beckingsale, "The Characteristics of the Tudor North," *Northern History* 4 (1969): 67; Davies, "Pilgrimage of Grace Reconsidered," p. 71. East Anglia was a potential trouble spot in 1536; like Yorkshire and Lincolnshire, Norfolk had a large concentration of monastic houses and more than a little economic unrest. See Alexander Savine, *English Monasteries on the Eve of the Dissolution* (Oxford: Clarendon Press, 1909), pp. 276–79, 285–87.

12. Christopher Haigh, *Reform and Resistance in Tudor Lancashire* (Cambridge: Cambridge University Press, 1975), pp. 105–6.

13. Garrett Mattingly, *Catherine of Aragon* (Boston: Houghton Mifflin Co., 1941), pp. 285–87; Reid, *King's Council in the North*, pp. 133, 137–38. Darcy (1467–1537) was a statesman, warrior and councilor under Henry VII and Henry VIII alike.

Married to a Neville, he was a social and religious conservative of considerable influence in the north.

14. M. E. James, "Obedience and Dissent in Henrician England: The Lincolnshire Rebellion, 1536," *Past and Present* 48 (1970): 14, 38–45.

15. Reid, *King's Council in the North*, pp. 130–35, 137.

16. M. H. and Ruth Dodds, *The Pilgrimage of Grace 1536–1537 and the Exeter Conspiracy 1538*, 2 vols. (Cambridge: Cambridge University Press, 1915), 1: 14–26 and ff.

17. Elton, *Reform and Reformation*, pp. 246–70. See also Elton, *Reform and Renewal*, passim; and Elton, "Politics and the Pilgrimage of Grace," in Barbara C. Malament, ed., *After the Reformation: Essays in Honor of J. H. Hexter* (Philadelphia: University of Pennsylvania Press, 1980), pp. 25–56. Williams, *The Tudor Regime*, pp. 316–24, provides an excellent survey of the scholarship of the Pilgrimage of Grace.

18. R. B. Smith, *Land and Politics in the England of Henry VIII: The West Riding of Yorkshire, 1530–46* (Oxford: Clarendon Press, 1970), pp. 166–67, 175. Not all of the northern barons rose in support of the rebellion; it is more than coincidence that the trouble was centered in areas of influence of lords later implicated in the risings, such as Darcy and Westmorland, while lands of loyal lords such as Derby and Shrewsbury remained quiet. R. B. Smith has noted that once Derby (a son-in-law of Norfolk) "had decided to oppose the rebels, he found it easy enough to raise a force against them." In fact south Lancashire, where Derby held sway, did not rise at all. Only around Blackburn, where Darcy's friend Sir Richard Tempest was steward, was there trouble. All of this supports the suspicion that the northern risings were far from spontaneous.

On Shrewsbury's role in suppressing the risings, see Bernard, *Early Tudor Nobility*, pp. 30–58, where he argues that Shrewsbury played a decisive role through his "immediate and unhesitating" loyalty at a time when many expected the Pilgrimage to widen into a general rebellion of conservative aristocrats against the crown. Bernard also suggests that Shrewbury's early show of loyalty helped convince Norfolk to take the king's side; had Talbot gone the other way, Howard might have as well.

19. Knowles, *The Religious Orders in England*, 3: 322–23; Haigh, *Lancashire Monasteries and the Pilgrimage of Grace*, pp. 61–66. See also *LP* 11: 701, and James, "Obedience and Dissent," pp. 1–14.

20. Helen Miller, *Henry VIII and the English Nobility* (Oxford: Basil Blackwell, 1986), pp. 150–51; *Span. Cal.* 5(2): 268–69; *LP* 11: 601.

21. *Sp. Cal.* 5(2): 268–69. Elton, "Politics and the Pilgrimage of Grace," pp. 49–51, argues that at least Darcy among the northern leaders was pushed into rebellion because of the eclipse of his Aragonese party at court; his purpose was not re-

bellion, but "to procure a reversal of policy by persuading the king that a change of ministers would lead to loyal peace." Bernard, *Early Tudor Nobility*, pp. 34–39, suggests that Darcy was a conservative who sympathized with the rebels' aims for largely religious reasons: in October, Darcy's son Sir Arthur told Shrewsbury that "yff abbays myght stond my lord his father myght make to serve the kynges hyghnes v thouzande mene." (PRO SP 1/117/191).

22. *Sp. Cal.* 5(2): 269.

23. *LP* 11: 601–3, 625–26, 701, 727; Miller, *English Nobility*, p. 151.

24. Knowles, *The Religious Orders in England*, 3: 321–23; Haigh, *Lancashire Monasteries and the Pilgrimage of Grace*, p. 58; Bernard, *Early Tudor Nobility*, pp. 36–40. An original badge appears in a color plate in Robinson, *The Dukes of Norfolk*, opposite p. 48.

25. On Norfolk's arrangements for men and supplies, see *LP* 11: 601, 625, 642, 659, 660, 671, 738, 754, 755. Typically, Norfolk was concerned about funds; even before starting the campaign he was seeking an additional £10,000 to £20,000 to finance the expedition.

26. *LP* 11: 752, 771, 778, 793, 799, 800, 816; *S.P. Hen. VIII*, 1: 473–78; Scarisbrick, *Henry VIII*, pp. 342–43. As late as 21 October, Sir William Paulet and Sir William Kingston wrote to Cromwell, expecting the rebels to disperse at the sight of Norfolk, as much out of fear as loyalty. See *LP* 11: 824.

27. *LP* 11: 846. Bernard, *Early Tudor Nobility*, pp. 41–43, argues that, far from moving too fast and almost denying Norfolk a chance at martial glory, Shrewsbury may have saved Henry's throne by his decisive action in confronting Aske and the rebels.

28. Norfolk's holograph letter of 25 October is PRO SP 1/109/96 (*LP* 11: 864), printed in Dodds and Dodds, *Pilgrimage of Grace*, 1: 259–60. See also Reid, *King's Council in the North*, pp. 137–39.

29. *S.P. Hen. VIII*, 1: 493–95.

30. Ibid., 495–96.

31. Reid, *King's Council in the North*, p. 140.

32. *S.P. Hen. VIII*, 1: 496–97; *LP* 11: 909; Davies, "Pilgrimage of Grace Reconsidered," p. 73.

33. *LP* 11: 909, 921, 995.

34. Ibid., 995, 1009, 1014.

35. PRO SP 1/111/67–71 (*LP* 11: 1045). Norfolk probably did not need the evidence of this exchange of letters to be assured of Darcy's guilt; in a letter of 29 October, Norfolk had exclaimed bitterly "fie, fie on the traitor Darcy!" See *LP* 11: 909.

36. *S.P. Hen. VIII*, 1: 498–505. The choice of Fitzwilliam—a Cromwell man—to accompany Norfolk surely was not a coincidence.

37. Ibid., 466–67.
38. Ibid., 506–510.
39. *LP* 11: 1115.
40. Ibid., 1120, 1126, 1138, 1167.
41. Norfolk's letters apparently did not survive and are not printed in *LP* or *S.P. Hen. VIII*, but their tenor is clear from Henry's reply on 2 December, which is *S.P. Hen. VIII*, 1: 518–19, and the new instructions, pp. 511–18.
42. Scarisbrick, *Henry VIII*, pp. 344–45.
43. *LP* 11: 1276, 1311. Norfolk was to be paid £3,000 a year, with wages for a personal retinue of 200 soldiers. See *LP* 11: 1363, 1410, and Reid, *King's Council in the North*, pp. 147–48.
44. *LP* 12 (1): 32, 43; *S.P. Hen. VIII*, 1: 523–24; Arthur G. Dickens, *Lollards and Protestants in the Diocese of York* (Oxford: Clarendon Press, 1959), pp. 92–106.
45. *LP* 12 (1): 98, 99, 100, 101, 148, 252. Norfolk's original instructions called for him to tour the area beyond Trent to administer an oath of loyalty and to supervise grand juries to indict those rebels who remained defiant. This provision was the basis for most of the subsequent trials and executions under Norfolk's lieutenancy.
46. *LP* 12 (1): 292, 293, 319, 320, 321; Davies, "Pilgrimage of Grace Reconsidered," pp. 55, 59.
47. *LP* 12 (1): 401, 416, 419, 426, 448, 468, 498; M. E. James, "The First Earl of Cumberland and the Decline of Northern Feudalism," *Northern History* 1 (1966): 55, 68. Scott M. Harrison, *The Pilgrimage of Grace in the Lake Counties, 1536–7* (London: Royal Historical Society, 1981), esp. pp. 71–79 and 124–25, has recently argued for a primarily religious basis for the risings in the Lake Counties, although noting economic grievances as well. Norfolk himself thought the Carlisle rising was provoked by economic causes, noting "they [the rebels] have been so sore handled in past time, which as I and all here think was the only cause of this rebellion." (*LP* 12[1]: 478.)
48. *LP* 12(1): 609.
49. Ibid., 594, 698, 710, 712, 1156. Not all of the proceedings went smoothly. On 23 March a York jury refused to convict one William Levenyng of complicity in Bigod's rebellion. Many of the jurymen were friends of Levenyng's who refused to be cowed by Norfolk's demand for a favorable verdict; see ibid., 731.
50. Ibid., 846–63. See also "The Pilgrimage of Grace" (Notes and Documents), *English Historical Review* 5 (1890): 330–45, for Aske's examination. For the executions, see *LP* 12(2): 41, 156, 166, 203, 229, 261.
51. Elton, *Reform and Reformation*, p. 262.
52. Haigh, *Lancashire Monasteries and the Pilgrimage of Grace*, pp. 86–101; *S.P. Hen. VIII*, 1: 537–40.

53. *LP* 12(1): 416, 546, 777, 1023, 1035, 1172, 1257; 12(2): 35; *S.P. Hen. VIII*, 5: 78. See also Joyce Youings, *The Dissolution of the Monasteries* (London: George Allen and Unwin, 1971), pp. 54–55.

54. *LP* 12(1): 777, 809, 810. Norfolk continued to complain of ill health well into the summer, all the while requesting recall. See *S.P. Hen. VIII*, 5: 91–93, 96–98.

55. *LP* 12(1): 846, 863.

56. Slavin, *Politics and Profit*, pp. 68ff.

57. This incident is detailed in *Lisle Letters*, 4: 340–42; see also *LP* 12 (1): 1286; 12(2): 291, 431, 479, 732.

58. *LP* 12(1): 804, 968, 1029, 1058; *S.P. Hen. VIII*, 5: 68–69; *The Hamilton Papers: Letters and Papers Illustrating the Political Relations of England and Scotland in the XVIth Century*, ed. Joseph Bain, vol. 1, 1532–43 (Edinburgh, 1890): 40.

59. *LP* 12(2): 430; *S.P. Hen. VIII*, 5: 99–101, 104–6.

60. *S.P. Hen. VIII*, 1: 549–50; Reid, *King's Council in the North*, pp. 150–51.

61. *S.P. Hen. VIII*, 5: 91–93.

62. Ibid., 1: 551–55; *LP* 12 (2): 100, 238; Reid, *King's Council in the North*, p. 151.

63. *S.P. Hen. VIII*, 5: 101–11; 1: 565–68.

64. *LP* 12(2): 850, 916; *S.P. Hen. VIII*, 5: 116–19.

65. *VCH Middlesex*, 2: 336; *LP* 12(2): 911, 923, 939.

66. *LP* 12(2): 1049, 1060.

67. *LP* 13(1): 1, 5, 24.

68. Ibid., 504.

69. Ibid., 593, 671, 995.

CHAPTER 7   Norfolk and Cromwell, 1538–1540

1. *LP* 12(2): 1004.

2. Henry VIII to Sir Thomas Wyatt, 10 October 1537, ibid., 869.

3. Scarisbrick, *Henry VIII*, pp. 355–59; *LP* 13(1): 995, 1101, 1102.

4. Scarisbrick, *Henry VIII*, pp. 359–60; *LP* 13(2): 277.

5. *LP* 13(1): 1135, 1147, 1375.

6. Scarisbrick, *Henry VIII*, p. 361; *LP* 13(2): 6.

7. *S.P. Hen. VIII*, 1: 577; see also Casady, *Henry Howard*, pp. 67–68.

8. *S.P. Hen. VIII*, 1: 576–78; *LP* 13(1): 78; Casady, *Henry Howard*, pp. 60–61, 68.

9. Casady, *Henry Howard*, pp. 57, 84; Elton, *Policy and Police*, p. 69.

10. BL Cott. Cleo. E iv, f. 122 (Norfolk and others to Cromwell, 4 August 1538); *LP* 13(2): 34; Elton, *Policy and Police*, p. 342.

11. *LP* 13(2): 306, Audley to Cromwell, 8 September 1538.

12. *LP* 13(2): 386, 554.

13. Scarisbrick, *Henry VIII*, pp. 363–65; Elton, *Reform and Reformation*, pp. 279–80. For the investigations of the Poles, see *LP* 13(2): 232, 695, 702, 743, 754, 755, 765, 766, 771, 772, 779, 796, 800–5, 817–31. For Gardiner's escape, see Redworth, *Stephen Gardiner*, pp. 86–87.

14. *LP* 13(2): 968, 979, 986; Scarisbrick, *Henry VIII*, pp. 364–65; L. B. Smith, "English Treason Trials and Confessions in the Sixteenth Century," *Journal of the History of Ideas* 15 (1954): 473–75.

15. See Ives, "Fall of Anne Boleyn," pp. 168–69, and G. R. Elton, "Tudor Government, The Points of Contact, III. The Court," *TRHS*, 5th series, 26 (1976): 211–28, and Elton, *Reform and Reformation*, pp. 280–81.

16. *LP* 14(1): 21, 23, 30, 1011; Scarisbrick, *Henry VIII*, p. 361.

17. *LP* 14(1): 36, 62; Scarisbrick, *Henry VIII*, p. 362.

18. *LP* 14(1): 398.

19. Ibid., 625, 697, 674, 731; *Hamilton Papers*, 1: 52.

20. *LP* 14(1): 651 (29, 31, 57); G. R. Elton, "Thomas Cromwell's Decline and Fall," *Cambridge Historical Journal* 10 (1951): 156.

21. *LP* 14(1): 764, 907.

22. Elton, "Cromwell's Decline and Fall," pp. 162–63; Lehmberg, *Later Parliaments*, p. 43.

23. Elton, *Reform and Reformation*, pp. 278–79, 283–84.

24. Ibid., pp. 283–84; Lehmberg, *Later Parliaments*, pp. 55–57; see also Glyn Redworth, "A Study in the Formulation of Policy: The Genesis and Evolution of the Act of Six Articles," *Journal of Ecclesiastical History* 37 (1986): 42–67.

25. L. B. Smith, *Tudor Prelates and Politics, 1536–1558* (Princeton: Princeton University Press, 1953), pp. 189–91. Philip Hughes, *The Reformation in England*, revised edition, three volumes in one (New York: Macmillan and Co., 1963), 1: 349–52, gives a good summary of the content of the Ten Articles.

26. Smith, *Tudor Prelates and Politics*, pp. 193–98. The instability of the religious settlement is demonstrated in Elton, *Policy and Police*, esp. pp. 1–45, which catalogues prosecutions for religious offenses by both Protestants and Catholics against the Henrician church. See also Scarisbrick, *Henry VIII*, pp. 384–423, for an excellent discussion of the royal supremacy and theology that underlies much of what follows here.

27. Elton, "Cromwell's Decline and Fall," pp. 165–67; Redworth, "Six Articles," pp. 49–53.

28. *Journals of the House of Lords*, 1: 105; Elton, "Cromwell's Decline and Fall," p. 165.

29. *Journals of the House of Lords*, 1: 109 (Latin text; my translation).

30. *LP* 14(2): 186, 379, 423; Elton, "Cromwell's Decline and Fall," p. 166. For

Gardiner's role behind the "whip with six strings" see James A. Muller, *Stephen Gardiner and the Tudor Reaction* (New York: Macmillan and Co., 1926), p. 81 and notes, and Redworth, *Stephen Gardiner*, pp. 96ff.

31. Elton, *Reform and Reformation*, p. 287; Lehmberg, *Later Parliaments*, pp. 65–66. Cranmer may have been particularly unsettled by the mention of clerical marriage, for he had been married before becoming archbishop and knew that the king knew it. See Burnet, *History of the Reformation*, 1: 412–13.

32. *Journals of the House of Lords*, 1: 111; LP 14(1): 1065; Elton, "Cromwell's Decline and Fall," pp. 166–67; Redworth, "Six Articles," pp. 58–59.

33. LP 14(1): 1219; Elton, "Cromwell's Decline and Fall," pp. 167–68; *Journals of the House of Lords*, 1: 126–27; Lehmberg, *Later Parliaments*, pp. 69–71; Elton, *Reform and Reformation*, p. 288.

34. Burnet, *History of the Reformation*, 1: 426–27.

35. Scarisbrick, *Henry VIII*, pp. 367–69.

36. Marillac to Montmorency, 1 September 1539, LP 14(2): 118.

37. Scarisbrick, *Henry VIII*, pp. 369–71, 374–75; Elton, *Reform and Reformation*, p. 289. See LP 14(2): 127, 222, 286, for the negotiations with Cleves and the marital treaty.

38. LP 14(2): 572; 15: 14, 22, 23, 822, 823; Scarisbrick, *Henry VIII*, pp. 370–71; Elton, "Cromwell's Decline and Fall," pp. 169–71.

39. *S.P. Hen. VIII*, 8: 265–68; Knecht, *Francis I*, pp. 289–99.

40. LP 15: 202; *S.P. Hen. VIII*, 8: 245–52.

41. *S.P. Hen. VIII*, 8: 254–58.

42. Ibid., 258–60.

43. Ibid., 254–58; LP 15: 224. See also Smith, *Tudor Prelates and Politics*, pp. 73–74, 96–97 and 141–44, for Bonner's background and beliefs. Bonner was a staunch conservative who supported Cromwell out of political expediency. He likely owed his consecration at London to Gardiner, whose lead he followed on religious matters.

44. *S.P. Hen. VIII*, 8: 265–69.

45. Ibid., 261–65.

46. Ibid., 275–76.

47. LP 15: 285, 289, 329.

48. Ibid., 370, 812; Elton, "Cromwell's Decline and Fall," p. 171; Redworth, *Stephen Gardiner*, pp. 107–15.

49. LP 15: 306, 312, 334, 411; Muller, *Gardiner and the Tudor Reaction*, pp. 79–89; Redworth, *Stephen Gardiner*, pp. 105–6, 118–19. Cromwell's fall, in Redworth's reading, grew out of Henry's unhappiness with the Cleves marriage, "his lust for Katherine Howard, and the fact that the Lutheran alliance, the policy for which Cromwell preeminently stood, had become a disposable commodity." Norfolk

and Gardiner were thus permitted to hound Cromwell to his death because Henry had lost faith in his minister; as with Wolsey, it was the king's choice to make and unmake ministers, and Henry was not, as Elton has portrayed him, a fool to be led around by the nose.

50. *LP* 15: 429; Elton, "Cromwell's Decline and Fall," pp. 172–73.

51. *LP* 15: 442.

52. Ibid., 500.

53. Slavin, *Politics and Profit*, pp. 46–50; Pollard, *Henry VIII*, p. 394. The best contemporary account of these events is in Charles Wriothesley, *A Chronicle of England During the Reigns of the Tudors, A.D. 1485 to 1559*, ed. William Douglas Hamilton, 2 vols. (London, 1875–77), 1: 115. No dated patents survive for Sadler and Wriothesley's appointments.

54. *LP* 15: 541; Elton, "Cromwell's Decline and Fall," p. 174.

55. *Journals of the House of Lords*, 1: 128–29, 137; Lehmberg, *Later Parliaments*, p. 92.

56. *LP* 15: 21, 613, 686; Smith, *Tudor Tragedy*, pp. 103, 117–18 and notes.

57. Elton, "Cromwell's Decline and Fall," p. 175. See also *LP* 15: 850, for an account of this conversation, which took place around 6 June. For Wriothesley's response, see Redworth, *Stephen Gardiner*, p. 122.

58. *LP* 15: 697, 733(64).

59. Ibid., 737, 758. Redworth, *Stephen Gardiner*, pp. 116–18, argues that Marillac got most of his information from Cromwell and seldom saw the king and that his reports therefore cannot be trusted. Redworth nevertheless has difficulty explaining the events surrounding Samson's consecration and arrest, and can say only that Henry remained the main agent of politics, with Gardiner "holding up a mirror to reflect the king's own theological self-image and political doubts."

60. *LP* 15: 766, 804; Elton, "Cromwell's Decline and Fall," p. 177.

61. Elton, "Cromwell's Decline and Fall," pp. 169, 177; Burnet, *History of the Reformation*, 1: 444; *S.P. Hen. VIII*, 8: 275–76.

62. Elton, "Cromwell's Decline and Fall," pp. 151, 176; Arthur G. Dickens, *The English Reformation* (New York: Schocken Books, 1964), pp. 172–73.

63. Lehmberg, *Later Parliaments*, p. 106.

64. Ibid., pp. 107–9; Elton, "Cromwell's Decline and Fall," pp. 177–81.

65. *LP* 15: 804, 824; Elton, "Cromwell's Decline and Fall," pp. 177–81; Scarisbrick, *Henry VIII*, pp. 379–80. Redworth, *Stephen Gardiner*, pp. 122–26, argues that heresy was *not* the main charge against Cromwell, but only an afterthought, pointing out that the first draft of Cromwell's attainder makes no mention of heresy. Redworth sees Cromwell's fall as Henry's doing, and the various charges against Essex as trumped up after the fact in order to justify a judicial murder Henry had already decided to carry out. Gardiner mainly served as a "legal lackey" in carrying

out Henry's will. It is an interesting argument, and, like much of what Redworth has to say, would be even more attractive if he had more compelling evidence.

66. Scarisbrick, *Henry VIII*, pp. 380–83; Elton, *Reform and Reformation*, p. 293.
67. *S.P. Hen. VIII*, 8: 349–50; *LP* 15: 770, 792, 793, 812.
68. *Journals of the House of Lords*, 1: 149; *LP* 15: 776, 821–24.
69. *LP* 15: 850, 851, 872; *Journals of the House of Lords*, 1: 153–54.
70. Elton, "Cromwell's Decline and Fall," p. 184.
71. Smith, *Tudor Tragedy*, pp. 123–25; *LP* 15: 902; Ellis, *Original Letters*, ser. 1, vol. 1, p. 202.
72. *LP* 15: 926.
73. Ibid., 966; Elton, *Tudor Revolution*, pp. 317ff. See also Williams, *The Tudor Regime*, pp. 423–24.
74. *LP* 15: 954.
75. Scarisbrick, *Henry VIII*, p. 426.

CHAPTER 8 Catherine Howard: From Triumph to Treason, 1540–1542

1. *LP* 14(2): 572; 15: 21; Smith, *Tudor Tragedy*, pp. 64–65.
2. Smith, *Tudor Tragedy*, pp. 37–45, and *DNB*, s.v.
3. Smith, *Tudor Tragedy*, pp. 22–23, 44. In an appendix, pp. 209–11, Smith examines the questions of Catherine's age and her place among her siblings. She may have been born as early as 1518 or as late as 1524. If she was, as Smith thinks, born around 1521, she was likely the eldest daughter of Edmund Howard and Joyce Culpeper, but this, too, is uncertain.
4. *LP* 15: 670, 719, 986, 987, 994, etc; 16: 2, 9, 32.
5. *LP* 16: 169, 198, 202, etc. This series of council meetings, through 7 January 1541, extends to no. 433.
6. Casady, *Henry Howard*, p. 84 and note.
7. *LP* 15: 942(44); 16: 503 (22), 780 (7).
8. For Wingfield (1485?–1552) and Gage (1479–1556), see *DNB*, s.v., and *LP* 15: 966; 16: 139, 751.
9. *LP* 16: 137; Elton, *Star Chamber Stories*, pp. 90–91.
10. *LP* 16: 146, 147. Neither Wingfield nor Gage was present.
11. *S.P. Hen. VIII*, 1: 650–52; Elton, *Star Chamber Stories*, pp. 91–92.
12. Slavin, *Politics and Profit*, pp. 137–39; Lehmberg, *Later Parliaments*, p. 102.
13. *LP* 16: 67, 77, 286; Elton, *Reform and Reformation*, pp. 208–10. The charges against Grey are printed in full in *S.P. Hen. VIII*, 3: 248–63. The factional focus of Grey's troubles is made clearer when it is noted that the new deputy sent to Ireland in July 1540 was Anthony St. Leger, formerly of Henry's privy chamber, who was a Howard client. On 16 November 1540, St. Leger sent his first report on Irish

affairs to Norfolk, explaining: "But the specially cawse, I wryte to Your Grace is, first, considering how miche I am bownd to love and sarve your bloode, with whom I have hadde my bringing up, and also for that I knowe no noble man in Ynglande hath such knowledge of the qualities of this land, and the people therof, as Your Grace." See *S.P. Hen. VIII*, 3: 267–68, and, for St. Leger, Peter J. Pireronus, "The Life and Career of Sir Anthony St. Leger of Ulcombe, Kent (1496?–1559), Lord Deputy of Ireland: A Biographical Study in the Evolution of Early Tudor Anglo-Irish Policy" (Ph.D. dissertation, Michigan State University, 1972).

14. *LP* 16: 363, 422, 423; Slavin, *Politics and Profit*, p. 140.

15. *LP* 16: 461, 466, 469; Slavin, *Politics and Profit*, pp. 141–44.

16. Muller, *Gardiner and the Tudor Reaction*, p. 95; *LP* 16: 503, 650.

17. Wingfield and Gage also went north with Henry. Comprehensive lists of council attendance and of the entourage accompanying the king appear throughout *LP* 16.

18. *LP* 15: 831 (52), 942 (81); 16: 678, 878, etc. See also Smith, *Tudor Tragedy*, pp. 155–56, 158, 161.

19. These events are discussed at considerable length in Smith, *Tudor Tragedy*.

20. *LP* 16: 1320, 1321, 1328; Smith, *Tudor Tragedy*, pp. 179–80.

21. Marillac to Francis I, 8 November 1541, *LP* 16: 1322.

22. Ibid., 1331.

23. *Calendar of the Manuscripts of the Marquis of bath Preserved at Longleat, Wiltshire*, 3 vols. (London: Historical Manuscript Commission, 1904–1908), 2: 8–9; Smith, *Tudor Tragedy*, p. 185.

24. *LP* 16: 1336, 1337, 1339. 1341, 1342.

25. Ibid., 1399; Smith, *Tudor Tragedy*, pp. 189–90.

26. *Sp. Cal.* 6(1): 465; *LP* 16: 1366; Smith, *Tudor Tragedy*, pp. 197–98.

27. *LP* 16: 1353, 1354, 1358, 1361, etc.; Slavin, *Politics and Profit*, pp. 147–48.

28. *LP* 16: 1369; Stanford E. Lehmberg, "Parliamentary Attainder in the Reign of Henry VIII," *Historical Journal* 18 (1975): 694–95.

29. *LP* 16: 1395, 1426; Wriothesley, *Chronicle During the Reigns of the Tudors*, 1: 131.

30. *Sp. Cal.* 6(1): 412; *LP* 16: 1426.

31. *LP* 16: 1409, 1413, 1414, 1416, 1422–25, 1430, 1432.

32. *S.P. Hen. VIII*, 1: 271.

33. *LP* 16: 1457, 1471. William Howard remained imprisoned until 1542; for his pardon, see *LP* 17: 714 (23).

34. *Sp. Cal.* 6(1): 452.

35. *LP* 17: 2, 34.

36. *Journals of the House of Lords*, 1: 165–76; Lehmberg, "Parliamentary Attainder," pp. 694–95. The finished act is 33 Hen. VIII, c. 21.

37. *LP* 17: 100, 106. Perhaps Norfolk was not so upset by his relatives' disgrace as might be expected. On 13 February Marillac reported that the duke hoped that his stepmother would not survive her imprisonment, for he stood to inherit her considerable lands should she succumb. Marillac went on to say that "the times are such that he [Norfolk] dare not show that the affair touches him, but he approves all that is done." See *LP* 17: 100.

38. Ives, "The Fall of Anne Boleyn," p. 180; Slavin, *Politics and Profit*, pp. 149–50; Ives, *Faction in Tudor England*, pp. 1–5, 26–29.

CHAPTER 9   The Last Years of Henry VIII, 1540–1547

1. Knecht, *Francis I*, pp. 295–300.
2. *LP* 15: 926; Elton, *Reform and Reformation*, p. 305.
3. *LP* 16: 238, 269.
4. Ibid., 449, 496, 497, 503 (52); *S.P. Hen. VIII*, 5: 184.
5. Gordon Donaldson, *Scotland: James V to James VII* (New York and Washington: Praeger, 1966), pp. 25–26; Slavin, *Politics and Profit*, pp. 96–97.
6. BL Cott. Cal. B vii, f. 228–29.
7. *LP* 16: 533, 632.
8. Ibid., 612, 613, 650. James commented that, concerning English subjects, "quha be trew or rebellis is misknawin." In December 1541 the Scots were still trying to secure several of the rebels requested in March; see *S.P.Hen. VIII* 5: 186 and *LP* 16: 1412.
9. *LP* 16: 650.
10. Ibid., 737, 769.
11. Ibid., 770.
12. Ibid., 733, 763, 769, 785; Scarisbrick, *Henry VIII*, p. 427.
13. *LP* 16: 850, 851, 903.
14. Ibid., 885, 922, 941; Scarisbrick, *Henry VIII*, p. 434.
15. *LP* 16: 905, 941, 973, 1074; Smith, *Tudor Tragedy*, p. 176.
16. *LP* 16: 1088.
17. Ibid., 1090.
18. Ibid., 1121, 1208; *S.P. Hen. VIII*, 1: 688.
19. *LP* 17: 34, 51, 84.
20. Ibid., 167.
21. Ibid., 143. See also Barrett L. Beer, *Northumberland: The Political Career of John Dudley, Earl of Warwick and Duke of Northumberland* (Kent, Ohio: Kent State University Press, 1973), p. 13; L. B. Smith, *Henry VIII: The Mask of Royalty* (London: Jonathan Cape, 1971), pp. 176–77.
22. *LP* 17: 145, 251; Elton, *Reform and Reformation*, p. 306.

23. *LP* 17: 235. A crown was worth about 5s. at this time, making Norfolk's assessment about £1,500 and the total to be collected £75,000. According to Marillac, Norfolk took the demand "very ill."
24. *LP* 17: 221, 227, 248, 251.
25. Ibid., 266, 293, 319, 320, 325, 329, 349, 361, 363, 386.
26. Ibid., 290, 392, 415; Smith, *The Mask of Royalty*, p. 176.
27. Wallop to Norfolk, 21 June 1542, *LP* 17: 423.
28. Scarisbrick, *Henry VIII*, p.428; Donaldson, *Scotland: James V to James VII*, p. 59.
29. *LP* 17: 439, 441, 446, 447.
30. Ibid., 540, 577, 586.
31. Ibid., 452, 542, 571.
32. Ibid., 601.
33. Smith, *The Mask of Royalty*, p. 181.
34. *LP* 17: 640. 660, 661, 710, 714; BL Add. Ms. 5754, f. 90, Norfolk, Sussex and Hertford to Sir George Lawson, 12 August [1542]. This volume also includes about two dozen pay warrants issued in the autumn of 1542 for the northern army; see ff. 4–26.
35. *LP* 17: 663, 673; Mackie, *The Earlier Tudors*, p. 405.
36. *LP* 17: 719; *Hamilton Papers*, 1: 129, 136. Citations to this collection are by document numbers. The original documents are in BL Add. Ms., 33,646, 33,647 and 33,648.
37. *Hamilton Papers*, 1: 140; *Sp. Cal.* 6(2): 124.
38. See Mackie, *The Earlier Tudors*, p. 405; Smith, *The Mask of Royalty*, p. 182, and C. S. L. Davies, *Peace, Print and Protestantism, 1450–1588* (St. Albans, Hertfordshire: Paladin, 1977), p. 214.
39. *LP* 17: 670, 671, 679, 700, 704, 709, 710, 730, 731; the two latter, Norfolk's letters to the council and to Sir Anthony Browne and Southampton, are printed in full in *Hamilton Papers*, 1: 143, 144.
40. *LP* 17: 714(23), 746.
41. *Hamilton Papers*, 1: 143, 150–54.
42. Ibid., 153, 161.
43. Ibid., 158, 163.
44. *LP* 17: 807, 809; *Hamilton Papers*, 1: 168.
45. *Hamilton Papers*, 1: 170, 171; *LP* 17: 813.
46. *LP* 17: 823.
47. Ibid., 824.
48. *Hamilton Papers*, 1: 178.
49. *LP* 17: 855, 865, 866.
50. *Hamilton Papers*, 1: 189.

51. *LP* 17: 836(2), 860; *Hamilton Papers*, 1: 190.

52. BL Add. Ms., 32,648, f. 8–9, Norfolk, Tunstall, Southampton and Browne to the council, York, 2 October 1542. "Costrelles" or costrels are small-eared jugs or kegs, perhaps 2–4-gallon, used to carry beer or other liquids; see *OED*.

53. BL Add. Ms., 32,648, f. 10, dated York, 2 October "at ij at afternoon."

54. BL Add. Ms., 32,648, f. 13–16. This is a draft of the finished dispatch of 4 October, which is summarized in *LP* 17: 903.

55. *LP* 17: 895.

56. BL Add. Ms., 32,648, f. 17–20. Another letter, Angus to Norfolk, 2 October 1542, was apparently enclosed in this one (and is bound as f. 21). Angus, writing from Berwick, assured Norfolk that dissention in the Scottish council would prevent the Scots from resisting an English invasion. Angus was partly right, but his advice seems to have been mistrusted, for the commissioners at York took pains to conceal the date of the pending assault from the Scottish envoys. These letters are summarized in *LP* 17: 906, 896.

57. BL Add. Ms., 32,648, f. 27.

58. *LP* 17: 919, 920; BL Add. Ms., 32,648, f. 44.

59. Southampton must have been near death on 12 October, for Norfolk noted in a letter that day that the lord privy seal was too weak to sign the letter to the privy council: "his hande did so tremble that he can not wright and is so ill that I feare hym to be in extreme danger." Three days later, Southampton was dead. See BL Add. Ms. 32,648, f. 44 (which indeed lacks Southampton's signature), f. 46, and *LP* 17: 950, 951. Norfolk protested that he had rather "have one of myne armys broken then to mys his company," but two weeks later he was begging Gardiner and Wriothesley to help him obtain Southampton's London house, Bath Place. See *LP* 17: 997.

60. *LP* 17: 953, 975.

61. Ibid., 933, 958, 969, 970. Among other things, Rutland, who had been at Berwick with 3,000 men for over a month, had fed his troops with Norfolk's supplies rather than harvest the grain that stood in the fields.

62. *Hamilton Papers*, 1: 223.

63. C. S. L. Davies, "Provisions for Armies, 1509–50: A Study in the Effectiveness of Early Tudor Government," *Economic History Review*, ser. 2, 17 (1964): 234–36.

64. *Hamilton Papers*, 1: 224, 224 (1), 226; *LP* 17: 998.

65. *Hamilton Papers*, 1: 231.

66. Norfolk to the privy council, 3 November 1542, *S.P. Hen. VIII*, 5: 213–19. "Sparcle" means "scatter" or "break up"; see *OED*.

67. *LP* 17: 1057, 1120; Beer, *Northumberland*, p. 14.

68. *LP* 17: 1121; *S.P. Hen. VIII*, 5: 232–35.

Notes to Pages 209–215

69. *LP* 18(1): 72, 79, Mackie, *The Earlier Tudors*, pp. 405–6; Smith, *The Mask of Royalty*, pp. 183–88. See also Head, "Henry VIII's Scottish Policy," pp. 1–24, and M. H. Merriman, "The Assured Scots: Scottish Collaborators with England During the Rough Wooing," *Scottish Historical Review* 48 (1968): 10–34.

70. *LP* 18(1): 72, 79, 86, 90, 94, etc. (council meetings); ibid., 44 (Chapuys to Charles V, 15 January 1543). Norfolk was in frequent attendance in council through the end of March, but was absent from 26 March to 23 April, when he returned for the feast of the Garter. See *LP* 18(1): 451.

71. Rymer, *Foedera*, 14: 768–76; *LP* 18(1): 603; Smith, *The Mask of Royalty*, p. 199.

72. *LP* 18(1): 661, 719, 727, 728, 804, 805; Rymer, *Foedera*, 14: 786–92.

73. *LP* 18(1): 681, 754, 759.

74. Smith, *The Mask of Royalty*, pp. 191–92.

75. *LP* 18(2): 504, 526.

76. Ibid., 19(1): 237, 249, 271(3, 5), 272(13).

77. Ibid., 118, 273, 274.

78. Ibid., 25, 258; Helen Miller, "Attendance in the House of Lords in the Reign of Henry VIII," *Historical Journal* 10 (1967): 343; Lehmberg, *Later Parliaments*, pp. 189–99.

79. *LP* 19(1): 227, 237, 249, 292, 314, 508, 514, 534, 540, 594, 602; Scarisbrick, *Henry VIII*, pp. 443–45.

80. Elton, *Reform and Reformation*, pp. 301–2, 306–7.

81. *LP* 19(1): 654, 672, 674, 675, 690, 694, 701. Norfolk signed dozens of warrants for payment for ordnance, supplies, and wages for his vanguard. Many are collected in BL Add. Ms., 5753, f. 34–139 (and catalogued in *LP* 19[1]: 632, 634, 635, 663, and 19[2]: 152, 243).

82. *LP* 19(1): 686, 687, 700, 709, 783, etc.; *S.P. Hen. VIII*, 8: 90–96.

83. *LP* 19(1): 836, 849, 863, 868, 873, 876, 907, 919; Casady, *Henry Howard*, p. 120.

84. *LP* 19(1): 976; 19(2): 3, 9, 89, 176, 230; *S.P. Hen. VIII*, 10: 15–16.

85. *LP* 19(2): 249; Scarisbrick, *Henry VIII*, pp. 448–49; Smith, *The Mask of Royalty*, pp. 209–10.

86. *LP* 19(2): 278, 279, 285, 303, 307, 344.

87. Ibid., 353, 354, 374, 377, 383, 395, 399; *S.P. Hen. VIII*, 10: 96–97, 101–5. See also Nott, *Henry Howard*, vol. 1, appendix, nos. 18 and 19.

88. *LP* 19(2): 414, 436; *S.P. Hen. VIII*, 10: 106–7, 114–17.

89. *S.P. Hen. VIII*, 10: 49–50, 98–100; *LP* 19(2): 436.

90. *LP* 19(2): 443, 445, 454–56, 463, 470, 479, 484, 505. See also Scarisbrick, *Henry VIII*, pp. 450–51, and Smith, *The Mask of Royalty*, pp. 212–13.

91. *LP* 19(2): 560–61, 574, 665, 667, 690; 20(1): 125 (3, 24), 215, 258, 270, 282, 297.

92. Casady, *Henry Howard*, p. 127; Mackie, *The Earlier Tudors*, p. 407.
93. *LP* 20(1): 297, 347, 381, 566, 623.
94. Ibid., 671, 672, 717.
95. Ibid., 833, 876, 881, 926, 984, 999, 1027.
96. See ibid., introduction, lvii–lix and notes.
97. Scarisbrick, *Henry VIII*, p. 455; *LP* 20(1): 1236, 1268, 1276.
98. *LP* 20(2): 209, 496(8); Casady, *Henry Howard*, pp. 130–31.
99. For attendance in council, see *The Acts of the Privy Council*, Volume I, 1542–47, 93 vols., ed. John Roche Dasent (London, 1890–1949), 1: 239ff. Hereafter cited as *APC*.
100. Nott, *Henry Howard*, 1: 178.
101. Thomas Hussey to Surrey, 6 November 1545, *LP* 20(2): 738; Casady, *Henry Howard*, pp. 135–38; Smith, *The Mask of Royalty*, p. 214. A number of Surrey's letters to Henry VIII and others are printed in Nott, *Henry Howard*, 1: 174ff.
102. *LP* 20(2): 435, 439, 445, etc.; see esp. Gardiner to Paget, 6 November 1545, ibid., 741. On 16 January 1546, Gardiner signed the Treaty of Utrecht with Charles V, a mutual nonaggression pact which restored some diplomatic balance and became the first step toward an eventual settlement with France. See *LP* 21(1): 71, and Smith, *The Mask of Royalty*, p. 221.
103. For analyses of the struggle at court at the end of Henry's reign, compare Elton, *Reform and Reformation*, pp. 328–32; Smith, *The Mask of Royalty*, pp. 238–40; Beer, *Northumberland*, pp. 20–26; and the account I have followed most closely here, Scarisbrick, *Henry VIII*, pp. 478–96.
104. *LP* 21(1): 124.
105. See Casady, *Henry Howard*, pp. 160–64; Scarisbrick, *Henry VIII*, p. 462; Smith, *The Mask of Royalty*, pp. 218–19.
106. Casady, *Henry Howard*, pp. 177–78.
107. *LP* 21(1): 610, 1007, 1014, 1015, 1058; Scarisbrick, *Henry VIII*, pp. 463–64; Casady, *Henry Howard*, pp. 176–77.
108. *LP* 21(1): 835, 849, 1383(72). See also Elton, *Reform and Reformation*, pp. 329–30; Hughes, *The Reformation in England*, 2: 63–68; Wriothesley, *Chronicle During the Reigns of the Tudors*, 1: 169–70.
109. Casady, *Henry Howard*, p. 179.
110. Ibid., pp. 179–80; *LP* 21(2): 555.
111. *LP* 21(1): 1384, 1398.
112. Elton, *Reform and Reformation*, p. 330; *LP* 21(1): 1537 (31–34).
113. Scarisbrick, *Henry VIII*, p. 482; Casady, *Henry Howard*, pp. 184–86. Norfolk was at court as late as 1 November, but the exact date of his departure and that of Surrey's arrival are unclear. See *LP* 21(2): 333, 334.
114. Casady, *Henry Howard*, p. 187. Smith, *The Mask of Royalty*, pp. 154–55.
115. Casady, *Henry Howard*, pp. 187–88.

Notes to Pages 223–230

116. Ibid., pp. 188–90; Smith, *The Mask of Royalty*, p. 255; *LP* 21(2): 604.
117. *S.P. Hen. VIII*, 1: 891–92; Casady, *Henry Howard*, pp. 190–92; *LP* 21(2): 533, 541; Redworth, *Stephen Gardiner*, pp. 234–35.
118. *LP* 21(2): 533, 546; Casady, *Henry Howard*, pp. 191–93.
119. *S.P. Hen. VIII*, 11: 391–92.
120. Ibid., pp. 385–88.
121. *LP* 21(2): 540, 541. Norfolk's letter is quoted in Herbert, *Henry the Eighth*, p. 565. See also Helen Miller, "Henry VIII's Unwritten Will: Grants of Lands and Honours in 1547," in E. W. Ives, R. J. Knecht and J. J.Scarisbrick, eds., *Wealth and Power in Tudor England: Essays Presented to S. T. Bindoff* (London: Athlone Press of the University of London, 1978), pp. 87–91.
122. PRO SP 1/227/82–83 and 88.
123. *LP* 21(1): 1425; 21(2): 555.
124. PRO SP 1/227/90–96.
125. BL Cott. Titus, B i, ff. 94–97. Additional evidence of the Howard investigation, including interrogation of family servants, is to be found in PRO SP 1/227/130, 131, 181.
126. *Sp. Cal.* 8: 531 and 533–34; *LP* 21(2): 554; Nott, *Henry Howard*, 1, appendix, no. 33.
127. Smith, *The Mask of Royalty*, pp. 257–58; Wriothesley, *Chronicle During the Reigns of the Tudors*, 1: 177. An account of Surrey's trial is in Nott, *Henry Howard*, 1, appendix, no.33.
128. BL Harl. Ms., 297, f. 257.
129. On the former, see James Gairdner in his introduction to *LP* 21(2), p. xlvii, and Hughes, *The Reformation in England*, 2: 73–74; for the latter, see Casady, *Henry Howard*, pp. 204–5.
130. The original act, not printed in *Statutes of the Realm* (but abstracted in *LP* 21[2]: 753), is quoted in Lehmberg, *Later Parliaments*, pp. 232–34.
131. Ibid., p. 235.
132. *LP* 21(2): 761. See also the accounts in Smith, *The Mask of Royalty*, p. 259, and Scarisbrick, *Henry VIII*, pp. 495–96.
133. Redworth, *Stephen Gardiner*, pp. 245–48.

CHAPTER 10 The Final Years, 1547–1554

1. *CPR*, 1547–48, p. 180.
2. Elton, *Reform and Reformation*, pp. 333–37.
3. *Sp. Cal.* 9: 45; *CPR*, 1548–49, p. 160; *CPR*, 1550–53, p. 3; *CPR*, 1553, p. 195.
4. Van der Delft to Charles V, 27 April 1547, *Sp. Cal.* 9: 85; Jasper Ridley, *Thomas Cranmer* (Oxford: Clarendon Press, 1962), p. 265.
5. Ethel M. Richardson, *The Lion and the Rose: The Great Howard Story*, 2 vols.,

pagination consecutive (New York: E. P. Dutton, 1922), p. 87. I have been unable to confirm Richardson's assertion that Beauchamp Tower was Norfolk's prison from manuscript sources or in the printed state papers for Edward's reign.

6. PRO SP 46/1/154; *APC* 2: 206, 381, 400.

7. PRO SP 46/2/80–81. Two drafts of this warrant survive; the original would have been sent to Markham and used as authorization to receive money quarterly.

8. PRO E. 101/60/22, a book of six leaves recording expenses of prisoners in the Tower, 13 December 1547–28 September 1548.

9. Ibid., ff. 2r., 4r.; PRO SP 46/2/80–81.

10. Elton, *Reform and Reformation*, pp. 346–52. For the troubles in Norfolk, see also Davies, *Peace, Print and Protestantism*, pp. 275–80, and S. T. Bindoff, *Ket's Rebellion* (London: Historical Association, 1949).

11. Van der Delft to Charles V, 18 January 1550, *Sp. Cal.* 10: 14.

12. *APC* 3: 88, 254.

13. *Sp. Cal.* 10: 454; *APC* 3: 479.

14. PRO LR. 2/113/129; LR. 2/115/1.

15. *APC* 2: 15–17. This memorandum, and a number of attached schedules of Norfolk's personal property, are printed in full in Nott, *Henry Howard*, 1, appendix, nos. 39–47. For a discussion of the motives and actions of the Edwardian regents, see Miller, "Henry VIII's Unwritten Will," pp. 87–105.

16. *CPR*, 1547–48, pp. 33, 126, 211. Fulmerston was also granted, in February 1549, a parcel of former Howard lands worth almost £150 a year; see ibid., 1548–49, pp. 298–99.

17. Ibid., 1547–48, pp. 171, 201.

18. Ibid., pp. 221, 253.

19. Ibid., pp. 27, 169. See also Lawrence Stone, *The Crisis of the Aristocracy, 1558–1641* (Oxford: Clarendon Press, 1965), pp. 346–47.

20. *CPR*, 1547–48, p. 245.

21. Ibid., pp. 46, 53.

22. Ibid., 1550–53, pp. 136, 182–83; Beer, *Northumberland*, p. 144.

23. Mary received most of the remaining furnishings along with the house; see *CPR*, 1548–49, p. 20, and PRO SP 46/1/119.

24. *CPR*, 1547–48, pp. 27, 33, 46, 126, 211, 253; 1548–49, p. 201; 1549–51, pp. 332–33; 1553, p. 157.

25. The Auditors of the Land Revenues book on the Howard lands, PRO LR. 2/113, records rents paid through the reign and, in some cases, notes properties leaving crown hands. About half of the manors recorded were still in crown hands when Mary came to the throne.

26. Helen Miller, "Subsidy Assessments of the Peerage in the Sixteenth Century," *BIHR* 28 (1955): 18. Paget's distribution scheme is in *APC* 2: 15–17, and lists

grants to Hertford and other councilors totalling £2,000 in annual rents. About one-third of the lands to satisfy these annuities came from Norfolk's estates. According to Neville Williams, *Thomas Howard, Fourth Duke of Norfolk* (New York: E. P. Dutton, 1964), p. 28, the Howard properties sold or leased by the crown had a total value of £926 a year. This figure may be too low, but it is certainly not too high.

27. The original drafts, based on the inventory of Kenninghall by Sirs John Gates, Richard Southwell and Wymand Carew, are PRO LR. 2/116 and 117; from these, a fair copy, LR. 2/115, was drawn up. Gates and his fellow surveyors submitted this final report and were cleared of responsibility in September 1551.

28. PRO LR. 2/115/1–10, 16, 17–19, 20, 22, 23, 37; LR. 2/116/13. This exhaustive survey even ran to kitchen stores—barrels of salt fish, wheat, oats and malt—and the horses in the stables, listed partially by name, beginning with "Furst, an olde horse called button" (LR. 2/115/83–86, 77r). For the return of Bess Holland's jewels, see the indenture between Robert Holdiche and Elizabeth and George Holland, 7 February 1547, Folger Library, Washington, D.C., Ms. Xd. 157.

29. W. K. Jordan, *Edward VI: The Threshold of Power* (Cambridge, Mass.: Belknap Press of Harvard University, 1970), pp. 103ff.; Elton, *Reform and Reformation*, pp. 335–37.

30. Elton, *Reform and Reformation*, pp. 350–51. The best recent work on Edwardian politics is Dale E. Hoak, *The King's Council in the Reign of Edward VI* (Cambridge: Cambridge University Press, 1976).

31. Elton, *Reform and Reformation*, pp. 359–71; Davies, *Peace, Print and Protestantism*, p. 281–88.

32. Jordan, *Edward VI: The Threshold of Power*, pp. 517ff., argues that Edward himself, determined to avoid a papist on a throne, was the moving force behind these alterations in the succession. See also Elton, *Reform and Reformation*, pp. 374–75; D. M. Loades, *The Reign of Mary Tudor: Politics, Government and Religion in England, 1553–1558* (New York: St. Martin's Press, 1979), pp. 62–63; and Davies, *Peace, Print and Protestantism*, pp. 288–90. Northumberland, like Henry VIII, ignored the claims of the descendants of Margaret Tudor who should have held precedence over the issue of Mary, the younger sister. This line eventually supplied the successor to the Tudors in James VI of Scotland in 1603.

33. *Sp. Cal.* 11: 80, 114.

34. John Stow, *The Annales, or a General Chronicle of England* (London, 1615), p. 613. H. F. M. Prescott, *Mary Tudor* (London: Eyre and Spottiswoode, 1952), pp. 176–78. By far the most useful recent study of the reign is Loades, *The Reign of Mary Tudor*, which by implication says a great deal about the general form of Tudor politics.

35. Wriothesley, *Chronicle During the Reigns of the Tudors*, 2: 96. According to

APC 4: 315, Norfolk was not sworn of the council and restored to the Garter until 10 August. This date may refer to taking the oath as a councilor, for the duke clearly functioned in that capacity earlier.

36. Wriothesley, *Chronicle During the Reigns of the Tudors*, 2: 96–97; Williams, *Thomas Howard, Fourth Duke of Norfolk*, pp. 27–28; Elton, *Reform and Reformation*, pp. 376–77; *APC* 4: 315–89.

37. See Antonio di Guaras, *The Accession of Queen Mary*, trans. R. Garnet (London, 1892), pp. 102–3, and Holinshed, *Holinshed's Chronicles*, 4: 4, for accounts of the trial.

38. *Sp. Cal.* 11: 183–84.

39. Beer, *Northumberland*, pp. 157–61; Elton, *Reform and Reformation*, p. 377.

40. PRO SP 46/163/68–72.

41. *APC* 4: 347; Ridley, *Thomas Cranmer*, pp. 354–57.

42. Di Guaras, *The Accession of Queen Mary*, pp. 122–25; *The Chronicle of Queen Jane and of Two Years of Queen Mary*, ed. John G. Nichols (London: Camden Society 1850), pp. 27–28, 30–31.

43. William Jerdan, ed., *Rutland Papers* (London, 1842), pp. 118–19.

44. PRO C. 65/162/22, 34; Lehmberg, "Parliamentary Attainder," p. 698.

45. PRO C. 65/162/22; *Sp. Cal.* 11: 401; Loades, *The Reign of Mary Tudor*, p. 97 and note 167, citing PRO SP 12/1/57, an Elizabethan report on "what lands, etc., hath been granted by the late Queen during her reign," says that Norfolk received lands to a yearly value of £1,626 14s. 4d. His grandson and heir Thomas, earl of Surrey, received lands worth 1,000 marks. Probably Norfolk recovered actual lands lost by his attainder, save those retained by Oxford and others, but the grant to Surrey looks like a round figure.

46. Elton, *Reform and Reformation*, pp. 379–80; Davies, *Peace, Print and Protestantism*, pp. 295–96. For the tension at court, see E. Harris Harbison, *Rival Ambassadors at the Court of Queen Mary* (Princeton: Princeton University Press, 1940), and D. M. Loades, *Two Tudor Conspiracies* (Cambridge: Cambridge University Press, 1965).

47. Loades, *Two Tudor Conspiracies*, pp. 24–46, 53–56. Norfolk had not been in council more than a few days since 23 December 1553, and was absent during the critical days in mid-January when the Spanish treaty was sealed and plans for the rebellion laid, discovered, and their discovery suppressed. See *APC* 4: 381–89 for Norfolk's attendance.

48. Loades, *Two Tudor Conspiracies*, p. 58; *Chronicle of Jane and Mary*, pp. 37–38.

49. *Calendar of State Papers, Domestic Series, of the Reigns of Edward VI, Mary and Elizabeth, Part I, 1547–1580* (London, 1856), 2: 21. (Hereafter cited as *SP Edward, Mary and Elizabeth*. Citations are to document numbers.) See also John Proctor, "The History of Wyatt's Rebellion," [London, 1555], in Thomas Seccombe, ed., *An English Garner: Tudor Tracts, 1532–1558* (Westminster: Archibald Constable, 1903), p. 222.

50. E. Harris Harbison, "French Intrigues at Queen Mary's Court," *American Historical Review* 45 (1940): 548; see also Proctor, "Wyatt's Rebellion," p. 222.

51. *Chronicle of Jane and Mary*, p. 38; Proctor, "Wyatt's Rebellion," p. 227.

52. *LP* 20(1): 622, 623; 20(2): appendix, 2; *CPR*, 1553, pp. 254, 316, 328, 355, 414; HMC *Reports*, series 77, DeLisle Papers, 1: 15; Lehmberg, *Later Parliaments*, p. 214.

53. *SP Edward, Mary and Elizabeth*, 2: 23, 23(i); Loades, *Two Tudor Conspiracies*, pp. 60–61.

54. Proctor, "Wyatt's Rebellion," pp. 229–30.

55. *Chronicle of Jane and Mary*, pp. 38–39.

56. Proctor, "Wyatt's Rebellion," p. 230.

57. *Chronicle of Jane and Mary*, p. 39.

58. Ibid., p. 40; *SP Edward, Mary and Elizabeth*, 2: 28, 30; 3: 2.

59. Loades, *Two Tudor Conspiracies*, pp. 66–74.

60. Elton, *Reform and Reformation*, p. 381; *APC* 5: 3–18. Mary also ordered the executions of Lady Jane Grey and Guilford Dudley, despite the lack of any evidence of their complicity in Wyatt's rebellion.

61. Blomefield, *Topographical History of Norfolk*, 3: 268.

62. R. Green, *The History, Topography, and Antiquities of Framlingham and Saxstead* (London, 1834), p. 80.

63. *APC* 5: 18; *Sp. Cal.* 12: 258. The date of the wedding is given in *DNB* and in Cokayne, *Complete Peerage*, as May 1555. This letter contradicts that, but may refer only to a formal betrothal. Mary Fitzalan was born in 1540, so would not have been unusually young to marry in 1554 or 1555; she died in childbirth in 1557.

64. *APC* 5: 42, 51.

65. PRO Probate 11/37/103–5 (formerly Prerogative Court of Canterbury, Register of Wills, 14 More). Norfolk's inquisition *post mortem*, PRO Chancery 142/103/56, includes a copy of the will, which differs in only a few words and in some spellings.

66. HMC *Reports*, series 10, Gawdy, p. 3; Williams, *Thomas Howard, Fourth Duke of Norfolk*, pp. 31–32; PRO Probate 11/37/103.

67. Norfolk's monument is illustrated in Katherine A. Esdaile, *English Church Monuments, 1510 to 1840* (New York: Oxford University Press, 1946), plates 45 and 46; see also the plate and description in Robinson, *The Dukes of Norfolk*, pp. 38–39, and the description of the motto in Green, *Framingham*, p. 81. This description is based on my examination in July 1984, for which my thanks to the rector of St. Michael's, Framlingham. A Victorian antiquarian who opened the Howard tombs in 1841 found three coffins and additional bones in the third duke's sepulcher. These may be the remains of the first and second Howard dukes, moved to Framlingham from Thetford in the 1540s. See BL Add. Ms., 19,193, f. 8.

68. PRO Probate 11/37/104–5; PRO C. 142/103/56.

Notes to Pages 247–251

CHAPTER 11   An English Duke, 1524–1554

1. K. B. McFarlane, *The Nobility of Later Medieval England* (Oxford: Clarendon Press, 1973), pp. 15, 146–49, 172–76.
2. Urban, "Anne Lady Howard," pp. 147–52; Nott, *Henry Howard*, 1: vii. A land settlement made between Norfolk and the king in 1545 supplies the name of a second son, Henry, who also predeceased Anne.
3. Harris, "Marriage Sixteenth Century Style," pp. 371–82.
4. Smith, *Tudor Tragedy*, pp. 23–24.
5. Bapst, *Deux Gentilshommes-poètes*, pp. 171–72.
6. *LP* 4: 13, 221, 1241; Cokayne, *Complete Peerage*, s.v. "Oxford."
7. *LP* 4: 2203, 5508. Elizabeth, born c. 1517, was thus about eight at her father's death.
8. Ibid., 6803 (14); Bapst, *Deux Gentilshommes-poètes*, p. 173. PRO Probate 11/37/103–105.
9. Cokayne, *Complete Peerage*, s.v. "Oxford."
10. Casady, *Henry Howard*, pp. 34–36; *LP* 5: 941.
11. *LP* 5: 720(9); Nott, *Henry Howard*, 1: xxiii.
12. Casady, *Henry Howard*, pp. 36–37, 50–53; Williams, *Thomas Howard, Fourth Duke of Norfolk*, pp. 1–4; *LP* 13(1): 505.
13. Nott, *Henry Howard*, 1: xxviii; their common ancestor was Anthony Woodville, lord Rivers, whose daughters Elizabeth and Catherine married Edward IV and Henry Stafford, second duke of Buckingham. For Mary's residence at Kenninghall, see PRO SP 1/227/82–83, and PRO LR 2/115 and 116, passim.
14. *LP* 13(1): 13, 78, 690, 691, 1375; 14(1): 651; *S.P. Hen. VIII* 1: 888–91. See also Nott, *Henry Howard*, 1, appendix, no. 37, where the grant for Swaffenham is printed in full.
15. *LP* 5: 390, 432, 563, 683.
16. Cokayne, *Complete Peerage*, s.v. "Bridgewater."
17. *Sp. Cal.* 4(1): 762; *LP* 4: 6248 (21).
18. Wriothesley, *Chronicle During the Reigns of the Tudors*, 1: 54, 70; Lehmberg, *Later Parliaments*, pp. 35–36. Howard's attainder, 28 Hen. VIII, c. 24, is in *Statutes of the Realm*, ed. A. Luders et al., 11 vols. (London, 1810–28), 3: 680.
19. Head, "Attainder of Lord Thomas Howard," pp. 3–16.
20. Harris, "Marriage Sixteenth Century Style," pp. 372–73. Much of what is known about the marital problems of Norfolk and his duchess comes from her letters to Cromwell in the 1530s. These are in the British Library, Cott. Titus B i, ff. 184, 388–92, 394–95, and printed in Nott, *Henry Howard*, 1, appendix, nos. 27–30. Norfolk's reply to some of Elizabeth's charges is printed as no. 31.
21. *LP* 3: 2383; Casady, *Henry Howard*, pp. 17–18. In 1537, Elizabeth wrote to

Cromwell that Norfolk had taken up with Bess Holland eleven years before; see BL Cott. Titus B i, ff. 184, 388 (the leaves of this letter are separated in the bound volume). Thomas Hussey was Norfolk's treasurer by 1543; in 1545 Hussey was a member of Parliament for Norfolk's borough of Grimsby, and was later a witness to the duke's will. See *LP* 20(1): 965; 20(2): 658; PRO Probate 11/37/105.

22. Nott, *Henry Howard*, 1, appendix, nos. 27–32 (pp. lxvi and ff.); *LP* 6: 474.

23. BL Cott. Titus B i, f. 388.

24. Ibid., f. 392.

25. Ibid., ff. 394–95; Casady, *Henry Howard*, pp. 18–20. At his arrest in 1546 Norfolk remarked that Elizabeth knew nothing to incriminate him since they did not live together. He must not have been too upset by the estrangement, for he recalled that Cromwell had once said to him, "my lord, you are an happy man thus; your wife knoweth no such by you, for if she did she would undo you." See BL Cott. Titus B i, f. 101r. For Bess Holland's house and jewels, see PRO SP 1/227/82v. and PRO LR. 2/115/4v.–5v., 19r.–20r., 23r.

26. Folger Library, Washington, D.C., ms. Xd. 157, an indenture between Robert Holdiche, Norfolk's former steward, and Elizabeth Holland and her brother George. Holdiche returned Bess Holland's jewels "by virtue of letters addressed from the King's Majesty's most honorable council," listing the items returned. Interestingly, Bess Holland's brother George signed the indenture "for and in the name of my said sister." If the duke's consort were illiterate, it would lend weight to Elizabeth Howard's charges that Bess was of mean estate.

27. Casady, *Henry Howard*, pp. 60–63.

28. Ibid., pp. 88–91.

29. *LP* 18(1): 73, 226, 327, 351; *APC*, 1: 104.

30. "Instructions for my Lorde Privey Seale as towching the whole communication betwixt John Barlow, Deane of Westbury, Thomas Barlow Prebendary there, clerkys, and George Constantine of Lawhaden, in their journey from Westbury unto Slebath in Sowthwales," *Archaelogia* 23 (London, 1831): 56ff.

31. Casady, *Henry Howard*, pp. 67–68, 178–81.

32. Ibid., pp. 198–99; PRO Probate 11/37/103. Someone—perhaps Mary, but the memorandum does not say—was granted £100 in June 1552 "for some relief toward the sustention of the Children of the late earl of Surrey." See PRO SP 10/14/45.

33. For Henry VIII's relations with the Tudor nobility, see Helen Miller, *Henry VIII and the English Nobility* (Oxford: Basil Blackwell, 1986).

34. D. M. Loades, *Politics and the Nation, 1450–1660: Obedience, Resistance and the Public Order* (Brighton, Sussex: Harvester Press, 1974), p. 132; *LP* 21(2): 476 (29). On court politics and the importance of patronage, see Ives, *Faction in Tudor England*, and Starkey, *Henry VIII*.

35. *LP* 2: 207, 1154; 4: 137(23), 2002, and many other grants during the reign.

36. *Paston Letters*, 5: 108, 249. Anthony Wingfield, the king's vice-chamberlain and captain of the guard, was sworn of the council following Cromwell's fall—apparently as a reward for his aid in toppling the lord privy seal. See *S.P. Hen. VIII* 1: 889.

37. *LP* 12(2): 1150(42), 1311(28). On St. Leger, see Pireronus, "Anthony St. Leger."

38. *LP* 5: 166 (12); 13(1): 646 (48); 17: 363 (66). In October 1536, when about to leave for the north to deal with the Pilgrimage of Grace, Norfolk sent Henry a list of those he had left in East Anglia to maintain order. This tally—including Sir William Drewery, Sir Thomas Jermyn, Roger Townshend, Robert Holdiche, Nicholas Hare, Sir Thomas Bedingfield, Sir John Tyndale, Sir John Heydon, Sir Humphrey Wingfield, Sir Thomas Rushe and Sir John Jerningham—is a cross section of the influential gentry loyal to the duke. Many of these names are found elsewhere in connection with the Howards. Only one such family has a modern study: C. E. Moreton, *The Townsends and Their World: Gentry, Law and Land in Norfolk, c. 1450–1551* (Oxford: Clarendon Press, 1992).

39. See, for example, *LP* 2: 789; 14(1): 1056.

40. Smith, *Tudor Tragedy*, p. 22, where he cites PRO E. 405/109–110 (Treasury Lists, 1539–41).

41. *LP* 4: 3105, 3590, 4931.

42. Ibid., 19(1): 610; 21(1): 476 (21, 63). For Blage and the Howards, see Starkey, *Henry VIII*, pp. 149–50.

43. *LP* 10: 79, 91, 436; 13(1): 384, 646, 1115; 13(2): 57, 84, 85; 14(1): 1056.

44. Ibid., 14(1): 398, 764, 806; 14(2): 572, 782.

45. Ibid., 14(1): 693, 764, 806.

46. Ibid., 15: 436 (88), 613 (22); 20(2): 496 (68).

47. Ibid., 16: 679; 18(1): 226(85), 446, 967; 18(2): 231, 271, 271, 365; 19(1): 610 (3); 20(1): 215.

48. Ibid., 20(2): 658; 21(2): 200.

49. *DNB*, s.v. "Richard Southwell"; *LP* 5: 1139 (11). Southwell's home was at Rising, Norfolk, near Kenninghall, which led the editors of *DNB* to surmise that Southwell was raised with Henry Howard. This is possible, but as there was a thirteen-year difference in their ages, they cannot have been the boyhood companions suggested by Casady, *Henry Howard*, p. 29.

50. *DNB*, s.v. "Richard Southwell"; *LP* 10: 79, 191, 436.

51. *LP* 14(1): 706, 808; Lehmberg, *Later Parliaments*, pp. 43–45.

52. Casady, *Henry Howard*, pp. 70–71; Lehmberg, *Later Parliaments*, p. 129.

53. *DNB*, s.v. "Richard Southwell"; Williams, *Thomas Howard, Fourth Duke of Norfolk*, pp. 14–15; PRO Probate 11/37/104r.

54. Green, *History of Framlingham and Saxstead*, p. 24.

Notes to Pages 260–264

55. "The Catorer's Book of Thomas Howard, Earl of Surrey, at his Houses of Stoke by Neyland, Suffolk, and Hunsdon, Hertfordshire, 1523–24," University of California at Berkeley, Ms. HF 5616 E5 N6 (formerly Ms. Ac. 523), fols. 116 and following; *LP* 3: 1366; 4: 2002; 5: 166 (12); 13(1): 646 (48); 17: 362 (66), 443 (24); 18(1): 226 (8); 20(1): 622, 623.

56. *LP* 21(1): 1041, 1051,; 21(1): 536; *S.P. Hen. VIII* 1: 889.

57. Folger Library, Washington, D.C., Ms. Xd. 157; PRO LR. 2/113/128–29; PRO SP 1/227/82–83; *CPR*, 1547–48, pp. 53, 75, 76; *CPR* 1550–53, p. 144; *CPR* 1553, p. 348.

58. HMC *Reports*, ser. 77, DeLisle Papers, 1: 372–86; 2: 1–2; PRO Probate 11/37/104r.

59. *LP* 12(1): 1252, 1307; 12(2): 248; 13(2): 365; 14(1): 541.

60. *VCH Norfolk*, 2: 391–93, 406; *LP* 15: 942(43); 19(1): 938; 19(2): 166 (36); 21(2): 553. The grant of Thetford to Fulmerston is recited twice, in *LP* 14(1): 651 (46) and 16: 678 (1). In the former, he is called Richard Fulmerston of Thetford, while the latter (which gives his wife's name as Alice) says he is from Ipswich.

61. *LP* 19(1): 610 (116); 20(2): 658, 738; 21(2): 553.

62. PRO SP 1/227/90–96; *CPR*, 1547–48, pp. 211, 230; *CPR* 1548–49, pp. 298–99; *CPR* 1549–51, p. 350.

63. *CPR* 1548–49, p. 154; *CPR* 1553, pp. 357–58.

64. HMC *Reports*, ser. 55, Various Collections, 7: 120–21.

65. "The Catorer's Book," and "The Booke of Emptions particular ffare and expensus of thoushold of the right high and mighty Prince Thomas, Duc of Norff, high Threasure of England from 1 Oct. 18 Henry VIII to Sept. 19 H. VIII," Pembroke College, Cambridge, Ms. 300, printed in part in Richardson, *The Lion and the Rose*, pp. 69–82.

66. "The Catorer's Book," passim, but esp. ff. 10r., 139r; "The Book of Emptions," in Richardson, *The Lion and the Rose*, p. 72.

67. "The Book of Emptions," in Richardson, *The Lion and the Rose*, pp. 79–82.

68. "The Catorer's Book," f. 10; Williams, *Thomas Howard, Fourth Duke of Norfolk*, p. 15.

69. Richardson, *The Lion and the Rose*, p. 87; *LP* 16: 101. Sabellius (fl. 225) was an early Christian writer whose works were interpreted to praise monarchy and attack the papacy.

70. See H. L. R. Edwards, *Skelton: The Life and Times of an Early Tudor Poet* (London: Jonathan Cape, 1949), pp. 204–8; Maurice Pollet, *John Skelton, Poet of Tudor England*, trans. John Warrington (London: J. M. Dent and Sons, 1971), p. 120; Melvin J. Tucker, "The More-Howard Connections of John Skelton," *Moreana* 37 (1973): 19–21; and Greg Walker, *John Skelton and the Politics of the 1520s* (Cambridge: Cambridge University Press, 1988), pp. 60ff.

71. Casady, *Henry Howard*, p. 27, and *DNB*, s.v.

Notes to Pages 264–269

72. James K. McConica, *English Humanists and Reformation Politics Under Henry VIII and Edward VI* (Oxford: Clarendon Press, 1965), p. 117. Tavener wrote to thank Cromwell for instigating a pension at Norfolk's hands; see *LP* 5: 1763.

73. McConica, *Humanists and Politics*, pp. 210–11.

74. Casady, *Henry Howard*, p. 111.

75. *The Chronicle of Iohn Hardyng, Together With the Continuation by Richard Grafton*, ed. Henry Ellis (London, 1812), pp. 1–5. This edition is an annotated reprint of Grafton's first edition of 1543.

76. *Faculty Office Registers, 1534–49. A Calendar of the First Two Registers of the Archbishop of Canterbury's Faculty Office*, ed. D. S. Chambers (Oxford: Clarendon Press, 1966), pp. 33, 119, 227, 236, 254, 257, 267; Green, *History of Framlingham and Saxstead*, p. 127; Blomefield, *Topographical History of Norfolk*, 1: 222, 312, 460; 2: 198; 3: 640, 644; 5: 107–9, 199–202, 261, 311, 313–16, 328, 349, 353, 410–11, 433, 449–50; 9: 58, 285, 465; *LP* 20(2): 1068 (15).

77. Lehmberg, *Reformation Parliament*, and *Later Parliaments*. Elections were held in 1529, 1536, 1539, 1542, and 1545.

78. Lehmberg, *Reformation Parliament*, p. 17; *LP* 4: 5993.

79. *LP* 10: 816. This is a memorandum of 1536, drawn up by Norfolk's clerk, reviewing arrangements for elections.

80. Lehmberg, *Reformation Parliament*, p. 17; *LP* 4: 5993.

81. *LP* 7: 56 (miscatalogued in 1534); Lehmberg, *Later Parliaments*, pp. 5–7, 46. George Gifford served on a number of commissions in East Anglia in the 1540s; in 1536, he left Norfolk's service to work for Cromwell in the monastic dissolutions.

82. Lehmberg, *Later Parliaments*, pp. 40–50; *Journals of the House of Lords*, 1: 103–7.

83. Lehmberg, *Later Parliaments*, pp. 56–57 and notes. In March 1540, Hare was imprisoned briefly in the power struggles that preceded Cromwell's fall; see *LP* 15: 289, 291.

84. Lehmberg, *Later Parliaments*, pp. 129–34.

85. Nott, *Henry Howard*, 1: 343; Lehmberg, *Later Parliaments*, p. 134; Casady, *Henry Howard*, pp. 97–99, 123. The Cleres, sons of Sir Robert Clere of Ormesby, Norfolk, were among the companions of Surrey examined before the council in 1542 for disreputable behavior.

86. Lehmberg, *Later Parliaments*, pp. 183, 196.

87. Ibid., pp. 211–16.

88. Ibid., pp. 205, 215; PRO Probate 11/37/104r.

89. Lehmberg, *Later Parliaments*, pp. 202–3.

90. Ibid., p. 204.

91. Ibid., p. 234.

92. Ibid., pp. 43, 134, 211–15. See also Williams, *The Tudor Regime*, pp. 401–2, 451–52.

93. The best account of the battle for control in Henry's final months is Starkey, *Henry VIII*, pp. 147–67.

94. Elton, *Reform and Reformation*, pp. 348–50.

95. Dairmaid MacCullough, "Kett's Rebellion in Context," *Past and Present* 84 (1979): 53–57; Joan Thirsk, ed., *The Agrarian History of England and Wales*, vol. IV, 1500–1640 (Cambridge: Cambridge University Press, 1967), pp. 276–78.

96. PRO C. 142/103/56; PRO Probate 11/37/103–5. In 1525–26, receiver general's accounts show Norfolk with a gross landed income of £2,800 and a net of £1,900; see Arundel Castle Ms. Q. 2/2, cited in R. Virgoe, "The Recovery of the Howards in East Anglia, 1485–1529," in E. W. Ives, R. J. Knecht and J. J. Scarisbrick, eds., *Wealth and Power in Tudor England: Essays Presented to S. T. Bindoff* (London: Althone Press of the University of London, 1978), p. 18.

97. PRO LR 2/113, 114.

98. Tucker, *Life of Thomas Howard*, p. 72; *Rot. Parl.*, 6: 479.

99. *LP* 1: 414, 520; *A Descriptive Catalogue of Ancient Deeds, Preserved in the Public Record Office*, 6 vols. (London, 1890–1915), 4: A7551; 5: A13566.

100. *Rot. Parl.*, 6: 479; *LP* 1: 1103, 3442; 13(2): 1215.

101. *LP* 1: 2684 (2); 2: 1363; 4: 1503; Rymer, *Foedera*, 14: 43–45.

102. *LP* 3: 2382; Blomefield, *Topographical History of Norfolk*, 9: 283, 452–53.

103. *Ven. Cal.* 2: 1287; McFarlane, *Nobility of Later Medieval England*, pp. 209, 211.

104. Miller, "Subsidy Assessments of the Peerage," pp. 19–20. For the return of the Howard-Mowbray lands, see J. R. Lander, "Attainder and Forfeiture, 1453 to 1509," *Historical Journal* 6 (1961): 138–40; the grant is *LP* 1: 2684 (1).

105. *LP* 21(1): 1383 (104). The absence of an inquisition *post mortem* for the second duke impedes investigation of the Howard lands; see Tucker, *Thomas Howard*, p. 136, note 61. In 1538 Norfolk noted that he still held lands worth £1,075 left him by his father, after substantial exchanges and sales; see *LP* 13(2): 1215.

106. *LP* 3: 2700; Arundel Ms. G. 1/4, and Pembroke College (Cambridge) Ms. B.5, cited in Virgoe, "Recovery of the Howards," p. 18.

107. Arundel Ms. Q 2/2, cited in Virgoe, "Recovery of the Howards," p. 18; *LP* 13(2): 1215.

108. *LP* 1: 2684(1); 4: 5132; 13(2): 1215; *Journals of the Houses of Lords*, 1: 89–90; Lehmberg, *Later Parliaments*, p. 136; *The Itinerary of John Leland, In or About the Years 1535–1543*, ed. Lucy Toulmin Smith, 5 vols. (Oxford, 1907–10; reprint, Carbondale, Ill.: Southern Illinois University Press, 1964), 1: 102; 5: 14.

109. Blomefield, *Topographical History of Norfolk*, 1: 93, 215, 219–20; Samuel Lewis, *A Topographical Dictionary of England*, s.v.

Notes to Pages 274–282

110. 21 Hen. VIII, c. 22, 26, in *Statutes of the Realm*, 3: 307–9; *VCH Hertfordshire*, 3: 327–38; *LP* 13(2): 1215.

111. *Journals of the House of Lords*, 1: 142, 149, 151, 155; "Historical Notes of Medieval London Houses," *London Topographical Record* 10 (1916): 77–78.

112. Dickens, *The English Reformation*, p. 159. On Shrewsbury, see Bernard, *Early Tudor Nobility*, pp. 30ff.

113. *LP* 15: 942 (44). Norfolk paid £1,329 10d. for Butley and its attendant manors, and agreed to pay yearly pensions totalling 60s. 19d. to its former inmates.

114. *Statutes of the Realm*, 3: 584–85.

115. *LP* 15: 498, 942(43); *VCH Norfolk*, 2: 363–68; HMC *Reports*, ser. 55, Various Collections, vol. 7., pp. 120–21. In 1547 the house and site of Thetford priory were granted to Edward Seymour—just the sort of man from whom Norfolk may have hoped to protect it. See *CPR*, 1547–48, p. 126.

116. *LP* 12(1): 1330 (26); *VCH Norfolk*, 2: 378–80.

117. *LP* 12(2): 1311 (30); *VCH Norfolk*, 2: 258–59.

118. *LP* 15: 942 (44); 16: 780 (7).

119. Blomefield, *Topographical History of Norfolk*, 1: 120–21; *Statutes of the Realm*, 3: 733–39; Savine, *English Monasteries*, p. 283.

120. *LP* 12(2): 1311 (24); 20(2): 266, 496 (68); *VCH Norfolk*, 2: 329, 430–32, 458–59; Blomefield, *Topographical History of Norfolk*, 9: 111–12, 133.

121. *LP* 12(2): 1311 (30); 18(1): 476 (16); 20(1): 282 (52), 624; 20(2): 496 (68); for Edwardian alienations, see *CPR*, 1547–48, pp. 113–14, 171, 200, 221; 1548–49, pp. 298–99; 1549–51, pp. 61, 69, 354; 1550–53, pp. 182–83.

122. Miller, "Subsidy Assessments," pp. 18–20.

123. PRO SP 1/227/130–31; *LP* 13(2): 1215. Between at least 1522 and 1529, Howard also received a pension of one thousand ducats from Charles V and, from 1527 to the 1540s, a French pension of 437 ½ crowns. See on these *Sp. Cal.* 4(1): 355 and *LP* 4: 3619.

124. Williams, *Thomas Howard, Fourth Duke of Norfolk*, p. 32.

125. Miller, "Subsidy Assessments," pp. 18, 21, 28–30.

126. PRO LR 2/115, 116, 117.

127. The patent for the admiralty is recited in Rymer, *Foedera*, 13: 402.

128. *LP* 2: 2459.

129. Ellis, *Original Letters*, ser. 3, vol. 1, p. 63.

130. *LP* 4: 1500, 1576.

131. G. R. Elton, "Tudor Government: The Points of Contact, III: The Court," *TRHS*, 5th series, 26 (1976): 212.

132. PRO SP 60/1/65.

133. Ellis, *Original Letters*, ser. 3, vol. 1, p. 223.

134. *S.P. Hen. VIII* 2: 85; BL Add. Ms. 24,965, f. 78.

135. See, for example, *LP* 4: 3150, 3590, 6395, for assays of the mint in 1527 and 1530.

136. *LP* 4: 1049 (25); 21(2): 476 (63). Dozens of other examples could be cited, often involving multiple appointments, as for escheators, each of whom had authority over a shire or two.

137. Williams, *The Tudor Regime*, p. 91.

138. Elton, *Star Chamber Stories*, pp. 90–92. Norfolk's letter of self-defense is *S.P. Hen. VIII* 1: 650–52.

139. *LP* 21(2): 556.

140. See on this Sidney Anglo, *Spectacle, Pageantry and Early Tudor Policy* (Oxford: Clarendon Press, 1969), passim.

141. *LP* 3: 3161; 4: 578 (50); 6: 415.

142. Ibid., 12(1): 1330 (27); 19(1): 812; Cockayne, *Complete Peerage*, 11, appendix C, pp. 43ff.

143. *LP* 15: 222, 608, 812, 970; *S.P. Hen. VIII* 8: 254–76.

144. *The Lisle Letters*, ed. Muriel St. Clair Byrne, 6 vols. (Chicago and London: University of Chicago Press, 1981), 4: 176–77; *LP* 12(2): 971, 1004.

145. PRO SP 1/103/60.

146. *LP* 13(1): 1520; Walter C. Richardson, *The History of the Court of Augmentations, 1536–1554* (Baton Rouge: Louisiana State University Press, 1961), pp. 223, 494. Hare was paid a salary £20 *per annum*.

147. See G. R. Elton, "Tudor Government: The Points of Contact, II: The Council," *TRHS*, 5th series, 25 (1975): 195–211.

148. John Hussee to Lord Lisle, 5 January 1537, in *Lisle Letters*, 4, no. 910.

CONCLUSION

1. William Camden, *Britain*, p. 483.
2. Elton, "Cromwell's Decline and Fall," p. 153.
3. Smith, *Tudor Tragedy*, pp. 27–29.
4. Mattingly, *Catherine of Aragon*, p. 369.
5. Smith, *Tudor Tragedy*, p. 33.
6. For a discussion of the passing of the medieval ethos, see Arthur B. Ferguson, *The Indian Summer of English Chivalry: Studies in the Decline and Transformation of Chivalric Idealism* (Durham, N.C.: Duke University Press, 1960), esp. pp. 20 and 76–77.

BIBLIOGRAPHY

UNPUBLISHED MANUSCRIPTS

Berkeley, California. University of California. Manuscript HF 5616 E5 N6. "The Catorer's Book of the Household and Expenses in Provisions and Beer of Thomas Howard, Earl of Surrey, at His Houses of Stoke by Neyland, Suffolk, and Hunsdon, Hertfordshire, 1523–24."
London, England. British Library. Additional Manuscripts; Harleian Manuscripts; Cottonian Manuscripts.
London, England. Public Record Office. Chancery (C. 142); Exchequer (E. 101); Land Revenues, Auditor's Accounts (LR. 2); Probate (P. 11); State Papers (SP. 1, 49, 60, 227).
San Marino, California. Huntington Library. Ellesmere Manuscript 2655. "Minutes of Proceedings from 8 Henry VII to 18 Henry VIII . . . Court of Star Chamber."
Washington, D.C. Folger Library. Manuscript Xd. 157. Receipt for Bess Holland's jewels, 7 February 1547.

PUBLISHED MANUSCRIPTS

The Acts of the Privy Council, 1542–1628. Edited by John Roche Dasent. 43 volumes. London: Public Record Office, 1890–1949.
Calendar of Letters, Dispatches and State Papers, Relating to the Negotiations Between England and Spain. Edited by G. A. Bergenroth, Pascual de Gayangos and Martin S. Hume. 13 volumes. London, 1862–1954.
Calendar of State Papers, Domestic Series, of the Reigns of Edward VI, Mary and Elizabeth. Part 1, 1547–1580. London, 1856. Kraus Reprint, 1967.
Calendar of State Papers and Manuscripts Relating to English Affairs, Residing in the Archives and Collections of Venice and Other Libraries of Northern Italy. Edited by Rawdon Brown. 9 volumes. London, 1864–98. Kraus Reprint, 1970.
Calendar of the Carew Manuscripts, Preserved in the Archiepiscopal Library at Lambeth, 1515–1574. Edited by J. S. Brewer and William Bullen. 6 volumes. London, 1867–73.
Calendar of the Charter Rolls, 5 Hen. V–8 Hen. VIII, 1427–1516. London: His Majesty's Stationer's Office, 1927.
Calendar of the Close Rolls, Henry VII, 1485–1500. London: Her Majesty's Stationer's Office, 1955.

353

Bibliography

Calendar of the Manuscripts of the Marquis of Bath Preserved at Longleat, Wiltshire. 3 volumes. London: Historical Manuscripts Commission, 1904–8.

Calendar of the Patent Rolls, Edward IV, Henry VI, 1467–1477. London: Eyre and Spottiswoode, 1901.

Calendar of the Patent Rolls, Edward VI, 1547–1553. 6 volumes. London: His Majesty's Stationer's Office, 1926–29.

Calendar of the Patent Rolls, Henry VII, 1485–1495 and 1494–1509. 2 volumes. London: His Majesty's Stationer's Office, 1914–16.

Calendar of the Patent Rolls, Philip and Mary. Volume 1, 1553–1554. London: His Majesty's Stationer's Office, 1937.

Calendar of the State Papers Relating to Scotland Preserved in the State Paper Department of Her Majesty's Public Record Office, 1509–1589. Edited by Markham John Thorpe. 2 volumes. London, 1858.

Cromwell, Thomas. *Life and Letters of Thomas Cromwell.* Edited with an introduction by Roger Bigelow Merriman. 2 volumes. Oxford: Clarendon Press, 1902.

A Descriptive Catalogue of Ancient Deeds Preserved in the Public Record Office. 6 volumes. London, 1890–1915.

Ellis, Henry, ed. *Original Letters Illustrative of English History.* 11 volumes. London, 1824–46.

Faculty Office Registers, 1534–49. A Calendar of the First Two Registers of the Archbishop of Canterbury's Faculty Office. Edited by D. S. Chambers. Oxford: Clarendon Press, 1966.

Fox, Richard. *The Letters of Richard Fox.* Edited by P. S. and H. M. Allen. Oxford: Clarendon Press, 1929.

Gardiner, Stephen. *The Letters of Stephen Gardiner.* Edited by James A. Muller. Cambridge: Cambridge University Press, 1933.

The Great Tournament Roll of Westminster: A Colotype Reproduction of the Manuscript. Edited with an explanatory text and notes by Sydney Anglo. 2 volumes. Oxford: Clarendon Press, 1968.

The Hamilton Papers: Letters and Papers Illustrating the Political Relations of England and Scotland in the XVIth Century. Volume 1, 1532–43. Edited by Joseph Bain. Edinburgh, 1890.

The Harleian Miscellany; or a Collection of Scarce, Curious, and Entertaining Pamphlets and Tracts, as Well in Manuscript as in Print, Found in the Late Earl of Oxford's Library, Interspersed With Historical, Political and Critical Notes. 10 volumes. London, 1808–13.

Household Book of John, duke of Norfolk, and Thomas, earl of Surrey, Temp. 1481–1490. From the Original Manuscript in the Library of the Society of Antiquaries. Edited by John Payne Collier. Roxburghe Club Publications, no. 61. London, 1844.

Bibliography

The Household of Edward IV: The Black Book and Ordinances of 1478. Edited by A. R. Myers. Manchester, 1959.

Howell, T. B., comp. *A Complete Collection of State Trials and Proceedings for High Treason and Other Crimes and Misdemeanors From the Earliest Period to the Year 1783.* Volume 1, 9 Hen. II to 43 Eliz., 1163–1600. London, 1816.

Illustrations of British History, Biography and Manners. Edited by E. Lodge. 3 volumes. London, 1791.

"Instructions for my Lorde Privey Seale as towching the whole communication betwixt John Barlow, Deane of Westburg, Thomas Barlow Prebendary journey from Westburg unto Slebath in Sowthwales." *Archaelogia* 23 (1931).

Journals of the House of Lords, Beginning Anno Primo Henrici Octavi. Volume 1, 1509–77. London, [1808].

Letters and Papers, Foreign and Domestic, of the Reign of Henry VIII. Edited by J. S. Brewer, James Gairdner and R. H. Brodie. 21 volumes. London, 1862–1910.

Letters and Papers Illustrative of the Reigns of Richard III and Henry VII. Edited by James Gairdner. 2 volumes. Rerum Britanicarum Medii Aevi Scriptores, no. 24. London, 1861–63.

The Lisle Letters. Edited by Muriel St. Clair Byrne. 6 volumes. Chicago: University of Chicago Press, 1981.

Materials for a History of the Reign of Henry VII, From Original Documents Preserved in the Public Record Office. Edited by William Campbell. 2 volumes. Rerum Brittanicarum Medii Aevi Scriptores, no. 60. London, 1873–77.

More, Thomas. *The Correspondence of Thomas More.* Edited by E. F. Rogers. Princeton: Princeton University Press, 1947.

The Paston Letters, A. D. 1422–1509. New Complete Library Edition. Edited by James Gairdner. 6 volumes. London: Chatto and Windus, 1904.

Paston Letters and Papers of the Fifteenth Century. Edited by Norman Davis. Oxford: Clarendon Press, 1971.

"The Pilgrimage of Grace." Notes and Documents. *English Historical Review* 5 (1890): 330–45.

Report on the Manuscripts of the Most Honorable the Marquis of Bath Preserved at Longleat. Volume 4. Edited by Marjorie Blatcher. London: Historical Manuscripts Commission, 1968.

Rotuli Parliamentorum, ut et Petitiones et Placita in Parliamento. 6 volumes. [London, 1771–83].

Rutland Papers; Original Documents Illustrative of Court and Times of Henry VII and Henry VIII. Selected From the Private Archives of His Grace the Duke of Rutland. Edited by William Jerden. Camden Society Old Series, no. 21. London, 1842.

Rymer, Thomas. *Foedera, Conventiones, Litterae et cujuscunque Generis Acta Publica inter Reges Angliae et alios quosuis Imperatores, Reges, Pontifices, Principes vel Com-*

Bibliography

munitates ab Ineunte Saeculo Duodecimo, viz. ab Anno 1101, ad nostra usque Tempora Habita aut Tractata. Second Edition, with additional material edited by Robert Sanderson. 20 volumes. London, 1727–35.
Smyth, John, ed. *The Berkeley Manuscripts. The Lives of the Berkeleys, Lords of the Honor, Castle and Manor of Berkeley; in the County of Gloucester, From 1066 to 1618.* Edited by John MacLean. 2 volumes. Gloucester, 1883–85.
State Papers, King Henry the Eighth. 11 volumes. London, 1830–52.
Statutes of the Realm. Edited by A. Luders et al. 11 volumes. London, 1810–28.
Wright, Thomas, ed. *Three Chapters of Letters Relating to the Suppression of the Monasteries.* Camden Society Old Series, no. 26. London, 1843.

CHRONICLES AND CONTEMPORARY BIOGRAPHIES

Armstrong, C. A. J., ed. and trans. *The Usurpation of Richard the Third: Dominicus Mancinus ad Angelum Catonem de Occupatione Regni Anglie per Ricardum Tercium Libellus.* Second Edition. Oxford: Clarendon Press, 1969.
Bayne, Roland, ed. *The Life of Fisher.* Early English Text Society Extra Series, no. 117. London: Oxford University Press, 1921.
Camden, William. *Britain, or a Chorographicall Description of the Most Flourishing Kingdomes, England, Scotland, and Ireland, and the Islands Adjoyning, Out of the Depth of Antiquitie.* Translated by Philemon Holland. London, 1637.
Cavendish, George. *The Life and Death of Cardinal Wolsey.* In *Two Early Tudor Lives*, edited by R. S. Sylvester and D. P. Harding. New Haven: Yale University Press, 1962.
Chrónica Del Rey Enrico Octave de Inglaterra, escrita por un autor coetáneo, y ahora por primera vez impressa é illustrata, con introduccion, notas y apéndices, por el Marquis de Molins. Libros de Antaño, n. IV. Madrid, 1874.
The Chronicle of Queen Jane and of Two Years of Queen Mary, and Especially of the Rebellion of Sir Thomas Wyatt. Written by a Resident of the Tower of London. Edited by John G. Nichols. Camden Society Old Series, no. 48. London, 1850.
Dowling, Thaddeus. *Annales Breves Hiberniae. Annals of Ireland.* Edited by Richard Butler. Dublin, 1849.
Godwin, Francis. *Annales of England. Containing the Reignes of Henry the Eighth. Edward the Sixt. Queen Mary. Written in Latin by the Right Honorable and Right Reverend Father in God, Francis, Lord Bishop of Hereford. Thus Englished, corrected and inlarged with the author's consent, by Morgan Godwyn.* London, 1630.
Grace, James. *Annales Hiberniae.* Edited, with a translation and notes, by Richard Butler. Dublin, 1842.
The Great Chronicle of London. Edited by A. H. Thomas and I. D. Thornley. London, 1938.

Bibliography

Guaras, Antonio di. *The Accession of Queen Mary. Being the Contemporary Narrative of A. de Guaras, a Spanish Merchant Resident in London.* Translated by R. Garnett. London, 1892.

Hakluyt, Richard. *The Principle Navigations, Voyages, Traffiques and Discoveries of the English Nation.* 12 volumes. Glascow: James MacLehose and Sons, Publishers to the University, 1903–5.

Hall, Edward. *Hall's Chronicle; Containing the History of England, During the Reigne of Henry the Fourth and the Succeeding Monarchs, to the Reign of Henry VIII.* Edited by Henry Ellis. London, 1809.

———. *The Triumphant Reigne of Kyng Henry VIII.* Edited with an introduction by Charles Whilbey. 2 volumes. London: T. C. and E. C. Jack, 1904.

Hardyng, John, and Richard Grafton. *The Chronicle of Iohn Hardyng, Together With the Continuation by Richard Grafton, to the Thirty-fourth Year of King Henry the Eight.* Edited by Henry Ellis. London, 1812.

Holinshed, Raphael. *Holinshed's Chronicles of England, Scotland and Ireland.* 6 volumes. London, 1808.

The Itinerary of John Leland, In or About the Years 1535–1543. Edited by Lucy Toulmin Smith. 5 volumes. Oxford, 1907–10. Reprint, Carbondale: Southern Illinois University Press, 1964.

"The Manner of the Triumph at Calais, 1532." In *An English Garner: Tudor Tracts, 1532–1588*, edited by Thomas Seccombe. Westminster: Archibald Constable, 1903.

Proctor, John. "The History of Wyatt's Rebellion: With the order and manner of resisting the same. Whereunto, in the end, is added: An Earnest Conference with the degenerate and seditious rebels for the source of the cause of their daily disorder." [Second Edition, London, 1555]. In *An English Garner: Tudor Tracts, 1532–1588*, edited by Thomas Seccombe. Westminster: Archibald Constable, 1903.

Roper, William. *The Life of Sir Thomas More.* In *Two Early Tudor Lives*, edited by R. S. Sylvester and D. P. Harding. New Haven: Yale University Press, 1962.

Smith, George, ed. *The Coronation of Elizabeth Wydeville, Queen Consort of Edward IV, on May 26th 1465. A Contemporary Account Now First Set Forth from a XV Century Manuscript.* London: Ellis, 1935.

Stow, John. *The Annales, or a General Chronicle of England, Begun First by Maister John Stow and After Him Continued and Augmented with Matters Forreyne and Domestique, Aunciend and Moderne, unto the End of this Present Yeere 1614, By Edmond Howes, gentleman.* London, 1615.

Vergil, Polydore. *The Anglica Historia of Polydore Vergil.* Translated and edited by Denis Hay. Camden Society, Third Series, no. 74. London: Camden Society, 1950.

Ware, James, ed. *Two Histories of Ireland: The One Written by Edmund Campion [1571] and the Other by Meredith Hanmer, Doctor of Divinity*. Dublin, 1633. Reprint, New York: Da Capo Press, 1971.

Wriothesley, Charles. *A Chronicle of England During the Reignes of the Tudors, From A.D. 1485 to 1559*. Edited by William Douglas Hamilton. 2 volumes. Camden Society, Second Series, nos. 20–21. Westminster, 1875–77.

SECONDARY SOURCES

Anglo, Sydney. *Spectacle, Pageantry and Early Tudor Policy*. Oxford: Clarendon Press, 1969.

Bagwell, Richard. *Ireland Under the Tudors, With a Succinct Account of the Earlier History*. 2 volumes. London, 1885–90. Reprint, London: Holland Press, 1963.

Bapst, Edmond. *Deux Gentilshommes-poètes de la Cour de Henry VIII*. Paris, 1891.

Bates, Cadwallader John. *Flodden Field: A Collection of Some of the Earliest Evidence Concerning the Battle of Branxton Moor, 9th September 1513*. Newcastle upon Tyne, 1894.

Baumer, Franklin L. *The Early Tudor Theory of Kingship*. New Haven: Yale University Press, 1940.

Bean, John M. W. *The Decline of English Feudalism, 1215–1540*. Manchester: University Press, 1968.

Beckingsale, B. W. "The Characteristics of the Tudor North." *Northern History* 4 (1969): 67–83.

———. *Thomas Cromwell, Tudor Minister*. Totowa, N.J.: Rowan and Littlefield, 1978.

Beer, Barrett L. *Northumberland: The Political Career of John Dudley, Earl of Warwick and Duke of Northumberland*. [Kent, Ohio]: Kent State University Press, 1973.

Bennett, H. S. *The Pastons and Their England: Studies in an Age of Transition*. Cambridge Studies in Medieval Life and Thought, edited by G. G. Coulton. Cambridge: Cambridge University Press, 1927.

Bennett, Michael. *The Battle of Bosworth*. Gloucester: Alan Sutton, 1985.

Bernard, G. W. *The Power of the Early Tudor Nobility: A Study of the Fourth and Fifth Earls of Shrewsbury*. Brighton, Sussex: Harvester Press, 1985.

———. *War, Taxation and Rebellion in Tudor England: Henry VIII, Wolsey and the Amicable Grant of 1525*. Brighton, Sussex: Harvester Press, 1986.

Bindoff, S. T. *Ket's Rebellion*. London: Historical Association, 1949.

———. *Tudor England*. Baltimore: Penguin Books, 1950.

Bingham, Caroline. *James V, King of Scots 1512–1542*. London: William Collins and Sons, 1971.

Blomefield, Francis. *An Essay Toward a Topographical History of the County of Norfolk*. 11 volumes. London, 1805–10.

Bibliography

Bradshaw, Brendan. *The Dissolution of the Religious Orders in Ireland Under Henry VIII.* Cambridge: Cambridge University Press, 1979.

———. *The Irish Constitutional Revolution of the Sixteenth Century.* Cambridge: Cambridge University Press, 1979.

Brenan, Gerald. *A History of the House of Percy, From the Earliest Times Down to the Present Century.* Edited by W. A. Lindsay. 2 volumes. London: Freemantle and Co., 1902.

Brenan, Gerald, and E. P. Statham. *The House of Howard.* 2 volumes, pagination consecutive. London, 1907. Reprint, Ann Arbor: University Microfilms, 1972.

Brodrick, George C. *English Land and English Landlords: An Enquiry into the Origin and Character of the English Land System With Proposals for its Reform.* London, 1881. Reprint, New York: Augustus M. Kelley, 1968.

Brown, P. Hume. *The History of Scotland: Volume I, To the Accession of Mary Stewart.* Cambridge: Cambridge University Press, 1909.

Bruce, Marie L. *Anne Boleyn.* New York: Coward, McCann and Geoghegan, 1972.

Buck, Sir George. *History of Richard III (1619).* Edited by Arthur Noel Kincaid. Gloucester: Alan Sutton, 1979.

Burke, Bernard. *A Genealogical History of the Dormant, Abeyant, Forfeited and Extinct Peerages of the British Empire.* London, 1866.

Burnet, Gilbert. *The History of the Reformation of the Church of England.* Revised with a preface by E. Nares. 3 volumes. New York, 1843.

Burton, John Hill. *The History of Scotland.* New Edition. 8 volumes. Edinburgh, 1899.

Bush, Michael L. "The Problem of the Far North: A Study of the Crisis of 1537 and its Consequences." *Northern History* 6 (1971): 40–63.

Casady, Edwin. *Henry Howard, Earl of Surrey.* Modern Language Association of America Revolving Fund Series, vol. 8. New York: Modern Language Association of America, 1938.

Caspari, Fritz. *Humanism and the Social Order in Tudor England.* Chicago: University of Chicago Press, 1954.

Chambers, D. S. "Cardinal Wolsey and the Papal Tiara." *Bulletin of the Institute of Historical Research* 38 (1965): 20–30.

Chambers, Raymond W. *Thomas More.* Westminster, Md.: Newman Press, [1936].

Chrimes, S. B. *Henry VII.* Berkeley and Los Angeles: University of California Press, 1972.

Cokayne, George Edward. *The Complete Peerage, or a History of the House of Lords and all its Members from the Earliest Times.* 13 volumes. London: St. Catherine's Press, 1910–40.

Colvin, H. M. "Castles and Government in Tudor England." *English Historical Review* 83 (1968): 225–34.

Bibliography

Crabites, Pierre. *Clement VII and Henry VIII*. London: George Routledge and Sons, 1935.

Davey, Richard. *The Nine Days Queen: Lady Jane Grey and Her Times*. Edited with an introduction by Martin S. Hume. New York: G. P. Putnam's Sons, 1909.

Davies, C. S. L. *Peace, Print and Protestantism 1450–1558*. St. Albans, Hertfordshire: Paladin, 1977.

———. "The Pilgrimage of Grace Reconsidered." *Past and Present* 41 (1968): 54–76.

———. "Provisions for Armies, 1509–50: A Study in the Effectiveness of Early Tudor Government." *Economic History Review*, series 2, 17 (1964): 234–48.

Deans, Richard S. *The Trials of Five Queens*. London: Methuen and Co., 1909.

Dickens, Arthur G. *The English Reformation*. New York: Schocken Books, 1964.

———. *Lollards and Protestants in the Diocese of York*. Oxford: Clarendon Press, 1959.

Dictionary of National Biography. Edited by Leslie Stephens and Sidney Lee. 63 volumes. London, 1885–1900. Reprinted in 22 volumes, London, 1921–22.

Dietz, Frederick C. *English Government Finance, 1485–1558*. Second edition. New York: Barnes and Noble, 1964.

Dodds, M. H., and Ruth Dodds. *The Pilgrimage of Grace, 1536–1537 and the Exeter Conspiracy, 1538*. 2 volumes. Cambridge: Cambridge University Press, 1915.

Donaldson, Gordon. *Scotland: James V to James VII*. New York: Praeger, 1966.

Dunham, William H. "The Ellesmere Extracts from the 'Acta Consilii' of King Henry VIII." *English Historical Review* 58 (1943): 301–18.

———. "Henry VIII's Whole Council and its Parts." *Huntington Library Quarterly* 71 (1943): 7–46.

———. "The Members of Henry VIII's Whole Council, 1509–27." *English Historical Review* 59 (1944): 187–210.

Eaves, Richard Glen. *Henry VIII's Scottish Diplomacy, 1513–1524: England's Relations with the Regency Government of James V*. New York: Exposition Press, 1971.

Edwards, H. L. R. *Skelton: The Life and Times of an Early Tudor Poet*. London: Jonathan Cape, 1949.

Einstein, Lewis. *Tudor Ideals*. New York: Harcourt, Brace and Co., 1921.

Ellis, Stephen G. *Tudor Ireland: Crown, Community and the Conflict of Cultures*. Harlow: Longman, 1985.

Elton, G. R. "The Early Journals of the House of Lords." *English Historical Review* 89 (1974): 481–512.

———. *England 1200–1640: The Sources of History*. Studies in the Use of Historical Evidence, general editor G. R. Elton. Ithaca: Cornell University Press, 1969.

———. *England Under the Tudors*. London: Methuen and Co., 1955.

———. "King or Minister? The Man Behind the English Reformation." *History*, new series, 39 (1954): 216–32.

Bibliography

———. *Policy and Police: The Enforcement of the Reformation in the Age of Thomas Cromwell.* Cambridge: Cambridge University Press, 1972.

———. "Politics and the Pilgrimage of Grace." In *After the Reformation: Essays in Honor of J. H. Hexter,* edited by Barbara C. Malament. Philadelphia: University of Pennsylvania Press, 1980.

———. *Reform and Reformation: England, 1509–1558.* Cambridge: Harvard University Press, 1977.

———. *Reform and Renewal: Thomas Cromwell and the Common Weal.* Cambridge: Cambridge University Press, 1973.

———. "Sir Thomas More and the Opposition to Henry VIII." In *Studies in Tudor Politics and Government.* 2 vols. Cambridge: Cambridge University Press, 1974. 1: 129–56.

———. *Star Chamber Stories.* London: Methuen and Co., 1958.

———. "Thomas Cromwell's Decline and Fall." *Cambridge Historical Journal* 10 (1951): 150–85.

———. "Thomas Cromwell Redivivus." *Archiv für Reformationsgeschichte* 68 (1977): 192–208.

———. "Tudor Government: The Points of Contact. I. Parliament." *Transactions of the Royal Historical Society* 5th series, 24 (1974): 183–200.

———. "Tudor Government: The Points of Contact. II. The Council." *Transactions of the Royal Historical Society* 5th series, 25 (1975): 195–211.

———. "Tudor Government: The Points of Contact. III. The Court." *Transactions of the Royal Historical Society* 5th series, 26 (1976): 211–28.

———. *The Tudor Revolution in Government: Administrative Changes in the Reign of Henry VIII.* Cambridge: Cambridge University Press, 1953.

Erickson, Carroly. *Bloody Mary.* Garden City, N. Y.: Doubleday and Co., 1978.

Esdaile, Katherine A. *English Church Monuments, 1510 to 1840.* New York: Oxford University Press, 1946.

Fenlon, Dermott. *Heresy and Obedience in Tridentine Italy: Cardinal Pole and the Counter-Reformation.* Cambridge: Cambridge University Press, 1972.

Ferguson, Arthur B. *The Indian Summer of English Chivalry: Studies in the Decline and Transformation of Chivalric Idealism.* Durham, N.C.: Duke University Press, 1960.

Fisher, H. A. L. *The History of England, From the Accession of Henry VII to the Death of Henry VIII (1485–1547).* The Political History of England, edited by William Hunt and Reginald L. Poole, volume 5. London: Longmans, Green and Co., 1919.

Friedmann, Paul. *Anne Boleyn: A Chapter in English History.* 2 volumes. London, 1884.

Froud, James Antony. *The History of England from the Fall of Cardinal Wolsey to the Defeat of the Spanish Armada.* 12 volumes. London, 1862–70.

Gairdner, James. "On a Contemporary Drawing of the Burning of Brighton in the Time of Henry VIII." *Transactions of the Royal Historical Society* 3rd series, 1 (1901): 19–31.

Gammon, Samuel R. *Statesman and Schemer: William, Lord Paget, Tudor Minister.* Hamden, Conn.: Archon Books, 1973.

Gladish, Dorothy M. *The Tudor Privy Council.* Retford [Nottinghamshire]: Printed at the Office of "The Retford, Gainsborough and Worksop Times," 1915.

Green, R. *The History, Topography and Antiquities of Framlingham and Saxstead in the County of Suffolk.* London, 1834.

Gunn, S. J. *Charles Brandon, Duke of Suffolk, c. 1484–1545.* Oxford: Basil Blackwell, 1988.

Guy, John A. *The Public Career of Thomas More.* Brighton, Sussex: Harvester Press, 1980.

———. "Wolsey, the Council and the Council Courts." *English Historical Review* 91 (1976): 481–505.

Haigh, Christopher. *The Last Days of the Lancashire Monasteries and the Pilgrimage of Grace.* Manchester: Chetham Society, 1969.

———. *Reform and Resistance in Tudor Lancashire.* Cambridge: Cambridge University Press, 1975.

Hammond, E. A. "Doctor Augustine, Physician to Cardinal Wolsey and King Henry VIII." *Medical History* 19 (1975): 215–49.

Hanham, Allison. "Hastings Redivivus." *English Historical Review* 90 (1975): 821–27.

———. "Landlords and Tenants in the Later Middle Ages: The Buckingham Estates." *Past and Present* 43 (1969): 146–50.

———. "Richard III, Lord Hastings and the Historians." *English Historical Review* 87 (1972): 233–48.

Harbison, E. Harris. "French Intrigues at Queen Mary's Court." *American Historical Review* 45 (1940): 545–60.

———. *Rival Ambassadors at the Court of Queen Mary.* Princeton: Princeton University Press, 1940.

Harris, Barbara J. *Edward Stafford, Third Duke of Buckingham, 1478–1521.* Stanford: Stanford University Press, 1986.

———. "Landlords and Tenants in the Later Middle Ages: The Buckingham Estates." *Past and Present* 43 (1969): 146–50.

———. "Marriage Sixteenth Century Style: Elizabeth Stafford and the Third Duke of Norfolk." *Journal of Social History* 15 (1982): 385–408.

Harrison, Scott M. *The Pilgrimage of Grace in the Lake Counties, 1536–7.* London: Royal Historical Society, 1981.

Harvey, Nancy L. *The Rose and the Thorn: The Lives of Mary and Margaret Tudor.* New York: Macmillan and Co., 1975.

Head, David M. "'Beyng Ledde and Seduced by the Devyll': The Attainder of Lord Thomas Howard and the Tudor Law of Treason." *Sixteenth Century Journal* 13 (1982): 3–16.

———. "Henry VIII's Scottish Policy: A Reassessment." *Scottish Historical Review* 61 (1982): 1–24.

Headley, John M. "The New Debate on More's Political Career." *Thought: The Fordham University Quarterly* 52 (1977): 270–78.

Herbert, Edward, Lord Herbert of Cherbury. *The Life and Raigne of King Henry the Eighth*. London, 1649.

Hexter, J. H. *Reappraisals in History*. New York: Harper and Row, 1963.

"Historical Notes of Medieval London Houses." *London Topographical Record* 10 (1916).

Hoak, Dale E. *The King's Council in the Reign of Edward VI*. Cambridge: Cambridge University Press, 1976.

Hood, Christobel, ed. *The Chorography of Norfolk: An Historicall and Chorographicall Description of Norffolck*. Norwich: Jarrold and Sons, 1938.

Hoskins, W. G. *The Age of Plunder: King Henry's England, 1500–1547*. London and New York: Longman, 1976.

Hughes, Philip. *The Reformation in England*. Revised edition. 3 volumes. New York: Macmillan and Co., 1963.

Hume, Martin S. *The Wives of Henry the Eighth, and the Parts They Played in History*. New York: McClure, Phillips and Co., 1905.

Hunt, A. Leigh. *The Capital of the Ancient Kingdom of East Anglia . . . Being a Complete and Authentic History of the Ancient Borough Town of Thetford*. London, 1870.

Hurstfield, Joel. "The Revival of Feudalism in Early Tudor England." *History* 37 (1952): 131–45.

———. "Was There a Tudor Royal Despotism After All?" *Transactions of the Royal Historical Society* 5th series, 17 (1967): 83–108.

Ives, E. W. *Anne Boleyn*. Oxford: Basil Blackwell, 1986.

———. "Court and County Palatine in the Reign of Henry VIII: The Career of William Brereton of Malpas." *Transactions of the Historic Society of Lancashire and Chester* 123 (1972): 1–38.

———. "Faction at the Court of Henry VIII: The Fall of Anne Boleyn." *History* 57 (1972): 169–88.

———. *Faction in Tudor England*. London: Historical Association, 1979.

———. "The Genesis of the Statute of Uses." *English Historical Review* 82 (1967): 673–97.

———. "Patronage at the Court of Henry VIII—Sir Ralph Egerton of Ridley." *Bulletin of the John Rylands Library* 52 (1970): 346–74.

Jacob, E. F. *The Fifteenth Century, 1399–1485*. Oxford: Clarendon Press, 1961.

James, M. E. "The First Earl of Cumberland and the Decline of Northern Feudalism." *Northern History* 1 (1966): 43–69.

———. "Obedience and Dissent in Henrician England: The Lincolnshire Rebellion, 1536." *Past and Present* 48 (1970): 1–72.

Jones, Paul von B. *The Household of a Tudor Nobleman.* University of Illinois Studies in the Social Sciences, vol. 6, no. 4. Urbana: University of Illinois Press, 1918.

Jordan, W. K. *Edward VI: The Threshold of Power.* Cambridge, Mass.: Belknap Press of Harvard University, 1970.

———. *Edward VI: The Young King.* Cambridge, Mass.: Belknap Press of Harvard University, 1968.

Kelly, Henry A. *The Matrimonial Trials of Henry VIII.* Stanford: Stanford University Press, 1976.

Kelly, Michael. "The Submission of the Clergy." *Transactions of the Royal Historical Society* 5th series, 15 (1965): 97–119.

Kendall, P. M. *Richard the Third.* New York: W. W. Norton and Co., 1955.

Kitching, C. J. "The Quest for Concealed Lands in the Reign of Queen Elizabeth I." *Transactions of the Royal Historical Society* 5th series, 24 (1974): 63–78.

Knecht, R. J. *Francis I.* Cambridge: Cambridge University Press, 1982.

Knowles, Dom David. *The Religious Orders in England, Volume 3: Henry VIII, The Tudor Age.* Cambridge: Cambridge University Press, 1959.

Lander, J. R. "Attainder and Forfeiture, 1453–1509." *Historical Journal* 6 (1961): 120–51.

———. *Conflict and Stability in Fifteenth Century England.* London: Hutchinson and Co., 1969.

———. *Government and Community: England, 1450–1509.* Cambridge: Harvard University Press, 1980.

Lehmberg, Stanford E. *The Later Parliaments of Henry VIII, 1536–1547.* Cambridge: Cambridge University Press, 1977.

———. "Parliamentary Attainder in the Reign of Henry VIII." *Historical Journal* 18 (1975): 675–702.

———. *The Reformation Parliament, 1529–1536.* Cambridge: Cambridge University Press, 1970.

———. "Sir Thomas Audley: A Soul as Black as Marble?" In *Tudor Men and Institutions: Studies in English Law and Government,* edited by A. J. Slavin. Baton Rouge: Louisiana State University Press, 1972.

Levine, Mortimer. "The Fall of Edward, Duke of Buckingham." In *Tudor Men and Institutions: Studies in English Law and Government,* edited by A. J. Slavin. Baton Rouge: Louisiana State University Press, 1972.

———. *Tudor Dynastic Problems, 1460–1571.* New York: Barnes and Noble, 1973.

Lewis, Samuel. *A Topographical Dictionary of England.* 4 volumes. London, 1831.

Bibliography

Loades, D. M. *Politics and the Nation, 1450–1660: Obedience, Resistance, and the Public Order.* Brighton, Sussex: Harvester Press, 1974.

———. *The Reign of Mary Tudor: Politics, Government and Religion in England, 1553–1558.* New York: St. Martin's Press, 1979.

———. *The Tudor Court.* Totowa, N.J.: Barnes and Noble, 1987.

———. *Two Tudor Conspiracies.* Cambridge: Cambridge University Press, 1965.

McConica, James K. *English Humanists and Reformation Politics Under Henry VIII and Edward VI.* Oxford: Clarendon Press, 1965.

MacCullough, Dairmaid. "Kett's Rebellion in Context." *Past and Present* 84 (1979): 36–59.

———. *Suffolk and the Tudors: Politics and Religion in an English County, 1500–1600.* Oxford: Clarendon Press, 1986.

MacCurtain, Margaret. *Tudor and Stuart Ireland.* Dublin: Gill and MacMillan, 1972.

McEwen, John. "The Battle of Floddon, September 9th, 1513." *History Today* 8 (1958): 337–45.

McFarlane, K. B. *The Nobility of Later Medieval England: The Ford Lectures for 1953 and Related Studies.* Oxford: Clarendon Press, 1973.

McKee, Alexander. *Henry VIII's Mary Rose.* New York: Stein and Day, 1973.

Mackie, J. D. *The Earlier Tudors, 1485–1558.* Oxford: Clarendon Press, 1952.

———. "Henry VIII and Scotland." *Transactions of the Royal Historical Society* 4th ser., 29 (1947): 93–114.

Manning, Owen and William Bray. *The History and Antiquities of the County of Surrey.* 3 vols. London, 1804–14. Reprint. Ilkley, Yorkshire: E. P. Publishing, 1974.

Martienssen, Anthony. *Queen Katherine Parr.* New York: McGraw-Hill, 1973.

Mathews, David. *The Courtiers of Henry VIII.* London: Eyre and Spottiswoode, 1970.

Mattingly, Garrett. *Catherine of Aragon.* Boston: Houghton Mifflin Co., 1941.

———. *Renaissance Diplomacy.* Boston: Houghton Mifflin Co., 1955.

Merriman, M. H. "The Assured Scots: Scottish Collaborators with England During the Rough Wooing." *Scottish Historical Review* 48 (1968): 10–34.

Mertes, Kate. *The English Noble Household, 1250–1600: Good Governance and Politic Rule.* Oxford: Basil Blackwell, 1988.

Miller, Helen. "Attendance in the House of Lords in the Reign of Henry VIII." *Historical Journal* 10 (1967): 325–51.

———. "The Early Tudor Peerage, 1485–1547." *Bulletin of the Institute of Historical Research* 24 (1951): 88–91.

———. *Henry VIII and the English Nobility.* Oxford: Basil Blackwell, 1986.

———. "Henry VIII's Unwritten Will: Grants of Land and Honours in 1547." In *Wealth and Power in Tudor England: Essays Presented to S. T. Bindoff,* edited by

E. W. Ives, R. J. Knecht, and J. J. Scarisbrick. London: Athlone Press of the University of London, 1978.

———. "Subsidy Assessments of the Peerage in the Sixteenth Century." *Bulletin of the Institute of Historical Research* 28 (1955): 15–34.

Moreton, C. E. *The Townshends and Their World: Gentry, Law and Land in Norfolk, c. 1450–1551*. Oxford: Clarendon Press, 1992.

Muller, James A. *Stephen Gardiner and the Tudor Reaction*. New York: Macmillan and Co., 1926.

Murph, Roxane. *Richard III: The Making of a Legend*. Metuchen, N.J.: Scarecrow Press, 1977.

Nichols, John Gough. "Mary, Duchess of Richmond." *Gentleman's Magazine* new series, 23 (1845): 480–88.

Nott, George F., ed. *The Works of Henry Howard, Earl of Surrey, and of Sir Thomas Wyatt the Elder*. 2 volumes. London, 1815–16. Reprint, New York: AMS Reprint, 1965.

Oman, Charles W. C. *The Art of War in the Middle Ages*, A.D. *378–1515*. Revised and edited by John H. Beeler. Ithaca: Cornell University Press, 1953.

———. *A History of the Art of War in the Sixteenth Century*. New York: E. P. Dutton and Co., 1937.

Oxley, James E. *The Reformation in Essex to the Death of Mary*. Manchester: Manchester University Press, 1965.

Paget, Hugh. "The Youth of Anne Boleyn." *Bulletin of the Institute of Historical Research* 54 (1981): 162–70.

Parmiter, Geoffrey DeC. *The King's Great Matter: Anglo-Papal Relations, 1527–1534*. New York: Barnes and Noble, 1967.

Pastor, Ludwig, freiherr von. *The History of the Popes, From the Close of the Middle Ages*. Edited and translated by Antrobus, Kerr, Graf and Peeler. 40 volumes. St. Louis: B. Herder, 1899–1953.

Paul, J. E. *Catherine of Aragon and Her Friends*. New York: Fordham University Press, 1966.

Pickthorn, Kenneth. *Early Tudor Government: Henry VIII*. Cambridge: Cambridge University Press, 1934.

Pireronus, Peter J. "The Life and Career of Sir Anthony St. Leger of Ulcombe, Kent (1496?–1559). Lord Deputy of Ireland: A Biographical Study in the Evolution of early Tudor Anglo-Irish Policy." Ph.D. dissertation. Michigan State University, 1972.

Pollard, A. F. *Henry VIII*. London: Longmans, Green and Co., 1905.

———. "The Making of Sir Thomas More's Richard III." In *Historical Essays in Honor of James Tait*, edited by J. G. Edward, V. H. Galbraith, and E. F. Jacob. Manchester: Printed for the Subscribers, 1933.

———. *Wolsey*. London: Longmans, Green and Co., 1929.

Bibliography

Pollet, Maurice. *John Skelton, Poet of Tudor England.* Translated from the French by John Warrington. London: J. M. Dent and Sons, 1971.

Plucknett, T. F. T. "Some Proposed Legislation of Henry VIII." *Transactions of the Royal Historical Society* 4th series, 19 (1936): 119-44.

Prescott, H. F. M. *Mary Tudor.* London: Eyre and Spottiswoode, 1952.

Quinn, David B. "Henry VIII and Ireland, 1509-1534." *Irish Historical Studies* 12 (1961): 318-44.

Rae, Thomas I. *The Administration of the Scottish Frontier, 1513-1603.* Edinburgh: Edinburgh University Press, 1966.

Rawcliffe, Carole. *The Staffords, Earls of Stafford and Dukes of Buckingham, 1394-1521.* Cambridge: Cambridge University Press, 1978.

Redworth, Glyn. *In Defense of the Church Catholic: The Life of Stephen Gardiner.* Oxford: Basil Blackwell, 1990.

———. "A Study in the Formulation of Policy: The Genesis and Evolution of the Act of Six Articles." *Journal of Ecclesiastical History* 37 (1986): 42-67.

Reid, Rachel. *The King's Council in the North.* London: Longmans, Green and Co., 1921.

Reid, W. Stanford. *Trumpeter of God: A Biography of John Knox.* New York: Charles Scribner's Sons, 1974.

Reynolds, Ernest E. *The Field Is Won: The Life and Death of Saint Thomas More.* Milwaukee: Bruce Publishing Co., 1968.

Richardson, Ethel M. *The Lion and the Rose: The Great Howard Story.* 2 volumes. New York: E. P. Dutton and Co., 1922.

Richardson, Walter C. *The History of the Court of Augmentations, 1536-1554.* Baton Rouge: Louisiana State University Press, 1961.

———. *Mary Tudor: The White Queen.* Seattle: University of Washington Press, 1970.

Riddell, John. *Inquiry into the Law and Practices in Scottish Peerages.* 2 volumes. Edinburgh, 1842.

Ridley, Jasper. *Nicholas Ridley, A Biography.* London: Longmans, Green and Co., 1957.

———. *Thomas Cranmer.* Oxford: Clarendon Press, 1962.

Robinson, John M. *The Dukes of Norfolk: A Quincentennial History.* Oxford: Oxford University Press, 1982.

Robinson, W. R. B. "The Officers and Household of Henry, Earl of Worcester, 1526-49." *Welsh Historical Review* 8 (1976): 26-41.

Ross, C. R. *Richard III.* London: Eyre Methuen, 1981.

Routh, E. M. G. *Sir Thomas More and His Friends, 1477-1535.* London: Oxford University Press, 1934.

Rowse, A. W. *Tudor Cornwall: Portrait of a Society.* Second Edition. New York: Charles Scribner's Sons, 1969.

Bibliography

Russell, Conrad. *The Crisis of Parliaments: English History, 1509–1660.* London: Oxford University Press, 1971.
Russell, Joycelyne G. *The Field of the Cloth of Gold: Men and Manners in 1520.* New York: Barnes and Noble, 1969.
Salzman, L. F. *English Trade in the Middle Ages.* Oxford: Clarendon Press, 1931.
Savine, Alexander. *English Monasteries on the Eve of the Dissolution.* Oxford: Clarendon Press, 1909.
Scammell, G. V. "Shipowning in England, c. 1450–1550." *Transactions of the Royal Historical Society* 5th series, 12 (1962): 102–22.
Scarisbrick, J. J. *Henry VIII.* Berkeley and Los Angeles: University of California Press, 1968.
———. *The Reformation and the English People.* Oxford: Basil Blackwell, 1984.
———. "Thomas More: The King's Good Servant." *Thought: The Fordham University Quarterly* 52 (1977): 249–59.
Slavin, A. J. *Politics and Profit: A Study of Sir Ralph Sadler, 1504–1547.* Cambridge: Cambridge University Press, 1966.
Smith, Herbert M. *Henry VIII and the Reformation.* New York: Russell and Russell, 1962.
Smith, L. B. "English Treason Trials and Confessions in the Sixteenth Century." *Journal of the History of Ideas* 15 (1954): 471–98.
———. "Henry VIII and the Protestant Triumph." *American Historical Review* 71 (1966): 1237–64.
———. *Henry VIII: The Mask of Royalty.* Chicago: Academy Chicago, 1982.
———. *Tudor Prelates and Politics.* Princeton: Princeton University Press, 1953.
———. *A Tudor Tragedy: The Life and Times of Catherine Howard.* New York: Pantheon Books, 1961.
Smith, R. B. *Land and Politics in the England of Henry VIII: The West Riding of Yorkshire, 1530–40.* Oxford: Clarendon Press, 1970.
Snow, Vernon F. "Proctorial Representation and Conciliar Management During the Reign of Henry VIII." *Historical Journal* 9 (1966): 1–26.
Starkey, David. *The Reign of Henry VIII: Personalities and Politics.* New York: Franklin Watts, 1986.
Stone, Lawrence. *The Crisis of the Aristocracy, 1558–1641.* Oxford: Clarendon Press, 1965.
Sturge, Charles. *Cuthbert Tunstall: Churchman, Scholar, Statesman, Administrator.* London: Longmans, Green and Co., 1938.
Swales, T. H. "The Redistribution of the Monastic Lands in Norfolk at the Dissolution." *Norfolk Archaeology* 34 (1966): 20–22.
Thirsk, Joan, ed. *The Agrarian History of England and Wales.* Volume 4: 1500–1640. General editor H. P. R. Finberg. Cambridge: Cambridge University Press, 1967.

Bibliography

Thomson, J. A. F. "Richard III and Lord Hastings—A Problematical Case Reviewed." *Bulletin of the Institute of Historical Research* 48 (1975): 22–30.

Tjernagel, Neelak S. *Henry VIII and the Lutherans: A Study in Anglo-Lutheran Relations from 1521 to 1547.* St. Louis: Concordia Publishing House, 1965.

Tucker, Melvin J. *The Life of Thomas Howard, Earl of Surrey and Second Duke of Norfolk, 1443–1524.* London: Mouton and Co., 1964.

———. "The More-Howard Connections of John Skelton." *Moreana* 37 (1973): 15–24.

———. "The More-Norfolk Connection." *Moreana* 33 (1972): 5–13.

Urban, Sylvanus. "Anne Lady Howard." *Gentleman's Magazine* new series, 23 (1845): 147–52.

———. "Elizabeth Duchess of Norfolk." *Gentleman's Magazine* new series, 23 (1845): 259–67.

Victoria County Histories. A History of Hertfordshire. Edited by William Page. 4 volumes. London, 1902–23. Reprint, London: University of London Institute of Historical Research, 1971.

Victoria County Histories. A History of Staffordshire. Edited by William Page, M. W. Greenslade, J. G. Jenkins and L. Margaret Midgley. 8 volumes. London: Constable and Co., and the University of London Institute of Historical Research, 1908–67.

Victoria County Histories. A History of Suffolk. Edited by William Page. 2 volumes, series incomplete. London: Archibald Constable, 1907–.

Victoria County Histories. A History of the County of Middlesex. Edited by J. S. Cockburn, H. P. F. King, J. G. T. McDonnel and William Page. 5 volumes. London: Constable and Co., 1911–69.

Victoria County Histories. A History of the County of Norfolk. Edited by H. A. Doubleday. 2 volumes, series incomplete. London: Constable and Co., 1901–.

Victoria County Histories. A History of the County of Surrey. Edited by H. E. Malden. 5 volumes. London: Constable and Co., 1902–14.

Virgoe, R. "The Recovery of the Howards in East Anglia, 1485–1529." In *Wealth and Power in Tudor England: Essays Presented to S. T. Bindoff*, edited by E. W. Ives, R. J. Knecht and J. J. Scarisbrick. London: Athlone Press of the University of London, 1978.

Walker, Greg. *John Skelton and the Politics of the 1520s.* Cambridge: Cambridge University Press, 1988.

Warnicke, Retha M. "The Fall of Anne Boleyn: A Reassessment." *History* 70 (1985): 1–15.

———. *The Rise and Fall of Anne Boleyn.* Cambridge: Cambridge University Press, 1989.

Wedgewood, Josiah C., ed. *History of Parliament. Biographies of the Members of the Commons House, 1439–1509.* London: His Majesty's Stationer's Office, 1936.

Bibliography

———. *History of Parliament. Register of the Ministers and of the Members of Both Houses, 1439–1509*. London: His Majesty's Stationer's Office, 1938.
Wegg, Jervis. *Richard Pace, A Tudor Diplomatist*. London: Methuen and Co., 1932. Reprint, New York: Barnes and Noble, 1971.
Wernham, R. B. *Before the Armada: The Emergence of the English Nation, 1485–1558*. New York: Harcourt, Brace and World, 1966.
Williams, Neville. *The Cardinal and the Secretary*. London: Weidenfield and Nicholson, 1975.
———. *Henry VIII and His Court*. New York: Macmillan, 1971.
———. *Thomas Howard, Fourth Duke of Norfolk*. New York: E. P. Dutton and Co., 1964.
Williams, Penry. *The Tudor Regime*. Oxford: Clarendon Press, 1979.
Williamson, Hugh R. *Enigmas of History*. New York: Macmillan, 1957.
Williamson, J. A. *Maritime Enterprise, 1485–1558*. Oxford: Oxford University Press, 1913.
———. *The Tudor Age*. London: Longmans, Green and Co., 1953.
Wilson, Derek. *A Tudor Tapestry: Men, Women and Society in Reformation England*. Pittsburgh: University of Pittsburgh Press, 1972.
Woods, Robert L. "The Amicable Grant: Some Aspects of Thomas Wolsey's Rule in England, 1522–26." Ph.D. dissertation, University of California at Los Angeles, 1974.
———. "Politics and Precedent: Wolsey's Parliament of 1523." *Huntington Library Quarterly* 40 (1977): 297–312.
Wolffe, B. P. "Hastings Reinterred." *English Historical Review* 91 (1976): 813–24.
———. "When and Why Did Hastings Lose His Head?" *English Historical Review* 89 (1974): 835–44.
Wyndham, H. A. *A Family History, 1410–1688. The Wyndhams of Norfolk and Somerset*. London: Oxford University Press, 1939.
Youings, Joyce. *The Dissolution of the Monasteries*. London: George Allen and Unwin, 1971.
Zeeveld, W. Gordon. *The Foundations of Tudor Policy*. Cambridge: Harvard University Press, 1948.

Index

Act of Six Articles, 160–63, 267
Albany, duke of. *See* Stuart, John, duke of Albany
Amicable Grant of 1524: proposed in council, 77; problems in collections, 79–81; revoked, 81
Angoulême, duke of: proposed in marriage to Princess Elizabeth, 125
Annebaut, Claude d', admiral of France, 221
Anne of Cleves, queen of England: marriage to Henry VIII, 154; divorce, 171–72, 175–76
Aragonese faction at court: after fall of Wolsey, 105, 120–21; Norfolk not a member, 121; and trial of William lord Dacre, 123; and fall of Anne Boleyn, 127–28; and Pilgrimage of Grace, 135; and Exeter conspiracy, 156
Arran, earl of. *See* Hamilton, James, earl of Arran
Arthur, Prince of Wales, 318 (n. 14)
Arundel, Thomas, servant to Wolsey, 100
Ascham, Roger, 264
Aske, Robert: and Pilgrimage of Grace, 137–43; arrest and execution, 145
Askew, Anne, 220
Assured lords, after battle of Solway Moss, 208–10
Audley, Thomas: Speaker of Commons, 1532, 112; knighted, 113; made keeper of Great Seal, 113; chancellor, 155; supports Cromwell, 160–62; death, 212; resigns chancellorship, 212
Augustini, Antonio de, 101
Auld Alliance between Scotland and France, 46, 64; reaffirmed by James V, 146, 193–94; by Arran, 210

Barnes, Robert, 168–69, 174
Barton, Andrew: killed in sea battle with Howards, 28; and battle of Flodden, 33, 35
Barton, Elizabeth, "Maid of Kent," 121
Beaton, David, archbishop of St. Andrews, cardinal, chancellor of Scotland, 71–73, 147, 193–94
Bellay, Jean du, bishop of Bayonne, cardinal, French ambassador to England: reports, 90–91, 93, 94; approaches Norfolk to arrange truce, 215
Benet, William, 108–9, 320 (n. 43)
Berkeley, William, lord, 15, 296 (n. 12)
Bigod, Sir Francis, 143–45
Bishops' Book, 160
Blage, George, 220, 222, 257
Blage, Robert, 309 (n. 119)
Blount, Elizabeth, mother of Henry Fitzroy, 83
Boleyn, Anne, queen of England: early life and appearance at court, 86–87; relations with Wolsey, 88; presses Henry to remove Wolsey, 92–93;

Boleyn, Anne (*continued*)
  and fall of Wolsey, 101–2, 317 (n. 123); rumors of bad relations with Norfolk, 109–10; made marchioness of Pembroke, 114; pregnancy, 115; marries Henry, crowned queen, 116; worsening relations with Norfolk, 119–20, 124–25; miscarriage, 126; trial and execution, 128–29; religious views, 318 (n. 8)

Boleyn, George, lord Rochford, 123–24, 127–29

Boleyn, James, 265

Boleyn, Jane, lady Rochford, 184, 186, 189

Boleyn, Sir Thomas: at court, 1509–10, 26; treasurer of household to Henry VIII, 86; and Anne Boleyn, 87; gives masque celebrating death of Wolsey, 102; made earl of Wiltshire and Ormond, 105; sent to France with Norfolk, 124–25; and fall of Anne Boleyn, 129; replaced as keeper of privy seal by Cromwell, 131

Bonner, Edmund, bishop of London, 118, 167, 330 (n. 43)

Borgho, papal nucio in England: conversations with Norfolk, 106, 111, 316 (n. 113); presents papal brief, 112

Bosworth, battle of, 17–18

Boulogne: Thomas Howard and, 214–15; Henry Howard and, 217–19

Bourchier, Humphrey, 13

Bourchier, John, lord Berners, 19

Bourchier, Thomas, archbishop of Canterbury, 296 (n. 17)

Bowes, Sir Robert: and Haddon Ridge, 199–200

Brandon, Charles, duke of Suffolk: companion of Henry VIII, 26; created duke of Suffolk, 41; relations with Howards, 43–45; marries Mary Tudor, 44; character, 44–45, 281; at christening of Princess Mary, 47; invasion of France, 1527, 64; joins Norfolk in opposition to Wolsey, 76, 91–94; and Amicable Grant, 77–80; and signing of Treaty of the More, 82; president of council, 97; breakdown of alliance with Norfolk, 105; growing resentment of Anne Boleyn, 110; made knight of Order of St. Michael, 114; yields earl marshalship to Norfolk, 118, 284; and progress to York, 196; captures Boulogne, 213; death, 217; annuity paid to Norfolk, 277; religious beliefs, 315 (n. 93)

Brereton, William, 128–29

Brett, Alexander, 240–41

Brighton: burned by French, 1514, 42, 302 (n. 5)

Brooke, George, lord Cobham, 240–42

Browne, Sir Anthony, 217, 266–67, 321 (n. 60)

Browne, Anthony, Franciscan friar: executed for treason, 155

Bryan, Sir Francis, 75, 267

Buckingham, duke of. *See* Stafford, Edward, duke of Buckingham

Bulmer, Sir William, 34, 51–52

Butler, Sir James, 56

Butler, Sir Piers, pretended earl of Ormond, 52–53, 54, 58–59

Butler, Thomas, seventh earl of Ormond, 52

Butts, William, physician to Henry VIII, 89

Index

Calais, Thomas Howard and, 60–61, 114, 117, 124–25, 212, 214–15
Cambrai, Peace of, 91
Campe, Treaty of, 221
Campeggio, Lorenzo, bishop of Salisbury, papal legate, 50, 90–92
Carew, Nicholas: and fall of Anne Boleyn, 127; executed, 157
Carlisle: risings at, 1537, 144
Carre, Sir John, 25, 299 (n. 7)
Casale, Gregory, 116, 119–20
Castillion, Gaspard de Coligny, French ambassador in England, 150, 153
Catherine of Aragon, queen of England: arrival, 21; coronation, 25; and birth and death of Prince Henry, 27; reports victory at Flodden to Henry, 38–39; and birth of Princess Mary, 47; and Evil May Day, 49; Henry considers divorcing, 83, 86; refuses to submit to Henry, 107; refuses to renounce claims as queen and is divorced, 116; death, 126
Cesford Castle, razed by Thomas Howard, 62
Chabot, Philippe de, admiral of France, 123–24
Chapuys, Eustace, imperial ambassador to England: describes Norfolk, 7; and Norfolk's reaction to Pilgrimage of Grace, 7, 136; arrival at court, 92; and Norfolk's reaction to Wolsey's removal as chancellor, 94; reports on political situation, 1529–30, 97–101, 106–7; and Norfolk's efforts to win divorce, 108–9; and proposed match between Henry Howard and Princess Mary, 109–10; and Parliament of 1532, 111–12; conversations with Norfolk, 113–14, 209–11; reports English indignation with marriage to Anne Boleyn, 116; reports bad relations between Norfolk and Anne, 119–20, 124–25; and conflict between Norfolk and Cromwell, 132–33; leads negotiations for alliance, 198–200; reliability of reports, 317 (n. 1), 321 (n. 70)
Charles duke of Bourbon, constable of France, 64, 69, 86, 114
Charles duke of Orleans, son of Francis I, and proposed marriage to Princess Mary, 195–98
Charles V, king of Spain, Holy Roman Emperor: accession, 49; captures Francis I at Pavia, 76; repudiates betrothal to Princess Mary, 81–82; and reports on fall of Wolsey, 94–95; truce with Francis I, 158; and negotiations for English alliance, 197–200, 209; and treaty of Crépy, 213; mediates between Henry and Francis, 215–16, 338 (n. 102); reaction to fall of Howards, 224; and Thomas Howard's pension, 350 (n. 123)
Cheke, John, 233
Clement VII, Pope: captured by troops of duke of Bourbon, 86; and Henry's divorce case, 91; issues brief revoking case to Rome, 99; issues brief forbidding Henry to remarry, 101; orders Henry to return to Catherine, 112; approves Cranmer as archbishop of Canterbury, 115; threatens Henry's excommunication, 117; death, 123
Clere, Sir John, 259, 267
Clere, Thomas, 253, 267

Clerk, John, 264
Cognac, League of, 82, 85
Collectanea satis copiosa, 105–6, 111
Compton, Sir William, 26, 309 (n. 123)
Constable, Sir Marmaduke, 35
Courtenay, Edward, 230, 235–36, 239
Courtenay, Henry, marquis of Exeter, 105, 122, 127, 137–38, 156
Cranmer, Thomas, archbishop of Canterbury: and progressive party after fall of Wolsey, 105; made archbishop, 115, 319 (n. 36); approves Henry's divorce from Catherine of Aragon, 116; declares marriage to Anne Boleyn void and dispenses marriage to Jane Seymour, 129; resistance to Act of Six Articles, 161; mediates between Norfolk and Cromwell, 163; and fall of Cromwell, 175; and fall of Catherine Howard, 185; political position in the 1540s, 190, 218; and death of Henry VIII, 228; visits Norfolk in Tower, 230; and Prayer Book, 234; arrest and execution, 237; his marriage, 330 (n. 31)
Crépy, Treaty of, 213
Crome, Dr. Edward, 220
Cromwell, Thomas: servant to Wolsey, 98–100; early life, 103–4; seeks seat in Parliament of 1529 from Norfolk, 104; and murder of Sir William Pennington, 110; in Parliamentary session of 1532, 110–12; becomes leading minister, 116–19; made principal secretary, 121; sends Norfolk to France, 1535, 124–25; and fall of Anne Boleyn, 126–29; made baron and lord privy seal, 131; and death of duke of Richmond, 132–33; northern hostility toward, 134–35, 142; and Norfolk and Pilgrimage of Grace, 136–37; orders Norfolk to remain in north, 146; receives conciliatory letter from Norfolk, 148; political position, 1536–38, 149–51; chastised by Henry, 153; and Cleves marriage, 154, 164–65; and Act of Six Articles, 160–63; rivalry with Norfolk, 163–64; created earl of Essex, 170; stalls Cleves divorce, 171–72; arrest, 172–73; execution, 176; and letters from Elizabeth Howard, 251–52
Culpeper, Thomas, 186–87

Dacre, Thomas, lord: and battle of Flodden, 35–37; warden of west marches, conflict with Surrey, 61–62; raids along Scots borders, 62–64; appointed deputy in north, 67–68, 308 (n. 96); signs truce with Scots, 75
Dacre, William, lord: trial and acquittal of, 122–23
Dandiprats: Norfolk suggests coining, 77, 311 (n. 30)
Darcy, Thomas, lord: and Cadiz expedition, 1511, 29; opposes English divorce of Catherine, 108; and Pilgrimage of Grace, 134–35, 137, 139, 140–41, 143–44, 324–25 (n. 13), 326 (n. 35); trial and execution, 145
Daubeney, Catherine, lady Bridgewater: arrest and attainder, 188–89; marriage, 250
Daubeney, Henry, earl of Bridgewater, 250
Delft, Francis van der, imperial ambassador to England, 215

Index

Denny, Sir Anthony: and fall of Howards, 222–28; and Norfolk's lands, 232–33
Dereham, Francis, 184–88
Dethicke, Gilbert, Hammes Pursuivant, 284
Douglas, Archibald, earl of Angus, 70–75, 336 (n. 56)
Douglas, George, 70–73
Douglas, Margaret, lady, daughter of Queen Margaret of Scotland: and contract of marriage with Lord Thomas Howard, 132, 250–51; marries earl of Lennox, 251
Drury, Sir Robert, 79
Dudley, Ambrose, earl of Warwick, 236–37
Dudley, Guildford, 235–37
Dudley, John, lord Lisle: appointed warden of marches, 208; defends against French armada, 216–17; and fall of Howards, 220–28; made earl of Warwick, 231; and Norfolk's lands and possessions, 232–34; seizes power, made duke of Northumberland, 234; and Lady Jane Grey, 235–36, 341 (n. 32); trial and execution, 236–37

East Anglia: disturbances in, 79–81, 88–89, 243; Norfolk's patronage in, 255–57; his land acquisitions in, 275–76
Edward IV, king of England, 13–16
Edward V, king of England, 16
Edward VI, king of England: birth, 149; betrothed to Queen Mary of Scotland, 209; accession, 229; device for succession, 234–35; death, 235

Elections to Commons, Thomas Howard and, 265–69
Elizabeth I, queen of England: birth, 118; proposed marriage to duke of Angoulême, 125; and possible French marriage, 1541–42, 197; restored to succession, 1544, 211; Mary considers executing, 242
Evil May Day riots, 1517, suppressed by Howards, 49, 304 (n. 33)

Factionalism: defined, 5–7, 10–11; at court, 1531, 104–5; and fall of Anne Boleyn, 126–28, 322–23 (n. 99); and Exeter conspiracy, 156–57; and fall of Cromwell, 173–75; after fall of Catherine Howard, 190; in 1546, 218–19; and fall of Howards, 220–28; and Edwardian regency, 229–30, 234; role in Tudor politics, 289–90, 324 (n. 3)
Falieri, Ludovico: describes Thomas Howard, 1
Ferdinand, king of Aragon, 29–30, 44, 46, 47
Fisher, John, bishop of Rochester, cardinal: opposes Henry's divorce, 115; execution, 122
Fitzgerald, Gerald, eighth earl of Kildare, lord deputy of Ireland, 52
Fitzgerald, Gerald, ninth earl of Kildare, 52–55, 59, 305 (n. 48)
Fitzroy, Henry, bastard son of Henry VIII: created earl of Nottingham and duke of Richmond and Somerset, 83; made admiral and lord lieutenant of the north in succession to Norfolk, 83; death and burial, 132–33; wed to Mary Howard, 249
Fitzwilliam, William, earl of Southamp-

Index

Fitzwilliam, William (*continued*)
  ton, 87, 124, 140–41, 172, 185, 198, 202, 206, 326 (n. 36), 336 (n. 59)
Flodden, battle of, 34–38, 301–2 (nn. 43, 45, 51)
Fox, Richard, bishop of Winchester, lord privy seal, 22, 27–28
Framlingham, Suffolk, ducal castle, 15, 69, 235, 263
Francis I, king of France: accession and character, 44; captured at Pavia, 76; released, makes alliance with Henry, 82; suggests marriage with Mary Tudor, 85; meets Henry at Calais, 114; meets with Norfolk, 117–18, 166–68; offers marital alliance, 153–54; renews truce with Charles, 158; signs Treaty of Crépy, 213; sends armada to attack England, 216–17; reaction to fall of Howards, 224
Fulmerston, Richard, steward to Norfolk, 225, 232, 261–62, 347 (n. 60)
Fynglas, Patrick, 57

Gage, Sir John, 104, 181, 206, 217, 266
Gardiner, Stephen, bishop of Winchester: at Rome arguing Henry's case, 90; and 1529 Parliamentary elections, 93; given charge of Great Seal, 94; and relations with Wolsey, 97; and fall of Wolsey, 105; joins Norfolk in support of divorce, 111, 319 (n. 36); meets with Clement VII, 118, 321 (n. 63); Cromwell replaces as principal secretary, 121; and Exeter conspiracy, 156–57; and Act of Six Articles, 160–62; and fall of Cromwell, 168–72, 330–32 (nn. 49, 65); and Catherine Howard, 171; and Cleves divorce, 176; attack on progressives in council, 182–83, 219–20; diplomatic disagreement with Norfolk, 193–97; Norfolk seeks support from, 205; peace negotiations with France, 215, 218, 338 (n. 102); retires from court, 219–20; excluded from Edward's regency, 229; arrested, 230; release and restoration, 236; and Spanish match, 238–39; executor of Norfolk's will, 244; Norfolk appoints archdeacon of Norwich, 265, 314 (n. 87); personality, 321 (n. 63)
Gawdy, Bassinbourne: carries word of Norfolk's death to court, 244
Gentry: role in Tudor politics, 9–10, 255–56, 346 (n. 38)
Gifford, George, 266, 348 (n. 81)
Goodman, Jane, bastard daughter of third duke, 244
Grafton, Richard, 264
Greenwich, Treaty of, 1527, 85
Grey, Elizabeth, 26
Grey, Jane, lady, pretended queen of England, 235–37
Grey, Leonard, lord: executed for treason, 182
Grey, Thomas, marquis of Dorset: and Spanish expedition of 1512, 29–30; sent north to support Surrey, 65
Griffith, Rhys ap: and Spanish expedition of 1512, 29; attainder, 108, 250, 318 (n. 16)

Haddon Ridge, battle of, 200
Hall, Edward, quoted, 29, 36, 49, 77, 79–81
Hall, Mary, 184
Hamilton, James, earl of Arran: and

Index

Angus's seizure of power, 71–75; made governor of Scotland, 209–10

Hare, Sir Nicholas: Speaker of Commons, 1538, 159; executor of Norfolk's will, 244; in Parliament of 1539, 266–67; deputy steward of augmentations, 285; and fall of Cromwell, 348 (n. 83)

Harper, Sir George, 240–41

Hastings, William, lord, 16, 296–97 (n. 18)

Henry, dauphin of France, 213–14

Henry, prince, son of Henry VIII, birth and early death, 27

Henry VII, king of England: victory at Bosworth, 17–18; and Thomas Howard, earl of Surrey, 18–19, 22; death and funeral, 22–23

Henry VIII, king of England character, 7, 10, 22, 25, 142, 145, 153, 199, 223, 228, 278; accession and coronation, 22–25; court ceremonials, 25–27; birth and death of first son, 27; and French campaign, 1513, 33, 38–39; and noble creations of 1514, 40–41; outrage with Suffolk's marriage to Mary Tudor, 44; renews peace with France, 45; signs alliance with Ferdinand, 46; and birth of Princess Mary, 47; pardons Evil May Day rioters, 49; appoints Surrey lieutenant of Ireland, 52–53, 305 (n. 48); and fall of duke of Buckingham, 53–54; sends Surrey instructions on Ireland, 55–58, 306 (nn. 57, 63); attends Field of Cloth of Gold, 56; recalls Surrey, 58; and Scotland, 1523–24, 61–62, 68, 75; plans invasion of France, 76; and Amicable Grant, 76–77; rescinds Grant, 81; considers divorcing Catherine of Aragon, 83, 86; interest in Anne Boleyn, 86–88, 313 (n. 64); impatience with Wolsey's work on divorce, 90–91; last meeting with Wolsey, 92–93; removes Wolsey as chancellor, 94; wavers toward Wolsey, 95–96; grants Wolsey pardon, 97; pardons Norfolk for abduction of earl of Derby, 98; and final destruction of Wolsey, 100–101, 314 (n. 84); Cromwell becomes leading advisor, 104–5, 119; and murder of Sir William Pennington, 110; refuses to return to Catherine, 112; meeting with Francis I, 114–15; learns Anne is pregnant, orders English divorce, 115; marriage and coronation of Anne, 116; and birth of Elizabeth, 118; and threatened excommunication, 118; and deaths of More and Fisher, 122; proposed marriage of Elizabeth and Angoulème, 125; falls from horse, 126; and fall of Anne Boleyn, 126–29; marries Jane Seymour, 129; anger with Norfolk over burial of Richmond, 132–33; and outbreak of Pilgrimage of Grace, 135–36; orders Norfolk to stay in East Anglia, relents, 136–37; refuses to negotiate with rebels, 137–38; instructs Norfolk on dealings with Aske, 140, 142–43; orders retribution, 145–46; orders Norfolk to remain in north, 146; appoints Tunstall to replace him, 148; and birth of Prince Edward and death of Jane Seymour, 149; chastises Cromwell, 153; and Exeter conspiracy, 156–57; religious views, 159, 320 (n. 47);

Henry VIII (*continued*)
and Act of Six Articles, 160–63;
marries Anne of Cleves, 164–65;
role in fall of Cromwell, 164–65,
173–75, 330–31 (n. 49); marries
Catherine Howard, 176–80; and
fall of Catherine Howard, 184–89;
return to war in 1540s, 192–93; royal
progress to York, 196–97; orders
mobilization and loan, 198; appoints
Norfolk lieutenant in north, 200;
sends instructions, 202–3, 205; displeasure
with Norfolk's accomplishments,
207; alliance with Charles
V, 209–10; marries Catherine Parr,
212; and war in France, 212–13; and
Norfolk's defense of Boulogne, 214–
15; worsening health, 221, 228; and
fall of Howards, 221–28; death, 228
Herbert, William, earl of Pembroke, 242
Heron, Giles, 182, 266
Heron, "Bastard" John of Ford, 34–35
Hertford, earl of. *See* Seymour,
Edward, earl of Hertford and duke
of Somerset
Holbein, Hans, 153
Holdiche, Robert, receiver of land
revenues for third duke, 232, 260–61
Holland, Elizabeth, mistress to third
duke, 233, 251, 260, 275, 345 (nn. 21, 26)
Holland, George, secretary to third
duke: and will, 243
Home, Alexander, lord, 34
Howard, Agnes, dowager duchess of
Norfolk, 118, 180, 188–90, 264, 272, 334 (n. 37)
Howard, Anne, first wife of third
duke: marriage 20, 247; births and
deaths of children, 21–22, 247;
lands, 26, 271–72; death, 30, 247
Howard, Catherine, queen of England:
in court of Anne of Cleves, 171,
179–80; marries Henry VIII, 176,
180; investigation of marital misconduct,
184–86; arrest, 186; attainder
and execution, 189; birth, 332 (n. 3)
Howard, Charles, 183
Howard, Sir Edmund, brother of
third duke: birth, 14; education and
upbringing, 19–20; and battle of
Flodden, 35–38; knighted, 38; and
marriage of Mary Tudor and Louis
XII, 43; and Evil May Day riots, 49;
later career and death, 179
Howard, Sir Edward, brother of third
duke: birth, 14; education and upbringing,
19–20; knighted, 21; and
funeral of Henry VII, 26; service at
sea, 28–29; death, 31
Howard, Elizabeth, second wife of
third duke: marriage, 31, 247; and
death of duke of Buckingham, 54; at
court for holidays, 68; visits Norfolk
in Tower, 231; death and tomb, 244;
marital problems, 251–52, 344–45
(nn. 21, 25)
Howard, George, 183
Howard, Henry, styled earl of Surrey,
son of third duke: birth, 51, 247;
marries Frances de Vere, 84, 110,
249; rumors of proposed marriage
to Princess Mary, 109–10, 249; not
permitted to assist Norfolk against
Pilgrimage of Grace, 136–37; blocks
marriage of Mary Howard and
Thomas Seymour, 154–55, 220–21;
joins father in north, 201; with Norfolk
in France, 211–13; commander

Index

of Boulogne, 217–19; arrest, 222–23; trial and execution, 226, character, 253–54

Howard, John, lord, first Howard duke of Norfolk: birth and early life, 13, 295 (n. 5); service under Edward IV, 14–15; and Edward's funeral, 15–16; created duke of Norfolk and earl marshal, 16–17; and Richard III's usurpation, 16–17, 296 (n. 11); killed at Bosworth, 18

Howard, Mary, duchess of Richmond, daughter of third duke: birth, 51, 247; and christening of Elizabeth, 118; and proposed marriages to Thomas Seymour, 154–55, 220–21, 254; in court of Anne of Cleves, 179; visits Norfolk in Tower, 231; personal property, 233–34; married to duke of Richmond, 249; and fall of Howards, 254

Howard, Thomas, earl of Surrey and second Howard duke of Norfolk: birth and early life, 13; service to Edward IV, 13–15; and Edward's funeral, 15–16; created earl of Surrey, 16; and Richard III's usurpation, 16–17; captured at Bosworth and attainted, 18; release and restoration as earl by Henry VII, 19; service to Henry VII, 19–22; made lord treasurer, 22; and death of Henry VII, 22–23; and accession of Henry VIII, 24–25; rivalry for primacy at court, 1509–10, 27–28; and battle of Flodden, 33–38; created duke of Norfolk, 40–41; and marriage of Mary Tudor and Louis XII, 43–44; in House of Lords, 1515, 45–46; and christening of Princess Mary, 47; and Wolsey's creation as cardinal, 47; suppresses Evil May Day riots, 49, 304 (n. 33); final illness and death, 68–69; valuation of lands and income, 69, 272; resigns as treasurer, 307 (n. 90)

Howard, Thomas, earl of Surrey and third Howard duke of Norfolk: described, 1–2; character, 3–4, 21, 30, 46, 60, 74, 102, 145, 147, 150, 227, 252, 281–82, 286–89, 309 (n. 109), 321 (n. 63); birth, 14; education and upbringing, 19–20, 263; marries Anne Plantagenet, 20, 247; early career under Henry VII, 20–21; knighted, 21; death of Anne and children, 21–22, 30, 247; and death of Henry VII, 22–23; and accession of Henry VIII, 24–25; elected to Order of the Garter, 1510, 26; and defeat of Andrew Barton, 28; Spanish campaign, 1512, 29–30; marries Elizabeth Stafford, 31; as admiral, 32, 41–42, 46, 50, 279–80; and battle of Flodden, 33–38; created earl of Surrey, 40–41, 302 (n. 1); and marriage of Mary Tudor and Louis XII, 43–44; in House of Lords, 1515, 45–46; and Wolsey's creation as cardinal, 47; and christening of Princess Mary, 48; punished for keeping retainers, 48, 255; and Evil May Day riots, 49; and Treaty of London, 1518, 50–51; births of children, 51, 247–48; and punishment of Sir William Bulmer, 51–52; appointed lord lieutenant of Ireland, 52–53; arrives in Dublin, 54; deals with Irish lords, 54–55; and piracy, 55–56, 306 (n.

379

Howard, Thomas (*continued*) 63); advises Henry on Irish affairs, 57–58, 123; recalled, 58; assessment of Irish mission, 59; raids Brittany, 59–60, 307 (n. 88); commander of Calais, 60–61; appointed lieutenant general against Scots, 61; conflict with Lord Dacre, 61–62; raids along Scots border, 62–64; reports on Scottish affairs, 62–68; confronts invasion of Albany, 66–67; and death of father, 69; rivalry with Wolsey, 70; orchestrates return of Angus to Scotland, 70–73; Wolsey's frustration with, 73–74; alliance with Suffolk against Wolsey, 76; and plans for war, 1524, 76; appointed to collect Amicable Grant, 77, 311 (n. 31); problems with collections, 78–80; suppresses rebellion in Suffolk, 79–81; and pardon of rebels, 81; forced into exile by Wolsey, 1525–27, 82; and Treaty of the More, 82; yields admiralty and lieutenancy of north to Richmond, 83; rebuilds palace of Kenninghall, 84, 150, 273; arranges family marriages and wardships, 84–85; and conflict with Wolsey, 85, 87; supports Henry's desire to wed Anne Boleyn, 87–88; exiled from court, 88–90; and legatine court, 91; presses Henry to remove Wolsey, 92–93; and Wolsey's surrender of Great Seal, 94, 315 (n. 91); return to prominence, 94–95; announces More's appointment as chancellor, 95; dinner with Wolsey, 96; abducts earl of Derby to wed a half-sister, 98; urges Henry to order Wolsey to York, 98; and Henry's divorce case, 99, 108–9; and arrest and death of Wolsey, 100–102; position after fall of Wolsey, 103; collapse of aristocratic anti-Wolsey faction, 105; harangues Chapuys on divorce case, 106; sent to force Catherine to submit, 107; relations with Anne Boleyn, 109, 116; marriage of Henry Howard, 109–10; in Parliament, 1532, 110–12; and Supplication Against the Ordinaries, 112; religious beliefs, 113, 263; asks Catherine to renounce claims, 116; mission to France, 116–19, 321 (n. 62); and birth of Elizabeth, 118; recovers office of earl marshal from Suffolk, 118; orders Princess Mary to serve Elizabeth, 119; and Cromwell's rise as leading minister, 119–20; examination and trial of More, 121–22; trial of William lord Dacre, 122–23; and reception of Phillipe de Chabot, admiral of France, 123–24; final breach with Anne, 124; mission to France, 1535, 124–25; exiled at Kenninghall, 125; and fall of Anne Boleyn, 126–29; sent to rebuke Princess Mary, 131; and death and burial of duke of Richmond, 132–33; and outbreak of Pilgrimage of Grace, 135–37; meets with Aske, 139–40, 142–43; commissioned king's lieutenant, 143; executions of rebels, 144–46, 327 (nn. 45, 49); seeks return to court, 146–48; replaced by Tunstall, 148; at christening of Prince Edward and funeral of Jane Seymour, 149; exiled by Cromwell, 149–50; returns to court, 153; fails to arrange marriage of Mary Howard and Thomas Seymour, 154–55; and Exeter conspiracy, 155–56; sent to north, 158; and Parliamentary elections of 1538, 159; and Act of Six Articles, 160–63; rivalry with Cromwell, 163–64; and Cleves marriage, 164–65; sent to France, 165–68; in Parliament of 1540, 169–72; and fall of Cromwell, 170–76; and Cromwell's arrest, 172; and Cleves divorce, 175–76; pushes Cromwell's attainder and execution, 175–76; and rise of Catherine Howard, 179–80; accused of corruption, 181, 283; rewards from Catherine's rise, 183; and fall of Catherine Howard, 184–88; escapes imprisonment, 189, 334 (n. 37); status after Catherine's execution, 190–91; inspects northern defenses, 193–95; opposes imperial alliance, 193–97; marital negotiations with French, 195–98; general mobilization and loan, 198, 335 (n. 23); negotiations with Scots, 200–201; lord lieutenant against Scots, 200–208; reports difficulties of supply, 204–5; burns Kelso, 207; defends results of campaign to Henry, 207–8; and war with France, 210–11; siege of Montreuil, 212–14; retreat to Boulogne and Calais, 214–15; returns to England, 215–16; cautions Surrey, 217–18; attempts to arrange marital alliance with Seymours, 220–21; withdraws to Kenninghall, 222; hears of Surrey's arrest, 224; arrest and interrogation, 224–25; confession and attainder, 226–27; rumors of execution, 228; conditions of imprisonment, 230–31; seeks release after death of Henry VIII, 230–31; lands and possessions dispersed, 232–34, 340–41 (n. 26); estimates of wealth, 233, 277, 318 (n. 15), 349 (n. 96), 350 (n. 123); release and restoration, 235–36, 341–42 (n. 35); and Mary's coronation, 237–38; reversal of attainder, 238; and Wyatt's rebellion, 238–41, 342 (n. 47); final illness and death, 242–44; will, 243–44, 343 (n. 65); tomb, 244–45, 343 (n. 67); family ties, 247–51; marital problems, 251–52, 345 (n. 25); problems with children, 253–55; patronage, 255–57, 283; and Anthony Rouse, 257–58; and Sir Richard Southwell, 258–60; and Robert Holdiche, 260–61; and Richard Fulmerston, 261–62; household books, 262–63, 308 (n. 97); and Parliamentary elections, 265–68; and Ket's Rebellion, 270; land acquisitions, 271–72; as treasurer, 273, 283; and dissolution of monasteries, 273–76; military experience evaluated, 279–81; view of role of nobility, 281; relations with Henry VIII, 281–82; as earl marshal, 283–85; and court of augmentations, 285; and privy council, 285–86; assessment of career, 287–91; his comital seal, 308 (n. 96)

Howard, Thomas, fourth duke of Norfolk: birth, 150, 249; restored as earl of Surrey, 238; wed Mary Fitzalan, 243, 343 (n. 63); named heir in Norfolk's will, 243–44; succeeds as duke, 244–45

Howard, Thomas, lord, half-brother of third duke: at christening of Elizabeth, 118; attainder and death, 132, 250

Howard, Thomas, viscount Bindon, son of third duke: birth, 51, 248; marries Elizabeth Marney, 84, 248;

Howard, Thomas (*continued*)
pardoned, restored as baron by Edward VI, 230; visits father in Tower, 231; and Norfolk's will, 248; at court in 1540s, 269
Howard, Sir William (d. 1308), 12
Howard, William, lord, half-brother of third duke: at christening of Elizabeth, 118; ambassador to France, 183; arrested and attainted, 188–89, 333 (n. 33); pardoned, joins Norfolk in north, 201; made admiral by Mary, 241; and Wyatt's rebellion, 241–42
Hussey, Sir John, 308 (n. 94)
Hussey, Thomas, treasurer to third duke, 253

Ireland: Thomas Howard as lord lieutenant, 52–59; Norfolk offers advise on, 89, 123; misrule under Lord Lisle, 182

James IV, king of Scotland: marries Margaret Tudor, 21; and Andrew Barton affair, 28, 33; desire for war with England, 33–34; and battle of Flodden, 34–37; death at Flodden, 37
James V, king of Scotland: minority, 46; declared of age, 71; reaffirms Auld Alliance, 1537, 146; reaches majority, affirms pro-French policy, 193–95; refuses to meet Henry at York, 199; death, 208
Jedburgh: burned by Thomas Howard, 63–64
Jermyn, Sir Thomas, 79
Jerningham, Sir Henry, 240
Junius, Hadrian, 264

Kelso: burned by Thomas Howard, 207
Kenninghall, Norfolk, ducal mansion: Norfolk resident there, 77, 89; rebuilt as palace, 1526–28, 84, 273; searched and inventoried, 225, 341 (nn. 27, 28); granted to Mary, 233; Norfolk draws up will there, 243; dies there, 244; origins of manor's name, 273
Kerr, Sir Robert, 34
Ket's Rebellion, 243, 270
Knevet, Sir Thomas: companion of young Henry VIII, 26; married to Muriel Howard, 26; death at sea, 31
Knight, William, servant to Wolsey: reports on Spanish campaign, 1512, 30; and Anne Boleyn, 87; sent to Rome, 88

Lassells, John, 184–85
Lawson, Sir George, 203
Lee, Edward, archbishop of York, 138
Legh, Thomas, appointed controller of customs for London, 257
Leland, John, 264
Leo X, pope: preaches crusade against Turks, 1518, 50
London, Treaty of, 1518, 50–51, 59–60
Louis XII, king of France: marries Mary Tudor, 42–44; death, 44

Manners, Thomas, earl of Rutland, 199, 336 (n. 61)
Manox, Henry, 185–86, 188
Margaret of Savoy, regent of Netherlands, 85
Marillac, Charles de, French ambassador to England: and Norfolk's

Index

opposition to Cleves match, 164; reports Cromwell "tottering," 169, 331 (n. 59); and Cromwell's arrest, 172–73; calls Norfolk chief minister, 176; reports dissension in privy council, 177; and fall of Catherine Howard, 188–89, 334 (n. 37); hopes Henry will ally with France, 193; reports on Norfolk's northern mission, 193–95; and marital negotiations with Norfolk, 195–98; receives Henry's defiance, 210

Markham, Sir John, lieutenant of the Tower of London, 230–31

Marney, Elizabeth: marries Thomas Howard, son of third duke, 84; wardship, 248

Marney, John, lord, 84, 248

Mary, queen of England, daughter of Henry VIII: birth, 47; betrothal to Charles V repudiated, 81–82; suggested as bride of Francis I, 85; ordered to serve Princess Elizabeth, 119; proposals for French marriage, 195–97; restored to succession, 1542, 211; granted Kenninghall, 233; and lady Jane Grey, 235–36; coronation, 237–38; marries Philip of Spain, 239; and Wyatt's rebellion, 242; supervisor for Norfolk's will, 244

Mary, queen of Scotland, 208

Mendoza, Diego Hortado de, imperial ambassador to England, 152

Mendoza, Iñigo de, bishop of Burgos, imperial ambassador to England: bias of reports, 87; reports Norfolk as leading opponent of Wolsey, 87; reports Wolsey is dragging feet on divorce, 89

Middleton, Sir Christopher, 48, 280

Monastic lands: acquired by Norfolk, 274–76

Monteagle, lord, wardship, 62, 248, 307–8 (n. 94)

Montmorency, Anne de, constable of France, 114, 165–67

More, Sir Thomas: and Peace of Cambrai, 92; deserts Wolsey, 93, 315 (n. 89); appointed chancellor, 95; and Parliament of 1529, 107; resigns as chancellor, 113; trial and execution, 121–22; relations with Norfolk, 122, 319–20 (n. 39)

More, Treaty of the, 82

Morlaix: burned by Thomas Howard, 60

Mowbray, Anne, 15

Mowbray, John, fourth Mowbray duke of Norfolk, 14–15

Musgrave, Sir William, 208

Neville, Sir Edward, 156

Neville, Ralph, earl of Westmorland, romance with Elizabeth Stafford, 31, 251, 325

Noailles, de, French ambassador to England, 239

Norfolk, dukes of. *See* Howard, John, lord, first Howard duke of Norfolk; Howard, Thomas, earl of Surrey and second Howard duke of Norfolk; Mowbray, John, fourth Mowbray duke of Norfolk

Norris, Henry, 128–29

Norris, Mary, 179

Paget, Sir William: made clerk of privy council, 177; made Henry's principal secretary, 216; and fall of

Paget, Sir William (*continued*)
  Howards, 222–28; and division of Howard lands and property, 232–34; and Wyatt's rebellion, 239
Parliament of 1485, and attainder of the Howards, 18
Parliament of 1489: and reversal of Surrey's attainder, 19
Parliament of 1515: elections, 45; sessions, 45–46; and Surrey's unsuccessful claim for precedence, 46
Parliament of 1529: Norfolk's role in elections, 93; and proceedings against Wolsey, 96; Norfolk's role in second session, 105
Parliament of 1536: elections, 130, 266
Parliament of 1538, 159–63
Parliament of 1553: and restoration of Howards, 238
Parliamentary session of 1532, 110–13
Parliamentary session of 1534, 120
Parliamentary session of 1542, 189
Parliamentary session of 1543, 209
Parliamentary session of 1544, 211
Parliamentary session of 1547: and attainder of Howards, 227–28
Parr, Catherine, 212, 220
Parr, William, earl of Essex: made marquis of Northampton and receives Howard lands, 232; trial, 236–37
Paston, John, 17–18
Paston family: relations with Howards, 13–14, 17–18
Pate, Richard, 168, 284
Paul III, Pope: elected, 123; mediates Franco-Imperial truce, 154; threatens Henry's excommunication, 156–58
Paulet, William, lord St. John: and parliamentary elections of 1529, 104; and funeral of Jane Seymour, 149; questions Norfolk after arrest, 225; made treasurer after fall of Somerset, 236; and Pilgrimage of Grace, 326 (n. 26)
Pavia, battle of, 76
Pechy, Sir John, 57, 305 (n. 54)
Peerage, wealth of, 277–78
Pennington, Sir William, 110
Percy, Henry, earl of Northumberland, 127, 134
Philip, son and heir of Charles V: installed as duke of Milan, 192; weds Mary Tudor, 239
Pilgrimage of Grace: background and causes, 133–35, 325 (n. 18), 325–26 (n. 21); Norfolk's role in suppression, 136–46
Plantagenet, Richard, duke of York and Norfolk: marries Anne Mowbray, 15; disappearance, 16
Pole, Sir Geoffrey, 156
Pole, Reginald, cardinal, 156, 158, 239
Pole, Richard de la, Lancastrian pretender to the throne, 64
Praemunire: charges against Wolsey, 93; charges against English clergy, 111–12
Privy chamber: role in Henrician politics, 8, 128–29, 269–70
Privy council: formally organized, 1540, 177; and corruption charges against Norfolk, 181; role in politics, 285–86
Pynson, Richard, 301 (n. 43)

Radcliffe, Robert, earl of Sussex, 145, 160
Reynard, Simon, imperial ambassador to England, 235, 238, 243
Rich, Sir Richard, 244, 268

Index

Richard III, king of England, 16–18
Rouse, Anthony, 257–58
Rush, Thomas, 104
Russell, John, lord, 97, 212–15
Ruthal, Thomas, bishop of Durham, 39, 46

Sadler, Sir Ralph: servant to Cromwell, 104; made king's secretary, 170; arrested but cleared, 1541, 182–83; leads investigation of Catherine Howard, 187
Sampson, Richard, bishop of Winchester, 172, 331 (n. 59)
Scotland: Thomas Howard and, 28, 33–38, 61–68, 70–73, 158, 193–95, 200–208
Seymour, Edward, earl of Hertford and duke of Somerset: made viscount Beauchamp, 129; becomes ally of Cromwell, 131–32; made earl of Hertford; burns Edinburgh, 211–12; negotiates for French peace, 215; returns to borders, 216; and fall of Howards, 220–28; made treasurer, earl marshal and duke of Somerset, 229; and Norfolk's lands and possessions, 232–34; fall and execution, 234; affray with Henry Howard, 253
Seymour, Jane, queen of England: becomes Henry's companion, 127; and fall of Anne Boleyn, 128; marries Henry VIII, 129; birth of Edward and death, 149
Seymour, Sir Thomas: proposed marriages to Mary Howard, 154–55, 220–21
Shrewsbury, earl of. *See* Talbot, George, earl of Shrewsbury
Skelton, John, 263–64
Smeaton, Mark, 128–29

Solway Moss, battle of, 208
Somerset, Charles, lord Herbert and earl of Worcester, 39, 41
Somerset, duke of. *See* Seymour, Edward, earl of Hertford and duke of Somerset
Southampton, earl of. *See* Fitzwilliam, William, earl of Southampton
Southwell, Sir Richard, 94, 110, 223–25, 244, 258–59, 266–67
Stafford, Edward, duke of Buckingham, 31, 53–54, 305–6 (nn. 52, 54)
Stafford, Edward, duke of Buckingham: and marriage of Thomas Howard and Elizabeth Stafford, 30–31; attainder and execution, 50–51
Stafford, Elizabeth. *See* Howard, Elizabeth, second wife of third duke
Stafford, Henry, duke of Buckingham, 17
Stanley, Sir Edward, 35–37, 39
Stanley, Edward, earl of Derby, 98, 250, 316 (n. 113)
Star chamber, court of: Wolsey presides over council meetings in, 48, 51, 81, 303–4 (nn. 27, 37), 312 (n. 49)
St. Leger, Sir Anthony, 332–33 (n. 13)
St. Michael's Church, Framlingham, and tomb of Norfolk, 244–45, 343 (n. 67)
Stuart, John, duke of Albany: regent for James V, 46–47; returns to Scotland, 64; leads invasion of England, 66–67; removed as regent, 70–71
Stuart, Matthew, earl of Lennox: supports Angus's seizure of power, 74–75; marries Margaret Douglas, 251

Index

Suffolk, duke of. *See* Brandon, Charles, duke of Suffolk
Supplication Against the Ordinaries, 1532, 111–12, 319 (n. 36)
Surrey, earl of. *See* Howard, Henry, styled earl of Surrey, son of third duke; Howard, Thomas, earl of Surrey and second Howard duke of Norfolk
Talbot, George, earl of Shrewsbury, 105, 107; and Pilgrimage of Grace, 137–38, 142, 325 (nn. 18, 21), 326 (n. 27)
Ten Articles, 160
Thetford, Cluniac Priory of St. Mary: burial place of John Howard, 18; burial place of second duke, 69; burial place of Henry Fitzroy, 132; lands granted to Somerset, 232; grants of lands after dissolution, 261, 274–75
Thirlby, Thomas, bishop of Westminster, 224
Tournon, François de, archbishop of Bourges, cardinal, 117–18
Townshend, Sir Roger, 155, 259, 265–67
Tudor, Margaret, daughter of Henry VII, queen of Scotland: married to James IV, 21; flees to England, 1516, 46–47; returns to Scotland and opposes Albany, 62–68; and Angus's return and seizure of power, 71–75; correspondence with Norfolk, 1537, 147
Tudor, Mary, daughter of Henry VII: marries Louis XII, 42–44; marries Suffolk, 44; and succession of Jane Grey, 235, 341 (n. 32)
Tuke, Brian: servant to Wolsey, 91, 92, 301 (n. 45); deserts Wolsey, 93

Tunstall, Cuthbert, bishop of London, bishop of Durham: and opposition to Wolsey, 87; and Peace of Cambrai, 92; warns Wolsey against holding northern convocation, 100–101; named president of council of the north, 148–49; and Act of Six Articles, 161; assessment of career, 290

Venice, English relations with, 60, 108–9
Vere, Francis de, countess of Surrey, 238, 248–49
Vere, John de, fifteenth earl of Oxford, 249
Vergil, Polydore, and account of Surrey attacking Wolsey, 48

Wallop, Sir John, 55, 199
Walsh, Thomas, 309 (n. 119)
Walsh, Walter, groom of privy chamber, 101–2
Warham, William, archbishop of Canterbury, chancellor: councilor to Henry VII, 22; and power struggle at court, 1509–10, 27–28; resigns chancellorship, 41; in House of Lords, 1515, 45–46; denies Surrey precedence in Lords, 46; and Amicable Grant, 77–79; refuses to grant Henry's divorce, 108; death, 115
Wark Castle: attacked by Albany, 67
Weston, Sir Francis, 128–29
Whelplay, George, 181
Wingfield, Sir Anthony: and arrest of Cromwell, 172; elected to Garter, 181; and privy council, 181, 217; in Parliament of 1536, 266
Winter, Thomas, 265, 314 (n. 87)
Wolsey, Thomas, archbishop of York,

chancellor: early career, 27–28; becomes leading councilor, 32–33; made archbishop of York and chancellor, 41; arranges marriage of Mary Tudor and Louis XII, 43–44; made cardinal, 47; and laws against retainers, 47–48; and Evil May Day riots, 49; and Treaty of London, 1518, 50–51; punishment of Sir William Bulmer, 51–52; and Surrey's appointment as lieutenant of Ireland, 53; and fall of Buckingham, 53–54; approves Surrey's recall, 58; rivalry with Norfolk, 70; frustration with Norfolk's handling of Scottish affairs, 73–74; opposition to war, 77; and Amicable Grant, 77–81; takes blame for Grant, 81; forces Norfolk into eclipse, 82; and Treaty of the More, 82; conflict with Norfolk, 1527, 85, 87, 88–90, 95–96; attempts to arrange French marriage for Henry, 87, discovers threat of Anne Boleyn, 88; and legatine court, 90–91; *praemunire* charges against, 93; surrenders Great Seal to Norfolk and Suffolk, 94, 315 (n. 91); and pardon from Henry, 97; ordered to York, 98–99; plans northern convocation, 100–101; arrested, dies on journey to London, 101–2

Wooten, Nicholas, 224

Wriothesley, Sir Thomas: made king's secretary, 170; and Cleves divorce, 172; investigated, 182; Norfolk seeks support from, 205; made chancellor, 212; joins progressive faction, 218; and fall of Howards, 220–28; forced from power, 230

Wyatt, Sir Thomas, 238–42

Wyndham, Sir Edward, 243, 259

Wyndham, Thomas, 182